LET'S GIT NEKKID TRIVIA: THE BARE-BONES PATH TO QUIZ SUCCESS

By John P. Campbell

Campbell's High School/College Quiz Book
Campbell's Potpourri I of Quiz Bowl Questions
Campbell's Potpourri II of Quiz Bowl Questions
Campbell's Middle School Quiz Book #1
Campbell's Potpourri III of Quiz Bowl Questions
Campbell's Middle School Quiz Book #2
Campbell's Elementary School Quiz Book #1
Campbell's 2001 Quiz Questions
Campbell's Potpourri IV of Quiz Bowl Questions
Campbell's Middle School Quiz Book #3
The 500 Famous Quotations Quiz Book
Campbell's 2002 Quiz Questions
Campbell's 210 Lightning Rounds
Campbell's 175 Lightning Rounds
Campbell's 2003 Quiz Questions
Campbell's 211 Lightning Rounds
Omniscience™: The Basic Game of Knowledge in Book Form
Campbell's 2004 Quiz Questions
Campbell's 212 Lightning Rounds
Campbell's Elementary School Quiz Book #2
Campbell's 176 Lightning Rounds
Campbell's 213 Lightning Rounds
Campbell's Potpourri V of Quiz Bowl Questions
Campbell's Mastering the Myths in a Giant Nutshell Quiz Book
Campbell's 3001 Quiz Questions
Campbell's 2701 Quiz Questions
Campbell's Quiz Book on Explorations and U.S. History to 1865
Campbell's Accent Cubed: Humanities, Math, and Science
Campbell's 2501 Quiz Questions
Campbell's Accent on the Alphabet Quiz Book
Campbell's U.S. History 1866 to 1960 Quiz Book
Campbell's 177 Lightning Rounds
Campbell's 214 Lightning Rounds
Campbell's Potpourri VI of Quiz Bowl Questions
Campbell's Middle School Quiz Book #4
Campbell's 2005 Quiz Questions
Campbell's Constant Quiz Companion: The Middle/High School Book of Lists, Terms, and Questions
Campbell's High School/College Book of Lists

REVIEWS FROM AROUND THE GLOBE FOR JOHN CAMPBELL'S

LET'S GIT NEKKID TRIVIA: THE BARE-BONES PATH TO QUIZ SUCCESS

"This book doesn't even come up to the level of good, clean dirty fun."
The Censor

"A complete education by daylight."
The Sunrise

"A great book to curl up with in the evening."
The Sunset

"People who love green cheese will love this book."
The Moon

"This book will sparkle in the evening sky long after you have dropped off to sleep."
The Stars

"It's a pity that the U.S. secretary of education might ban this book from public schools across the nation."
The Watch and Ward Society

"It's a pity that the pope might ban this book from parochial schools across the nation."
The Holy See

"The smell of a burning book is an awful sight to hear about and taste."
The Mixed Metaphor

"Ce livre est impossible à lire parce que je suis mort."
Le Penseur

"The best quiz book ever if you can find an unexpurgated, unbowlderized, or unburned copy."
The Daily News

"This book should have an A$^+$ emblazoned across its cover, which is more than Hester Prynne was forced to wear, although today she probably wouldn't get more than a C$^-$."
The Weekly News

"If you were a Gentleman C student, then this book is a must to enable you to move on up, at least to being an Esquire C student."
The Monthly News

"Whether you are an *idiot* or a *savant*, this book can teach you a thing or two."
The Idiot Savant

"This book will rekindle warm memories of your favorite courses and professors and then burst into flame like a Phoenix. If you survive the conflagration, you will be reborn."
The Spontaneous Combustion

"I shall avert my eyes from ever laying them upon this book again and again and again."
The Puritan

"This book evokes memories of everything students either loved or hated about school."
The Madeleine

"Who cares about learning the names of all those cats and dogs!"
The Equestrian

"If the Index of Forbidden Books were still being published, this book would certainly be on the list."
The Index of Forbidden Books

"Well, you might learn a lot from reading this book but we find nothing at all titillating about it."
The Peep Show

"This book is more profound and down-to-earth than the Flat Earth Society."
The Planetarian

"It's earthshaking to realize that this book might even be banned worldwide, especially in foreign languages into which it hasn't yet been translated."
The Globe

"It's so ethereal to realize that this book might even be banned in outer space."
The Galaxy

LET'S GIT NEKKID TRIVIA: THE BARE-BONES PATH TO QUIZ SUCCESS

JOHN P. CAMPBELL

PATRICK'S PRESS

Columbus, Georgia

Copyright (C) 2005 by John P. Campbell

All rights reserved. No part of this book may be reproduced or utilized in any form or by any means, electronic or mechanical, including photocopying, recording or by information storage or retrieval system, without permission in writing from the Publisher, except for brief quotes used in connection with reviews written specifically for inclusion in a magazine or newspaper. For information, write: Patrick's Press, Box 5189, Columbus, Georgia 31906. Call 1-800-654-1052 to request a color catalogue or place an order.

Printed in the United States of America

CIP data suggested by the author

Campbell, John P., 1942-
Let's Git Nekkid Trivia: the Bare-Bones Path to Quiz Success

   Includes index.
   Summary: Lists on a wide variety of categories including: Americana, bible and religion, entertainment, geography, history, language, literature, mythology, publishing, sex, science, and trivia
   1. Lists and questions and answers. [1. Lists and answers]
I. Title II. Title: *Let's Git Nekkid Trivia: the Bare-Bones Path to Quiz Success*
III. Title: *Let's Git Nekkid Trivia* IV. Title: *Git Nekkid Trivia* V. Title: *Nekkid Trivia*

AG195.C2005a   2005   031'.02

ISBN: 0-944322-41-7

First Edition
First Printing, October 2005

Acknowledgments

I am once again very indebted to my editor Rinda Brewbaker for her editing ability and contributions to this work.

I also appreciate the help of all those who assisted in researching or proofreading this material, especially Lloyd Busch, Judy Gunter, and David Taggart.

I also thank Jackie Taylor for typesetting this book.

To

Those Ken Jenkins wannabees who aspire to emulate his success, or at least go confidently, knowing they have the foundation for being successful. May they find their time well spent with this book's coverage of a wide variety of subjects.

And to Lewis Grizzard*, for this book's title was inspired in part by this former Atlanta *Journal-Constitution* columnist and humorist who explained that the word *naked* means you are not wearing clothes but the word *nekkid* means you're not wearing clothes and are up to something.

*Some of his titles are: *If Love Were Oil, I'd Be About a Quart Low; Elvis Is Dead and I Don't Feel So Good Myself; My Daddy Was a Pistol and I'm a Son of a Gun; Shoot Low Boys — They're Riding Shetland Ponies; Don't Bend Over In the Garden, Granny — You Know Them Taters Got Eyes*

PREFACE

If you are planning on being the next Ken Jennings or just participating on quiz shows, start today if you haven't already started and work daily using a long-range plan. You might not get on a show for two, three, maybe five years, but be as ready as you can when your moment comes. Read as much as you can: books, magazines, and newspapers, including their movie, TV, and song/album reviews. Play trivia games whenever and wherever possible. Develop some obsessions, such as *Star Trek*, Julia Roberts' movies, and the U.S. Civil War while memorizing lists such as U.S. and world capitals, the Presidents, their terms of office, and their numerical ranking, etc., etc., etc. And, of course, never ever forget anything you ever learn.

Constantly review this book and any other quiz books you have. Knowledge is like any skill—a lot of it comes through repetition and drilling. If *practice, practice, practice* are the 3 keys to getting to Carnegie Hall, then *review, review, review* are the 3 keys to being ready at crunch time on a quiz show. If nothing else, you will feel much more confident of your ability.

All quiz books can be of some help, and for further practice, especially for academic purposes, *Campbell's High School/College Quiz Book* from Patrick's Press is one of the best. You can purchase a CD-ROM of this book as well as one for *Nekkid Trivia* for quick and easy reference.

Your suggestions and comments will be appreciated. Please send them to me in care of PATRICK'S PRESS, Box 5189, Columbus, Georgia 31906.

John Campbell

Foreword

Possibly the most important question that could ever be asked is:

"What is the capital of Burkina Faso, a country you may remember was formerly called Upper Volta"?

Answer: Ouagadougou (often shortened to Ouaga).

Several reasons why this question and answer are so important: one, you will be one of the few who will know the answer; two, it is fun to say the answer; three, knowing this answer can change your life dramatically as was once stated by a game show contestant who related that while he was a college student asking other students trivia questions, he asked this, his favorite question. Only one student in the group knew the answer, and he eventually married her.

Additionally, if you are depressed, Eeyorish, melancholic, mournful, feeling low, having the blues, in the doldrums, down in the dumps, in the Slough of Despond, or have hit bottom, then saying the answer will cheer you up.

Though some say the name Ouagadougou means "come here village," its etymology is uncertain, so who is to say that it doesn't mean "I'm having a great day."

You just never know when that one question and one answer can change your life.

TABLE OF CONTENTS

Your First Thought 1
   Likely Answerable After the First Clue 3
Adultery 4
Bible 6
   The Ten Commandments 6
   Biblical People/Places/Things 7
      People 7
      Places 9
      Things 10
   Biblical Pairs 12
Religion 14
   Judaism 14
   Hinduism 16
   Buddhism 17
      Its Founder 17
   Christianity 18
   Islam 20
      Its Founder 21
Books Challenged/Banned 23
Campaign Propaganda 25
Homo All the Time 27
Cats, Dogs, Horses 28
   Cats and Dogs 28
Cats 28
   Domestic Cat Breeds 28
   Famous Cats 29
   Language Cats with *Cat* in the Answer 30
   Language Cats Otherwise 31
   Literary Cats in the Answer 31
   Literary/Film Cats 32
   Potpourri of Cats with *Cat* in the Answer 33
   Potpourri of Cats Otherwise 33
Dogs 35
   Cartoon/Film/Pop Culture/TV Dogs 35
   Comic Strip Dogs 36
   Dog Breeds 37
   Homo Sapiens and Their Dogs 39
   Language Dogs Beginning with the Word *Dog* 40
   Language Dogs With *Dog* in the Answer 40
   Language Dogs Otherwise 41
   Literary Dogs in the Answer 42
   Literary/Film Dogs Otherwise 42
   Potpourri of Dogs with *Dog* in the Answer 44
   Potpourri of Dogs Otherwise 44
Horses 46
   Famous Horses 47
   Homo Sapiens/Pop Culture-Related Horses 48

- Horse Breeds and Other Horses 49
- Language Horses with *Horse* in the Answer 50
- Language Horses Otherwise 51
- Literary/Fine Arts/Film Horses 52
- Myth-Related Horses 54
- Potpourri of Horses with *Horse* in the Answer 54
- Potpourri of Horses Otherwise 55
- Sport Horses 57
- Harness Racing 58

Dragons 59
- Literary/Fine Arts Dragons 59
- Potpourri of Dragons 60

"Frankly, My Dear..." 62
The Good and the Bad 64
- The Good 65
- 1-Word, 2-Word "Goods" 65
- Foreign "Goods" 65
- Homo Sapiens "Goods" 66
- Language "Goods" 66
- Literary "Goods" 67
- Potpourri of "Goods" 68
- The Bad 69
- 2-Word "Bads" 69
- Entertainment/Music "Bads" 69
- Language "Bads" 70
- Potpourri of "Bads" 71

Naked, Not Nekkid 73
- Entertainment/Music/TV "Nakeds" 75

Nobel Prizes 76
- Winners (Listed chronologically) 76

Ooh-La-La! 79
- Beginning "La La" 79
- Interior "La La" 80
- Geography "La La" 81
- Literary/Fine Arts "La La" 82
- Potpourri of "La La" 83

S-E-X: Everything You've Ever Wanted to Know About It 85
- Beginning S-E-X 85
- Beginning Separated S-E-X 85
- Elsewhere S-E-X 86

Sexual Trivia 87
- Censoring 87
- Famous Actress 87
- Proper Names Linked Sexually 88
- Potpourri of Sexual Trivia 90

Just "Sexual" 92
Americana 95
Benjamin Franklin 97

Poor Richard's Almanac	98
Declaration of Independence	99
U.S. Constitution	101
U.S. Government	103
The White House	105
"The Star-Spangled Banner"	107
Statue of Liberty	108
American Revolution	109
Leading Toward War	109
The War Chronologically	109
War Potpourri	111
War of 1812	113
The Alamo	116
The Alamo in Film	116
Mexican War	117
Spanish-American War	119
U.S. Presidents	121
Presidents and Their Vice Presidents	121
Presidential Nicknames	122
Presidential Quotations	123
Presidential Firsts	124
Presidential Onlys, Seconds, and Lasts	125
Middle Names of Presidents	126
Presidents and Their Monograms	126
Presidential Matriculations	126
Other Presidents and Their Colleges	127
Presidents and College Sports	127
Presidents and Academia	127
Questions on Presidents	128
Presidential/Vice Presidential Twos	129
Red, White, and Blue	131
Red, White, or Blue	132
Red	132
1-Word Reds	132
2-Word Reds	133
Red Idioms	133
Geography Reds	134
Homo Sapiens Reds	135
Literary Reds	137
Potpourri of Reds in the Answer	138
Potpourri of Reds Otherwise	139
White	141
1-Word Whites	141
2-Word Whites	141
White Idioms	142
Geography Whites	142
Homo Sapiens-Related Whites	144
Literary/Entertainment Whites	144
Potpourri of Whites in the Answer	146

Potpourri of Whites Otherwise	147
"White" People	148
Blue	149
1-Word Blues	149
2-Word Blues	149
Blue Idioms	150
Fine Arts/Music Blues	151
Geography Blues	152
Literary/Entertainment Blues	153
Potpourri of Blues in the Answer	154
Potpourri of Blues Otherwise	155
U.S. Colleges and Universities	157
Ivy League Schools: Their Nicknames and Locations	157
Major Colleges/State Universities: Their Nicknames and Locations	157
Aviation	159
Aircraft Related	159
Aircraft/Pilots	159
No Fear of Flying Here	162
U.S. Airports	162
World Airports	162
Countries and Their Airlines	163
U.S. Airport Codes	163
World Airport Codes	164
Ships, Boats, Subs	165
Vessels/Commanders (15th-18th century)	166
Vessels/Commanders (19th century)	167
Vessels/Commanders (20th-21st century)	167
Saints	171
Male Saints	171
Female Saints	173
Male Patron Saints	174
Female Patron Saints	175
Sinners (A.K.A. Notorious Homo Sapiens)	176
James Butler Hickok	176
William H. Bonney	176
October 26, 1881, Gunfight	176
Missouri Outlaws	176
Saloonkeeper and Judge	177
College Crime	177
1920s New England Murder Case	177
Famous Kidnapping	178
Caryl Chessman	178
Famous Espionage Case	178
1968 Trial	179
Cult Suicide	179
Murderer	179
Cult Tragedy	179
Terrorist Attack	180
9/11/2001	180

Potpourri of Crime	180
Thespians and Other Entertainers	**183**
Multiple Oscar-Winning Performances	184
Academy Award Winners	185
Best Actor	185
Best Actress	186
Best Picture	187
Nicknames of Entertainers	187
Pseudonyms/Real Names	190
Language/Alphabet	**196**
Multiple Languages	198
Language Potpourri	198
International Phonetic Alphabet	199
Greek Alphabet	**201**
1-Word Answers	201
2-Word Answers	202
Greek-Letter Societies	203
Potpourri of Completions	204
Letters from A to Z	**205**
Letters A-H	206
Letters I-P	207
Letters Q-Z	209
Common 2-Letter Abbreviations	211
Alpha-Numerically	**213**
Beginning with a Letter	213
Beginning with a Numeral	214
Diacritical Marks: Umlauts and Tildes	**215**
Umlauts	215
Tildes	217
Eponyms	**218**
Articles of Clothing and Grooming	218
Foods	219
Awards	220
Gimme an *A-A*	**221**
Homo Sapiens A-A	221
Potpourri of A-A	221
Athletes and A-A Nicknames	223
Gimme a *B-B*	**224**
Homo Sapiens B-B	224
Geography B-B	226
Literary/Film/TV/Music B-B	227
Homo Sapiens-Related B-B	229
Potpourri of B-B	230
Athletes and B-B Nicknames	232
Gimme a *C-C*	**233**
Homo Sapiens C-C	233
Geography C-C	234
Literary/Film/TV/Music C-C	235
Potpourri of C-C	236

- Athletes and C-C Nicknames 238
- Gimme a *D-D* 239
  - Homo Sapiens D-D 239
  - Literary/Film/TV/Music D-D 240
  - Potpourri of D-D 240
  - Athletes and D-D Nicknames 242
- Shared Names 243
  - Four or More Clues 243
  - Three Clues 244
  - Two Clues 246
  - Name Sharing 247
- Kiddie Lit 249
  - Fictional Characters 249
  - Legendary Creatures/Things 253
  - Harry Potter 254
  - Robin Hood 254
  - Peter Pan 255
  - Giant Lumberjack in American Folklore 255
- Adult Lit 256
  - Real Names/Literary Pseudonyms or Pen Names 256
  - Fictional Characters 257
  - Fictional Places 261
  - World Literature/Classical Authors 261
  - Epics 262
  - World Authors/Their Nationalities/Their Works 263
- Publishing: Newspapers and Magazines 267
  - U.S. Cities and Their Newspapers 267
  - World Cities and Their Newspapers 267
  - Publishing History 268
  - Potpourri of Publishing 271
  - Fictional Newspapers 271
  - Magazines 272
  - Magazine Potpourri 274
- Mythology 276
  - Greek and Roman Mythology 276
  - "In the Beginning" in Greek and Roman Mythology 276
  - Marketplace Myths 277
  - Geography Myths 279
- Food 282
  - British 282
  - French 282
  - German 283
  - Greek 284
  - Italian 284
  - Italian Pasta 285
  - Japanese 286
  - Mexican 286
- Mmm-Mmm Good 287
- Potpourri of Onlys 290

Lonelys	292
U.S. Geography	294
States and Their Capitals	294
States and Their Nicknames	294
State Capitals	296
Onlys in U.S. Geography	300
World Geography	302
Nations and Their Capitals	302
Continents	305
Seven Summits of the World	305
Longest Rivers by Continent	305
Largest Countries by Continent	305
15 Largest Countries in Area	305
Onlys in World Geography	306
Countries Bordering Only One Other Country	307
Toponyms	308
U.S. Related	308
Food and Drink in the U.S.	309
World Related	310
Articles of Clothing and Fabric	311
Food and Drink Worldwide	313
Medicine and Human Anatomy	315
Eye	316
Teeth	316
Body Parts	316
Bones of the Body	317
Adjectives Pertaining to Parts of the Body	317
Inflammatory Conditions	318
Specialized Language	319
Vitamins	320
Medical Specialists	320
Potpourri	321
Just Trivia	322
Thirty-Three Threes	325

YOUR FIRST THOUGHT*

Author who in "Self-Reliance" said: "To believe your own thought, to believe that what is true for you in your private heart is true for all men—that is genius"
Answer: Ralph Waldo Emerson.

*Sometimes a question can be answered solely on the basis of knowing one name that fits the general category after the first few clues, as in giving "your first thought" response "Hans Christian Andersen" to the question *Danish short story author* who wrote "The Emperor's New Clothes," "The Ugly Duckling," and "The Little Mermaid"

Adrian IV—*English pope* (1154-1159) born Nicholas Breakspear, who shares the name of the last German pope prior to Joseph Alois Ratzinger, who became Benedict XVI in 2005, though he was actually born in Utrecht in what was then Germany and is now part of the Netherlands

Vitus Jonassen Bering—*Danish navigator* who explored the northeastern coast of Asia for Czar Peter I (the Great) of Russia from 1728 to 1730

Niels Bohr*—*Danish physicist* who won the 1922 Nobel Prize in physics for his theory of the structure of the atom

Tycho Brahe—*Danish astronomer* who discovered a new star in 1573

Constantin Brancusi—*Romanian-born French sculptor* known for *Sleeping Muse* and *Bird in Space*

Catherine II (the Great)—*German-born Russian empress* who ruled from 1762 to 17986

Frédéric Chopin—*Polish-French composer* who had a 10-year liaison with writer George Sand

Joseph Conrad—*Polish-born author who wrote in English* and is known for "Heart of Darkness"

Nicolaus Copernicus—*Polish astronomer* who revolutionized science with his heliocentric theory of planetary movement

Emily Dickinson—*Amherst poet* known for having only 7 of her poems published in her lifetime

Anne Frank—*German Jewish diarist* whose 1947 *Diary of a Young Girl*, written during her 2 years in hiding in Amsterdam, was published 2 years after she died in a Nazi concentration camp

Sigmund Freud—*Viennese-born physician* whose writings include *The Interpretation of Dreams*

Hammurabi—*Babylonian lawgiver* whose code of laws in the 18th century B.C. is one of the earliest such examples written and defined in an orderly manner

Hannibal—*Carthaginian general* who was the son of Hamilcar Barca and crossed the Alps with his elephants

Vaclav Havel**—*Czech president and playwright* who founded the Civic Forum, a political organization, in 1989

Thor Heyerdahl—*Norwegian ethnologist and adventurer* who sailed the *Kon-Tiki* from South America to Polynesia

Henrik Ibsen—*Norwegian playwright* who wrote *A Doll's House*

Eugène Ionecso—*Romanian-born French playwright* who wrote *The Bald Soprano* and *Rhinoceros*

*In giving the surname, Bohr would be correct; he does, however, have a son, Aage Niels Bohr, who shared the 1975 Nobel Prize for physics. **He was elected president of the new Czech Republic in 1993; Karel Capek, author of *R.U.R: Rossum's Universal Robots*, is a better known playwright.

John Paul II—*Polish pope*, born Karol Józef Wojtyla, who served from 1978 to 2005 and was the first non-Italian pope since 1523

Johannes Kepler—*German astronomer* who used Tycho Brahe's work to lay the groundwork for Newton's work

Soren Kierkegaard—*Danish religious philosopher* considered the founder of existentialism

Edward Lear—*English limerick writer* who wrote *Book of Nonsense* and "The Owl and the Pussy-Cat"

Carolus Linnaeus***—*Swedish botanist and taxonomist* who founded the binomial system of nomenclature and originated the modern scientific classification of plants and animals

Luxembourg—*European (grand) duchy* bordering France, Belgium, and Germany

Gregor Mendel—*Austrian geneticist and monk* known as the founding father of modern genetics

Edvard Munch—*Norwegian artist* who painted *The Scream*

Tenzing Norgay—*Sherpa mountaineer guide* who with Sir Edmund Hillary climbed to the summit of Mount Everest in 1953

Jacques Offenbach—*German-born French composer* who is credited with the creation of 19th-century French operetta

Ignacy Jan Paderewski—*Polish statesman, pianist, and composer* who served briefly as premier in 1919

I.M. Pei—*Chinese-American architect* known for the Louvre's glass pyramid

Samuel Pepys—*English diarist* whose work covers the 1660 to 1669 period

Puerto Rico****—*U.S. island commonwealth* since 1952 whose capital is San Juan

Paul Revere—*American silversmith and patriot* known for his famous April 18, 1775, ride

Eero Saarinen*****—*Finnish-born American architect* known for St. Louis's Gateway Arch

Jean Sibelius—*Finnish composer* known for *Finlandia*

August Strindberg—*Swedish playwright and novelist* who wrote *Miss Julie*

Kiri Te Kanawa—*New Zealand soprano* who made her debut with the Met as Desdemona in Verdi's *Otello* and was made Dame Commander of the Order of the British Empire in 1984

Nikola Tesla—*Croatian-born American inventor* known for his induction coil

Dylan Thomas—*Welsh poet* who wrote the poem "Do Not Go Gentle into That Good Night"

Heitor Villa-Lobos—*Brazilian composer* known for his 9 *Bachianas brasileiras* blending Brazilian folk tunes with Johann Sebastian Bach's style

Lech Walesa—*Polish Solidarity leader* who became his country's president, serving from 1990 to 1995

***His name in Swedish is Carl von Linné. ****The Northern Mariana Islands is also a commonwealth. *****The surname Saarinen would be correct, as Eliel Saarinen, father of Eero, is also a Finnish-American architect.

However, some first clues help only in narrowing the choices, as in the following:

Edda—*13th-century Icelandic literary* work consisting of 2 books, the *Elder* or *Poetic* _____ and the *Younger* or *Prose* _____

Saga—*12th-13th-century Icelandic prose narrative* such as *Volsunga* _____, a retelling of the legends of the German epic *Nibelungelied*

Inigo Jones—*English architect* known for designing the Banqueting Hall at London's Whitehall Palace

Sir Christopher Wren—*English architect* who redesigned many churches after the Great London Fire in 1666

Maria Theresa—*Austrian archduchess* and queen of Hungary and Bohemia who brought unity to the Hapsburg monarchy
Marie-Louise—*Austrian archduchess* whom Napoleon married in 1810 as his second wife
Francis Ferdinand*—*Austrian archduke* whose assassination triggered WWI
Maximilian—*Austrian archduke* who served as emperor of Mexico from 1864 to 1867 before being executed
Confucius—*Chinese philosopher* whose life and thoughts are recorded in the *Analects*
Lao Tzu (Laozi)—*Chinese philosopher* considered the author of *Tao-te-Ching*, Taoism's central text
*Or Franz Ferdinand

Of course, some first clues help little in narrowing down the choices, as in the following:
Seamus Heaney—*Irish poet* who won the 1995 Nobel Prize in literature
Oscar Wilde—*Irish poet* and dramatist whose only novel is *The Picture of Dorian Gray*
William Butler Yeats—*Irish poet* and dramatist who won the 1923 Nobel Prize in literature
Lord Acton—*British lord* and historian known for saying "Power tends to corrupt, and absolute power corrupts absolutely"
Lord Byron—*British lord* and poet who wrote *Childe Harold's Pilgrimage*
Lord (Horatio) Nelson—*British lord* and naval commander known for his naval victory at Trafalgar
Alfred, Lord Tennyson—*British lord* and poet who wrote *In Memoriam*
Herodotus—*Greek historian* known as the "Father of History"
Thucydides—*Greek historian* who wrote the *History of the Peloponnesian War*
Xenophon—*Greek historian* who wrote the *Anabasis*

LIKELY ANSWERABLE AFTER THE FIRST CLUE

The Bartered Bride—Bedrich Smetana *opera* whose Czech title is *Prodaná Nevesta*
The Blue Boy—Thomas Gainsborough *painting* formally entitled *Jonathan Buttall*
Cavalleria rusticana—Pietro Mascagni *opera* set in a Sicilian village and including Santuzza and Lola
Gone With the Wind—Margaret Mitchell's *only novel*
Guggenheim Museum—*Circular museum* in New York City designed by Frank Lloyd Wright
Iliad*—*Homeric epic* about the Trojan War whose title means "a poem of Ilium"
Jane Eyre—Charlotte Brontë *novel* in which a governess at Thornfield Hall falls in love with Mr. Rochester
The Merry Widow—Franz Léhar's *most popular operetta* in music history, one including Hanna Glawari and Valencienne
(I) Pagliacci—Ruggiero Leoncavallo's *popular opera* inspired by Mascagni's *Cavalleria Rusticana* with the two, referred to as "Cav and Pag," often being performed together
Porgy and Bess—George Gershwin's black *"folk opera"* that includes Crown and Serena
A Ship of Fools—Katherine Anne Porter's *only* novel
To Kill a Mockingbird—Harper Lee's *only* novel
Wuthering Heights—Emily Brontë *novel* set in the Yorkshire moors and featuring the Earnshaw and Linton families
*The first of Homer's two epics with the *Odyssey* being the other possibility

ADULTERY

Name given to the Bible including the line: "Thou shall commit adultery" (Exodus xx, 14)
Answer: *The Wicked Bible* or *The Adulterous Bible* (misprint by the King's printers at Blackfriars in 1631)

Anna Karenina—Tolstoy novel featuring a Russian princess who abandons her husband and child to join her lover, Count Vronsky, and kills herself by throwing herself under a train
The Awakening—Kate Chopin's 1899 novel in which a New Orleans woman, dissatisfied with her passionless husband, commits adultery and kills herself by drowning in the ocean
Bathsheba—Biblical woman with whom David committed adultery and whose husband, Uriah the Hittite, he arranged to have killed in battle so he could marry her
Saul Bellow—American author of *Herzog*, a novel in which an author in his second failed marriage has a number of affairs
Lord Byron—English author who wrote in *Don Juan*: "What men call gallantry, and gods adultery,—Is much more common where the climate's sultry."
Jimmy Carter—U.S. President who confessed in an interview with *Playboy* during his campaign, "I have looked on a lot of women with lust. I've committed adultery in my heart many times. This is something that God recognizes I will do—and I have done it—and God forgives me for it."
Catherine the Great—Russian empress who had a succession of lovers, some of whom—Grigori Orlov and Grigori Potemkin—exercised great political influence
Geoffrey Chaucer*—English author of the tale told by The Miller in which Alison betrays her husband with her lover, Nicholas
Clytemnestra—Agamemnon's wife, who falls in love with Aegisthus while awaiting her husband's return from the Trojan War
Ethan Frome—Edith Wharton's 1911 novel in which a New England farmer falls in love with his sickly wife's cousin and companion, Mattie Silver
The Great Gatsby—F. Scott Fitzgerald's 1925 novel in which Daisy Buchanan accidentally runs over and kills Myrtle Wilson, her husband's mistress
Guinevere—King Arthur's wife who has an illicit affair with a knight of the Round Table
Henry VIII—English king who accused his wives Anne Boleyn and Catherine Howard of adultery and had them executed
Heracles (Hercules)—Alcmene's son born of a relationship with Zeus after he disguised himself as her husband, Amphitryon
Koran—Sacred book of Islam that, like the Bible, forbids adultery
Lady Chatterly's Lover—D.H. Lawrence's novel in which Connie (Constance) takes the gamekeeper, Oliver Mellors, as her lover because her husband is paralyzed from the waist down
La(u)ncelot—Knight of King Arthur's Round Table whose love affair with Arthur's wife led to his downfall
Madame Bovary—Gustave Flaubert novel in which Emma commits adultery, then kills herself with arsenic
Massachusetts—New England colony in which the 18-year-old married woman Mary Latham was hanged in 1643 with her lover James Britton, in what was the only such hanging in colonial times

*In *The Canterbury Tales*

Matthew—New Testament book with the line: "But I say unto you, That whosoever looketh on a woman to lust after her hath committed adultery with her already in his heart" (5:28)

Mourning Becomes Electra—Eugene O'Neill's 1931 trilogy in which Christine Mannon betrays her husband, Ezra, by having an affair with Captain Adam Brant

(I) *Pagliacci*—Ruggiero Leoncavallo opera in which Tonio the clown tells Canio of his wife's affair with Silvio after she rejects him

The Scarlet Letter—Nathaniel Hawthorne novel in which Hester Prynne and the Rev. Arthur Dimmesdale commit adultery

7th—Of the Ten Commandments, the one saying "Thou shalt not commit adultery" according to Exodus 20:14

Leo Tolstoy—Russian author of *The Kreutzer Sonata*, in which a bored Madame Pozdnishef takes her music partner Trukhashevsky as a lover

Ulysses—James Joyce novel in which Molly Bloom, wife of the central character Leopold Bloom, has an affair with Blazes Boylan

John Updike—American author whose 1968 novel *Couples*, set in the affluent New England community of Tarbox, deals with the theme of martial infidelity

BIBLE

Comedian who said during his last illness: "I've spent a lot of time searching through the Bible for loopholes"
Answer: W.C. Fields.

1) Name the 3 sons of Adam and Eve.
Answer: Cain, Abel, and Seth (listed in order of birth).

2) Name the 3 biblical patriarchs, that is, the founding fathers of the Jews.
Answer: Abraham, Isaac, and Jacob.

3) Name the first 3 kings of Israel.
Answer: Saul, David, and Solomon.

4) Name the 3 sons of Noah who, according to Genesis 7, were exiled forever from their homes by the great flood.
Answer: Shem, Ham, and Japheth.

5) Name Daniel's 3 companions who were thrown into the fiery furnace for not obeying King Nebuchadnezzar's command to worship a golden idol and were rescued by the Lord.
Answer: Shadrach (Hananiah), Meshach (Mishael), and Abednego (Azariah).

6) Give the 3 generally accepted names for the Three Wise Men of the East, the Three Kings of the Orient, or the Magi who followed a star to worship the baby Jesus in Bethlehem, arriving there on January 6, a day called the Epiphany, Twelfth Day, Twelfth-tide, Feast of Lights, or Feast of the Three Kings.
Answer: Melchior (or Melichior, meaning "King of Light"); Balthasar (or Balthazar, meaning "The Lord of the Treasures"); and Gaspar (or Caspar, meaning "The White One").

7) Identify the 3 gifts the Three Wise Men, or Magi, brought to the Christ child.
Answer: Gold, frankincense, and myrrh.

8) Name the authors of the 4 Gospels, that is, the first 4 books of the New Testament, which tell about the life and teachings of Jesus.
Answer: Matthew, Mark, Luke, and John (also referred to as the Evangelists, as in the title of Jacob Jordaens' painting *The Four Evangelists*, c. 1625, featuring Matthew, Mark, Luke, and John).

THE TEN COMMANDMENTS (According to Exodus 20: 1-17)*
Gods—Thou shalt have no other _____ before me;
Graven—Thou shalt not make any _____ image, or any likeness of anything in heaven above, on the earth, or in the sea;
Vain—Thou shalt not take the name of the Lord thy God in _____;
Sabbath—Remember the _____ day, to keep it holy;

*All Bible quotations are from the King James Version

Honor—_____ thy father and mother;
Kill—Thou shalt not _____;
Adultery—Thou shalt not commit _____;
Steal—Thou shalt not _____;
Witness—Thou shalt not bear false _____ against thy neighbor; and
Covet—Thou shalt not _____ thy neighbor's house, wife, manservant, maidservant, ox, ass, nor anything that is his.

BIBLICAL PEOPLE/PLACES/THINGS

PEOPLE (see also Biblical Pairs)
Aaron—First high priest of the Hebrews, Moses' older brother who supervised the making of the Golden Calf

Abraham—First of the biblical patriarchs, the one tested by God by being asked to kill his son Isaac but stopped at the last moment when an angel intervened saying he had proven his faith in God, and the one revered as the "father" of Judaism, Christianity, and Islam

Antichrist—Christ's great antagonist and spreader of evil who is to be conquered by Christ at the Second Coming before the Last Judgment

Apostles—Another name for Jesus' 12 Disciples, or followers who spread His religious beliefs

Barabbas—Prisoner and thief who, by popular choice of the Jews, was released by Pilate instead of Christ

Beelzebub—Literally, "Lord of flies, the prince of demons" in the New Testament, or Satan

Chosen people—Term for the Israelites or Jews, who, according to the Old Testament, were picked by God to possess their own land, grow into a great nation, and fulfill His purpose on earth

Daniel—Hebrew prophet who after being captured and taken to Babylon (as part of the Babylonian Captivity) prayed only to God and was protected by Him after being thrown into a lion's den

David—Second king of the Israelites who defeated Goliath, married Bathsheba, and fathered Solomon

Delilah—Samson's mistress who discovered that his strength was in his hair and betrayed him to the Philistines after having it all cut off while he slept

Esau—Isaac and Rebecca's eldest son who was tricked into selling his birthright to his twin brother Jacob for a bowl of stew, or pottage

Gabriel—God's messenger who appeared to the Virgin Mary and to Zacharias and whose trumpet will announce Judgment Day

Gideon—Judge and warrior of Israel who led 300 men in the defeat of the Midianites

Goliath—Philistine giant killed by David with his sling shot

Good Samaritan—Foreign traveler who helps an injured man after the victim's countrymen pass by without offering help, leading Jesus to tell the Judeans to be more like the stranger

Herod Antipas—King from 4 B.C. to A.D. 39 who was responsible for the beheading of John the Baptist

Herod the Great—King from 37 to 4 B.C. who ordered the slaughter of the infant boys in and around Bethlehem in an attempt to kill the infant Jesus (known as the Massacre of the Innocents)

Isaac—Second of the Hebrew patriarchs, whose name means "one laughs"; the elderly Abraham and Sarah's son who had twins, Esau and Jacob, by his wife Rebecca

Ishmael—Son of Abraham and his maid Hagar, both of whom are driven away by Abraham after the birth of Isaac

Israelites—Hebrews who were living in slavery in Egypt and then considered God's Chosen People when they were led out by Moses to live in the promised land of Canaan, later called Jews

Jacob—Esau's brother who with his mother Rebecca's help conspired to deprive his twin of his father's blessing, the patriarch who later while sleeping at a place called Bethel dreamed about a ladder reaching from earth to heaven and whose sons founded the 12 tribes of Israel—he was called Israel after wrestling with the angel of the Lord

Jeremiah—Old Testament "weeping prophet" who lived during the period when Jerusalem was conquered by the Babylonians and to whom is attributed the book *Lamentations* as well as a book named after him

Jesus—Divine son of God, born to Mary and Joseph, a carpenter, who taught about the coming kingdom of God but was crucified by his enemies on Calvary, only to arise after 3 days and later ascend into heaven—worshipped by Christians as Jesus Christ

Jezebel—Phoenician princess and wife of King Ahab considered an abomination because she brought the worship of Baal into the kingdom of the Israelites

Job—God-fearing man who endured much suffering but never lost his faith in God

John the Baptist—Zacharias and Elizabeth's son, the preacher who told of the coming of the Messiah, baptized Christ in the river Jordan, and was later arrested and beheaded

Jonah—Hebrew prophet whom God punished for disobedience by having him thrown overboard and swallowed by a "giant fish" during a storm and who, after 3 days in the belly of the fish, was pardoned and freed

Joseph—Jacob's 11th son, who was sold into slavery in Egypt by his jealous brothers where he rose to high office and was reconciled with his family

Joshua—Moses' successor who led the Israelites into the Promised Land

Judas (Iscariot)* —Disciple who for 30 pieces of silver betrayed Jesus to the authorities with a kiss in the Garden of Gethsemane and later hanged himself

Lazarus—Mary and Martha's brother who died and lay in a grave for 4 days before Jesus raised him from the dead

Lot—Abraham's nephew whose wife was turned into a pillar of salt because she disobeyed by looking back at the burning city of Sodom from which they were escaping

Lucifer—Archangel who for rebelling against God was thrown out of heaven and into hell, where he became known as Satan

Mary—Mother of Jesus who conceived by means of the Immaculate Conception—also called the Virgin Mary, the Blessed Virgin, and Madonna, the Italian meaning "my lady"

Mary Magdalene**—Woman out of whom Jesus cast 7 demons and who then followed Jesus the rest of His life, today known as His closest adviser

Messiah—Hebrew word meaning "the anointed one" for the redeemer of the Israelites as prophesied in the Old Testament—the equivalent of the Greek word *Christ*, meaning "anointed one"

Methuselah—Patriarch who lived 969 years, the oldest man mentioned in the Bible

Moses—Israelite leader who led the Israelites out of slavery in Egypt and received the Ten Commandments from God on Mount Sinai

*According to Matthew 27:3-10 (according to the Acts of the Apostles, 1:16-20, he died by falling and "all his bowels gushed out"). **Erroneously said to have been a prostitute.

Nazarite—Old Testament term for one who refrained from alcohol, from cutting one's hair, and from touching a dead body

Nimrod—Cush's son known as a mighty hunter

Noah—Patriarch commanded by God to build the Ark because the Deluge, or the Flood, was going to cover the earth following 40 days and 40 nights of rain—he took aboard 7 people and 2 of every animal species

Paul—"Apostle to the Gentiles" who was born Saul and spread the message of Christ after converting to Christianity following a vision on the road to Damascus

Peter—Apostle who, just as Jesus had predicted, denied 3 times that he was one of His followers—a fisherman born Simon renamed by Jesus, who said he was the rock upon which He would build His church

Philistines—Traditional enemies of the Israelites

Pontius Pilate—Roman governor in Jerusalem who allowed Jesus to be crucified after washing his hands of the matter, saying he found Jesus innocent of the charges brought against him

Prodigal son—Son who left home with his share of his father's goods and "wasted his substance with riotous living," returned home, was forgiven by his father and feasted with a fatted calf to celebrate

Rachel—Jacob's second wife, mother of Joseph and Benjamin

Rebekah (Rebecca)—Jacob's mother who helped him deceive his blind father Isaac to get his brother Esau's birthright

Ruth—Moabite widow who stayed with Naomi, her mother-in-law, and then married Boaz—she was known for her kindness and loyalty

Salome—Herodias' daughter and dancer who performed for King Herod Antipas and at the urging of her mother demanded the head of John the Baptist on a platter

Samson—Israelite judge noted for his great strength who after being betrayed by Delilah and blinded and imprisoned by the Philistines, then regained his strength and died while knocking down his enemies' largest temple

Satan—Christ's tempter and adversary or the Devil, today pictured with horns on his head, a tail, and hooves like that of a goat

Saul—First king of Israel who waged war against the Philistines, had his nerves soothed by David's playing the lyre, became unstable, was wounded in battle, and committed suicide

Solomon—David and Bathsheba's wealthy son and king of Israel who built the first temple and was noted for his many wives and his wisdom

Thomas (Didymus)—Apostle who doubted the resurrection of Jesus until he saw the wounds from the crucifixion

PLACES

Armageddon—Scene where the last, great decisive battle between the forces of good and evil is to be fought at the end of the world, just prior to Judgment Day according to Revelation (16:16)

Babel (Tower of)—Tower people erected in Babylonia following the flood to try to reach the heavens, leading God to make them speak different languages as punishment for their arrogance

Bethlehem—Town in which Jesus was born in a manger in a stable because there was no room at the inn

Calvary—Hill near Jerusalem on which Jesus was crucified, also known as Golgotha, or the "Place of the Skull"

Canaan—Ancient name for Palestine, the Promised Land of the Israelites, over which they ruled following their flight from Egypt and said to be the "land flowing with milk and honey"
Eden—Beautiful garden and earthly paradise where Adam and Eve lived until they disobeyed God by eating the forbidden fruit
Gethsemane—Olive garden or grove at the foot of the Mount of Olives, scene of the agony and arrest of Jesus
Gomorrah—City whose name begins with *G* that God destroyed by fire and brimstone because its people were sinners
Heaven—Dwelling place of God, the angels, and those souls who have been granted salvation
Hell—Dwelling place of Satan and a place of eternal punishment for those souls not granted salvation
Holy Land—Land promised by God to the Israelites—also called the Promised Land and Canaan—an area bordered by the Mediterranean Sea, the Jordan River, Lebanon, and the Sinai Peninsula
Jericho—City the Israelites captured by following Joshua's God-given orders to blow trumpets and shout, thus bringing its walls down
Jerusalem—Holy city where Solomon built his temple and Jesus was crucified
Land of Nod—Place east of Eden to which Cain was banished by God after killing Abel
Mount of Olives (Mount Olivet)—Jerusalem site of the Sermon on the Mount and the Garden of Gethsemane where Jesus prayed before He was betrayed
Nazareth—Town in Galilee, in northern Israel, where Jesus lived as a child with His parents Mary and Joseph
Paradise—Garden of Eden, or Heaven
Pearly Gates—2-word phrase for the entranceway to heaven
Potter's field—Burial ground for paupers bought by the chief priests with the money that Judas returned to them
Promised Land—Canaan or Palestine, the land God promised Abraham his Israelite descendants would rule—they found it after fleeing Egypt and wandering in the desert for 40 years
Sodom—City from which God permitted Lot and his family to flee before He destroyed it by fire and brimstone because its people were sinners
Solomon's Temple—Central place of Jewish worship on Mount Moriah in Jerusalem that was destroyed by Nebuchadnezzar in 586 B.C.

THINGS
Apocalypse—Any of various Jewish and Christian anonymous writings depicting symbolically the ultimate destruction of evil and triumph of good, or another name for Revelation, the last book of the New Testament
Apocrypha—14 books of the Septuagint rejected by the Jews as not inspired by God, 11 of which were later accepted by the Roman Catholic Church
Ark of the Covenant—Wooden chest carried around on poles by the Hebrews and containing the 2 tablets on which the Ten Commandments God gave to Moses were written
Behemoth—Animal described in Job 40:15-24 whose name from the Hebrew means "great animal," perceived by most as a hippopotamus
Burning bush—Term for the plant from which God appeared to Moses in a flame of fire and ordered him to lead the Israelites out of slavery in Egypt and across the Red Sea

("sea of reeds"), which parted, allowing their escape and killing the Egyptians when they followed
Coat of many colors—Beautiful coat Joseph's father Jacob gave him, prompting his jealous brothers to sell him into slavery, then tell their father that the blood stains on the coat were the result of wild animals killing him—he became rich serving the pharaoh
Covenant—Solemn promise made by God to his people as set forth in the Old and New Testament on condition of obedience to God's will
Crown of thorns—Thorny branches Pilate's soldiers forced Jesus to wear on his head as a mockery of his claim to be king of the Jews
Crucifixion—Execution of Jesus by nailing and binding to a cross, on a hill called Calvary
Dead Sea Scrolls—Oldest known documents of the Bible, called the "greatest manuscript discovery of modern times," found by a Bedouin shepherd boy in the Wadi Qumran (Qumran Valley) in 1947 in caves near the Dead Sea
Easter—Christian holiday celebrating the Resurrection of Jesus Christ
Ecclesiastes (3:1)—Biblical book having the line "To every thing there is a season, and a time to every purpose under the heaven."
Epiphany—Festival held on January 6 commemorating the visit of the Magi to worship the baby Jesus in Bethlehem
Exodus—Old Testament book describing how Moses led the Israelites out of Egypt
The Fall (of man)—Term for Adam and Eve's sin of eating the forbidden fruit and their subsequent loss of grace and expulsion from the Garden of Eden
Fire and brimstone—Symbols of divine punishment in this world and the next for those who have done wrong
Forbidden fruit—Term for the fruit of the Tree of Knowledge of Good and Evil, which God commanded Adam and Eve not to eat
Golden Calf—Idol that Aaron directed be made from the people's jewelry and that the Israelites worshipped until Moses returned from Mount Sinai and destroyed it
Golden rule*—Precept stated in Matthew 7:12 as "Do unto others as you would have them do unto you"
Good Friday—Day on which Christ was crucified, 2 days before the Resurrection
Gospels—Term, literally meaning "good news," for the New Testament books concerning the life and teachings of Jesus
Judgment Day**—Day following the destruction of the world when the Lord will return to judge the living and the dead, sending the good to heaven and the wicked to hell
Last Supper—Meal with His disciples that Jesus presided over the night before His crucifixion
Leviathan—Great sea beast described in Job 41:1 whose name from the Hebrew means "that will gather itself together in folds," perceived by many as a crocodile
Loaves (5) and fishes (2)—Foods Jesus multiplied to feed the multitude who had gathered in the desert who came to watch Him heal the sick
Mammon—Riches personified as a false god in the New Testament
Manna—Food miraculously provided to the Israelites during their 40-year trip through the wilderness
Millennium—Period of a thousand years during which Christ will reign on earth, according to Revelation 20:1-5
Nativity—Birth of Jesus

*"Therefore all things whatsoever ye would that men should do to you, do ye even so them." **Also called Day of Judgment, Doomsday, and the Last Judgment

Noah's Ark—Vessel measuring 300 cubits by 50 cubits by 30 cubits that may have landed on Mount Ararat in northeastern Turkey
Original sin—Adam's act of disobedience in eating the fruit of the Tree of Knowledge of Good and Evil, traditionally resulting in the belief that all men are tainted with sin at birth
Palm Sunday—Sunday before Easter when Jesus made a triumphal entry into Jerusalem riding on a donkey after 3 years of preaching—also called Passion Sunday
Pentateuch—Greek word meaning "five books" or "five scrolls" designating the first five books of the Bible—also called the "Five Books of Moses" and the Torah
Proverbs—Wise sayings attributed to Solomon and others and found in the 20th book of the Old Testament
Psalm 23 (1-2)—Chapter and verses for the lines: "The Lord is my shepherd; I shall not want. / He maketh me to lie down in green pastures: he leadeth me beside the still waters."
Psalms—Songs and prayers, many of which were written by David, collected in one book of the Old Testament and used as part of Jewish and Christian worship
Rapture—In some Christian theologies, the bodily transporting of a person to heaven just before Armageddon
Resurrection—Rising of Jesus from the dead on the third day after His death and burial
Revelation(s)—Last book of the Bible, also known as the Apocalypse
Second Coming—Expected return of Christ at the Last Judgment
Septuagint—Earliest extant translation of the Pentateuch from the original Hebrew dating to 3 centuries before Christ's time and named from the ancient tradition that it was completed in 72 days by 72 Jewish scholars
Sermon on the Mount—Jesus' sermon that includes the Lord's Prayer and the 8 Beatitudes
666—Number of the Beast, or the devil, according to Revelation
Song of Solomon—Book of the Bible sometimes called Song of Songs, traditionally ascribed to David and Bathsheba's son and considered as an allegory of the union between Jesus and His church
Ten Commandments—The Decalogue, or Divine laws in the Bible
Torah—Hebrew name meaning "law" for the first 5 books of the Bible—also called the "Five Books of Moses" and the Pentateuch

BIBLICAL PAIRS
Adam and Eve—First man and woman who, according to Genesis, lived in the Garden of Eden before being expelled, forcing them to work and grow their own food
Cain and Abel—"Tiller of the soil" who became the first person in the Bible to commit a murder and his victim, his younger brother who was "the keeper of the sheep"
David and Bathsheba—King who arranged for Uriah the Hittite to be killed in battle so he could marry Uriah's wife, with whom he had already committed adultery, and this woman who became his wife and later bore him a son named Solomon
David and Goliath—Figure who used a slingshot to defeat a giant of a man who stood "6 cubits and a span" and the Philistine giant whom he defeated
David and Jonathan—Pair whose covenant of friendship described in I Samuel 18:1 has led to their names being used as a metaphor for "inseparable friends"
Isaac and Rebecca—2nd of the Hebrew patriarchs and his wife who was childless for 20 years before giving birth to the twins Esau and Jacob

Jacob and Rachel—Isaac's son who fathered the founders of the 12 tribes of Israel and his wife, Laban's daughter, whom he married after being first forced to marry her older sister Leah

Peter and Paul—Pair called, respectively, "The Apostle to the Jews" and "The Apostle to the Gentiles"

Ruth and Naomi—Moabite woman who followed her deceased husband's mother to Bethlehem, saying, ". . . whither thou goest, I will go," and the mother-in-law to whom she showed such loyalty

Samson and Delilah—Famous Hebrew known for his great strength and the beautiful Philistine woman who betrayed him after discovering that the secret of his strength lay in his long hair

Sarah and Abraham—Parents of Isaac, who was born to them in their old age fulfilling a promise from God

King Solomon and the Queen of Sheba—3rd king of ancient Israel who ruled from about 965 B.C. until his death and the queen best known for her visit to Jerusalem during the time this king was on the throne

RELIGION

German-born American scientist who said: "Science without religion is lame, religion without science is blind"
Answer: Albert Einstein.

1) Arrange the religions of Buddhism, Christianity, Judaism, Hinduism, and Islam in chronological order of their beginning.
Answer: Judaism (about the 1700s B.C., from the time of Abraham), Hinduism (about 1500 B.C.; some sources list Hinduism as older than Judaism), Buddhism (6th century B.C.), Christianity (1st century A.D.), and Islam (7th century A.D.).

2) Identify the 3 major religions born in the Middle East.
Answer: Christianity, Islam, and Judaism.

3) Jerusalem is a city of 3 Sabbaths. Identify these 3 days of the week observed, respectively, as days of rest and worship by the 3 major religious groups living there.
Answer: Friday (Muslim), Saturday (Jewish), and Sunday (Christian).

4) Name the following 3 holiest places within the walls of the Old City of Jerusalem: the wall that is the only surviving part of the Second Temple and Judaism's most sacred shrine; the Christian shrine standing on Calvary; and the golden-domed shrine of Islam.
Answer: Wailing Wall, Western Wall, or Happiness Wall; Church of the Holy Sepulcher; and Dome of the Rock (sometimes incorrectly called the Mosque of Omar), respectively.

JUDAISM
1) Name the 5 books called the Pentateuch, or Books of Moses, which constitute the Torah of the Jewish religion. According to Jewish tradition, Moses received these books from God.
Answer: Genesis, Exodus, Leviticus, Numbers, and Deuteronomy.

2) Name the 3 Jewish patriarchs or founding fathers.
Answer: Abraham, Isaac, and Jacob.

Bar Mitzvah—Ceremony to mark a boy's entry into adulthood at age 13
Bat Mitzvah—Ceremony to mark a girl's entry into adulthood at age 13
Bris (brith milah)—Circumcision ceremony on the 8th day after birth
Cantor—Worship leader who sings or chants the music and leads the prayers during Jewish services in a synagogue, such as those of the High Holy Days
Challah (hallah)—Loaf of rich white bread eaten on the Sabbath and holidays
Chanukah (Hanukkah)—8-day feast commemorating the victory of the Maccabees over the Syrians in 165 B.C. and the rededication of the Temple—known also as the Festival of Lights or Feast of Dedication
Diaspora—Dispersion or the scattering of Jews after the Babylonian exile

Gentile—Anyone not a Jew

Haggada(h)—Exodus passage read at the Passover Seder

The Holocaust—Word meaning "burnt whole" for the systematic killing of over 6 million European Jews by the Nazis before and during WWII

Jerusalem—Judaism's holiest city

Kabbala(h; Cabala)—Ancient mystical movement based on a symbolic interpretation of the Scriptures having as its main text the ancient Zohar, whose name means "bright light"

Kaddish—Mourners' prayer, or prayer in praise of God

Kol Nidre—Prayer recited in synagogues at the start of services on the eve of Yom Kippur

Kosher—Food prepared in accord with Jewish dietary laws

Latkes—Potato cakes, eaten especially on Chanukah

Masada—Ancient Hebrew fortress above the Dead Sea where Jewish Zealots committed mass suicide in A.D. 73 at the end of a Roman siege

Matzo (matza)—Thin, unleavened bread eaten by Jews on the 8 days of Passover

Menorah—9-branched candelabrum used during Chanukah

Passover—Festival celebrating the flight of the Israelites from Egyptian slavery—also known as Pesa(c)h

Pogrom—Organized persecution and massacre of Jews in Czarist Russia

Purim—Feast that commemorates the rescue of the Jews of Persia by Esther, the Jewish queen of King Ahasuerus, from Haman's plot to kill them—also known as the Feast of Lots

Rabbi—Hebrew word for "teacher" or "master" used to designate the leader in a place of worship

Rosh Hashana(h)—Jewish New Year, also known as the Day of Judgment, which begins a 10-period of repentance and spiritual renewal

Seder—Ceremonial feast on the eve of the first day of Passover when the story of liberation of the Israelites from Egyptian bondage is read from the Haggadah

Shabbat—The Sabbath, which begins at sundown on Friday

Shavuot—Festival commemorating Moses' receiving of the Ten Commandments—also called Feast of Weeks

Shofar—Ram's horn blown in synagogues on Rosh Hashanah

Star of David—6-pointed symbol of Judaism that was officially adopted in the 17th century by the Jewish community of Prague—also called Magen David, Shield of David, or Solomon's Seal

Sukot (Sukkot)—Feast known as the Feast of Tabernacles

Synagogue (temple)—Place of worship

Tallit(h)—Prayer shawl worn by men during morning prayer

Talmud—Body of Jewish civil and religious law consisting of 2 parts, the Mishna and the Gemara

Tora(h; Scrolls)—Parchment on which the Pentateuch is written in Hebrew

Yahweh (Jehovah)—Another name for God, from a modern transliteration of the Tetragrammaton YHWH

Yarmulke—Skullcap worn by Orthodox and conservative Jewish males at prayer, study, or meals

Yeshiva—Seminary where Orthodox rabbis are trained

Yom Kippur—Holiest day of the Jewish calendar for fasting, worship, and repentance—also called Day of Atonement

HINDUISM

Identify the 3 most important members, or *Trimurti*, making up the one universal spirit called *Brahman* in the Hindu religion, representing, respectively, the forces of creation, preservation, and destruction.

Answer: Brahma (creator of the universe), Vishnu (its preserver), and Shiva (its destroyer).

Angkor Wat—Hindu temple complex in Cambodia dedicated to Vishnu

Ashram—Sanskrit word for a secluded place for a community of Hindus wanting to live simply and meditate

Avatar—Incarnation or personification of a god on earth

Bhagavad-Gita—Sanskrit for "Song of the Blessed One" designating the 18-part discussion between the god Krishna and the warrior Arjuna that is a sacred text of Hinduism, found in the *Mahabharata*, an ancient Sanskrit epic

Brahman—Supreme and eternal spirit of the universe, or the universal spirit in everyone and everything

Brahmin—Highest priestly caste who carry out sacrifices

Caste system—System that determines the life of most Hindus, including the occupation they may hold

Chakra—Form of yoga, named from the Sanskrit for "wheel," referring to the centers in the body, usually 7, that Hindus consider sources of energy for psychic or spiritual power

Dharma (dhamma)—Moral and religious law of Hinduism (and Buddhism) and a person's observance of this law

Dhoti (dhotti)—Loincloth worn by Hindu men in India

Ganesh(a)—4-armed elephant-headed god of wisdom and son of Shiva, considered to be a remover of obstacles

Ganges—Most sacred river in India, where Hindus bathe and along which they visit their temples, especially in such holy cities as Varanasi and Allahabad

Guru—Teacher or spiritual leader

India—Country whose major religion is Hinduism and the one in which most Hindus live

Juggernaut—Incarnation of the Hindu god Vishnu carried on a large cart during religious rites under whose wheels worshippers often threw themselves and were crushed

Kali (Durga)*—Goddess of destruction and motherhood, wife of Shiva

***Kamasutra* (*Kama Sutra*)**—Love manual written about A.D. 400 and attributed to Vatsyayana, also known as Mallanaga—its name in Sanskrit means "love aphorisms"

Karma—Totality of a person's action and experiences in the successive states of existence; loosely, fate, destiny, or kismet

Krishna—Sanskrit word for "black" designating the incarnation of the god Vishnu

Lotus—Water lily used as a religious symbol

Lotus position—Yoga position used in meditation, sitting erect with the legs crossed

Mahabharata—Oldest of the 2 great Hindu epics, an 18-book Sanskrit one, the world's longest poem, ascribed to the Hindu sage Vyasa and including the *Bhagavad-Gita*—its title means "the great story" of the descendants of King Bharata

Mahatma—Title of respect used for a very spiritual person with high ideals

Mantra—Hymn from the *Veda*, a sacred book, chanted as an incantation or prayer

Moksha—State of perfect peace and happiness, achieved by the extinction of all desires and passions

*As Parvati or Uma, she is the beloved goddess of motherhood.

Nepal—Country whose official religion is Hindu and in which Buddha, the founder of Buddhism, was born
Om—Sanskrit word for "yes," repeated over and over while meditating
Purdah—Urdu and Hindi word for "veil" that designates the practice of, or the cloth used in, concealing the face of women in Hindu and Muslim communities
Rama—Popular Hindu god, a human form of the god Vishnu, depicted as a king carrying a bow and arrow
Ramayana—Latest of the 2 great Hindu epics, this one about the godlike Rama
Reincarnation—Rebirth of the soul in another body, a basic belief in Hinduism
Sacred cow—2-word phrase meaning "something cherished and above criticism" derived from the Hindu belief that cows contain the souls of dead persons and are therefore not to be eaten (other animals are also revered)
Samsara—Continuing cycle of birth, death, and reincarnation
Sutra—Collection of wise sayings or maxims
Suttee (sati)—Former Hindu custom requiring a widow to burn herself on the funeral pyre of her husband
Swami—Religious teacher
Untouchables**—Those at the bottom of India's caste system, the lowest under Hinduism
Upanishads—Group of metaphysical treatises dealing with man in relation to the universe that form the final section of each of the 4 sacred books of Hinduism
Vedas—Oldest Hindu scriptures, 4 sacred books written in an early dialect of Sanskrit
Yoga—Hindu philosophy that aims to achieve liberation of the self and union with the supreme being through fitness of body and mind
Yogi—One who practices yoga
**Also called Dalits, Scheduled Castes, Scheduled Tribes, or harijan

BUDDHISM
1) Identify the 4 Noble Truths of Buddhism.
Answer: Life is suffering (*dukkha*); suffering has its roots in desire (*tanha*), which leads to the cycle of rebirth (*samsara*); cessation of desire is the end of suffering (*nirvana*); and the way to escape from suffering and desire can be reached by the Noble Eightfold Path as taught by Buddha.

2) Identify the 8 components of the Noble Eightfold Path to righteousness in Buddhism.
Answer: Right views (understanding), right intentions (thought), right speech, right conduct (action), right livelihood, right effort, right mindfulness, and right meditation (concentration).

3) Identify the Three Fires, or causes of suffering, or *dukkha*, that Buddhists believe are extinguished in Nirvana.
Answer: Hate, greed (or restlessness), and dullness of mind.

ITS FOUNDER
Siddhartha Gautama—Real name of the founder of Buddhism
Buddha—Sanskrit title meaning "the Enlightened One" given to this founder
India—Country in which Buddhism was founded about 525 B.C. near Benares
Nepal—Neighboring country on whose border this founder was born

Fig—Type of tree called a bo or bodhi tree under which revelations came to him
Dalai Lama—Of the 2 Grand Lamas who are both considered as Buddha born again, the one regarded as the ruler of Tibet and the highest spiritual ruler of Lamaism—the name means "superior priest"
Panchen Lama—Lama regarded as the second leading spiritual ruler of Lamaism, second in importance to the first of the Grand Lamas

Bodhi—Spiritual enlightenment Buddhists strive to achieve
Bodhisattva—Enlightened person, a potential Buddha, especially one who rejects nirvana to assist mankind
Dharma—Teachings of Buddha or the cosmic order or law underlying all existence
Enlightenment—Spiritual awakening to the true nature of reality
Great Buddha—English meaning of *Daibutsu*, designating the large bronze statue of Buddhism's founder in Kamakura, Japan
India—Country in which the Dalai Lama has been living in exile in Dharmasala since China took control of Tibet in 1950
Karma—Lifetime of words, deeds, and thoughts believed to determine the fate of a person's next stage in existence, or loosely, fate, destiny, or kismet
Koan—Nonsense question in Zen Buddhism intended to free the mind, such as "What is the sound of one hand clapping?"
Lamaism—Tibetan branch of Buddhism
Lamasery—Monastery of Lama Buddhists
Lotus—Water lily used as a religious symbol
Lotus position—Yoga position used in meditation, sitting erect with the legs crossed
Mantra—Sacred utterance chanted as an incantation or prayer
Mount Fuji—Japan's highest mountain, which has long been sacred to the country's Buddhists
Nirvana—State of perfect peace and happiness, achieved by the extinction of all desires and passions
Noble Eightfold Path—8 steps or path to happiness
Reincarnation—Rebirth of the soul in another body
Samsara—Continuing cycle of birth, death, and reincarnation
Sangha—Community of believers founded by Buddha
Stupa—Buddhist shrine shaped like a dome and containing a sacred object
Sutra—One of Buddha's sermons or dialogues
Tripitaka—Collection of Buddha's teachings
Zen Buddhism—Sect of Buddhism whose followers seek to attain illumination of the mind and spirit through meditation, the form now practiced in Japan, Vietnam, and Korea

CHRISTIANITY
1) The term Trinity expresses the belief that in the one God there are 3 divine persons. Name these 3.
Answer: The Father, the Son, and the Holy Ghost (or Holy Spirit or Divine Spirit).

2) Name the 7 sacraments of both the Roman Catholic and the Eastern Orthodox churches.
Answer: 1) Baptism (christening), 2) confirmation, 3) Holy Eucharist (or Holy Communion or the Lord's Supper), 4) penance (or confession or reconciliation), 5) holy orders, 6) matrimony, 7) Anointing of the Sick (formerly Extreme Unction).

3) Identify the 3 sacraments that may be received only once in both the Roman Catholic and the Eastern Orthodox churches.
Answer: Baptism, confirmation, and holy orders.

4) Name the 7 Deadly, or Capital, Sins, so designated because they are believed to cause spiritual death.
Answer: Pride, wrath (anger), envy, lust (lechery), gluttony, avarice (covetousness), and sloth (laziness).

5) According to Roman Catholic belief, to what 4 places can the soul go to after the death of the body?
Answer: Heaven, hell, purgatory, and limbo.

6) What are, by tradition, the 3 basic statements of the Christian faith?
Answer: Ten Commandments, Lord's Prayer (or *Pater Noster*), and the Apostles' Creed.

7) Name the 3 members of the Holy Family, especially as used in art.
Answer: Jesus (especially the baby Jesus), Mary (or the Virgin Mary), and Joseph.

Advent—Word designating the birth of Jesus or, sometimes, the Second Coming, and the liturgical period including the 4 Sundays just before Christmas in Western churches
Apostles' Creed—Ancient Christian statement of belief beginning with the words "I believe in God, the Father Almighty"
Archbishop—Highest ranking bishop, one who oversees an archdiocese
Ascension—Christ's rising to heaven, commemorated on the 40th day after Easter Sunday
Baptism—Religious ceremony using water as a symbol of a person's acceptance into the Christian faith
Bible—Sacred book of Christianity, containing both the Old Testament and New Testament
Bishop—High-ranking member of the clergy who heads a diocese or district in Christian churches
Born-again Christian—Person who undergoes a personal conversion to the Christian faith signified by baptism, especially in the evangelical tradition
Canonization—Declaration of a deceased person a saint in a formal procedure
Cardinal—Any of the Roman Catholic Church officials called "Princes of the Church," ranking just below the pope and appointed by the pope to the college, or council, that chooses the next pope
Catechism—Book of questions and answers about religion used for teaching religious doctrine
Cathedral—Christian church building where a bishop has his *see*, or his seat of authority
Christen—To give a first name to, as is done in baptism
Christian—Someone who believes in Jesus as the Christ or the Messiah, or someone who believes in the religion based on Jesus' teachings
Clergy (clerics)—Ordained religious leaders
Confession—Practice of the Roman Catholic Church through which a person admits his sins to a priest, asks forgiveness, and does penance
Confirmation—Ceremony marking a person's admittance to full church membership
Contrition—Remorse for having sinned

Ecumenism—Movement to promote unity among Christian churches
Eucharist—Christian rite also called Holy Communion in which bread and wine are consecrated and given to worshippers to celebrate their union with Jesus Christ
Infidel—Person belonging to another religion, or a person with no religious beliefs
Jesus Christ—Founder of Christianity
King James Version—English translation of the Bible from the Hebrew and Greek published in 1611 as authorized by the king, also called the Authorized Version
Lent—40 weekdays from Ash Wednesday to Easter Sunday
Messiah—Hebrew word meaning "the anointed one," the equivalent of the Greek *Christ*, meaning "anointed one"
Pentecost—Festival on the 50th day after Passover celebrating the descent of the Holy Spirit upon the Apostles
Pilgrimage—Journey made by a pilgrim to a holy site
Pope—Leader of the Roman Catholic Church, or pontiff, the first of whom was Peter
Priest—Clergyman authorized to administer the sacraments and ranking just below a bishop in the Roman Catholic, Eastern Orthodox, and Episcopal Churches
Roman Catholic Church—Christian church headed by the pope, or Bishop of Rome
Saint—Holy person, especially one who has died and is considered to be with God in heaven—or, in the Roman Catholic Church, one who has been officially canonized
Tithe—Tenth of one's annual income contributed to support a church or its clergy
Transubstantiation—Roman Catholic and Eastern Orthodox Church doctrine that in the Eucharist the elements of bread and wine become the body and blood of Christ
Vatican (Palace)—Headquarters of the Roman Catholic Church and the residence of the pope

ISLAM

1) Identify the 5 Pillars of Islam, whose name is the Arabic word meaning "surrender" or "submission."
Answer: Witness (or *shadada*; "There is no God but the one God, and Muhammad is His prophet"); prayer (or *salat*; said 5 times a day, at daybreak, noon, midafternoon, sunset, and evening); almsgiving (or *zakat*); fasting (or *sawm*; during the month of Ramadan); and pilgrimage (or *hajj*; to the Kaaba, the holiest shrine of Islam in Mecca).

2) According to the Koran, who are the 4 archangels?
Answer: Gabriel, Michael, Azrael, and Israfel.

3) Identify the 2 holy cities in the Hejaz, the Moslem (Muslim) holy land in the western part of Arabia.
Answer: Mecca and Medina (both are located in Saudi Arabia).

4) Identify the 2 symbols that appear on the flags of several nations with a Muslim majority, such as Pakistan and Turkey.
Answer: Crescent and star.

5) Excluding the first prophet Adam and the last one, the founder of Islam, name the other 4 most important ones, all of whose names are found in the Bible.
Answer: Noah (Nuh), Abraham (Ibrahim), Moses (Musa), and Jesus (Isa).

RELIGION

ITS FOUNDER

Muhammad (Mohammed)*—Prophet who founded Islam about A.D. 622 and who believed and preached that there was only one God and that he was God's messenger—his name means "Praised One"

Allah—Islam's one god, a word meaning "The God"

Mecca—This prophet's Saudi Arabian birthplace, the holiest site in Islam to which all Moslems try to make a pilgrimage at least once in their lives

Gabriel—Angel who transmitted the revelations of God to this prophet and brought the milk white horse that carried this prophet to Seventh Heaven

Al-Borak—His milk white horse with the wings of an eagle, a human face with horses' cheeks, and capable of speaking—its name means "the lightning"

Khadija—This prophet's wife and first disciple who convinced him that the vision of this angel came from God

Koran (Quran)—Sacred text of Islam—its name means "a book" or "a recitation" in which God's revelations and this prophet's teachings are recorded

Medina—Islam's 2nd holiest city, once called Yathrib, to which this prophet fled from his enemies and where he later died and was buried

Hegira—Forced journey of this prophet from his birthplace to the city where he died in 622 A.D.—the Muslim calendar begins with this year

Hadith—Written collections in which this prophet's sayings and acts, the *Sunna*, are found

Sunna—Words and practices of this prophet

Fatima—His youngest child, considered to be the "supreme lady" of Paradise

*Also spelled Mohammad and Mahomet

Adam—Islam's first prophet

Ayatollah—Arabic word meaning "sign of God" designating a Shiite religious leader

Black Stone—Most sacred object in all of Islam, an object located in a corner of the Kaaba and believed to be a sign that Allah sent to mankind

Caliph*—Supreme ruler, the title taken by Muhammad's successors as head of Islam

Dome of the Rock—Shrine in Jerusalem on Temple Mount over the rock from which Muhammad is said to have ascended into heaven—erroneously called Mosque of Omar

Hajj—Pilgrimage to Mecca to pay homage at the Kaaba, a trip every Muslim is expected to make at least once in a lifetime

Halal—Word to describe food prepared in accord with Islamic dietary laws

Houri—Beautiful female guide in Paradise

Imam—Prayer leader in a Muslim house of worship

Infidel—One belonging to any faith other than Islam

Jerusalem—Islam's holiest city after Mecca and Medina

Jihad (*jehad*)—Arabic word for a war by Moslems against enemies of Islam, carried out as a religious duty

Jinni (djinni)—Demons in animal or human form in Muslim folklore

Kaaba—Empty cubical structure in the center of the Great Mosque in Mecca known to Muslims as the House of God

Madrasa(h)—Islamic school or college, especially one attached to a Muslim house of worship

*Caliphate is the land ruled by a caliph.

Minaret—Muslim house of worship's tall prayer tower

Moors—Arabicized Berbers who established Muslim rule in the Iberian Peninsula in the 8th century but who by the late 1200s had lost most of their land there

Mosque—Muslim temple or house of worship

Muezzin—Person in a minaret who calls Muslims to prayer 5 times a day

Mulla(h)—Muslim teacher of religious law

Muslim (Moslem)—Arabic word for "one who submits," the name given to one who believes in this one God and accepts the Prophet Muhammad as his messenger

Ramadan—Sacred month of Islam during which a Muslim may not eat or drink between sunrise and sunset

Rasul—Word meaning "messenger" designating one to whom God has made a revelation to guide humanity

Salaam aleikum—Muslim greeting translated as "Peace (be) to you"

Sharia—Islamic law, whose name means "the way that leads to God"

Shiites—Members of the Shiah, the division of Islam second in size to that of the Sunnis

Sunnis—Division of Islam to which most Muslims belong

BOOKS CHALLENGED/BANNED*

Longest-serving justice on the U.S. Supreme Court who in 1956 said: "Book banning is as old as books"
Answer: William O. Douglas.

Identify the U.S. President who said, "Don't join the book burners. Don't think you are going to conceal faults by concealing evidence that they never existed," doing so in a speech at Dartmouth College on June 14, 1953.
Answer: Dwight D. Eisenhower.

Harry Allard—*The Stupids* (series); *Bumps in the Night*
Isabel Allende—*The House of Spirits*
Maya Angelou—*I Know Why the Caged Bird Sings*
Anonymous—*Go Ask Alice*
Margaret Atwood—*The Handmaid's Tale*
Jean Auel—*Clan of the Cave Bear*; *Earth's Children* (series)
Marion Dean Bauer—*On My Honor*
Judy Blume—*Deenie*; *Forever*; *Blubber*; *Tiger Eyes*; *Are You There, God? It's Me, Margaret*
Ray Bradbury—*The Martian Chronicles*; *Fahrenheit 451*
Forrest Carter—*The Education of Little Tree*
Brock Cole—*The Goats*
J.L. and C. Collier—*My Brother Sam Is Dead*; *Jump Ship to Freedom*
Jane Conly—*Crazy Lady*
Caroline Cooney—*The Face on the Milk Carton*
Robert Cormier—*The Chocolate War*; *We All Fall Down*; *Fade*
Chris Crutcher—*Running Loose*
Roald Dahl—*James and the Giant Peach*; *The Witches*
William Faulkner—*As I Lay Dying*
Ken Follett—*The Pillars of the Earth*
Jean Craighead George—*Julie of the Wolves*
William Golding—*Lord of the Flies*
Bette Greene—*The Drowning of Stephan Jones*; *Summer of My German Soldier*
John Grisham—*The Client*
Judith Guest—*Ordinary People*
Martin Handford—*Where's Waldo?*
Nathaniel Hawthorne—*The Scarlet Letter*
Ursula Hegi—*Stones From the River*
S.E. Hinton—*Taming the Star Runner*; *The Outsiders*
Aldous Huxley—*Brave New World*
James Joyce—*Ulysses*
Daniel Keyes—*Flowers for Algernon*
Stephen King—*Christine*; *The Stand*; *Cujo*; *Different Seasons*; *The Dead Zone*
Rudyard Kipling—*Just So Stories*
John Knowles—*A Separate Peace*

*Banned book week is in September; John Campbell's *Let's Git Nekkid Trivia: The Bare-Bones Path to Quiz Success* may be added to this list.

Harper Lee—*To Kill a Mockingbird*
Madeleine L'Engle—*A Wrinkle in Time*
C.S. Lewis—*The Lion, the Witch, and the Wardrobe*
Lois Lowry—*The Giver; Anastasia Krupnik* (series)
Mark Mathabane—*Kaffir Boy*
Herman Melville—*Moby-Dick*
N. Scott Momaday—*House Made of Dawn*
Toni Morrison—*Beloved; The Bluest Eye; Song of Solomon*
Walter Dean Myers—*Fallen Angels*
Phyllis Reynolds Naylor—*Alice* (series)
Katherine Paterson—*Bridge to Terabithia; The Great Gilly Hopkins*
Robert Newton Peck—*A Day No Pigs Would Die*
Dav Pilkey—*Captain Underpants*
Anne Rice—*Sleeping Beauty Trilogy* (under the pseudonym A.N. Roquelaure)
Willo Davis Roberts—*The View from the Cherry Tree*
Thomas Rockwell—*How to Eat Fried Worms*
J.K. Rowling—All the *Harry Potter* books
Louis Sachar—*The Boy Who Lost His Face*
J.D. Salinger—*The Catcher in the Rye*
Alvin Schwartz—*Scary Stories* (series); *Cross Your Fingers, Spit in Your Hat*
Maurice Sendak—*In the Night Kitchen*
Dr. Seuss—*The Lorax*
William Shakespeare—*Twelfth Night*
Shel Silverstein—*A Light in the Attic*
Neil Simon—*Brighton Beach Memoirs*
John Steinbeck—*The Red Pony; Of Mice and Men*
R.L. Stine—*Beach House; Goosebumps* (series)
Amy Tan—*The Joy Luck Club*
Mildred D. Taylor—*Roll of Thunder, Hear My Cry*
Mark Twain—*The Adventures of Huckleberry Finn; The Adventures of Tom Sawyer*
John Updike—*Rabbit is Rich*
Kurt Vonnegut Jr.—*Breakfast of Champions; Slaughterhouse-Five*
Alice Walker—*The Color Purple*
James Welch—*Fools Crow*
Laura Ingalls Wilder—*Little House in the Big Woods*
Richard Wright—*Native Son; Black Boy*
Paul Zindel—*The Pigman*

Campaign Propaganda

British novelist and critic who said in *The Olive Tree:* "The propagandist's purpose is to make one set of people forget that certain other sets of people are human"
Answer: Aldous Huxley.

In 1950, *Time* magazine printed the following speech that reportedly appeared in George Smathers' pamphlets and stump speeches in his campaign to unseat Senator Claude Pepper of Florida, though Smathers denies ever having made such a speech:

"Are you aware that Claude Pepper is known all over Washington as a shameless *extrovert*? He is also reliably reported to practice *nepotism* with his sister-in-law, and he has a sister who was once a *thespian* in Greenwich Village. He has a brother who is a practicing *homo sapiens*, and he went to a college where men and women openly *matriculated* together. It is an established fact that Mr. Pepper before his marriage practiced *celibacy*. Worse than that, he has admitted to being a lifelong *autodidact*."

Identify by their given definitions the words used erroneously as accusations in the above campaign leaflet.
Autodidact—Person who is self-taught
Celibacy—Complete sexual abstinence
Extrovert—Person interested in others and the environment to the exclusion of self
Homo sapiens—Human being
Matriculated—Enrolled, especially as a student in a university
Nepotism—Favoritism shown to nephews and other relatives, especially in job appointments
Thespian—Actor or actress

Claude Pepper, a Democrat, who served in the U.S. Senate from 1936 to 1950 and in the U.S. House of Representatives from 1962 to 1989, championed causes of the elderly during his tenure and, in his last years as Congress's oldest member, defended Social Security and opposed retirement restrictions.

According to an apocryphal account, Claude Pepper was not only accused by his opponent of being an avowed *heterosexual* who practiced *premarital interdigitation* and was observed *osculating* a member of his staff but was also reprimanded by the Senate for *masticating* and *expectorating* in public places, and for having *knocked up a bird* while visiting England. This longtime *sexagenarian*, was a known member of a House *sextet*, sometimes engaged in *histrionics* on the Senate floor, spent considerable time reading about *horticulture* at home, and was clearly guilty of subscribing to *phonographic* magazines.

Identify the words or phrases from the prior paragraph having the following definitions.
Expectorating—Spitting
Heterosexual—Person with a sexual desire for those of the opposite sex
Histrionics—Melodramatics; affected display of emotions
Horticulture—Art or science of growing flowers, vegetables, etc.

Knocked up a bird—Telephoned a woman (British)
Masticating—Chewing (food, etc.)
Osculating—Kissing
Phonographic—Relating to the sounds made by a device for reproducing sound
Premarital interdigitation—Holding hands before marriage
Sexagenarian—Person in his 60s
Sextet—Music group composed of 6 people

HOMO ALL THE TIME

Author who in *The Naked Ape* said: "There are one hundred and ninety-three living species of monkeys and apes. One hundred and ninety-two of them are covered with hair. The exception is a naked ape self-named *Homo sapiens*"
Answer: Desmond Morris.

Mammals (Mammalia)—Class of animals to which human beings* belong
Primates—Order to which human beings, apes, monkeys, and lemurs belong
Hominidae—Family to which human beings and their closet prehuman ancestors belong
Hominoidae—Super family to which man, chimpanzees, gorillas, orangutans, gibbons, and siamangs belong
Homo*—Genus that includes modern humans and their close relatives
Homo sapiens—Only extant species of the genus *Homo*, so named from the Latin for "wise human being"
Homo sapiens sapiens—Subspecies whose name means "wise wise human being," to which all existing people belong

*Or the human race or humankind; humans belong to the kingdom *Animalia* and the phylum *Chordata*. **Homo* is the Latin word for "human being."

WORLD HISTORY TIME LINE

c. 13.7 billion B.C.—Universe is formed*
c. 4.5 billion B.C.—Planet Earth is formed
c. 3 billion B.C.—Primeval life appears in the oceans
c. 600 million B.C.—Earliest known fossils appear
Ethiopia—African country in which the earliest known hominid fossils, dating to c. 4.4 million B.C., are found in 1994
Australopithecus afarensis—"Southern Ape of Afar," called "Lucy," capable of walking upright and of running, dating to c. 3.2 million B.C., and found in Ethiopia in 1974
Stone Age—Age that begins c. 2.5 million B.C. and ends c. 12,000 B.C.**
Homo habilis—"Skillful Man," probably the earliest hominid to use stone tools and the earliest known species of the genus *Homo*, appearing c. 2 million B.C., and found at Olduvai Gorge in Tanzania in 1960
Homo erectus*—"Upright Man," having a larger brain than others before, having evolved from *Homo habilis*, appearing c. 1.6 million B.C., and found on the island of Java in 1891
Homo sapiens—Species who look like, walk like, and in some other ways act like modern man, appearing c. 130,000 B.C., and existing in Ethiopia based on fossils discovered there in the late 1990s
Neanderthal man**—Generally accepted *Homo sapiens* subspecies who used fire and advanced tools, appearing c. 125,000 B.C., and found in the Neander Valley near Duesseldorf, Germany, in 1856—this last surviving relative of *Homo sapiens* died out about 30,000 years ago
Cro-Magnon man—Earliest known European example of *Homo sapiens sapiens* that replaced Neanderthal man c. 35,000 B.C., anatomically identical to modern *Homo sapiens* and first discovered in a cave in Les Eyzies, in France in 1868

*Give or take a couple of million years, according to data provided in 2003 by the satellite known as the Wilkinson Microwave Anisotropy Probe, or WMAP, which has been orbiting in deep space since July 2001. **This "Age," or period of time, is relative and varies from one part of the world to another. ***Homo erectus* was the first known hominid species to extend its range outside of Africa. ****Classified as *Homo sapiens neanderthalensis*

Cats, Dogs, Horses

Word beginning with *D* designating animals such as cats, dogs, or horses that walk only on their toes without the heels touching the ground
Answer: Digitigrade.

CATS AND DOGS
1) What are the breeds of the 3 animals who make the trip in Sheila Burnford's *The Incredible Journey*, a story set in Canada?
Answer: Labrador retriever, bull terrier, and Siamese cat.

2) Identify the 2 animal characters involved in a spat in Eugene Field's "The Duel."
Answer: Gingham dog and calico cat.

3) Which idiomatic expression including the names of animals means "to pour very hard"?
Answer: To rain cats and dogs.

4) Identify the Robert Browning work that includes the lines: "Rats! / They fought the dogs and killed the cats."
Answer: *The Pied Piper of Hamelin*.

CATS

T.S. Eliot work including the lines: "Macavity, Macavity, there's no one like Macavity, / There never was a Cat of such deceitfulness and suavity. / He always has an alibi, and one or two to spare: / At whatever time the deed took place / MACAVITY WASN'T THERE!"
Answer: *Old Possum's Book of Practical Cats*, in *Macavity: The Mystery Cat*.

DOMESTIC CAT BREEDS
Abyssinian—Short-haired cat with grayish or reddish fur, originating in Egypt or Ethiopia and called the "Cat from the Blue Nile"
Angora—Long-haired breed that derives its name from Ankara, Turkey's former name
Balinese—Cat having long, silky fur like the Siamese but named after an Indonesian island
Birman—Long-haired cat of Burma whose light-colored coat resembles that of a Siamese
Bombay—Shorthaired black cat with yellowish eyes, developed in Kentucky and named for the former name of Mumbai, India, because the cat was said to resemble its black leopards
Burmese—Cat with a glossy coat and round yellow eyes, originating in Burma
Calico—Domestic cat marked with mottled colors of black, brown, orange, etc., and named after Calicut, India
Chartreux—Sturdy cat thought to have been brought to France by Carthusian monks
Cornish rex—Slender cat that originated in Cornwall, England

Devon rex—Sturdy cat that originated in Devonshire, England
Havana brown—Cat developed in Britain with a mahogany brown coat and forward-tilting ears, possibly named because its color resembles a Cuban cigar
Korat—Muscular cat of Thai origin having large, round greenish eyes
Himalayan—Cat with a stocky build and blue eyes, named after the Asian mountain system whose highest peak is Mount Everest
Maine coon (cat)—Bushy-tailed, long-haired cat resembling a raccoon and believed to have been developed in Maine
Manx—Tailless cat named after the Isle of Man where it originated
Norwegian forest cat—Ancient long-haired breed that is mentioned in Norse mythology
Persian—Cat with a long, thick, glossy coat, believed to have originated in Asia Minor
Ragdoll—Brave, long-haired cat developed in the U.S. and known for his limpness
Rex—Latin word for "king" for a breed with a short, curly coat and a long, slim tail
Russian blue—Muscular cat with green eyes and a bluish coat named after a European/Asian country
Siamese—Cat with blue eyes and a light-colored coat named after Siam, where it is thought to have originated
Somali—Cat developed from the Abyssinian and named after the country on the Horn of Africa
Tabby—Any light-colored cat with darker streaks and spots, especially a female
Turkish van—Ancient breed that originated in the Lake Van area of southeastern Turkey

FAMOUS CATS
All Ball—Koko the gorilla's pet kitten
Arlene—Female cat in the comic strip *Garfield*
Attila—Cat tormented by Grimmy, the bull terrier created by Mike Peters in *Mother Goose and Grimm*
Bill the Cat—Character in Berke Breathed's *Bloom County* comic strip who says "Ack!" and "Thbbbt!"
Bowser—Cat that cartoon character Mr. Magoo thinks is a dog
Brambley—Adelle Kelly's cat in Chris Browne's comic strip *Raising Duncan*
Bucky Katt—Sarcastic cat belonging to Rob Wilco in Darby Conley's comic strip *Get Fuzzy*
Felix the Cat—Cartoon character originally drawn by Pat Sullivan, later by Otto Messmer, and the first ever transmitted on TV, in the 1920s
Figaro—Geppetto's cat in Disney's *Pinocchio*
Garfield—Big orange comic strip cat belonging to Jon Arbuckle and created by Jim Davis
Gideon—Cat who schemes with a fox to convince Pinocchio to become an actor in the Disney film *Pinocchio*
Heathcliff—Bad-tempered comic strip cat created by George Gately
Hotdog—Dennis the Menace's cat in the comic strips
Kittycat—Family cat in *The Family Circus*
Krazy Kat—George Herriman's comic strip cat whose friend Ignatz Mouse is always throwing bricks in Coconino County, Arizona
Lucifer—Stepmother's mean cat in Disney's *Cinderella*
Misty Malarky Ying Yang—Amy Carter's Siamese cat in the White House
Mooch—Cat with a lisp created by Patrick McDonnell in the comic strip *Mutts*
Morris—Finicky cat in the advertisement for 9-Lives cat food

Mr. Jinks—Cartoon cat who chases the mice Pixie and Dixie and is known for saying "I hate meeces to pieces!"
Muffin—Earl and Opal's cat in Brian Crane's comic strip *Pickles*
Oil Can Harry—Cartoon cat foe of superhero Mighty Mouse
Puff—Dick and Jane's cat in primary readers
Scratchy—Cat terribly abused by the mouse Itchy on a show seen on the TV cartoon *The Simpsons*
Socks—Clinton family cat
Streaky—Supergirl's super cat with a lightning bolt streak in its fur in the Superman comics
Sylvester the Cat—Looney Tunes cartoon cat who is known for chasing Tweety Bird and saying "Thuffering Thucotash"
Tom—Hanna and Barbera's cartoon cat featured with Jerry, a house mouse

LANGUAGE CATS WITH *CAT* IN THE ANSWER

Alley cat—Homeless, crossbreed cat or a promiscuous person, especially a woman, with loose morals
(To) bell the cat—Expression meaning "to attempt a dangerous job, especially for the good of others," from an Aesop fable retold in William Langland's *Piers Plowman*
(To play a game of) cat-and-mouse—3-word hyphenated phrase designating a strategy of toying with or challenging an opponent while waiting for the moment to strike
Catcall—Shrill shout or whistle expressing scorn or disapproval
Caterwaul—To make a shrill wail, as that of a cat at rutting time
Catfight—Bitter quarrel, especially between 2 women
Cathouse—Brothel
Catnap—Short, light sleep
Catty—5-letter adjective meaning "spiteful" or "malicious"
Catwalk—Narrow platform down which models stroll to show off a designer's latest fashions or a narrow, elevated walk or platform, as one along the edge of a bridge
Cat burglar—Thief very adept at entering a home by skillful climbing to an upper story
Cat's meow*—Slang for a person, thing, or idea that is remarkable or noteworthy
(To be made a) cat's-paw (of)—Person deceived into performing a dangerous or unpleasant task
Cool cat—Slang for a fashionable person or a person with a low-keyed style
Copycat—Person who imitates another
Fat cat—Slang for a wealthy person, especially a donor to a political campaign, or a person used to certain privileges because of wealth
Fraidy-cat—Child's hyphenated term for a person who is easily frightened
(To) grin like a Cheshire cat—Expression meaning "to smile widely, especially in a self-satisfied or mysterious manner," after an animal in *Alice's Adventures in Wonderland*
Hellcat—Witch, or evil, vengeful, bad-tempered woman; a vixen
In the catbird seat—Expression meaning to be in a favorable position, a phrase popularized by Brooklyn Dodger baseball announcer "Red" Barber
(To) let the cat out of the bag—Phrase meaning "to reveal a secret, especially accidentally"
Pussycat—8-letter word for a cat or pussy, or an informal term for a person who is gentle and meek
Scaredy-cat—Hyphenated term for a person who is irrationally afraid

* *Cat's meow, cat's pajamas,* and *cat's whiskers* all have similar, if not identical, meanings.

LANGUAGE CATS OTHERWISE

Ailurophile—Person who loves cats
Ailurophobia—Abnormal fear of cats
Bricks—Word completing the British idiom *like a cat on hot* _____, meaning "incapable of remaining still"
Canary—Word completing the idiom *to look like the cat that ate (swallowed) the* _____, meaning "to look guilty but satisfied"
Curiosity—According to the proverb, this is what killed the cat
Dragged (brought)—Word completing the idiom *to look like something the cat* _____ *in*, meaning "appearing totally unkempt"
Feline—Any animal of the cat family or an adjective meaning "catlike"
Gray—According to the proverb, the color all cats are in the dark
Jazz—Type of music for which, according to old slang, a *hepcat* had enthusiasm
King—Word completing the expression *a cat may look at a* _____, conveying the idea that any ordinary person may look at or say anything to a very important person
Kittenish—Playful, frisky, like a kitten
Kitty—Word completing *to feed the* _____, meaning "to contribute money to a reserve fund"
Mice—According to the proverb, these creatures will play when the cat is away
More than one—According to the proverb, the number of ways to skin or kill a cat
9—According to the saying, the number of lives a cat has
Pussyfoot—To move cautiously; to avoid taking a definitive stand on something
Satisfaction—According to the proverb, this is what brought the cat back
Swing—Word completing the expression *not enough room to* _____ *a cat*, meaning "very little space"
Tin roof—2 words completing the idiom *like a cat on a hot* _____, meaning "nervous or ill at ease"
Tongue—According to the idiom, what the cat has gotten from someone if that person is unable to speak

LITERARY CATS IN THE ANSWER

Cheshire Cat—Character who is capable of appearing and vanishing gradually, leaving only a grin in Lewis Carroll's *Alice's Adventures in Wonderland*
Crookshanks—Hermione Granger's cat in the Harry Potter series
Dinah—Alice's cat in *Alice's Adventures in Wonderland*
Macavity—"Napoleon of Crime" in T.S. Eliot's *Old Possum's Book of Practical Cats*
Mehitabel—Archy the giant cockroach's friend whose battle cry is "toujours gai" in a Don Marquis tale
Mr. Mistoffelees—"The Original Conjuring Cat" in T.S. Eliot's *Old Possum's Book of Practical Cats*
Mrs. Norris—Argus Filch's cat in the Harry Potter series
Old Deuteronomy—Elderly cat who has buried 9 wives in T.S. Eliot's *Old Possum's Book of Practical Cats*
Puss in Boots—Red-booted fairy tale cat who through a series of clever tricks pleases the king and wins the princess's hand for his master in the tale *Le Chat Botté*
Pussycat—Animal that "went to sea" with the Owl "in a beautiful pea-green boat" in an Edward Lear poem
The Rum Tum Tugger—"Curious Cat" who is "a terrible bore" in T.S. Eliot's *Old Possum's Book of Practical Cats*

Skimbleshanks—"The Cat of the Railway Train" in T.S. Eliot's *Old Possum's Book of Practical Cats*
Snowbell—Cat that doesn't like Stuart Little in an E.B. White tale

LITERARY/FILM CATS
The Aristocats—Disney film set in Paris where Duchess, the mother cat, lives with her 3 kittens with the Bonfamille
Margaret Atwood—Canadian author who wrote *Cat's Eye*
Bast(et)—Goddess of love, life, and fertility in Egyptian mythology who was represented as having the body of a woman with the head of a cat
Rita Mae Brown—American author whose tiger cat Sneaky Pie, born in Virginia, helps her write Mrs. Murphy mysteries
Cabaret—1972 film in which Liza Minnelli as Sally Bowles performs at Berlin's Kit Kat Club
Cat Ballou—1965 film starring Lee Marvin in which Jane Fonda plays Cat
Cat on a Hot Tin Roof—1958 film starring Elizabeth Taylor as Maggie and Paul Newman as Brick
The Cat's Meow—2002 Peter Bogdanovich film about the mysterious death of Thomas Ince during a 1924 cruise on William Randolph Hearst's yacht
Colette—French author of *Gigi* who wrote *La Chatte* (*The Cat*) and after her 1906 divorce performed at such places as La Chatte Amoureuse
Dick Whittington—Legendary poor boy who ran away to London because its streets were allegedly paved with gold and silver and whose cat was bought for a large sum to kill rats in Barbary
T.S. Eliot—American-born British author who wrote *Old Possum's Book of Practical Cats*
Fiddle—Word completing the nursery rhyme, "Hey Diddle Diddle / The cat and the ____,—The cow jumped over the moon"
"Fisher"—Name completing the rhyme: "Lucy Locket lost her pocket, / Kitty ____ found it; / Not a penny was there in it, / Only a ribbon round it."
Thomas Gray—English poet of "Elegy Written in a Country Churchyard" who also wrote "Ode on the Death of a Favorite Cat Drowned in a Tub of Goldfishes"
Robert Heinlein—American author who wrote *The Cat Who Walks Through Walls* about a cat named Pixel
Hellcats of the Navy—1957 film starring Ronald Reagan and Nancy Davis
Kilkenny—Town in the nursery rhyme where the cats "fought and they fit, / And they scratched and they bit, / Till . . . / Instead of two cats, there weren't any."
Kitty—Name Anne Frank gave to her diary
Louis L'Amour—American who wrote the Western *Catlow*
Little Johnny Green—Nursery rhyme character who put pussy in the well
London—City in which the nursery rhyme pussy cat frightened a little mouse under the queen's chair
Macbeth—Shakespeare play in which the First Witch says to a cat she believes to be a witch, "I come Grimalkin"
Ogden Nash—Poet who wrote the lines, "The trouble with a kitten is / THAT / Eventually it becomes a / CAT," doing so in *The Face Is Familiar*
Edgar Allan Poe—American author in whose short story "The Black Cat" a cat named Pluto that is walled in a vault with the man's dead wife alerts others to the crime
Pride and Prejudice—Jane Austen novel featuring Mr. Bennet's 5 daughters named Elizabeth, Jane, Kitty (Catherine), Lydia, and Mary

Rat—What the cat takes in the nursery rhyme "The farmer in the dell"
Carl Sandburg—Poet whose poem "Fog" includes the line "The fog comes / On little cat feet"
Dr. Seuss—American author who wrote *The Cat in the Hat*
7—Number of cats in each sack in the nursery rhyme that begins "As I was going to St. Ives"
Siamese cats—Breed of Koko and Yum Yum, the cats featured in Lilian Jackson Braun's "The Cat Who" mystery series
Three Little kittens—Nursery rhyme characters who lost their mittens
James Thurber—American short-story writer and humorist who wrote "The Catbird Seat"
Mark Twain—Humorist who wrote the line, "One of the most striking differences between a cat and a lie is that a cat has only 9 lives," doing so in his *Pudd'nhead Wilson*
Kurt Vonnegut—American author whose *Cat's Cradle* opens with the line, "Call me Jonah"
Andrew Lloyd Webber—20th-century British composer and producer known for the musical *Cats*
What's New Pussycat?—1965 film starring Peter Sellers as Dr. Fitz Fassbender and Peter O'Toole as a fashion editor romantically involved with his models
Tennessee Williams—Playwright who wrote *Cat on a Hot Tin Roof*
Wuthering Heights—Emily Brontë novel in which Heathcliff's pet cat is named Grimalkin

POTPOURRI OF CATS WITH *CAT* IN THE ANSWER
Black cat—Animal considered bad luck if it crosses your path
Catnip—Popular name for *catamint*, a strong-smelling common plant of the mint family
Cat-o'nine-tails—Whip with 9 lashes used for punishing offenders, possibly so named in reference to the ancient Egyptian weapon made from the thongs of cat hide—sometimes called *the cat*
Cat's cradle—Game played by two children with a piece of string
Cat's-eye—Gem or stone having a changeable luster
Carrie Lane Chapman Catt—Woman who served as president of the National American Woman Suffrage Association 1900-1904 and 1915-1920 and founded the National League of Women Voters in 1920
Dead-cat bounce—Temporary stock market recovery after a severe drop off or a prolonged bear market
Fat Cats—Comic strip created by Charlie Podrebarac
Pas de chat—French term, literally "step of the cat," for a catlike, springing jump, putting one foot over the other as in ballet
Cat Stevens—Musician born Steven Georgiou who later adopted the Muslim name Yusuf Islam
Tom(cat)—Male cat, or sexually promiscuous male

POTPOURRI OF CATS OTHERWISE
"at" symbol (@)—Part of an e-mail address that is called *miau* or "cat tail" in Finland
Bahamas—West Indies island nation that includes Cat Island, located southeast of Nassau
Brigitte Bardot—French actress known as "The Sex Kitten"
Black Death (Bubonic Plague)—Plague epidemic of the Middle Ages spread by rats, possibly after hundreds of thousands of cats were killed because the people believed they symbolized evil

Chatoyant—Polished stone, such as the cat's eye, with a changeable luster

Frédéric Chopin—Polish-French composer whose *The Cat's Waltz* was so named because his cat scampered across the keyboard and he tried to imitate the sound

Cluster—Group of cats, a word also designating a number of things of the same sort gathered together

Clutter*—Group of cats, a word also designating a jumble of things scattered in disorder

Egypt—Ancient civilization in which the cat was worshipped and honored in works of art

Fanciers—Completion of the name of the major U.S. cat organization, the Cat _____' Association, or CFA

Harvey Haddix—St. Louis and Pittsburgh pitcher nicknamed "The Kitten"

Jim Katt—Longtime pitcher for Minnesota nicknamed "Kitty"

Kindle—Group of kittens, a word also meaning to build or start a fire

Kit/Kitty—Diminutive form for Catherine or Katherine

Kitten—Young cat

Kitty—Child's term for a kitten or a pet name for any cat; a poker pot; money combined for a particular objective; and the nickname of celebrity Katherine Hart Carlisle

Kitty Dukakis—Woman who wrote the 1990 autobiography *Now You Know*, which tells of her drug problem—her husband ran for President in 1988

Kitty Foyle—1940 film starring Ginger Rogers as the title character

Kitty Genovese—28-year-old who was stabbed to death on the street on March 13, 1964, in Queens, New York, as 37 of her neighbors "didn't want to get involved"

Kitty Hawk—North Carolina site where the Wright brothers first flew their heavier-than-air plane in 1903

Kitty Kelley—American author of unauthorized biographies of Frank Sinatra, Nancy Reagan, and Jackie Onassis

Kitty Wells—Woman born Ellen Muriel Deason known as the "Queen of Country Music"

Lake Erie—Southernmost of the Great Lakes, the one called *Lac du Chat*, or "Lake of the Cat," by French explorers

Litter—Group of kittens, a word also designating a granular material used in a container to absorb cat waste

Johnny Mize—Hall of Famer called "The Big Cat," who hit 359 home runs

Tabby—Term other than *queen* for a female cat or an old maid or spinster

Vibrissae—Cat's whiskers or tactile hairs

* *Clowder* is a variant of *clutter*.

Dogs

According to Noel Coward, the 2 groups that "go out in the mid-day sun"
Answer: Mad dogs and Englishmen.

1) Name the 7 major groups of dogs for exhibition in dog shows as classified by the AKC, or the American Kennel Club.
   Answer: Sporting dogs, hounds, working dogs, terriers, toy dogs, nonsporting dogs, and herding dogs.

2) Identify the 3 breeds of wolfhound.
   Answer: Irish wolfhound, the borzoi or Russian wolfhound, and the Scottish deerhound.

3) Identify the 2 months in which "dog days" or "canicular days" occur in the Northern Hemisphere.
   Answer: July and August (period of hot, sultry weather, usually from July 3 to August 11).

4) Which person in the Bible said to which person, "Am I a dog that thou comest to me with staves?"
   Answer: Goliath said those words to David (I Samuel 17:45).

CARTOON/FILM/POP CULTURE/TV DOGS
Astro—Jeston's family dog on *The Jetsons*
Augie Doggie—Doggie Daddy's puppy son on the TV cartoon *Huckleberry Hound*
Benji—Title mutt who saves 2 kidnapped children in a 1974 movie
Bingo—Sailor Jack's dog on Cracker Jack boxes
Bullet—Roy Rogers' wonder dog, a German shepherd
Clifford—The Big Red Dog on TV—a 20-foot-tall red dog who lives with Emily Elizabeth Howard on Bridwell Island and has the dog friends Cleo and T-Bone
Eddie—Martin Crane's Jack Russell terrier on TV's *Frasier*
Ginger—Barbie's dog
Goofy—Mickey Mouse's friend, a dog, originally named Dippy Dawg
Gromit—Clay animation canine who hosted the Westminster dog show's Internet broadcast in 2005 and is the sidekick of his cheese-loving human inventor named Wallace
Huckleberry Hound—Cartoon blue dog with a southern drawl wearing country boy's clothes, and created by Hanna-Barbera
Jock—Scottish terrier in *Lady and the Tramp* whose real name is Heather Lad o'Glencairn
Lady—Cocker spaniel living with Jim Dear and Darling in Disney's *Lady and the Tramp*
Mighty Manfred—Tom Terrific's wonder dog
Nipper*—RCA company's logo white fox terrier who seeks "His Master's Voice"
Pete(y)—Dog with a ring around his left eye in the *Our Gang* or *The Little Rascals* series
Pluto—Mickey Mouse's dog
Rin Tin Tin—Rusty's German shepherd dog nicknamed "Rinty" featured in movies and TV shows

*Chipper, a Jack Russell terrier, is his sidekick.

Rowlf—Shaggy piano-playing dog on *The Muppet Show*
Santa's Little Helper—Simpsons' pet greyhound on *The Simpsons*
Scooby-Doo—Cartoon Great Dane created by Hanna-Barbera
Smiley—Baxter family dog in *Hazel*
Snuffles—Quick Draw McGraw's tracking dog
Spike/Tyke—Gruff bulldog and his cute son in the Tom and Jerry cartoons
Tige—Buster Brown's bulldog who also lives in a shoe
Toby—Hunchbacked Punch and Judy's bull terrier in a puppet show
Tramp—Mongrel who "never gets caught by the dogcatcher" in Disney's *Lady and the Tramp*
Triumph—Insult comic dog on *Late Night With Conan O'Brien*
Trusty—Bloodhound friend of Lady in Disney's *Lady and the Tramp*
Yukon King—Alaskan husky of Sgt. Preston of the Northwest Mounted Police

COMIC STRIP DOGS
Ace—Bruce Wayne's bat-hound in the Batman comics
Andy—Mark Trail's Saint Bernard
Barfy/Sam—2 family dogs in *The Family Circus*
Daisy—The Bumstead's dog
Dawg—Hi and Lois Flagston's dog
Dogbert—Dog in Scott Adams' *Dilbert* who treats everyone with disdain, including his master, Dilbert
Duncan—Black Scottish terrier in Chris Browne's *Raising _____*
Earl—Dog created by Patrick McDonnell in *Mutts*
Electra—Cathy's little brown dog, her alter ego, in *Cathy*
Fuzz—Ziggy's dog in *Ziggy*
Grimmy—Cartoonist Mike Peters' bull terrier whose absentminded caretaker is Mother Goose
Hot Dog—Jughead Jones' dog in Archie comics
Krypto—Superboy's super "dog of steel"
Louie—Captain Crow's dog in Chip Dunham's *Overboard* who communicates through thought balloons
Marmaduke—Cartoonist Brad Anderson's Great Dane living with the Winslow family
Mr. Peabody—Historian/time traveller dog whose pet boy is named Sherman
Odie—Garfield's nemesis in *Garfield*
Offissa B(ull) Pupp—Canine constable in Coconino County in the Krazy Kat strip
Ol' Bullet—Snuffy Smith's dog in *Barney Google* who "ain't worth a hoot as a bird dog or a possum hound"
Otto—Sgt. Orville Snorkel's bulldog in *Beetle Bailey* who walks on all fours and wears a uniform
Poochie—Nancy's dog in *Nancy*
Raymond—Cecilia's dog in Chip Dunham's *Overboard* who walks on 2 legs, smokes cigarettes, and talks directly with humans
Roscoe—Earl and Opal's dog in *Pickles*
Ruff—Dennis the Menace's dog
Sandy—Little Orphan Annie's dog
Satchel Pooch—Friendly, naive dog belonging to Rob Wilco in Darby Conley's *Get Fuzzy*
Snert—Family dog in *Hagar the Horrible*
Snoopy—Charlie Brown's dog famous for saying "*Au contraire*"

Snowy—Tintin's loyal white-haired fox terrier whose name in French is Milou
Spike—Snoopy's brother in *Peanuts*
Vivian—Irving's little dog in *Cathy*

DOG BREEDS
Afghan (hound)—Swift hunting dog developed in Afghanistan
Airedale—Largest of the terriers, the so-called "king of terriers," developed in the Aire Valley in England
Akita—Large, powerful dog with pointed ears named after a city in Japan
Alaskan malamute—Large, strong sled dog developed named after an Eskimo or Inuit tribe
Basenji—African small dog that does not make a true barking sound, though it can make a singing sound, so named because of its monkeylike tail and face
Basset hound—Hunting hound with a long body, short forelegs, and drooping ears
Beagle—Small hunting dog whose name is from the French for "wide throat"
Bloodhound—Breed of large-sized dogs with an acute sense of smell, frequently used for hunting lost persons or escaped prisoners
Border collie—Sheep dog originally bred in the border region between Scotland and England
Borzoi—Russian wolfhound whose name means "swift"
Boston terrier—Small dog bred in the U.S. in 1870 whose name includes that of a state capital
Briard—Large sheep herding dog with a coarse, bushy coat named after the French region of Brie
Brussels griffon—Small, sturdy dog developed in Belgium, part of whose name is from the French word for a mythical monster
Bulldog—Short-haired, square-jawed sturdily built dog noted for its stubborn-looking expression, the national dog of England
Cairn terrier—Terrier so named in Scotland for its ability to dig under piles of stones to hunt small animals
Chesapeake Bay retriever—Duck-hunting dog named after a large U.S. East Coast body of water
Chihuahua—World's smallest breed of dogs, named after a Mexican state and often called the "royal dog of the Americas"
(Chinese) shar-pei—Chinese breed whose skin folds into wrinkles and whose tongue is blue-black
Chow chow—Medium-size dog of Chinese origin with a sturdy build and blue-black tongue
Collie—Sheepdog first bred in Scotland and popular as pets after Queen Victoria brought some to Windsor Castle in the 1860s
Dachshund—Breed of German origin with a long body and short legs and whose name means "badger dog"
Dalmatian—Firehouse dog, carriage dog, or coach dog that has black spots on a white coat and originated in Yugoslavia—only dog that can get gout
Dandie Dinmont terrier—Breed whose name is derived from Sir Walter Scott's *Guy Mannering*, a novel in which farmer Dandie Dinmont raises 2 of these dogs
Doberman pinscher—Strong, muscular breed named after German Ludwig _____ who helped develop this fierce guard dog
German shepherd—Dog first bred in Germany as a herding dog and now frequently trained for police work
Great Dane—Large, muscular dog developed in Germany in the 1500s and named after the country of Denmark

Greyhound—Tall, very swift dog of Egyptian origin used for track racing

Havanese*—Small sturdy breed of the Bichon family that may have originated on the island of Malta but later was developed in Cuba—its name is *Habeneros* in Spanish, and it is known as the "white Cuban" in England

Irish setter—Breed of setter with a silky, brownish-red coat

Irish wolfhound—Tallest or largest breed, originally bred in Ireland

Keeshond—18-inch-high breed developed in the Netherlands and now this country's national dog

Kerry blue terrier—National dog of Ireland, a terrier with a grayish-blue coat named after County Kerry

King Charles spaniel—Toy spaniel with a black-and-tan coat, popularized by the English king who served from 1660 to 1685

Labrador retriever—Of the 5 recognized breeds of retrievers, the one named after the mainland territory of Newfoundland

Lhasa apso—Small breed from Tibet named after its capital and after the word meaning "sentinel lion dog" because of its historical role as a watchdog

Maltese—Breed of very early lap dog named after an island in the Mediterranean

Mastiff—One of the world's 2 heaviest domestic dogs, now used as a guard dog or a watchdog

Mexican hairless—Mexican breed without fur on its body except for a few tufts on its head

Neapolitan (mastiff)—New AKC breed of mastiff as of 2004, named with the word for a citizen of Naples

Newfoundland—Muscular dog formerly famous for rescuing drowning people, now used as a guard dog, and named after a Canadian province

Norfolk/Norwich—Either breed of short-legged terrier, one with droopy ears and the other with erect ears, both named after counties in England

Papillon—Toy spaniel whose ears resemble butterfly wings and whose name is French for "butterfly"

Pekingese (Peke)—Small dog with long silky hair and a pug nose, originally from China and named after its capital, formerly the royal dog of China

Pit bull—Breed developed to attack bulls and bears and fight other dogs—once very popular until a spate of fatal attacks against people

Pointer—Muscular hunting dog with a short, smooth coat that stops still when it smells a bird and aims itself in its direction

Pomeranian (Pom)—Small dog named after a former Prussian province in northern Germany

Poodle—Intelligent, friendly dog classified as *toy*, *miniature*, and *standard*, and the national dog of France and Spain

Pug—Largest toy dog, one of Chinese origin with a short nose and wrinkled face

Retriever—Hunting dog trained to bring back birds or other small game

Rhodesian Ridgeback—Strong, short-haired hunting dog with a ridge on its back, developed in South Africa and also called the *African lion hound*

Rottweiler—Large, strong working dog with a short tail, named after a town in Germany

St. Bernard**—One of the world's 2 heaviest domestic dogs, from the Swiss Alps, taught to rescue lost persons, or those buried in snowdrifts or snowstorms

Saluki—Royal dog of ancient Egypt, a hunting breed resembling a greyhound and named after an ancient Arabian city—also called a *gazelle hound*

*Also called the Havana Silk dog **As of 2004, this dog no longer does rescue work in the mountains.

Samoyed—Working dog developed in Siberia whose Russian name means "cannibal"

Schipperke—Small dog with a foxlike head whose name in Flemish means "little boatman," formerly used as ship watchdogs—also called the *barge dog* and *little skipper*

Schnauzer—Strongly built dog of German origin with a wiry coat and whiskers whose 3 breeds are *standard*, *miniature*, and *giant*

Scottish deerhound—Dog of nobility originally bred to hunt wild deer in Scotland

Setter—Long-haired hunting dog trained to stand motionless and point its nose toward the prey—its 3 breeds are *English*, *Gordon*, and *Irish*

Shetland sheepdog—Working dog smaller than a collie and named after a group of islands in the Atlantic

Shih Tzu—Toy dog of Chinese origin whose name in Mandarin means "lion"

(Siberian) husky—Arctic sled dog of Siberian origin, whose name is possibly after an alteration of the word Eskimo

Skye terrier—Breed of terrier with a long body and short legs named after the largest of the Inner Hebrides

Spaniel—Large family of dogs whose name comes from *español*, the Spanish word for Spanish

Spitz—Family of dogs with a dense white coat and a tail curling over its back, whose name is German for "pointed"

Terrier—Any of various breeds, such as Irish, Manchester, Scottish, and Welsh, whose name literally means "of the earth" since it was once used to drive game out of holes

Vizsla—Medium-sized hunting dog named after a town in Hungary—also called the *Hungarian pointer*

Weimaraner—Hunting dog sometimes called the "gray ghost" because of its short, smooth, gray coat and its quiet movement while hunting—named after the German city of Weimar

Welsh corgi—Short-legged dog bred in Wales as either a Cardigan or a Pembroke, whose name literally means "dwarf dog"

Whippet—Slender, swift dog resembling a small greyhound and used for racing

HOMO SAPIENS AND THEIR DOGS

Barney—George W. Bush's Scottish terrier

Biche—Frederick the Great's favorite among the 35 Italian greyhounds

Blondi(e)—Adolf Hitler's German shepherd

Boatswain—Lord Byron's Newfoundland for which there is a monument at Newstead Abbey

Bounce—Alexander Pope's Great Dane

Buddy—President Clinton's chocolate Labrador retriever

Centaur Pendragon—Rudolph Valentino's Irish Wolfhound

Checkers—Cocker spaniel mentioned in a famous speech by Richard Nixon

Diamond—Isaac Newton's "gem" of a dog that supposedly started a fire, destroying his research

Fala—Franklin Delano Roosevelt's Scotch terrier—in full, Murray of _____ Hill

Flush—Elizabeth Barrett Browning's cocker spaniel

Igloo—Admiral Richard E. Byrd's fox terrier

Laika—First animal in space, aboard *Sputnik II* on November 3, 1957

Millie—Springer spaniel whose book was dictated to First Lady Barbara Bush

Nimrod—Sir Walter Scott's wolfhound, a Biblical "mighty hunter"

Spot—George W. Bush's English springer spaniel
Uga—University of Georgia's famous bulldog mascot

LANGUAGE DOGS BEGINNING WITH THE WORD *DOG*
Dog-and-pony show—Hyphenated expression meaning "a detailed presentation to gain approval for something"
Dogcatcher—Municipal pound employee who rounds up and impounds stray dogs
Dog days—Summer's hottest days, the period of hot sultry days from about July 3 to August 11 when a star of this name rises and sets with the sun (Latin *dies caniculares*)
Dog-eared—Turned-down corner of the leaf of a book; worn or used
Dog-eat-dog—Hyphenated expression meaning "heartlessly competitive"
Dogface—Slang for a U.S. Army infantryman in WWII
Dogfight—Violent battle, or combat between fighter planes in close proximity to each other
Dogged—Stubborn or persistent
Doggerel—Comic verse or bad poetry
Doggone—Damn, or darn
Doggy—Child's term for a little dog
Doggy (doggie) bag—Box or bag in which restaurant customers take home leftovers
Dog in the manger—Phrase derived from an Aesop story meaning "a person who selfishly refuses to give to others something he himself has no use for"
(To) dog it—Phrase meaning "to do less than what is required"
Dogleg—Sharp bend in a golf fairway
Dogmerd—Anthony Burgess's word for dog excrement
Dognap—To steal a dog in order to sell it to a medical research laboratory
(A) dog's age—Phrase meaning "a very long time"
(A) dog's life—Phrase meaning "a very unhappy existence"
Dogtired—Exhausted
Dogwatch—Informal term for any night shift, especially the last one, or a nautical duty period from either 4 to 6 P.M. or 6 to 8 P.M.
Dog paddle—Swimming stroke used to stay afloat
Dog tag—Slang for a military identification marker worn around the neck

LANGUAGE DOGS WITH *DOG IN THE ANSWER*
Barking dog—According to the expression, type of dog that never bites
Bulldog—To bring a steer to the ground, or a short-barreled large-caliber revolver, or a person who is stubborn or determined
(To) die like a dog—To come to a miserable, dishonorable end
Dirty dog—A morally reprehensible person
(To) give (throw) to the dogs—To cause someone to suffer an undesirable outcome, especially by placing blame on him or to sacrifice another person
(To) go to the dogs—To deteriorate or to worsen
Hangdog-look—Hyphenated phrase for a demeanor of shame or defeat
(To) hotdog—To show-off, especially in sports
In the doghouse—To be in trouble with someone else, especially as applied to one of a married couple
(To) put on the dog—To make a show of wealth or to act in an extravagant manner to impress others
(To) see a man about a dog—To excuse oneself, especially to go to the bathroom; to go out for a drink; to visit a prostitute

DOGS 41

Shaggy-dog story—Long, belabored story that ends anticlimactically
Three-dog night—A very cold night
Top dog—Primary person in an organization or group
Underdog—Person or group that is losing or is expected to lose the competition, or someone at a disadvantage in a struggle
(To) wag the dog—To create a diversion such as a war in order to deflect attention from personal problems
Watchdog—Dog used to guard one's property, as by barking, or person who works to prevent theft, unethical practices, etc.
Yellow dog—Cowardly, despicable person

LANGUAGE DOGS OTHERWISE

(To) bark up the wrong tree—To misdirect one's efforts by following the wrong path
Bitch—Female dog; a lewd woman; or a bad-tempered, aggressive woman
Bloodhound—Person who pursues relentlessly, or figuratively, any detective
Canicide—Killing of dogs
Canicular—Adjective meaning "having to do with the Dog Star or the dog days"
Canine—Any animal of the dog family or an adjective meaning "doglike"
Cur—3-letter word for a mongrel or a mixed-breed dog, or, as now used, a mean, loathsome person
Cynophobia—Fear of dogs
Cynosure—Any person or thing that is the center of attention, the Greek for "dog's tail," and a former name for Ursa Minor or for the North Star or Pole star
Day—Word completing the proverb *every dog has his* _____, meaning that something good happens to everyone at some time
Diggity—Word completing the expression *hot* _____ *dog!* for a cry of approval, similar to *hot dog!*
Feet—Part of the body known in slang as *the dogs*
Fleas—According to the proverb, what a person "will rise up with" if he "lies down with dogs"
Footsteps—Word completing the expression *to dog someone's* _____, meaning "to follow closely, either physically or as in collecting a debt"
Hair—Word completing the expression _____ *of the dog that bit one*, meaning "a small alcoholic drink that cures a hangover"
Kennel—Group of dogs, or a place where dogs are bred or kept
Life—Word completing the expression *there's* _____ *in the old dog yet*, meaning "the person may be old but he still has abilities on a certain level left"
Litter—Group of pups, or material used as bedding for animals
Love—Word completing the proverb _____ *me,* _____ *my dog*, meaning that if you care for another, you must do so despite all of his/her faults
Man—According to the proverb, a dog is his best friend
New tricks—According to the proverb, what you can't teach an old dog
One's bark is worse than one's bite—Phrase including the word *bark* said of "a person who seems more antagonistic than is the case"
Pack—Group of dogs, or group of wild animals running together
Pedigree—Record of the ancestors of a purebred dog
Pound—Enclosure maintained by a town for confining stray animals such as dogs
Pup (dog) tent—Small, portable tent for 2 people

Puppy* —Young dog, or an impudent, self-important, or foolish young man
Puppy love —Immature love between a boy and a girl
Purebred —Dog whose parents belong to the same breed
Sick —Word completing the simile *as _____ as a dog* referring to the state of one's health
Sleeping —Word completing the proverb *let _____ dogs lie*, meaning let well enough alone
Son of a bitch —Offensive phrase for someone or something considered despicable, or an interjection used to express surprise
Tail —Word completing the expression *with one's _____ between one's legs*, meaning "ashamed," in reference to a dog's sneaking away in this manner
Travois —Indian-made framework of long poles used as a sled and pulled by a dog or horse
Wagging —Word completing the expression *the tail _____ the dog*, meaning "an unimportant factor dominating a more important one"
Whelp —Unweaned puppy
Work —Word completing the simile *to _____ like a dog* meaning to labor very hard
Young pup —2-word term for a young person not to be taken seriously
*A *pup* is also a young dog.

LITERARY DOGS IN THE ANSWER
Argos (Argus) —Odysseus's dog that recognizes him after a 20-year absence in Homer's *Odyssey*
Asta —Wire-haired terrier of Nick and Nora Charles in *The Thin Man*
Buck —Half-St. Bernard, half-Scottish sheepdog that is stolen from his California home and later leads a wolf pack in *The Call of the Wild*
Cerberus —Mythological 3-headed dog that guards Hades
Charley —John Steinbeck's French poodle in *Travels With _____*
Cujo —Saint Bernard in the title of a Stephen King novel
Fang —Hagrid's enormous black boarhound in the Harry Potter series
Fluffy —3-headed dog guarding the trap door in *Harry Potter and the Sorcerer's Stone*
Jip —Both Dr. Dolittle's dog in Hugh Lofting's novels and Dora Spenlow's in Dickens' *David Copperfield*
Lassie —Collie named in the title of Eric Knight's novel *_____ Come Home*
Max —Dog that the Grinch disguises as a reindeer in a Dr. Seuss story
Nana —Saint Bernard that acts as a nursemaid for the 3 Darling family children in *Peter Pan*
Old Yeller —Mongrel dog that saves Little Arliss from a "she-bear" in a Fred Gibson novel—the "best doggone dog in the West" in the Disney film based on the novel
Shiloh —Beagle in a Phyllis Reynolds Naylor novel
Sounder —Coon dog that gets shot trying to protect his master in William Armstrong's novel
Spot —Dog who accompanies Sally, Dick, and Jane in a series of primers
Toto —Cairn terrier that accompanies Dorothy to Oz
White Fang —Klondike half-dog, half-wolf that ends his days in California in a Jack London story
Wolf —Rip Van Winkle's faithful dog

LITERARY/FILM DOGS OTHERWISE
Aesop —Greek fabulist who wrote "The Dog in the Manger"
"Barbara Frietchie" —John Greenleaf Whittier poem that includes the lines: "Who touches a hair of yon gray head,—Dies like a dog! March on!"

Dogs

"The Bear"—William Faulkner novella as part of *Go Down, Moses* that includes Sam Fathers, Old Ben, and a wild, mongrel dog called Lion

Beethoven—1992 film about a Saint Bernard, starring Charles Grodin

Bill Sikes—Villainous character having a white-coated shaggy dog named Bull's-eye in Dickens' *Oliver Twist*

Bulldog Drummond—Herman Cyril McNeile's detective who always catches his man

Cinderella—Disney film in which Bruno, the friendly lazy dog, is changed into a footman

Salvador Dali—Surrealist known for his 1928 motion picture *An Andalusian Dog* (*Un Chien andalou*), which he made in collaboration with Luis Buñuel

Death of a Salesman—Arthur Miller play including the lines: "So attention must be paid. He's not to be allowed to fall into his grave like an old dog."

Dogberry—Foolish constable in Shakespeare's *Much Ado About Nothing* whose name has come to designate any foolish, bungling, slow official, or a stupid, arrogant official

Dog Day Afternoon—1975 film starring Al Pacino as a bumbling bank robber

Frederick Forsyth—British author who wrote the novel *The Dogs of War*

Oliver Goldsmith—Irish-born English author who wrote "An Elegy on the Death of a Mad Dog" and *The Vicar of Wakefield*

Günter Grass—German 1999 Nobel Prize-winner for literature who wrote *Dog Years*

"greyhounds"—Fast dogs to whom Shakespeare refers in the following line in *Henry V*: "I see you stand like _____ in the slips, / Straining upon the start"

Heathcliff—Violent, disturbed character having dogs named Wolf and Gnasher in Emily Brontë's *Wuthering Heights*

The Hound of the Baskervilles—1902 Arthur Conan Doyle story featuring a "fiend dog" that is a cross between a mastiff and a bloodhound, the story in which Sherlock Holmes is "revived"

Julius Caesar—Shakespearean play that includes the line "Cry 'Havoc!' and let slip the dogs of war"

Laughed—What the "little dog" of nursery rhyme did after "The cow jumped over the moon"

Little boys—According to the rhyme, creatures that are made of "snakes (snips or frogs) and snails and puppy-dogs' tails"

Mother Hubbard—Old nursery rhyme character who went to get her poor dog a bone

Must Love Dogs—2005 romantic comedy starring Diane Lane and John Cusack

My Dog Skip—2000 film starring Frankie Muniz as a shy boy growing up in the 1940s Mississippi with his beloved Jack Russell terrier

Nurse—Person who takes the dog before the dog takes the cat in the nursery rhyme "The Farmer in the Dell"

Suzan-Lori Parks—Winner of the 2002 Pulitzer Prize in drama for *Topdog/Underdog*

Gary Paulsen—American author of the young adult novel *Dogsong*

Scylla—Ravenous mythological sea monster whose 6 heads, each having 3 rows of teeth, were said to resemble those of barking dogs

Straw Dogs—1971 film starring Dustin Hoffman in a violent Sam Peckinpah film

Booth Tarkington—American author of the novel *Penrod*, whose title character has a scraggly, wistful dog named Duke

Dylan Thomas—Welsh author who wrote *Portrait of the Artist as a Young Dog*

J.R.R. Tolkien—English author whose *Roverandom*, a fairy tale about a young dog, Rover, turned into a toy by a wizard, was published posthumously in 1998 though it was written years before his trilogy *The Lord of the Rings*

Turner and Hooch—1989 film starring Tom Hanks and a junkyard French mastiff who witnesses a murder

Mario Vargas Llosa—Peruvian author who wrote *The City and the Dogs*
Vietnam War—War during which Robert Stone's novel *Dog Soldiers* is set
Wag the Dog—1997 Barry Levinson film satire about a president who is caught in a sex scandal and creates a fake war in Albania weeks before the election
Where the Red Fern Grows—Wilson Rawls' novel featuring Billy Colman and his dogs Old Dan and Little Ann

POTPOURRI OF DOGS WITH *DOG* IN THE ANSWER
Bulldog—Nickname of Edward Braddock, the British general in the French and Indian War; pitcher Jim Bouton; and football player Clyde Turner
Bulldog edition—Earliest newspaper edition, especially one being sent to rural routes
Bulldogs—Nickname of the athletic teams at the University of Georgia and Mississippi State University
Dogbane—Plant so named because it was said to be poisonous to dogs
Dogpatch—Hometown of comic strip character L'il Abner
Dog soldier—Cheyenne warrior, or, later, any outlaw Western Indian warrior
Hot dogs—Food called *frankfurters*, *wieners*, and *red hots*
"Hound Dog"—Elvis Presley song that includes the line, "You ain't no friend of mine"
Iditarod sled-dog race—Race in Alaska known as the "Last Great Race on Earth"
Prairie dog—Small burrowing North American rodent that makes a barking cry like that of a small dog
Prairie dogging—Act of heads of workers popping up over cubicle partitions like small burrowing North American rodents
Sea dog—Sailor, a sea captain, or a pirate
Three Dog Night—Pop-rock trio whose popular hits were "One" and "Joy To The World"
Yellow-dog contract—Contract by which a worker agrees not to join a union while employed

POTPOURRI OF DOGS OTHERWISE
American Kennel Club—World's largest registry for purebred dogs, or the AKC
Arkansas—State known for the former Dogpatch Amusement Park, named for Al Capp's comic strip
Atlanta—State capital called the "Dogwood City," site of the Martin Luther King Jr. tomb
H.M.S. *Beagle*—Ship on which Charles Darwin traveled as a naturalist from 1831 to 1836
Canary Islands—Islands whose name first designated a wild dog found there and later a native small yellow bird
Canes Venatici—Constellation under the Big Dipper's handle called "the hunting dogs"
Canines—Cuspids, or sharp pointed teeth used for tearing and shredding meat, named from the Latin word for *dog*
Canis Major—Constellation whose Latin name means "Larger or Greater Dog," the one containing the Dog Star
Canis Minor—Constellation whose name means Lesser or Little Dog
The Citadel—Charleston, South Carolina, school whose athletic teams are called the "Bulldogs" and the "Cadets"
The Cynics—Philosophical movement founded by Antisthenes, whose name is thought to come from a Greek word for "doglike," possibly as a commentary on their very critical nature
Charles A. Dana*—*New York Sun* editor to whom is attributed the 1882 remark: "When a dog bites a man that is not news, but when a man bites a dog, that is news."
*Also attributed to John Bogart and Amos Cummings

Dogs

Dingo—Australian wild dog brought to the country by the Aborigines
Diogenes—Greek philosopher, most famous of the Cynics, who was nicknamed "The Dog"
Duke—Golden retriever entrusted with the secret family recipe for Bush's Baked Beans
W.C. Fields—Comedian to whom is attributed the line, "Anyone who hates children and dogs can't be all bad."
Gonzaga University—Spokane, Washington, school whose athletic teams are called the "Bulldogs" and the "Zags"
Greyhound—Nationwide bus company
Hush-puppy—Small ball of cornmeal dough fried in deep fat
Jezebel—Biblical queen who was thrown from a window and devoured by dogs according to II Kings 9:30-37
K-9—Police dog unit
Lazy—Word completing the typewriting test phrase: "The quick brown fox jumps over the _____ dog"
Groucho Marx—Comedian who said, "Outside of a dog, a book is man's best friend. Inside of a dog it's too dark to read."
McGruff—Canine detective featured on a U.S. Postal Service stamp with the line "Take the Bite out of Crime"
Missouri/North Carolina—States whose state flower and state tree are both the flowering dogwood, respectively
Mud puppy—North American salamander
Patti Page—Female singer known for "How Much Is That Doggie in the Window?"
Ivan Pavlov—Russian who discovered the conditioned reflex while working with dogs
Prime number sequence—Type of sequence Mark Haddon uses in numbering his chapters 2, 3, 5, 7, 11, 13 and 101, 103, 107 in the novel *The Curious Incident of the Dog in the Night-time*
St. Louis—Midwestern city known for its AKC Museum of the Dog, especially for its dog-related art
Salukis—Hunting dogs for which the athletic teams at the University of Southern Illinois-Carbondale are named
Sirius—Dog Star or Canicula, the brightest star seen from Earth at night
Spuds McKenzie—Bud Light spokesdog
Virginia—State whose state tree and state flower are both the dogwood
Waggley—Word completing the song line, "How Much Is That Doggie in the Window? / The one with the _____ tail"
Westminster Kennel Club Show—Top American dog show
Virginia Woolf—English author who wrote *Flush*, the biography of Elizabeth Barrett Browning's pet spaniel—she also wrote *To the Lighthouse*
Yale University—New Haven, Connecticut, school whose athletic teams are called the "Bulldogs" and the "Elis"

HORSES

Character in William Shakespeare play who said: "A horse! A horse! my kingdom for a horse!"
* **Answer: King Richard III (in *Richard III*).**

1) Name the 3 races that make up the Triple Crown of Horseracing.
Answer: Kentucky Derby, Preakness Stakes, and the Belmont Stakes.

2) Identify the 3 tracks at which the Triple Crown races are held.
Answer: Churchill Downs (in Louisville, Kentucky; Kentucky Derby); Pimlico (in Baltimore, Maryland; Preakness Stakes); and Belmont Park (in Elmont, Long Island; Belmont Stakes).

3) Name the first 5 of the 11 Triple Crown winners in horseracing.
Answer: Sir Barton (1919, with Johnny Loftus aboard); Gallant Fox (1930, with Earl Sande); Omaha (1935, with Willie Saunders); War Admiral (1937, with Charley Kurtsinger); and Whirlaway (1941, with Eddie Arcaro).

4) Name the 1943, 1946, and 1948 Triple Crown winners, the 6th to 8th winners.
Answer: Count Fleet (with Johnny Longden); Assault (with Warren Mehrtens); and Citation (with Eddie Arcaro; Arcaro was the first to win the Triple Crown twice), respectively.

5) Name the 1973, 1977, and 1978 Triple Crown winners, the 9th to 11th winners.
Answer: Secretariat (with Ron Turcotte); Seattle Slew (with Jean Cruquet); and Affirmed (with Steve Cauthen; the first horse to win $2 million), respectively.

6) Name the 3 fillies that have won the Kentucky Derby, in 1915, in 1980, and in 1988.
Answer: Regret, Genuine Risk, and Winning Colors, respectively.

7) Identify the 3 songs played respectively before the running of each of the Triple Crown races.
Answer: "My Old Kentucky Home" (Kentucky Derby), "Maryland, My Maryland" (Preakness Stakes), and "Sidewalks of New York" (Belmont Stakes).

8) Identify the 3 flowers associated with the Triple Crown races.
Answer: (The Run for the) Roses, (The Run for the) Black-eyed Susans, and (The Run for the) Carnations, respectively.

9) Identify the 3 official drinks* associated with the Triple Crown races.
Answer: Mint julep (Kentucky Derby), Black-Eyed Susan (Preakness), and Belmont Breeze (Belmont; previously it was the White Carnation).

*__Mint julep__: Kentucky bourbon and a syrup of mint, sugar, and water; __Black-Eyed Susan__: vodka, rum, triple sec, pineapple juice, and orange judice; and __Belmont Breeze__: Seagram's 7, sherry, orange juice, cranberry juice, lemon juice, simple syrup, 7UP, and club soda (the **White Carnation** was vodka, peach schnapps, orange juice and a splash of cream).

10) In betting terms, what are the first 3 places in a horse race?
Answer: Win, place, and show.

11) Identify the 5 English Classic races.
Answer: St. Leger Stakes (1776), The Oaks (1779), the Epsom Derby (1780), the 2,000 Guineas (1809), and the 1,000 Guineas (1814).

Bit—Part of the bridle that goes into a horse's mouth
Bridle—Head harness used to guide a horse
Brood mare—Mare kept for breeding
Canter—Horse's smooth, easy gait, named after the pace at which the pilgrims rode to Canterbury, England
Colt—Young male horse 4 years of age or under, or any young horse
Croup—Horse's rump
Dam—Mother of a horse
Filly—Female horse from the time of weaning to age 4
Foal—Young horse that is less than a year old
Gait—Horse's forward movement
Gallop—Fastest gait of a horse, consisting of a succession of leaping strides with all the feet off the ground at one time
Gelding—Male horse whose reproductive organs have been removed, thus prohibiting it from breeding
Hand—Unit of 4 inches used to measure the height of a horse
Herd—Large group of horses other than *pair, team,* and *span*
Hinny—Offspring of a male horse, or *stallion*, and a female ass, or *jenny*
Mare—Mature female horse
Mule—Hybrid animal resulting from a *mare* or female horse and a *jack* or male donkey
Paddock—Small field near a stable where horses are exercised, or a racetrack enclosure where horses are saddled
Pony—Horse less than 58 inches tall at the shoulder
Purebred—Adjective meaning "having ancestors that all belonged to the same breed"
Reins—Narrow straps of leather held by the rider to control the horse
Sire—Horse's father
Stallion—Mature male horse, especially one used for breeding
Tack—Harness for a horse, including the saddle and bridle
Trot—Horse's gait faster than a walk and with diagonal legs lifted together
Walk—Horse's slowest gait
Withers—Highest part of a horse, the ridge between a horse's shoulder bones
Yearling—Horse that is more than 1 and less than 2 years old (dating starts January 1)
Zebra—Striped member of the horse family whose 3 species are called *common, Grevy's,* and *mountain*
Zorse—Cross between a zebra and a horse

FAMOUS HORSES
Al-Borak—Muhammad's milk-white horse with the wings of an eagle, a human face with horses' cheeks, and a pace equal to the farthest range of human sight
Black Jack—Last U.S. Army horse, one born in 1947, so named from the nickname of U.S. General John Pershing

Bucephalus—Alexander the Great's horse whose name means "bull-headed"
Buttermilk—Dale Evans' horse
Champion—Gene Autry's horse called the "World's Wonder Horse"
Comanche—Captain Miles W. Keogh's horse, the lone U.S. cavalry survivor of the Battle of Little Big Horn
Comet—Superman's Super Horse in DC Comics
Copenhagen—Duke of Wellington's horse whose name is shared by Denmark's capital
Dallas—Barbie's golden palomino that shares its name with a Texas city
Hero—The Phantom's great white horse in the comics
Horse—Dimwitted horse of Dudley Do-Right, the Canadian mountie of cartoon and animated TV fame
Incitatus—Caligula's horse, one he loved so much that he adorned it with a jeweled collar, placed a marbled statue of it in its ivory stable, and even supposedly wanted to make it a consul
Macaroni—Caroline Kennedy's pony
Marengo—Napoleon's white stallion, named after a village in Northwestern Italy, the site of the victory on June 14, 1800, of the French over the Austrians
Mr. Ed—TV's talking palomino horse belonging to Wilbur
Nightmare—Casper the Friendly Ghost's ghostly horse
Phantom—Zorro's white horse
Pokey—Gumby's sidekick, an animated pony made of orange clay
Quick Draw McGraw—Horse character in Hanna-Barbera cartoons whose deputy is Baba Looey, a Mexican burro
Rex—Sgt. Preston (of the Yukon)'s horse
Scout—Tonto's horse earlier called White Feller, or Paint
Silver—Lone Ranger's horse
Spark Plug—Barney Google's horse in the *Barney Google* comic strip
Tarzan—The Wonder Horse of Ken Maynard, the first singing cowboy in the movies
Thunder or Papoose—Red Ryder's horse or his sidekick Little Beaver's horse
Tony—Tom Mix's "Wonder Horse" after Blue died
Topper—Hopalong Cassidy's white horse
Tornado—Zorro's black horse on TV
Traveller—Robert E. Lee's gray gelding originally called Jeff Davis and later Greenbrier
Trigger—Roy Rogers' golden palomino horse, sometimes called "the smartest horse in the movies" and formerly known as Golden Cloud
Venus—Belle Starr's black horse sharing the name of the Roman goddess of love
White Flash—Tex Ritter's horse in the movies
Whitey—Rutherford B. Hayes' horse; Zachary Taylor's favorite horse; and Hoot Gibson's horse in the movies
Winchester—Union Gen. Phil Sheridan's horse originally named Rienzi, then renamed after his famous ride to the Battle of Cedar Creek to rally his troops ("mostly on the gallop" in a Thomas Buchanan Read poem)

HOMO SAPIENS/POP CULTURE-RELATED HORSES
El Cid*—Spain's national hero whose battle horse was Babieca, a name meaning "Stupid"
Cinderella—Disney film in which Major, an old horse, is transformed into a coachman

*El Cid is Rodrigo, or Ruy, Diaz de Vivar.

The Cisco Kid—TV show on which Cisco rode Diablo and Pancho rode Loco
William F. Cody—Army scout and Indian fighter nicknamed "Buffalo Bill," whose buffalo-hunting horse was named Brigham
George Armstrong Custer—U.S. cavalry leader at the 1876 Battle of Little Bighorn whose horse was named Vic
Ulysses S. Grant—Civil War general and U.S. President some of whose many horses were named Cincinnatus, Egypt, Julia, Jeff Davis, and St. Louis
James Butler Hickok—Frontiersman nicknamed "Wild Bill" whose horse was Black Nell
Thomas J. Jackson—Civil War general nicknamed "Stonewall" whose Little Sorrel was also referred to as "Fancy"
Mighty Mouse—Superhero, who "came to save the day," featured with the time-traveling winged stallion named Luno
Non Sequitur—Wiley Miller's comic strip in which Lucy, a pygmy Clydesdale, is being trained by Danae as a guide horse for the blind
Thomas Paine—American author of *Common Sense* whose horse was named Button
John J. Pershing—General of the Armies who rode his horse Kidron through New York City's Victory Arch at the end of WWI
Paul Revere—Patriot and silversmith who rode the borrowed horse Brown Beauty during his famous April 18, 1775, ride
Richard III—Last Yorkist king of England, defeated at the Battle of Bosworth Field, whose favorite horse was White Surrey
William T. Sherman—Civil War general with the middle name Tecumseh whose horse was named Lexington or Sam
Dick Turpin—Legendary British highwayman associated with the horse Black Bess
John Tyler—10th U.S. President, who rode the horse General
William III—Dutch leader and king of England from 1689 to 1702 who suffered a fatal injury when his horse Sorrel, blind in one eye, stumbled throwing him

HORSE BREEDS AND OTHER HORSES
Appaloosa—Popular rodeo horse associated with the Nez Percé, named after the Palouse Indians or the Palouse River region, and sometimes called a *raindrop horse* or "Dalmatian of Horses" because of its black or brown spots
Arabian—Swift, graceful horse named after a breed developed by Bedouins in the deserts of Arabia
Belgian—Heavy, muscular draft or work horse named after the country of Belgium
Bronc(o)—Spanish word for "rough" for an any wild or partially untamed horse of the western U.S. plains
Clydesdale—Breed of large, heavy draft horse with heavily "feathered" legs called *hocks*, named after the valley of the Clyde River, Scotland
Falabella—Smallest breed of horses, only about 30 inches high and originally bred in Argentina
Hackney—English breed of sturdy, harness horses used for ordinary driving
Lipizzan(er)—Any breed of gray to white horses used especially in dressage exhibitions, a line that originated with the imperial Austrian stud farm near Trieste, Yugoslavia, and trained in Vienna at the Spanish Riding School
Morgan—Breed of strong riding horse, usually chestnut or black in color named after Justin _____, a Vermonter
✓**Mustang**—Small, wild horse of the southwestern U.S. plains, a variety descended from Spanish horses

Palomino—Spanish word for a golden-tan horse with a light blond or silvery mane and a white streak on the face
Percheron—Strong draft horse named after Perche, France, where they were bred
Pinto—Spanish word for a piebald horse, that is, one marked with patches of white and black or brown
Przewalski's horse*—Only true wild horse in existence today, named after Russian explorer Nikolai _____
Quarter horse—Horse that can run 1/4 of a mile in about 20 seconds
Shetland pony—Breed of small, hardy pony named after a group of islands in the Atlantic
Shire—Largest breed of horses, named after a region in England
Tennessee walking horse**—Breed of lightly built saddle horse developed in Tennessee
Thoroughbred—Breed developed by crossing Arabian and Turkish stallions with English mares, all of which can be traced to 3 stallions named Darley Arabian, Godolphin Arabian (or Barb), and Byerly Turk

*Another wild horse, the tarpan, now extinct, was called *a forest horse*. **Also called Tennessee walker

LANGUAGE HORSES WITH *HORSE IN THE ANSWER*
(To) back the wrong horse—Phrase meaning "to support the losing side or candidate"
Charley horse—Informal term for a muscle cramp, especially in the thigh
Clotheshorse—Person very interested in the latest fashion, or a frame on which to hang garments
Dark horse—Candidate unexpectedly nominated, or a person with little apparent chance of winning who does go on to win
(To) beat (flog) a dead horse—Phrase meaning "to pursue a futile goal"
Four Horsemen of the Apocalypse—Phrase from Revelation 6 designating any group of four who will bring evil and destruction to the world
Gift horse—According to the proverb, type of horse you do not look at in the mouth
High horse—According to the idiom, kind of horse on which a person is if he shows disdain for others or acts in an arrogant manner
Hobby horse—Child's toy consisting of a stick with a horse's head at one end, or an idea or scheme that becomes a preoccupation
(To) hold one's horses—Phrase meaning "to be patient"
Horse-and-buggy—Hyphenated phrase for something old-fashioned
(To) horse around—Phrase meaning "to engage in mischief"
(To) horse-collar—In baseball, hyphenated slang term meaning to keep the other team from scoring
Horsefeathers—Slang for nonsense
Horsehide—Slang for a baseball
Horselaugh—Loud, vulgar guffaw
Horseless—Adjective meaning self-propelled
Horsemanship—Art of riding, managing, and training horses
Horse of a different (another) color—Phrase meaning "a different matter completely"
Horse opera—Slang for a film set in the American West
Horseplay—Rough, rowdy fun—*to horse around* is "to engage in such fun"
Horse race—Figurative term for any contest, especially a very close or difficult one
Horse sense—Intelligence
Horse trade—Informal term for a shrewd compromise
One-horse (town)—Hyphenated term for something inferior, or of minor importance, such as an unimportant town

Sawhorse—Rack used to support a piece of wood being sawed

Stalking horse—Political candidate who serves as a decoy for a more serious unannounced candidate

(Straight/right) from the horse's mouth—Phrase meaning "information from an authoritative source"

Trojan horse—Phrase for "any devious scheme," alluding to the huge hollow wooden ruse the Greeks used to gain access to Troy

War horse—Person who has seen many fights; a veteran; an overused piece of music, literature, etc., or a charger

Wild horses—According to the expression, type of horses that could not drag information from a person

LANGUAGE HORSES OTHERWISE

Ass—Word completing the phrase *to make a horse's _____ of oneself or someone else*, meaning "to make an utter fool of oneself or of another"

Beggars—According to the proverb, those who would ride if wishes were horses

Caballero—Spanish word for "a horseman" or "a nobleman"

Cart—According to the proverb, type of object one does not put before the horse

(To) champ at the bit—Phrase similar to *bite the bridle* and meaning "to show impatience," referring to the way a horse chews on the bit when anxious to go

Charger—Horse ridden in battle or in a parade

Chivalry—Medieval system of knighthood, derived from the French word *cheval* for "horse"

Colt—Informal term for a young person lacking experience, from the term for a young male horse no more than 4 years old

Coltish—Adjective describing someone as "frisky or frolicsome," from the term for a young male horse no more than 4 years old

(To) come a cropper—Phrase meaning "to fall headlong from a horse" or "to come to ruin, or to suffer failure"

(To) cool one's heels—Phrase meaning "to wait or be kept waiting, from having to wait after a horse's hooves got too hot"

Drink—What according to the proverb you cannot get a horse to do after leading (taking) it to water

Eat—Word completing the idiom *to _____ like a horse*, meaning "to consume a great deal of food"

Equestrian—Person skilled in horseback riding, or adjective describing sculptures depicting someone on horseback

Equine—Any animal of the horse family, or the adjective meaning "horselike"

Filly—Informal term for a lively young woman, from the term for a female horse under 5 years of age

Garrison finish—Term for a last-second victory in a horse race, after American Edward _____, a jockey who won many races right at the end

Gaucho—Spanish word for mounted horseman in southern Latin America

(To) go by shank's mare—Phrase meaning "to go on foot"

Hackney—Trite or commonplace, as derived from the word for a carriage for hire, so named after a Greater London borough

Healthy (strong)—Word completing the simile *as _____ as a horse*

Hippology—Study of horses

Hippophile—Lover of horses

Hippophobia—Fear of horses

Hobson's choice—No choice at all, after Englishman Thomas _____, who in renting horses required the person to take the horse nearest the door, or the best rested one

Mare's-nest—Hyphenated term for an amazing discovery that is really a hoax or a delusion, or a very confused situation

(To) mount Pegasus—Phrase meaning "to begin writing a poem, to do creative work, or to achieve great success," alluding to the winged horse of the Muses that created their spring called Hippocrene on Mt. Helicon from the touch of its hoof

Nag—Old, worn-out horse, or slang for a racehorse, especially a second-rate one

Nail—Word completing the proverb about neglect breeding great mischief: "for want of a _____ the shoe is lost; for want of a shoe the horse is lost; for want of a horse the rider is lost"

Picador—Spanish word for a horseman who opens bullfights by provoking the bull

Piebald—Horse usually marked with patches of white and black

Pinto—Spanish word meaning "painted" for a horse or pony marked with patches of white and black or brown, or for a kind of kidney bean

Pony—Informal term like *trot* for a translation of a foreign language work, used especially as a crib sheet in school, or a small glass holding less than 2 ounces of alcohol

(To) pony up—Slang meaning "to pay something owed"

Skewbald—Horse usually marked with patches of white and brown or any other color except black

Stable (barn) door—According to the proverb, what you don't lock after the horse has been stolen

Steed—High-spirited riding horse, from the Old English word for "stud horse"

Stream (river)—Word completing the idiom *It's best not to swap (change) horses in the middle of a _____*

Thoroughbred—Figurative term borrowed from horseracing for a cultured, well-bred person or a high-spirited person

Troika—Any group of 3 persons or nations acting equally in authority or a Russian carriage drawn by a team of 3 horses abreast

(To) trot out—Phrase meaning "to bring out for others to see and consider"

The trots—Slang for a bout of diarrhea

LITERARY/FINE ARTS/FILM HORSES

Banbury Cross—Nursery rhyme place to which one rides "a cockhorse . . . to see a fine lady upon a white horse"

The Black—Arabian horse in Walter Farley's novels *The Black Stallion*

Black Beauty—Horse featured in Anna Sewall's book called "the *Uncle Tom's Cabin* for animals" since it is an autobiography of a horse mistreated by a groom and rescued by a kind woman

Boxer—Draft horse who represents the working class and is taken to the glue factory by the pigs in George Orwell's *Animal Farm*

Buckbeak—Half eagle, half-horse in *Harry Potter and the Prisoner of Azkaban*

Robert Burns—Scottish poet in whose poem "Tam o'Shanter" Tam's gray steed named Meg loses her tail to a witch

Chincoteague—Virginia island named in the title of Marguerite Henry's book *Misty of _____*

Clover or Mollie—Mare showing motherly concern for Boxer or the vain mare who leaves Animal Farm to work in a pub in Orwell's *Animal Farm*

The Faerie Queen—Edmund Spenser epic in which Sir Guyon reclaims his war horse Brigadore from Braggadocio

Flicka—Horse named in the title of Mary O'Hara's novel *My Friend* _____

Dick Francis—British mystery writer whose plots center on the sport of horse racing and whose first novel is *Dead Cert*—his autobiography is entitled *The Sport of Queens*

The Godfather—1972 film in which the head of the thoroughbred race horse Khartoum is put in his owner's bed

Götterdämmerung—German name for the opera in which Brünnhilde presents her war horse Grane (Grani) to Siegfried, the 4th of Wagner's Ring series

Gunpowder—Ichabod Crane's horse in Washington Irving's *The Legend of Sleepy Hollow*

Headless Horseman—Phantom, Brom Bones in disguise, who scares Ichabod Crane in *The Legend of Sleepy Hollow*

Horse Feathers—1932 Marx Brothers film set at Huxley College

The Horse Soldiers—John Ford's 1959 film set mainly during the U.S. Civil War

The Horse Whisperer—Robert Redford's 1998 film about a girl and her wounded horse

Houyhnhnm—Metaphorical name for a "horse endowed with reason," from a race of horses with reasoning powers and human virtues in Jonathan Swift's *Gulliver's Travels*

Humpty Dumpty—Egg-shaped nursery rhyme character whom "All the King's horses / And all the King's men" couldn't put together again after he falls off a wall

D.H. Lawrence—British author who wrote the short story "The Rocking-Horse Winner" about a small boy who rides himself to death

C.S. Lewis—British author whose stories in *The Chronicles of Narnia* series include *The Horse and the Boy*

Man Called Horse—1970 film starring Richard Harris as a British aristocrat who is captured and enslaved by Sioux Indians

Cormac McCarthy—American author who wrote *All the Pretty Horses*

Larry McMurtry—American author who wrote *Horseman, Pass By*

Paradise Lost—John Milton poem including the lines, "Behind her Death / Close following, pace for pace, not mounted yet / On his pale horse."

Pied Piper—Mythical person of Hamelin, Germany, for whom the leader of the horses in the novel *Misty of Chincoteague* is named

Katherine Anne Porter—American author who wrote *Pale Horse, Pale Rider*

The Red Pony—John Steinbeck's story about 3 events in the life of the boy Jody Tiflin, one of which is the death of his prize pony Gabilan after he leaves it out in the rain

Ros(c)inante—Don Quixote's bony horse in Cervantes's *Don Quixote*

Shadowfax—Gandalf the wizard's horse in J.R.R. Tolkien's *The Lord of the Rings*

Sir Gawain and the Green Knight—14th-century Arthurian romance featuring Gawain and his horse Gringalet

They Shoot Horses—Words completing the 1969 title _____, *Don't They?*, a film about a dance marathon set in Chicago's Aragon Ballroom

Velvet Brown—Teenage girl who rides her horse The Pie (Piebald) to victory in the Grand National title race in Enid Bagnold's *National Velvet*

The Velveteen Rabbit—Margery Williams story that includes these lines said by the Skin Horse: "Generally, by the time you are Real, most of your hair has been loved off, and your eyes drop out and you get loose in the joints and very shabby."

Alice Walker—American author of *The Color Purple* who wrote *Horses Make a Landscape More Beautiful*

Widow-Maker—Pecos Bill's horse, which no one else could ride

The Wizard of Oz—Film in which the Guardian of the Emerald City Gates says, "There's only one of him and he's it. He's the Horse of a Different Color, you've heard tell about."

William B. Yeats—Irish poet whose "Under Ben Bulben" includes the lines: "On limestone quarried near the spot / By his command these words are cut: / 'Cast a cold eye—On life, on death, / Horseman, pass by!'"

MYTH-RELATED HORSES

Arion—Fabulous winged horse with 2 human feet and the ability to speak, the one Hercules gave to Adrastus—it is the offspring of Demeter and Poseidon

Balius—Achilles' immortal steed, the offspring of Podarge and Zephyrus

Bellerophon—Glaucus' son who rode Pegasus to slay the Chimera and from which he fell when he tried to mount to Olympus

Centaur—Monster having the head, trunk, and arms of a man, and the body and legs of a horse

Diomedes—King of Thrace whose wild horses, known for eating humans, were captured by Heracles, who in turn fed them the king

Helios—Greek god of the Sun who drove his horse-drawn chariot across the sky each day

Hippocampus—Horse Neptune is depicted as riding, one with the forelegs of a horse but the posterior of a fish or dragon

Hippogriff—Fabulous winged monster resembling a griffin but having the body and hind quarters of a horse

Hippolytus—Theseus' son who rejected the amorous advances of his stepmother, Phaedra, and later died when his horses, frightened by a sea bull sent by Poseidon, dragged him into the sea

Laocoön (Laocoon)—Trojan priest of Apollo who proclaimed the Wooden Horse a deception and gave the warning, "I fear the Greeks even when bearing gifts"

Pegasus—Winged horse created from the blood or neck of Medusa

Poseidon—Greek god of the sea, called the "Lord of the Horses," who created the horse

Sea horse—Mythical sea creature, half fish and half horse

Sleipnir—Odin's 8-legged horse in Norse mythology

Trojan horse—Huge hollow wooden horse the Greeks used to gain access to Troy and raze it—Greek soldiers were hiding inside and came out at night and conquered Troy

Unicorn—Horselike animal having a single horn growing from the center of its forehead

Xanthus—Achilles' horse who in the *Iliad* was endowed by Hera with the power of speech

POTPOURRI OF HORSES WITH *HORSE* IN THE ANSWER

Crazy Horse—Sioux Indian who defeated Custer in 1876 and is portrayed in a gigantic unfinished sculpture in the Black Hills of South Dakota started by Korczak Ziolkowski

Draft horse—Horse that pulls heavy loads

Horsefly—2-winged insect belonging to the order diptera

Horse latitudes—Name given to the regions of 30° to 35° north and south latitudes possibly because of the animals thrown overboard there when ships were becalmed

Horseradish—Hot, white, fleshy root of the mustard family

Horseshoe—Symbol of luck, something nailed to barn doors in the Middle Ages to keep witches and others from stealing the horses

Horseshoe Bend—1814 Battle in Alabama at which Andrew Jackson defeated the Creek Indians

Horseshoe Falls—Another name for the Canadian Falls that with the American Falls make up Niagara Falls
Iron horse—Train or locomotive, as named by Indians
"Light-Horse Harry"—Nickname of major general Henry Lee known for his eulogy of President George Washington
One horsepower—English unit of measurement equaling 550 foot-pounds per second, or 746 watts
Rocking horse—Toy horse mounted on springs and ridden by a child
Sea horse—Bony fish of the genus *Hippocampus* that swims upright, has a prehensile tail, and a horselike head
Whitehorse—Capital of Canada's Yukon Territory
Workhorse—Reliable person who does a considerable amount of work, or a machine considered sturdy and dependable

POTPOURRI OF HORSES OTHERWISE
America—Group whose "A Horse With No Name" was a No. 1 hit in 1972
ASPCA*—After having witnessed brutality to horses and other animals in Russia, society Henry Bergh founded in 1866
Automobile—What was early in its history referred to as the "horseless carriage"
Gene Autry—"America's Favorite Cowboy" known for his "Back in the Saddle Again" theme
Basketball—Ball used in the 2-person game called *horse*
(A) Buffalo Bill—An expert horseman, scout, and sharpshooter, derived from William F. Cody's nickname
Daniel Boone—American frontiersman who blazed the Wilderness Road and is known for saying, "All you need for happiness is a good gun, a good horse, and a good wife."
Calgary—Alberta city famous for its Exhibition and Stampede—it uses the Rockies, a buffalo, a horse, and a steer as symbols
Ben Campbell—Colorado rancher and Cheyenne tribal member with the middle name Nighthorse who in 1992 became one of the first Native Americans elected to the U.S. Senate
"Camptown Races"—Stephen Collins Foster song that includes the lines: "G'wine to run all night! / G'wine to run all day! / I'll bet my money on de bobtail nag— / Somebody bet on de bey."
Cavalry—Soldiers who fight on horseback
Charles V—Holy Roman emperor from 1519 to 1556 who allegedly said, "I speak Spanish to God, Italian to women, French to men, and German to my horse."
Cheval-de-frise—French term, literally "horse of Friesland," for a piece of wood with spikes intended to impede a cavalry attack
Winston Churchill—British prime minister who said, "There is something about the outside of a horse that is good for the inside of a man."
Clydesdale—Breed of large horses featured in Budweiser beer commercials
Comanche—Warlike Indian tribe of the American West who were noted for their skill as horseback riders
Cossack—Word for "free person" that designates a famous horseman of southern Russia, or the Ukraine
Dada (Dadaism)—French word for "hobby-horse" used to designate an art and literary movement of 1915 to 1922 essentially rejecting society's values

*In full, American Society for the Prevention of Cruelty to Animals

Edgar Degas—French artist who painted contemporary scenes, especially horse races, ballet, cafés, and the circus

Delaware—State whose quarter depicts Caesar Rodney, signer of the Declaration of Independence and commander of the state militia, sitting astride a horse

Albrecht Dürer—15th-16th century German artist known for his woodcut *The Four Horsemen of the Apocalypse*

Eohippus—Earliest ancestor of the modern horse whose name means "dawn horse"

John Charles Frémont—American explorer known as the "Gray Mustang" and the "Pathfinder of the West"

Hippocampus—Sea-horse shaped ridge along the lower section of each lateral ventricle of the brain that is a center of memory and learning

Hippodrome—Oval track for horse races and chariot races in ancient Greece and Rome

Hippopotamus—Animal whose name means *river horse*

Italian Stallion—Rocky Balboa's nickname in the *Rocky* films

"Jingle Bells"—Song that includes the lines, "Dashing through the snow / In a one horse open sleigh"

Kentucky—State whose quarter depicts a stately mansion Federal Hill and a thoroughbred racehorse positioned behind a fence in the foreground

Lexington—Kentucky city called "The Capital of the Horse World" and named after a battle fought in Massachusetts in 1775

Abraham Lincoln—U.S. President known for saying, "It's best not to swap (change) horses in the middle of a stream," upon learning of his renomination

Jack London—American author who is the subject of Irving Stone's novel *Sailor on Horseback*

James Longstreet—Civil War leader known as "Lee's War Horse" and "War Horse of the Confederacy"

Mesohippus—Historically, the "middle horse," the one after the *Eohippus* and before the *Miohippus*

David Niven—English actor whose autobiographies are entitled *The Moon's a Balloon* and *Bring on the Empty Horses*

Oats—Cereal grass most commonly used as grain to feed horses

Pegasus—Mythic horse that the Exxon Mobil Oil Corporation adopted as its trademark

Wilson Pickett—Alabama-born R&B singer whose "Mustang Sally" was a 1966 hit

Pinto—Ford car known for bursting into flame in an accident, named from the Spanish word for "painted"

Pony edition—Newspaper or magazine edition that is smaller than the main edition

Pony Express—Mail delivery service between St. Joseph, Missouri, and Sacramento, California, that was established on April 3, 1860, and closed in late 1861

Pony League—Baseball group for youngsters aged 13 and 14

Ponytail—Hairdo in which long hair is tied tightly at the back of the head so that it hangs freely

Frederick Remington—19th-century American who sculpted the 1895 bronze equestrian piece called "Bronco Buster"

Rolling Stones—English rock group known for their 1971 "Wild Horses"

Theodore Roosevelt—U.S. President known as the "Cowboy President" and the "Man on Horseback"

St. Hippolytus—Patron saint of horses

Margaret Chase Smith—Maine senator who directed at Senator Joseph McCarthy the following statement in a Declaration of Conscience Speech on June 1, 1950: "But I don't want to see the Republican Party ride to political victory on the Four Horsemen of Calumny—Fear, Ignorance, Bigotry, and Smear."
Snickers—Mars candy bar named after a favorite horse of the Mars family
Tang—7th-10th century Chinese dynasty known for its ceramic horses—its name also designates an orange-flavored soft drink
Tattersall—Fabric pattern of thin lines of dark colors forming squares on a light background, named after a sporting enterprise and horse market in London opened by Richard _____
WWII—War during which the U.S. Army gave up the use of cavalry horses

SPORT HORSES
Alan Ameche—Baltimore Colts' running back nicknamed "The Horse"
Alydar—Only horse ever to be runner-up in all 3 Triple Crown races, in 1978
Aristides—Winner of the first Kentucky Derby, in 1875
Assault—Thoroughbred race horse nicknamed the "Clubfoot-footed Comet"
Australia—Country in which the Melbourne, a famous horse race established in 1861, is run on the first Tuesday in November
Belmont (Stakes)—Oldest of the Triple Crown of Horse races, having been first run in 1867
Citation—Thoroughbred race horse nicknamed "Big Cy," the first to win a million dollars
Derby—Annual horse race for 3-year-olds at Epsom Downs, England
Diomed—English horse foaled in 1777 who is the ancestor of all American Walking horses
Dressage—Guiding of a horse through various steps and gaits without using reins or noticeable signs, as in Olympic competition
Eclipse—English thoroughbred with an astronomical name foaled in 1764, the ancestor of most modern thoroughbreds
8—Seconds a rodeo contestant in a bareback bronc riding event must stay aboard to qualify while spurring the horse as it bucks
Equitation—Art of riding on horseback, or horsemanship
Furlong—Unit of length relegated mostly to horse-race tracks and equal to 40 rods, 1/8 mile, or 220 yards
Gallant Fox—Only Triple Crown winner to sire another Triple Crown winner, Omaha
Lou Gehrig—American baseball player known as the "Iron Horse," who played in 2,130 consecutive games
Horseracing—Sport known as "The Sport of Kings"
Horseshoes—Game involving players tossing objects at stakes 40 feet apart
John Henry—Famous gelding who won 25 grade stakes from 1974 to 1984, becoming the highest money earning thoroughbred ever
Kentucky Derby—Horse race for 3-year-old horses, male or female, held on the first Saturday in May
Knight—Chessman also referred to as a horse that makes an L-shaped move
Maiden—Any horse who has never won a race
Man o'War—Thoroughbred race horse with 20 wins and 1 loss nicknamed "Big Red"
John Martin—St. Louis "Gas House Gang" member known as "Pepper" and "The Wild Hoss of the Osage"
Bronislau Nagurski—Football running back known as the "Big Ukranian" and "Bronco"
Native Dancer—Thoroughbred race horse nicknamed the "Grey (Gray) Ghost"

Notre Dame—University at which "The Four Horsemen" played football
Oklahoma—University whose mascots are white Shetland ponies named Boomer and Sooner
Pommel horse—Gymnasium horse used by men for balancing and swinging exercises—also called a *side horse*
Royal Ascot—Fashionable race established by Queen Anne in 1711 and held at Ascot Heath in England
Seabiscuit—Racehorse Red Pollard rode to wins in the '30s and subject of a 2003 film based on Laura Hillenbrand's 2001 book tracing its life
Secretariat—1973 winner of the Belmont Stakes by 31-lengths nicknamed "Big Red"—the only Derby winner to finish under 2 minutes
Southern Methodist—Dallas, Texas, university whose athletic teams are called the "Mustangs"
Thoroughbred—Fastest of all horses, the type that can run the mile in about 1½ minutes at a speed just under 40 miles per hour
Traveller—University of Southern California's famous white horse mascot, an Andalusian
Upset—Only horse to defeat Man o'War
Whirlaway—Thoroughbred race horse nicknamed "Mr. Longtail"

HARNESS RACING

1) Name the 3 races that make up the Triple Crown of Harness Racing for trotters.
Answer: Hambeltonian (at the Meadowlands in East Rutherford, New Jersey), Yonkers Trot (at Yonkers Raceway in Yonkers, New York), and the Kentucky Futurity (at the Red Mile Harness Track in Lexington, Kentucky).

2) Name the 3 races that make up the Triple Crown of Harness Racing for pacers.
Answer: Cane Pace, the Little Brown Jug, and the Messenger Stakes (not always in this order and the races periodically move to different tracks).

3) Identify the 2 kinds of harness horses, one moving its front leg on one side and its hind leg on the other side at the same time, and the other one moving its legs on the same side of its body together.
Answer: Trotter and pacer, respectively.

Dan Patch—Legendary horse who never lost a race, after whom a 2-step dance was named and featured in a 1949 film
Hambletonian—Name for both the "Great father" of harness horses, the one who sired over 1,330 horses before his death in 1876, and the race known as "The Kentucky Derby of harness racing"
Messenger—First thoroughbred to sire great trotters
New York—State in which the Harness Horse Museum and Hall of Fame is located in Goshen
Old Henry Clay—"Father of American Trotting Horses" who lived from 1837 to 1867
Standardbred—Light horse, also called the American trotting horse, developed from the Thoroughbred as a trotter or pacer in harness races
Sulky—Two-wheeled cart with a seat for one person, used in harness racing

DRAGONS

Author who in *The Hobbit* said: "Never laugh at live dragons"
Answer: J.R.R. Tolkien.

LITERARY/FINE ARTS DRAGONS
Beowulf—Old English hero of the Geats who kills the monster Grendel and his mother and dies while slaying a dragon
Bilbo Baggins—Hero of J.R.R. Tolkien's novel *The Hobbit* whom the wizard Gandalf describes as "one of the best—as fierce as a dragon in a pinch"
Pearl S. Buck—American author who wrote *Dragon Seed* and *The Good Earth*
Cadmus—Phoenician prince in Greek mythology who killed a dragon at the spring at Thebes after it had killed all his servants whom he had sent for water
Centaur Pendragon—Rudolph Valentino's Irish Wolfhound
Delphi—Oracular shrine of Apollo known as the site where he killed a dragon or serpent
Donatello—European sculptor of the 15th century known for his *St. George Killing the Dragon* and *The Boy David*
Dragon Lady—Nickname of the Chinese *femme fatale* Lai Choi San in the comic strip *Terry and the Pirates*
Eragon—Christopher Paolini's teenage character who communicates telepathically with the dragon Saphira as they set out with Brom to get vengeance on Galbatorix
Fafnir—Hreidmar's son who turns himself into a dragon in order to guard Andvari's gold hoard in Icelandic prose legend
Gargoyle—Building ornament that Thomas Hardy describes in these lines from *Far from the Madding Crowd*: "It was too human to be called like a dragon, too impish to be like a man, too animal to be like a fiend, and not enough like a bird to be called a griffin"
Johnny Gruelle—American author who wrote *Raggedy Ann and the Paper Dragon*
Heracles—Strongman of myth who had to kill or put to sleep a dragon or serpent named Ladon in order to steal the Golden Apples in the Garden of the Hesperides
Hippocampus—Horse Neptune is depicted as riding, one with the forelegs of a horse but the posterior of a fish or dragon
Hogwarts—School in Harry Potter series having the motto *Draco Dormiens Nunquam Titillandus*, translated as "Never Tickle a Sleeping Dragon"
E. Howard Hunt—Member of the White House "Plumbers" in the Watergate break-in who later wrote the novel *Dragon Teeth*
Jabberwock—Giant fiendish dragon-like monster in Lewis Carroll's *Through the Looking Glass*
Jason—Argonaut leader to whom Medea gave a magic drug to put the dragon guarding the Golden Fleece to sleep
Ang Lee—Taiwanese-born U.S. film director known for *Crouching Tiger, Hidden Dragon*
Marianne Moore—Poetess with the initials M.M. who wrote the poem "O To Be a Dragon"
Ogden Nash—American author of the poem about a dragon named Custard who has big sharp teeth

Norbert—Norwegian Ridgeback Hagrid won in a game of cards in the Harry Potter series

Uther Pendragon—King Arthur's father whose surname means "chief or head dragon," the title given to a military chief

Perseus—Mythological hero who rescues Andromeda from a sea monster or dragon

Pilgrim's Progress—John Bunyan work in which Apollyon, a creature with wings like a dragon, tries to defeat Christian

Python—Dragon or serpent sent by Hera to kill Apollo's mother, Leto, during her pregnancy and later killed by Apollo at Delphi

Red Cross Knight—Knight who slays a dragon and marries Princess Una in Edmund Spenser's *The Faerie Queene*

Peter Paul Rubens—Flemish artist who painted *St. George and the Dragon* and *Raising of the Cross*

Shrek—2001 animated film in which a green-skinned ogre rescues the Princess Fiona from a firebreathing dragon

Siegfried—Richard Wagner's 1876 opera in which the hero kills Fafner the dragon and Mime the dwarf, then takes the magic ring

Sigurd—Icelandic hero in the epic *The Saga of the Volsungs* who kills the dragon Fafnir and bathes in its blood, making his flesh invulnerable except for one little spot on his body

Upton Sinclair—American author who won the 1943 Pulitzer for *Dragon's Teeth* but is better known for *The Jungle*

Smaug—Dragon from whom Bilbo Baggins, Gandalf, and others reclaim Lonely Mountain and its riches in *The Hobbit*

Snap-dragon-fly—Insect in Lewis Carroll's *Through the Looking Glass* whose body is made of plum-pudding, its wings of holly-leaves, and its head a raisin burning in brandy

(To) sow dragon's teeth—Phrase used figuratively to mean "to plant seeds of strife, or to stir up trouble, especially by peaceful intent," alluding to the action of Cadmus in following the advice of Athena

Philo Vance—Detective in S.S. Van Dine's *The Dragon Murder Case*

Laurence Yep—American author who wrote *Dragonwings*, *Dragon of the Lost Sea*, and *Dragon's Gate*

Yggdrasil—Ash tree near whose roots lived the serpent or dragon Nidoggr in Norse myth

POTPOURRI OF DRAGONS

Baal—Canaanite storm god who subdues Yam, the dragon of the sea

Bhutan—Asian country between India and Tibet whose square flag features a white "Thunder Dragon" with a jewel in each claw

China—Country whose yellow imperial flag showed a blue dragon chasing a red ball (the earth), representing the Manchu (Qing) Dynasty (in its traditional New Year's Day parade, a group of people wind through the streets wearing a large dragon costume)

Columbus—Georgia city that is the home of both the Riverdragons in the NBDL and Patrick's Press

Draco—Latin name of the constellation whose English name is Dragon

Daryl Dragon—Real name of The Captain of the duo The Captain and Tennille

Dragonet—Small dragon or a small, colorful marine fish

Dragonfly—Water insect that captures its prey in a basket formed by its 6 spiny legs and eats while flying—sometimes called a "horse stinger," a "mule killer," a "mosquito hawk," or a "devil's darning needle"

Dragonhead—Common name for some 45 species of the mint family

Dragon lady—Powerful or domineering woman or a femme fatale, derived from the evil Oriental woman in *Terry and the Pirates*

Dragon's blood—Cheap Rhine wine so called because of the story of Siegfried and what he bathed in to protect himself from injury

Sir Francis Drake—English explorer and adventurer known as *El Draque*, or "The Dragon," and "Terror of the Spanish Main"

Enter the Dragon—1973 film starring Bruce Lee in a martial arts contest on an island fortress

Komodo dragon—Largest extant lizard, the so-called *dragon lizard*, named after an island in Indonesia where it is found

Kowloon—Suburb of the city of Hong Kong or the Chinese rocky peninsula on which it is located, a name meaning "nine dragons"

Ku Klux Klan—Organization known for its Dens, Grand Cyclopes, Grand Titans, Grand Dragons, and Grand Wizard

Leviathan—Name designating a huge sea monster or dragon in Psalm 74:13 and Isaiah 27:1

Meteor—Shooting star sometimes called "a flying dragon"

Michael—Archangel who, according to Revelation 12:7-8, struggled with his angels against Satan in the shape of a dragon

Oolong—Dark tea from China and Taiwan whose name literally means "black dragon"

Puff—Magic dragon who lived in a land called Honalee in a Peter, Paul, and Mary song

Carl Sagan—1978 Pulitzer Prize-winner for *The Dragons of Eden: Speculations on the Evolution of Human Intelligence*—this astronomer is linked with the phrase "billions and billions of stars"

St. George—England's patron saint who allegedly slayed a dragon to rescue the daughter of the king of Libya

Satan—Figure said to be "the great dragon" in Revelation 12:9

Seine—French river flowing through Paris ravaged by the dragon La Gargouille until St. Romain of Rouen killed it

Siberia—Russian region bordering China where the 1,755-mile long Amur river the Chinese call the Heilung Kiang, or the "Black Dragon River," is located

Snapdragon—Plant with spikes of colorful flowers whose blossoms open like jaws, then snap shut again

South Africa—Country that shares with Lesotho the Dragon Mountains, or Drakensberg Mountains

Wales—Political division of the United Kingdom whose flag features a red dragon on a field of green and white

"F<small>RANKLY</small>, M<small>Y</small> D<small>EAR</small>..."

1939 film that includes the line: "Frankly, my dear, I don't give a damn"*
Answer: *Gone With the Wind*.

(Listed chronologically)
Jonathan Edwards—So-called "Artist of Damnation" who during the Great Awakening delivered his famous sermon "Sinners in the Hands of an Angry God" in 1741
Crispus Attucks—Leader at the 1770 Boston Massacre who allegedly said, "Come on, you bloodybacks, you lobster scoundrels, fire if you dare . . . fire and be damned, we know you dare not."
Lexington—Site where Captain John Parker, leading a force of 70 Minutemen on April 19, 1775, was told by the head of the British troops: "Lay down your arms, you damned rebels, and disperse."
Fort Ticonderoga—New York fort where Ethan Allen after demanding the British surrender it in 1775 allegedly first said to the British leader, "Come out of there, you damned old rat."
Andrew Jackson**—7th U.S. President to whom is attributed the statement, "It's a damn poor mind that can only think of one way to spell a word!"
Philip Nolan—Character in Edward Everett Hale's 1863 "The Man Without a Country" who says, "Damn the United States, I wish I may never hear of this United States again."
David Glasgow Farragut—Admiral at the 1864 Battle of Mobile Bay who said, "Damn the torpedoes! Captain Drayton, go ahead! Jouett, full speed!"
Pennsylvania—State of Thaddeus Stevens, a Radical Republican Congressman, who in 1867 wanted to bring the traitors in the South to their knees by having Congress divide up the "damned rebel provinces" and fill them with new settlers
Andrew Johnson—U.S. President who, upon learning that the House had begun impeachment proceedings against him, said, "Let them impeach and be damned!"
Chester A. Arthur—21st U.S. President who said, "I may be President of the United States, but my private life is nobody's damned business."
William H. Vanderbilt—Robber Baron and railroad mogul who said in 1882 about an extra fare charge, "The public be damned! I'm working for my stockholders."
Mark Twain—American humorist who once suggested that "writers should substitute the word 'damn' for every occurrence of 'very'" on the idea that their copy editors will cut the "damns" and will leave the copy just as it should be
Isaac C. Parker—"The Hanging Judge" of Fort Smith, Arkansas, whose court was known as the "Court of the Damned" since about 80 death sentences were carried out in his 21 years on the bench
Theodore Roosevelt—Person about whom Mark Hanna was speaking when he said, "Now, look, that damned cowboy is President of the United States."
Henry Ford—Automobile entrepreneur who said, "History is more or less bunk. It's tradition. We don't want tradition. We want to live in the present and the only history that is worth a tinker's damn is the history we make today."

*In Margaret Mitchell's book, the line appears as "I wish I cared what you do or where you go but I can't. . . . My dear, I don't give a damn." **Also attributed to Andrew Johnson.

Theodore Roosevelt—U.S. President who said: "Damn the law, I want the canal built!" insisting he had a "mandate from civilization" to get construction of the Panama Canal started

F. Scott Fitzgerald—American author whose novel *The Beautiful and the Damned* was published in 1921

Warren Harding—29th U.S. President who once said, "I have no trouble with my enemies. I can take care of my enemies all right. But my damn friends. . . . They're the ones that keep me walking the floor nights!"

Clarence Darrow—Attorney who became known as the "Defender of the Damned" for having saved college students Richard Loeb and Nathan Leopold from the death penalty in their trial for the murder of Bobbie Franks in the 1920s

Ernest Hemingway—American author whose 1926 *The Sun Also Rises* includes the lines: "'Oh, Jake,' Brett said, 'we could have had had such a damned good time together.'. . . 'Yes,' I said. 'Isn't it pretty to think so?'"

Eugene O'Neill—American author whose 1931 *Mourning Becomes Electra* includes the line, "The damned don't cry."

"The Devil and Daniel Webster"—1937 Stephen Vincent Benét short story including the line, "Even the damned may salute the eloquence of Mr. Webster."

Clark Gable—Actor playing Rhett Butler in 1939's *Gone With the Wind* who says to Vivien Leigh playing Scarlett O'Hara in parting, "Frankly, my dear, I don't give a damn!"

Bernard M. Baruch—U.S. representative to the U.N. Atomic Energy Commission who said in 1946: "We are here to make a choice between the quick and the dead. . . . If we fail, then we have damned every man to be the slave of fear. Let us not deceive ourselves: we must elect world peace or world destruction."

Harry S Truman—U.S. President who said, "I don't give a damn about 'The Missouri Waltz' but I can't say it out loud because it's the song of Missouri. It's as bad as 'The Star-Spangled Banner' so far as music is concerned."

Damn Yankees—1955 Broadway play based upon Douglass Wallop's *The Year the Yankees Lost the Pennant*

Richard Nixon—U.S. President who said, "I don't give a damn how it is done, do whatever has to be done to stop these leaks and prevent unauthorized disclosures," doing so during the Watergate crisis

THE GOOD AND THE BAD

Author who in *Animal Farm* said: "Four legs good, two legs bad"
Answer: George Orwell.

1) Identify the title of the 1966 film starring Clint Eastwood, Lee Van Cleef, and Eli Wallach.
Answer: *The Good, the Bad, and the Ugly*.

2) Identify the 3 words that complete the following line from Baruch Spinoza's *Ethics*: "Thus one and the same thing can be at the same time _____, _____, and _____. For instance, music is good to the melancholy, bad for him who mourns, and neither good nor bad for him who is deaf."
Answer: Good, bad, and indifferent.

3) Identify the 5-word phrase meaning "to spend more money while trying to get back some that has been lost."
Answer: (To) throw good money after bad.

4) Which 4 words designate the police interrogation technique by which 2 different policemen try to wear down a suspect by alternating between sympathy and a harsh manner?
Answer: Good cop, bad cop.

5) Which author in which work wrote the line: "I'm really a very good man; but I'm a very bad Wizard"?
Answer: Lyman Frank Baum in *The Wonderful Wizard of Oz*.

6) Identify the Shakespeare play that includes the line: "There's nothing either good or bad, but thinking makes it so," expressing the idea that interpreting something as good or bad depends solely on one's point of view.
Answer: *Hamlet* (said by Hamlet to Rosencrantz).

7) Identify the author who wrote the following poetic lines: "There was a little girl / Who had a little curl / Right in the middle of her forehead; / And when she was good / She was very, very good, / But when she was bad she was horrid."
Answer: Robert Louis Stevenson.

8) Identify the actress who said, "When I'm good, I'm very, very good; but when I'm bad, I'm better," doing so in the film *I'm No Angel*.
Answer: Mae West.

9) Identify the U.S. President known as "Good Bill/Bad Bill."
Answer: Bill Clinton.

10) Identify the first song on Led Zeppelin's 1969 debut album whose title fits this category.
Answer: "Good Times Bad Times."

THE GOOD

1-WORD, 2-WORD "GOODS"

Damaged goods—Materials that have been ruined or a "ruined" person, especially an unmarried woman who is no longer a virgin
Good Book—The Bible
Good-bye—Farewell, a contraction of *God be with ye*
Good cheer—Merrymaking, or good food and drink
Good egg—Agreeable, honest person, or "good ovum"
(In) good faith—Sincerity, absence of spite, or good intentions
Good fellow—Friendly, jovial person
Good-fellowship—Strong, jovial companionship
Good-hearted—Adjective meaning kind and generous
Good humor—Cheerful, friendly, pleasant mood
(The) good life—Wealthy, lavish life style
Goodies—Food treats, especially sweets
Good-looking—Handsome or beautiful
Good looks—Attractive personal demeanor
Good-natured—Having a pleasant disposition, or agreeable
Goodness—State of being good or generosity
Good night—Phrase used in parting when going to bed
Good riddance—A welcome exit
Goods—Merchandise or movable personal property
Good sense—Sound judgment
Good turn—Kind act
Good will—Kindly or friendly feeling
Good works—Acts of charity or kindness
Goody-goody—Alliterative term for a moral or pious person, or someone "holier-than-thou"
Straight goods—The truth
White goods—Household linens

FOREIGN "GOODS"

Adieu—French term for goodbye, suggesting finality
Adios—Spanish for goodbye or farewell
Aloha—Hawaiian for hello or goodbye
Au revoir—French for goodbye, meaning literally until we meet again
Auf Wiedersehen—German for goodbye or farewell
Bona fide—Latin for in good faith or genuine
Bona fides—Latin for proof of good faith, designating documents proving identity or authority
Bonjour—French for good day, good morning, or hello
Bonne chance—French for good luck
Bonne nuit—French for good night
Bon vivant—French for one who enjoys the good things of life
Bon voyage—French for (have a) good journey
Buenas noches—Spanish for good evening
(La) dolce vita—Italian for the good life
Gesundheit—German for good health, especially used after someone has sneezed

Hasta luego—Spanish for goodbye, meaning until later!
Laisser les bons temps rouler—Cajun French expression meaning "let the good times roll"
Pro bono—Latin meaning "donated for the public good (i.e. without a fee)"
Sayonara—Japanese for goodbye

HOMO SAPIENS "GOODS"
George W. Bush—U.S. President known as "The Good President" because of his frequent use of this adjective
Grover Cleveland—U.S. President known as "Grover the Good"
Calvin Coolidge—U.S. President who married Grace Anna Goodhue
Elizabeth I—English queen known as "Good Queen Bess"
Sigmund Freud—Austrian neurologist and psychiatrist, the founder of psychoanalysis, known as "the Good Doctor"
Jane Goodall—British primatologist known for her long-term observations of chimpanzees in the wild in Tanzania
Dwight Gooden—New York Mets pitcher known as "Dr. K"
Cuba Gooding Jr.—Actor starring in *Jerry Maguire*
Gladys Gooding—Organist for the New York Rangers, New York Knicks, and the Brooklyn Dodgers
Benny Goodman—Clarinet player and band combo leader known as the "King of Swing"
Ellen Goodman—Boston *Globe* columnist and 1980 Pulitzer Prize winner for Distinguished Commentary
John Goodman—Actor who starred on TV's *Roseanne*
B.F. Goodrich—Akron, Ohio, rubber manufacturer
Mark Goodson—American television producer and long-time partner of Bill Todman known for such game shows as *Beat the Clock*, *The Price Is Right*, and *To Tell the Truth*
Good Samaritan—Biblical traveler who helped an injured man after the victim's countrymen passed by without offering help, leading Jesus to tell the Judeans to be more like the stranger
Good Shepherd—Name used for Jesus in John 10:11
Charles Goodyear—American inventor of vulcanized rubber and founder of the company known today for its blimp
Rutherford B. Hayes—U.S. President known as "Goody Two-shoes" and "Old Eight to Seven"
Henry I—William the Conqueror's youngest son, known as *Beauclerc*, or the "Good Scholar" or the "Good Clerk," a complimentary term
Thurgood Marshall—First black on the U.S. Supreme Court
James Monroe—U.S. President known as "Era of Good Feeling President"
Samuel Osgood—First U.S. Postmaster General
William Howard Taft—U.S. President known as "Good Old Will"
St. Wenceslas—Bohemian martyr-prince made famous in the 19th-century carol "Good King ____"

LANGUAGE "GOODS"
Account—*To give a good ____ of oneself*, meaning "to behave creditably"
An end—According to the proverb, this is what all good things must come to
Break/leg—*To ____ a ____*, meaning "good luck" as said to an actor before a performance
Charlie—*Good-time ____*, slang for a friendly, fun-loving person
Dead Indian—According to the 19th-century pejorative, *The only good Indian is a ____*

THE GOOD AND THE BAD

Deed—*No good _____ goes unpunished*, according to this ironic proverb
Deliver—*To _____ the goods*, meaning "to do exactly what is called for"
Fight/fight—*To _____ the good _____*, from I Timothy 6:12, meaning "to struggle to the end for what is right" or "to live one's life according to religious rules and customs"
For good (and all)—Permanently
Get out—According to the expression, what one does "while the getting is good"
Gold (or done)—*As good as _____*, meaning "totally genuine" or "well behaved"
(A) good beginning—According to the proverb, this is what is half the battle
Good-for-nothing—Worthless person
Good intentions—*The road to hell is paved with _____*, expressing the idea that well-intended conduct can have bad results
(A) good man—According to the proverb, this is what is hard to find
Good measure—*Do for _____*, meaning to add to what is required
Good offense—*The best defense is a _____*, advocating taking aggressive action as a defense
Good old boy—Southern white male thought of as easygoing, friendly, and loyal to his peer group
(A) good reputation—According to the proverb, this is what is more valuable than money
Good things—According to the proverb, this is what comes to those who wait or what comes in small packages
Good turn—According to the proverb, one of these "deserves another"
Goods—*To get the _____ on*, or *to have the _____ on*, meaning "to acquire confidential, especially incriminating, information on someone"
Goods—*To sell a bill of _____*, meaning "to swindle someone"
Goody two-shoes—Straitlaced, self-righteous person, as derived from a good little girl of nursery tale fame
Goose—Word completing the proverb, *what's good for the _____ is good for the gander*
Graces—*In someone's good _____*, meaning "favored"
Guess—*Your _____ is as good as mine*, meaning "I don't know any more than you do"
Head/shoulders—*To have a good _____ on one's _____*, meaning "to be intelligent"
(An) ill wind—According to the proverb, this is what "blows no good"
In a good mood—In a happy or cheerful state of mind
(A) miss—According to the proverb, this is what is as good as a mile
No good—*To come to _____*, meaning "to have a bad result" or "to die unpleasantly"
No news—According to the proverb, this is what is good news
Word—*As good as one's _____*, meaning "acting according to what was promised"
Young—According to the expression, when "only the good die"

LITERARY "GOODS"

Margaret Atwood—Canadian author who wrote *Good Bones and Simple Murders* and *The Handmaid's Tale*
Jane Austen—English author who wrote the line, "It is a truth universally acknowledged, that a single man in possession of a good fortune, must be in want of a wife" in *Pride and Prejudice*
Margaret Wise Brown—American author known for *Goodnight Moon*
Raymond Chandler—American author whose last novel, 1953's *The Long Good-Bye*, features detective Philip Marlowe
Anne Frank—German author who wrote the line, "In spite of everything I still believe that people are really good at heart" in *The Diary of a Young Girl*

Oliver Goldsmith—Irish-born British author who wrote *The Good-Natur'd Man* as well as *She Stoops to Conquer*

Goodbye, Mr. Chips—James Hilton's sentimental tale of an English schoolmaster or the 1939 film starring Robert Donat

The Good Earth—Novel by Pearl Buck

"Good fences"—Words completing Robert Frost's line "_____ make good neighbors," in the poem "Mending Wall,"

"The Good Gray Poet"—Walt Whitman's "colorful" nickname

A Good Man Is Hard to Find—Flannery O'Connor's 1955 collection of short stories

Goody Two-shoes—Oliver Goldsmith's nursery tale character who is delighted with her new pair of shoes

Hamlet—Shakespeare play in which Horatio says to the title character: "Now cracks a noble, heart. Good-night, sweet prince, / And flights of angels sing thee to thy rest!"

Nathaniel Hawthorne—American author of the short story "Young Goodman Brown"

Joseph Heller—American author who wrote *Good As Gold* as well as *Catch-22*

Christopher Isherwood—American author whose *Goodbye to Berlin* and other stories are the basis for the play and film *I Am a Camera* and the musical *Cabaret*

John D. MacDonald—American author whose *The Deep Blue Good-By* features private investigator Travis McGee

Friedrich Nietzsche—German philosopher who wrote *Beyond Good and Evil* and announced the death of God

Robin Goodfellow—Another name for Puck, the happy, mischievous elf in English folklore

Romeo and Juliet—Shakespeare work that includes the lines: "Good night, good night! Parting is such sweet sorrow, / That I shall say good night till it be morrow."

Philip Roth—American author who wrote *When She Was Good* and *Goodbye, Columbus*

Jane Smiley—American author who wrote *Good Faith* and *A Thousand Acres*

Dylan Thomas—Welsh poet who wrote the poem "Do Not Go Gentle Into That Good Night"

POTPOURRI OF "GOODS"

As Good As It Gets—1997 film for which Jack Nicholson won a Best Actor Oscar

Baseball—Sport whose phrase *good field, no hit* designates a skilled fielder who is weak at bat

Daniel Boone—American frontiersman who blazed the Wilderness Road and is known for saying, "All you need for happiness is a good gun, a good horse, and a good wife."

Buenos Aires—World capital whose name means "Good Winds"

The Goodbye Girl—1977 film starring Richard Dreyfuss and Marsha Mason

"Good" cholesterol—The "good" by which high-density lipoproteins are known

Good Conduct Medal—U.S. military decoration awarded for outstanding behavior, efficiency, and fidelity while on active duty

Goodfellas—1990 film starring Robert De Niro and Ray Liotta

Good Friday—Day on which Christ was crucified, 2 days before the Resurrection

"Good Grief"—Exclamation of surprise or dismay or Charlie Brown's favorite 2-word expression in Charles Schulz's comic strip *Peanuts*

(Cape of) Good Hope—Cape at the southwest coast of South Africa

Good Housekeeping Seal of Approval—Consumer rating begun in 1910 by a magazine using its own labs to test products laboratories

Good Morning, Vietnam—1987 film starring Robert Williams as Armed Forces Radio disc jockey Adrian Cronauer

Good Neighbor Policy—Franklin Roosevelt's policy for economic and political relations with Latin America

Good News (Tidings)—Literal meaning of the word *Gospels* as used to designate the Christian accounts of Jesus' life

Good News Bible—Name given to the new American Bible Society's 1976 translation of the Bible

Good Samaritan Law—Statute designed to protect give legal protection to a medical person who gives emergency treatment without consent as at an accident scene

Good Times—1974 to 1979 TV sitcom spin-off from *Maude* featuring the Evans family

Good Will Hunting—1997 film set in Boston starring Matt Damon, Ben Affleck, and Robin Williams

Hair—Off-Broadway musical having "Good Morning Sunshine" as one of its principal songs

Elton John—Singer, songwriter, pianist born Reginald K. Dwight, known for "Goodbye Yellow Brick Road"

Little Richard—Macon, Georgia, singer known for his 1958 "Good Golly, Miss Molly"

*M*A*S*H*—TV sitcom whose final episode on February 28, 1983, was entitled "Goodbye, Farewell, and Amen"

Maxwell House—Coffee company whose slogan is "Good to the Last Drop"

Marilyn Monroe—Actress whose story is told in the 1975 film *Goodbye, Norman Jean*

Diana Ross—Detroit singer known for "Good Morning Heartache" from the movie *Lady Sings the Blues*

Tree of Knowledge of Good and Evil—Tree in the Garden of Eden whose fruit God commanded Adam and Eve not to eat

Charles Erwin Wilson—U.S. engineer who said in 1953, "For many years I thought what was good for our country was good for General Motors, and vice versa. The difference did not exist."

Walter Winchell—Journalist known for the opening line for his weekly radio broadcast: "Good evening, Mr. and Mrs. America and all the ships at sea! . . . Let's go to press."

THE BAD

2-WORD "BADS"

Bad apple—A "fruity" troublemaker
Bad blood—Hostile feeling between groups of people
Bad break—Unfortunate piece of luck
Bad dream—Nightmare
Bad egg—Incorrigible person, especially one who is a bad influence, or "bad ovum"
Bad faith—Intentional deception, or dishonesty in a transaction
Bad guys (men)—Villains in western movies
Bad handwriting—Cacography
(To) bad-mouth—To talk badly about, or criticize
Bad news (omen)—Woeful tidings
Bad patch—Period of bad luck
Bad rap—False criminal charge
Bad seed—Evil person from birth
Bad-tempered—Cross or irritable
Bad trip—Adverse drug experience
Not bad—Fairly good
Too bad—Expression of regret

ENTERTAINMENT/MUSIC "BADS"

The Bad and the Beautiful—1952 film starring Lana Turner and Kirk Douglas about a Hollywood producer

Bad Boys—1983 film starring Sean Penn and Esai Morales about troubled kids in Chicago

Bad Day at Black Rock—1955 film starring Spencer Tracy and Robert Ryan about a one-armed stranger in a western town

Badlands—1973 film starring Martin Sheen and Sissy Spacek based on the Charles Starkweather-Carol Fugate murder spree in Nebraska in 1958

The Bad News Bears—1976 film starring Walter Matthau and Tatum O'Neal about Little League Baseball

Erykah Badu—Singer born Erica Wright known for her "On and On" and her debut album *Baduizm*

Brigitte Bardot—French actress known as the "Bad Little Bad Girl" and "The Sex Kitten"

Milton Berle—Comedian labeled as the "Thief of Bad Gags" and "Uncle Milty"

Bon Jovi—New Jersey rock group known for 1988's "Bad Medicine"

Credence Clearwater Revival—California rock group known for 1969's "Bad Moon Rising"

Jim Croce—Singer/songwriter known for 1973's "Bad, Bad Leroy Brown"

W.C. Fields—Comedian who said, "Anyone who hates children and dogs can't be all bad"

"Happy Days Are Here Again"—Milton Ager and Jack Yellen song with the lines: "So long, sad times; / Go 'long, bad times!"

Michael Jackson—"King of Pop" known for his 1987 album *Bad*

Eartha Mae Kitt—Singer and actress known as "The Bad Eartha"

Prince—Singer who once changed his name to an unpronounceable syllable and is known as "His Royal Badness"

Will Rogers—Comedian who said, "I not only 'don't choose to run' (for President) but I don't even want to leave a loophole . . . so I won't 'choose.' I will say 'won't run' no matter how bad the country will need a comedian."

Neil Sedaka—Pop singer/songwriter known for 1963's "Bad Girl" and 1975's "Bad Blood"

Donna Summer—Singer born Adrian Donna Gaines known for 1979's "Bad Girls"

Mae West—Actress known as the "Screen's Bad Girl" and "Diamond Lil"

LANGUAGE "BADS"

The bad—*To go to _____*, meaning "to develop a bad or immoral character"

Badass—Slang for a troublemaker

Bad-ball hitter—Batter who swings at bad pitches, thus a person with questionable judgment

Bad Day at Black Rock*—A fateful day resulting in a disastrous end, from the title of a 1955 film western

Bad hair day—As expressed in terms of coiffure, a period of time when everything seems to go wrong

Badinage—Word of French origin for teasing talk or banter

Badman—Outlaw or villain

Bad name—*To give a _____ to*, meaning "to spoil someone's reputation"

Bad news—According to the idiom, what "travels fast"

Bad penny—According to the proverb, what "always turns up," meaning that something unwanted regularly shows up

Bad taste—*To leave a _____ in one's mouth*, meaning "to leave a bad impression or cause bitter feelings"

Bad way—*In a _____*, meaning "seriously sick or hurt" or "in an unfortunate predicament"

Bad workman—According to the proverb, this person always blames or quarrels with his tools

*Black Rock is also a term used for the CBS building because of its dark-gray granite.

C'est dommage—French for "It's too bad"
(To) feel bad—To experience sadness or regret
Grace—*With a bad* _____, meaning "reluctantly"
Graces—*In someone's bad* _____, meaning "out of favor with someone"
In a bad mood—In a cantankerous or depressed state of mind
Not so (too) bad—Fairly good
(Peck's) bad boy—*Peck's* _____, designating a mischievous boy or someone who behaves badly, as derived from the naughty main character who plays pranks on his father in George W. Peck novels
Run—_____ *of bad luck*, meaning "continuous spell of bad fortune"
Bad/Worse—*To go from* _____ *to* _____, meaning "to grow steadily poorer"

POTPOURRI OF "BADS"

Albatross—Bird whose killing in *The Rime of the Ancient Mariner* brings the ship bad fortune
Maxwell Anderson—American author who wrote *The Bad Seed*, a play based on a William March novel about an evil little girl
Bad Boys—Nickname of the 1989 Detroit Pistons championship team
Bad break—Words completing Lou Gehrig's statement, "On this day I consider myself the luckiest man on the face of the earth. I might have been given a _____ / but with all this I've got an awful lot to live for."
"Bad" cholesterol—The "bad" by which low-density lipoproteins are known
Baden-Baden—Alliterative name of a fashionable spa in Germany in the Black Forest
Agnes Baden-Powell—First commissioner of the Girl Guides
Lord or Robert Baden-Powell—Founder of the Boy Scouts
Badger—Nocturnal, burrowing carnivorous mammal, related to the weasel
Badger State—Nickname for the state of Wisconsin
Badlands—Region in South Dakota and Nebraska where erosion has produced unusual land formations
✓ **Badminton**—Game in which a net, shuttlecock, and rackets are used
Bad peace—Words completing Benjamin Franklin's maxim: "There never was a good war or a _____."
Badwater—Lowest point in North America, located in Death Valley at 282 feet below sea level
Bald eagle—Bird that Benjamin Franklin said was "a bird of bad moral character"
Barbados—West Indies country whose capital is Bridgetown
Ambrose Bierce—American author of "An Occurrence at Owl Creek Bridge" who is the subject of a biography subtitled *Alone in Bad Company*
Big Bad Wolf—Enemy of the 3 Little Pigs who threatens each by saying, "I'll huff, and I'll puff, and I'll blow your house down!"
Black cat—Animal considered bad luck if it crosses your path
Black Hawk War—War during which the Battle of Bad Axe was fought in 1832 in present-day Illinois
Cacodontia—Technical term for bad teeth
Carlsbad—Another name for Karlovy Vary, a famous health resort in the Czech Republic
Carlsbad Caverns—National park located in New Mexico famous for its underground caves
Jubal Anderson Early—Independent Confederate commander in the Shenandoah Valley nicknamed "Bad Old Man" and "Old Jube"

Germany—Country in which Baden-Württemberg is located
Ruth Bader Ginsburg—Supreme Court justice whose middle name is Bader
Gresham's Law—Economic hypothesis that bad money tends to drive out good money from circulation
Halitosis—Technical term for bad breath
Hope Diamond—World's largest blue diamond believed to bring bad luck to its owner
Iranian—Nationality of Shirin Ebadi, the first Muslim woman to win the Nobel Peace Prize, in 2003, for her fight for liberalization, democracy, and human rights in her country
Islamabad—Pakistan's capital
Jonah—Biblical figure whose name has come to designate a person considered to bring bad luck
Ladder—Object said to bring bad luck if you walk under it
Alice Roosevelt Longworth—U.S. President's daughter who said, "Harding was not a bad man. He was just a slob."
Marienbad—German name for the Czech Republic town Mariánské Lázně, which appears in the title of the 1961 film *Last Year at* _____, directed by Alain Resnais
H.L. Mencken—Editor and columnist for the *Sun* known as the "Bad Boy of Baltimore"
Obadiah—Biblical prophet whose name begins with *O*
Pakistan/India—Country in which the cities Hyderabads are located, one on the Indus River and another near Bombay
Raven—Largest of all perching birds and a bird of ill omen that allegedly brings bad luck and forebodes death
7—Years of bad luck said to result from breaking a mirror
Sinbad—Actor born David Adkins known for his role in TV's *A Different World*
Sinbad the Sailor—Merchant and sailor who makes 7 sea voyages in the *Arabian Nights*
Spain—Country in which Badalona is a suburb of Barcelona
Mark Twain—American author and humorist born Samuel Langhorne Clemens and known as the "Bad Boy from the Mississippi" and the "Bad Boy of Old Missouri"
Cynthia Voigt—American author who wrote *Bad Girls* and *Bad, Badder, Baddest* as well as *Dicey's Song*
Wisconsin—University whose athletic teams are called the "Badgers"

NAKED, NOT NEKKID

American poet who in his poem *Howl* wrote: "I saw the best minds of my generation destroyed by madness, starving hysterical naked, / dragging themselves through the negro streets at dawn looking for an angry fix"
Answer: Allen Ginsberg.

Actaeon—Mortal hunter who accidentally saw Artemis, the chaste Greek goddess of the hunt, naked in her bath and was then by her hand turned into a stag and chased and killed by his own dogs

Adam and Eve—Biblical couple who "were both naked" in the Garden of Eden "and were not ashamed," according to Genesis 2:25

John Quincy Adams—Only U.S. President interviewed while swimming naked in the Potomac River, being forced to do so when journalist Anne Royall sat on his clothes until he granted the interview

Amaryllis (belladonna)—Plant with rose-colored flowers also called *naked lady* and *belladonna lily*

Andromeda—Nearest spiral galaxy beyond the Milky Way that is the most distant celestial object visible to the naked eye

Ape—*Naked* _____, meaning "human being," loosely alluding to Charles Darwin's *The Origin of Species* in 1859

Archimedes—Greek mathematician and scientist who allegedly discovered the principle of displacement while sitting in a bath and then ran naked through the streets of Syracuse shouting, "*Eureka! Eureka!*" meaning "I've found it! I've found it!"

Au naturel—French phrase meaning "naked," "in simplest manner," or "cooked simply"

(In one's) birthday suit—What one is said to be wearing if naked

William Blake—British poet who wrote the following lines in his *Proverbs of Hell*: "The pride of the peacock is the glory of God. / The lust of the goat is the bounty of God. / The wrath of the lion is the wisdom of God. / The nakedness of woman is the work of God."

Tycho Brahe—Danish astronomer whose first name was given to a supernova star that appeared in the constellation Cassiopeia in 1572 because he observed it with the naked eye

William S. Burroughs—American author who wrote the cult novel *Naked Lunch*, dealing with an addict's world

Coco Channel—French fashion designer who said, "I wanted to give a woman comfortable clothes that would flow with her body. A woman is closest to being naked when she is well dressed."

Corporal works (acts) of mercy—Name given to the 7 compassionate acts required of Christians as enumerated in Matthew 25:35-45, one of which is to clothe the naked

e.e. cummings—Poet who used only lower case in writing these lines: "a pretty girl who naked is / is worth a million statues"

Cupid—Naked, winged cherub with bows and arrows used as a symbol of love on a valentine card

Lady Godiva—11th-century English woman who allegedly rode naked through Coventry covered only by her long hair as a condition of her husband's lifting the taxes imposed on the people

Francisco Goya—Spanish artist known for his *Naked Maja*

Gymnasium—From the Greek word for "to train naked," a place where exercises are done

Gymnosperms—Of the 2 large classes of seed plants, the one that consists of plants having uncovered seeds, i.e., not enclosed in fruit or ovaries, and whose name comes from 2 Greek words meaning "naked" and "seed"

Headlights—American equivalent of the British "naked lights"

Jaybird—*As naked as a _____*, meaning "nude"

Job—Biblical person who, after rending his mantle and shaving his head, worshipped saying "Naked came I out of my mother's womb, and naked shall I return thither" (1:21)

Magellanic Clouds—2 galactic clusters that can be seen with the naked eye, those "large and small" galaxies named after the 16th-century Portuguese explorer who led the first expedition that circumnavigated the world

Norman Mailer—American author who wrote *The Naked and the Dead*, a 1948 war novel loosely based on his own WWII experiences

Edouard Manet—French impressionist attacked by the critics for being too modern, especially when his *Luncheon in the Grass* showed a naked woman having a picnic with 2 clothed men

Matthew (25:35-36)—New Testament book in which Jesus says, "I was a stranger, and ye took me in:—Naked, and ye clothed me: I was sick, and ye visited me"

Naked eye—Manner of seeing something without the help of any scientific instrument

Naked mole-rat—Small, hairless African rodent with wrinkled skin that spends its entire life underground, the only known hairless rodents

Naked short selling—Selling of securities that are sold short and then neither borrowed nor delivered

Naked truth—Plain unadorned facts, as named from the fable in which the goddess Falsehood takes the goddess Truth's clothing while they are bathing and Truth decides to go naked

Noah—Biblical person whose son Ham found him lying drunk and naked and whose other 2 sons then covered his nakedness with a cloak

Pablo Picasso—Spanish artist known for *Les Demoiselles d'Avignon*, an early Cubist work featuring 5 naked prostitutes, 2 of whom have African masks for heads

Ramadan—Muslim month of dusk-to-dawn fasting that begins with the spotting of a new moon with the naked eye

Robinson Crusoe*—Fictional character who says: "One day, about noon, going towards my boat, I was exceedingly surprised with the print of a man's naked foot on the shore, which was very plain to be seen in the sand."

Peter Paul Rubens—16th-17th century Flemish artist known for depicting fleshy nude females, as in *The Judgment of Paris*, which features 3 naked goddesses in front of a shepherdboy holding a golden apple in his hand

Susanna—Woman in the Apocrypha who, after being seen bathing naked by two elders and rebuffing their advances, was falsely accused of adultery—she was acquitted and they were executed

Mark Twain—American humorist who wrote, "Clothes make the man. Naked people have little or no influence on society."

Valley Forge—Pennsylvania site where on December 23, 1777, George Washington wrote, "We have this day no less than 2,873 men in camp, unfit for duty because they are bare-footed and otherwise naked."

*In Daniel Defoe's *Robinson Crusoe*

Venus de Milo—Statue of a half-naked woman found by a peasant on the Greek island of Melos (Milos) in 1820 and now in the Louvre, often called the *Aphrodite of Melos*

Tennessee Williams—American author who in *A Streetcar Named Desire* wrote the lines, "I can't stand a naked light bulb, any more than I can a rude remark or a vulgar action."

William Wordsworth**—Romantic poet who wrote the following lines cited in Robert Redford's film *A River Runs Through It*: "Not in entire forgetfulness, / And not in utter nakedness, / But trailing clouds of glory do we come / From God, who is our home."

**From his "Intimations of Immortality From Recollections of Early Childhood"

ENTERTAINMENT/MUSIC/TV "NAKEDS"

Barenaked Ladies—Canadian group known for their albums *Gordon*, *Maybe You Should Drive*, and *Born on a Pirate Ship*

Marilyn Monroe—Actress who when asked "Didn't you have anything on?" replied, "I had the radio on."

Naked Boys Singing—Off-Broadway show celebrating the splendors of male nudity pulled from a list of discounted offerings for delegates at the 2004 Republican National Convention

Naked City—1958 to 1963 TV police drama set in New York City where the narrator intoned "There are eight million stories . . ."

The Naked City—1948 film documentary starring Barry Fitzgerald as Lt. Dan Muldoon

The Naked Edge—1961 film starring Gary Cooper and Deborah Kerr

The Naked Face—1984 film starring Roger Moore and Rod Steiger

The Naked Gun—Film series featuring Leslie Nielsen and Priscilla Presley based on TV's Police Squad

Naked Lunch—1991 science fiction fantasy drama based on the novel by William S. Burroughs

The Naked Maja—1858 film starring Ava Gardner and Anthony Franciosa about an 18th-century romance between artist Francisco Goya and the duchess of Alba

The Naked Spur—1953 film western starring James Stewart and Janet Leigh

The Naked Truth—1995 to 1998 TV sitcom starring Tea Leoni as Nora Wilde

NOBEL PRIZES

Scientist who said: "My factories may make an end of war sooner than your congresses. The day when two army corps can annihilate each other in one second, all civilized nations, it is to be hoped, will recoil from war and discharge their troops"
Answer: Alfred Nobel.

1) Name the 6 fields in which Nobel Prizes are awarded.
Answer: Physics, chemistry, physiology or medicine, literature, (world) peace, and economics.

2) Name the 4 South Africans who have won the Nobel Peace Prize, one in 1960, one in 1984, and 2 in 1993.
Answer: Albert J. Luthuli, Desmond Tutu, Nelson Mandela, and Frederik W. de Klerk, respectively.

3) Which 3 U.S. Presidents have won the Nobel Peace Prize?
Answer: Theodore Roosevelt (1906), Woodrow Wilson (1919), and Jimmy Carter (2002; as a former President).

4) Name the 3 people who shared the 1994 Nobel Peace Prize for signing a 1993 accord between the PLO and Israel that allowed limited Palestinian self-rule in the Gaza Strip and the West Bank town of Jericho.
Answer: (Israeli Prime Minister) Yitzhak Rabin, (Israeli Foreign Minister) Shimon Peres, and (PLO Chairman) Yasser Arafat (the first time the Nobel Peace Prize was ever awarded to 3 people).

5) Name the 3 scientists, 2 Americans and 1 British, who shared the 1962 Nobel Prize for physiology or medicine for their work with DNA.
Answer: James D. Watson, Francis H.C. Crick, and Maurice H.F. Wilkins, respectively.

6) Name the 2 leaders who shared the Nobel Peace Prize in 1978 for their efforts to bring about a settlement of the Arab-Israeli conflict. They are the leaders of Israel and Egypt.
Answer: Menachem Begin and Anwar el-Sadat.

Swedish—Nationality of Alfred Bernhard Nobel, the chemist who invented dynamite and originated the Nobel Prizes
Oslo (Norway)—Scandinavian city in which the Nobel Peace Prize is presented
Stockholm (Sweden)—Scandinavian city in which the other 5 Nobel Prizes are presented
1901—Year the first Nobel Prize was awarded
Economics—Nobel Prize established by the Bank of Sweden and awarded for the first time in 1969
Nobelium—Chemical element 102 named either after Alfred Nobel or the Nobel Institute in Stockholm, where it was discovered

WINNERS (Listed chronologically)
Jean Henri Dunant—Swiss founder of the International Red Cross who shared the first Nobel Peace Prize, in 1901

Wilhelm K. Roentgen—German scientist who discovered X-rays in 1895 and won the first Nobel Prize in physics in 1901
Literature—Field in which Frenchman Sully Prudhomme was the first to win a Nobel, in 1901
Marie Curie—First woman to win the Prize, a French scientist born in Poland, who shared the Nobel in physics in 1903 and won it in chemistry in 1911—the first person to win 2 Nobel Prizes
Ivan Pavlov—Russian who won the 1904 Nobel Prize for his work on the physiology of the digestive system
Rudyard Kipling—First British writer to win the Nobel Prize in literature, in 1907
International Red Cross—Organization that won the Nobel Peace Prize in 1917, 1944, and 1963
Albert Einstein—German-Swiss-U.S. scientist who won the 1921 Nobel Prize in physics for his work on the photoelectric effect
Niels Bohr—Danish physicist and winner of the 1922 Nobel Prize in physics whose son Aage Niels ____ shared the 1975 Nobel Prize for physics
Sinclair Lewis—First American to win the Nobel Prize in literature, in 1930
Karl Landsteiner—First American to win a Nobel Prize for physiology or medicine, for discovering the 4 main human blood types, in 1930
Jane Addams—Hull House founder and co-winner of the Nobel Peace Prize, in 1931
Irène Joliot-Curie—Daughter of Nobel Prize winners who shared the Nobel Prize in chemistry in 1935 with her husband Frédéric Joliot
Eugene O'Neill—Second American to win the Nobel Prize in literature, in 1936
Pearl S. Buck—First American woman to win a Nobel Prize in literature, in 1938
Ralph Bunche—First black American to win the Nobel Peace Prize, in 1950
Bertrand Russell—British philosopher and mathematician who won the 1950 Nobel Prize for literature for his philosophic writings
Albert Schweitzer—Alsatian-born philosopher, physician, musician, and missionary who opened a hospital in Lambaréné, Gabon, in 1913 and won the Nobel Peace Prize in 1952
Literature—Category in which Winston Churchill won a Nobel Prize in 1953
George C. Marshall—American who won the Nobel Peace Prize in 1953 for his European Recovery Program
Linus Pauling—American who won 2 Nobel prizes, one in chemistry in 1954 and the other in peace in 1962
John Bardeen—American physicist who was the first person to win a Nobel Prize twice in the same field, sharing it in 1956 and again in 1972
Frederick Sanger—British chemist who was the second person to win a Nobel Prize twice in the same field, by himself in 1958 and sharing it in 1980
Boris Pasternak—Soviet author of *Dr. Zhivago*, who declined the Nobel Prize for literature in 1958
Dag Hammarskjöld—U.N. secretary-general posthumously awarded the Nobel Peace Prize, in 1961
Maria G. Mayer—German-born physicist who was the 2nd woman to win the Nobel Prize in physics, sharing it in 1963
Jean-Paul Sartre—French author of *The Age of Reason*, who declined the Nobel Prize for literature in 1964
Martin L. King Jr.—Second black American to win the Nobel Peace Prize, in 1964
North Vietnamese—Nationality of Le Duc Tho, the man who shared the 1973 Nobel Peace Prize with Henry Kissinger and declined the prize

Sir Arthur Lewis—British man who was the first black to win the Nobel Prize in economics, sharing the 1979 award

Mother Teresa—Woman born Agnes Gonxha Bojaxhiu to Albanian parents in present-day Skopje, Macedonia, who won the 1979 Nobel Prize for peace

Lech Walesa—Polish Solidarity leader and winner of the 1983 Nobel Peace Prize

Toni Morrison—Second American woman and first black American woman to win the Nobel Prize in literature, in 1993

John Nash—Mathematician whose doctoral thesis "Noncooperative Games" was published in the 1950s and who shared the 1994 Nobel Prize in economic science

Ooh-La-La!

In addition to Tinky Winky, Dipsy, and Po, the 4th character on the children's TV series *Teletubbies*
Answer: Laa Laa (Laa-Laa; Laalaa).

BEGINNING "LA LA"

La Bamba—1987 film biography about Ritchie Valens, one of the 3 rock 'n' roll stars who died on February 3, 1959*

La Belle Epoque—French phrase containing the word *belle* that designates the period between the end of the Franco-Prussian War in 1871 and the outbreak of WWI in 1914

La Bohème—Giacomo Puccini opera set in 19th-century Paris featuring the painter Marcello and the poet Rodolfo trying to work in their freezing garret

La Bouche—American dance duo of Lane McCray and Melanie Thornton named from the French for "the mouth"

La Brea tar pits—Los Angeles site known as one of the world's richest sources of Ice Age fossils

La Cage aux Folles—1987 film about a Saint-Tropez nightclub, starring Robin Williams

La Comédie française—France's national theatre, also known as *Le Théatre française* or *La Maison de Molière*

L.A. Confidential—1997 film about crime and corruption in Hollywood in the 1950s, starring Kevin Spacey and Russell Crowe

La Crosse—Largest Wisconsin city on the Mississippi River, named from the French for "the crutch" or "crook"

La Cucaracha—Spanish word for "cockroach" identifying a folk song and a dance

La Dame aux camélias—Alexandre Dumas fils' 1852 play adapted from an 1848 novel

La Défense—Paris suburb of office towers and apartments where La Grande Arche is located

La Dolce Vita—1960 Federico Fellini film starring Marcello Mastroianni or the Italian for "the good life"

La Femme Nikita—1997-2001 TV series starring Peta Wilson as Nikita or the 1990 film starring Anne Parillaud

La Gioconda—Amilcare Ponchielli's opera whose title is translated into English as "The Joyful Girl" or "The Ballad Singer"

La Jolla—Residential and resort community north of San Diego whose name means "the jewel" in Spanish

"La La"—Title of an Ashlee Simpson song from her 2004 album *Autobiography*

La La Land—Nickname for Hollywood or for Los Angeles, symbolizing its entertainment industry

L.A. Law—1986-1994 TV legal drama featuring a Los Angeles law firm

La Leche League—International organization of women that helps mothers to breast-feed their babies

La Mancha—Spanish province named in the title of Cervantes' novel *Don Quixote de*

"La Marseillaise"—French national anthem

*Others were Buddy Holly and J.P. Richardson, known as "The Big Bopper"

La Navidad—First European settlement in the New World, on the island of Hispaniola, in 1492

La Niña—Spanish for "the little girl," naming the "cold water event" that is the reversal of the conditions caused by El Niño, the phenomenon causing the warming of waters

La Paz—Bolivian capital, the world's highest, whose name means "(The) Peace" in Spanish

La Rochelle—French city on the Bay of Biscay established by the Edict of Nantes in 1598 as a Protestant community

La Salle**—Explorer who descended the Mississippi River to the Gulf of Mexico in 1682, claiming the entire valley for France

La Salle University—Philadelphia college whose athletic teams are called the "Explorers"

La Scala—Famous opera house in Milan, Italy—the "Theatre at the Stairway"

La Traviata—Giuseppe Verdi opera translated in English as *The Wayward One*, or *The Woman Gone Astray*, or *The Fallen Woman*, based on the play *La Dame aux camélias*

**Robert Cavelier, Sieur de la Salle

INTERIOR "LA LA"

A la carte—French phrase used in English for "according to the menu" or "with a separate price for each item on the menu"

A la king—French phrase, literally "in the kingly style," for diced and creamed with mushrooms, pimentos, and green peppers

A la mode—French phrase used in English for "in fashion" and "pie served with ice cream"

"Au Clair de la Lune"—Title of the song with the lines "Mon ami Pierrot, / Prête-moi ta plume / Pour écrire un mot."

Jean de La Bruyère—French satirist known for *The Characters of Theophrastus*

Antoine de la Mothe Cadillac—French colonial governor who founded Detroit in 1701

C'est la vie—French phrase used in English for "That's life!"

Cherchez la femme—French phrase used in English for "look for the woman" (as the probable explanation for the cause of the trouble)

Churchy la Femme—Pogo's turtle friend in the comic strip *Pogo*

Crème de la crème—French phrase used in English for "the top level" and "the very best"

Walter de la Mare—English novelist and poet known for *Memoirs of a Midget* and "The Listeners"

De La Salle—Concord, California, high school that won 151 consecutive football games from 1991 to 2004

Madame de la Fayette—French author who wrote *La Princesse de Clèves*

Finita la commedia—Italian phrase used in English for "the farce (show) is over"

Robert Marion La Follette—U.S. senator from Wisconsin known as "Battling Bob" who served from 1906-1924 or his son, a U.S. senator from 1925-1947

Jean de la Fontaine—French poet best known for his *Fables* and whose surname literally means "the fountain"

(Fiorello) La Guardia—New York mayor from 1933-1945 featured in the Pulitzer Prize-winning musical *Fiorello!* or the name of a New York City airport

Hasta la vista—Spanish phrase used in English for "see you later!"

Ile de la Cité—Parisian island on which the Cathedral of Notre Dame is located

Irma La Douce—1963 film starring Jack Lemmon and Shirley Maclaine about a Paris streetwalker

Jack La Lanne—"Godfather of Fitness" whose first name is Jack

Man of La Mancha—Broadway musical based on the adventures of Don Quixote
Jake La Motta—Role of the middleweight boxing champion nicknamed "The Bronx Bull" for which Robert De Niro won a Best Actor Oscar in the 1980 film *Raging Bull*
Notre Dame de la Paix—Yamoussoukro, Ivory Coast, basilica, known as Our Lady of Peace in English and completed in 1989 as the world's largest church (according to Guinness)—it is a replica of St. Peter's Basilica in Rome but is taller because of the gold cross at its top
Lash La Rue—Movie cowboy known for using a bullwhip as a weapon
Place de la Concorde—Paris square featuring an Egyptian pillar called the Obelisk of Luxor
Plus ça change, plus c'est la même chose—French phrase used in English for "the more things change, the more they stay the same"
Río de la Plata—Funnel-shaped bay between Argentina and Uruguay, an estuary whose name means "river of silver"
Duc de la Rochefoucauld—French writer known for his 1665 *Maxims*
Tony La Russa—Longtime major league baseball manager, from 1979 to 2005, with the first name Tony
Georges de La Tour—French artist whose religious scene *The Penitent Magdalene* appears in Ariel's underwater home in *The Little Mermaid*
Vive la différence—French phrase used in English for "Long live the difference," said of the differences between the sexes
Vive la France—French phrase used in English for "Long live France"

GEOGRAPHY "LA LA"
Arc de Triomphe—Monument begun by Napoleon in 1806 on which François Rude sculpted the relief *La Marseillaise*
Argentina—Country whose seaport of La Plata was renamed Eva Perón in 1952 but returned to its original name after the overthrow of President Perón in 1955
Canary Islands—Spanish islands of which La Palma is a part
English Channel—Body of water between England and France called La Manche, "The Sleeve," in French
France—Country in which La Hague, a promontory on the English Channel is located
Georgia—State in which the city of La Grange, meaning "the farm," is located 40 miles north of Columbus
Hispaniola—Present day name of the island whose climate and trees reminded Columbus so much of Spain that he named it *La Isla Española*, meaning the Spanish Island
Honduras—Central American country whose chief Caribbean port is La Ceiba, located 115 miles north of Tegucigalpa
James Bay—Southern arm of the Hudson Bay into which La Grande River flows
Little Rock—U.S. state capital the French once called *la Petite Roche*
Los Angeles—California city known as L.A.
Louisiana—U.S. state whose postal code is LA
Paris—City where Jim Morrison is buried in Père-Lachaise cemetery, named after Père La Chaise
Pyrenees—Mountains in which Andorra la Vella is the capital of Andorra
Quebec—Canadian province known as "La Belle Province"
St. Lawrence River—River called by Jacques Cartier "*La Grande Rivière*," or "The River of Canada"
San Antonio—Texas city where *La Villita* or "Little Village" is located along the riverfront

Spain—Country in which La Coruña is a seaport on the Atlantic Ocean
Switzerland—Country in which La Tène, French for "The Swallows," is an archaeological site at the end of Lake Neuchâtel
Venezuela—Country in which the seaport town of La Guaira serves as a port for Caracas

LITERARY/FINE ARTS "LA LA"
Honoré de Balzac—French writer known for *La Comédie Humaine* (*The Human Comedy*)
Frédéric Auguste Bartholdi—French sculptor known for his colossal copper statue called *La Liberté Eclairant le Monde**
Kathleen Battle—Temperamental opera star who was dismissed in 1994 from the Metropolitan Opera for "unprofessional actions" during the production of *The Daughter of the Regiment*, or *La Fille du Régiment*
Charles Baudelaire—French poet whose long essay *Le Peintre de la Vie Moderne* (*The Painter of Modern Life*) inspired Édouard Manet and other impressionists to portray contemporary scenes
Vincenzo Bellini—19th-century Italian composer known for his operas *La Somnambula* and *Norma*
Alexander Calder—U.S. artist who created the stabile *La Grande Vitesse* (*The Grand Rapids*) in Grand Rapids, Michigan
Albert Camus—French author who wrote *La Peste* or *The Plague*
Cinderella—English title of Gioacchino Rossini's opera *La Cenerentola*, the story of a heroine who works in the home while her stepsisters go to a ball
Jean Cocteau—French playwright known for his 1934 *La Machine Infernale*, or *The Infernal Machine*
Claude Debussy—French composer whose orchestral work *La Mer* is translated into English as *The Sea*
René Descartes—French "Father of Modern Philosophy" who wrote *Discours de la Méthode* (*Discourse on Method*) in 1637
Gaetano Donizetti—Italian composer of *The Daughter of the Regiment*, or *La Fille du Régiment*
George Gershwin—American composer and pianist known for *La, La Lucille*, "Swanee," and *Rhapsody in Blue*
The Girl of the Golden West—English title of *La Fanciulla del West*, a Puccini opera set in a California mining town
Philip Glass—American minimalist composer whose *La Belle et la Bête*, or *Beauty and the Beast*, was first presented in the U.S. in 1994
John Keats—British poet who wrote *La Belle Dame sans merci* and *The Eve of St. Agnes*
The Lady of the Lake—English title of Gioacchino Rossini's opera *La Donna del Lago*, the story of the woman from whom King Arthur received his magical sword Excalibur
Nicholas Nickleby—Charles Dickens' work in which Miss La Creevy, a spinster painter, is friend to the Nicklebys
Marriage—Word completing the title of William Hogarth's _____ *à la Mode*, a series of 6 paintings satirizing upper-class customs in England during the 18th century
Mona Lisa—Leonardo da Vinci painting stolen from the Louvre in August, 1911, also known as *La Joconde* or *La Gioconda*
Claude Monet—French impressionist who painted outdoors to capture the fleeting effects of nature, as in *Bathers at La Grenouillere*

*Translated as "Liberty Enlightening the World," the official name of the Statue of Liberty

Odalisque—Word for a female slave or concubine in an Oriental harem that completes the title of French artist Jean Auguste Ingres' 1814 painting *La Grande* _____

Jacques Offenbach—German-born French composer known for his 1864 satiric operetta *La Belle Hélène* and his fantasy opera *The Tales of Hoffman*

(I) Pagliacci—Ruggiero Leoncavallo opera that closes with the line "*La commedia è finita*," or "The comedy is ended"

I.M. Pei—Chinese-American architect who designed La Pyramide, the glass pyramid at the Louvre's new entrance

Marcel Proust—French author whose 16-volume *Remembrance of Things Past* or *A la recherche du temps perdu* was written after he ate a madeleine, a small rich tea cake that evoked much nostalgia

Giacomo Puccini—19th-20th century Italian composer known for his operas *Tosca*, *La Bohème*, and *Madama Butterfly*

Raphael—Renaissance artist whose *La Fornarina*, or "the baker's daughter," a 1520 nude portrait, toured the U.S. in 2004-2005

Maurice Ravel—French composer whose works include the orchestral piece *La Valse* and who featured the flute in "La flûte enchantée" in his *Shéhérazade* for orchestra in 1898

Pierre Auguste Renoir—French impressionist who painted *Le Moulin de la Galette* and whose son was a film director

Auguste Rodin—French sculptor of *La Porte de l'enfer*, or *The Gates of Hell*, commissioned in 1880

Rose—Word completing the title of Michel Fokine's 1-act ballet *Le Spectre de la* _____, in which Vaslav Nijinsky demonstrated his genius and body control by a dramatic leap through an open window

Georges Seurat—French artist who developed a system of painting called pointillism, qualities of which appear in his *Sunday Afternoon on the Island of La Grande Jatte*

Shangri-La—Himalayan mountain kingdom where James Hilton's novel *Lost Horizon* is set

The Song of Roland—English title for the medieval poem *La Chanson de Roland*, considered the first great work of French literature

Henri de Toulouse-Lautrec—French painter and lithographer whose works include *At the Moulin de la Galette*

Venice—Italian city whose La Fenice Opera House burned down in 1996 and was reopened in 2003

Giuseppe Verdi—Italian composer whose opera *La Forza del destino* is *The Force of Destiny* in English

POTPOURRI OF "LA LA"

A la—French phrase used in English for "in the manner or style of"

"Alouette"—Word completing the French song line, "Oh _____, gentille _____; / _____, je te plumerai. / Je te plumerai la tête"

Marie Antoinette—18th-century Queen of France linked with the phrase "*la brioche*" from her alleged comment, "Qu'ils mangent de la brioche!" translated as, "Let them eat cake!"

Around the World in 80 Days—Movie in which *La Coquette*, a hot air balloon, takes Passepartout and Phileas Fogg from Paris to Spain

Josephine Baker—St. Louis-born African-American actress/dancer who gained fame in Paris and was nicknamed "La Bakhair," "Our Fifine," and "La Perle Noire"

Casablanca — Movie in which Rick Blaine and Ilse Lund meet for the last time at La Belle Aurore, a Paris café, before seeing each other in Africa

Chartreuse — Yellow or green liqueur or greenish-yellow color, named after the liqueur produced at *La Grande _____*, a Carthusian monastery, in France

Cesar Chavez — Farm worker organizer known for saying "Viva la huelga!" or "Long live the strike!"

Foreign Legion — French organization formed in 1831 whose name in French is *La Légion Etrangère*

Jiminy Glick — Character Martin Short plays in the 2005 film _____ *in La La Wood*

Joan of Arc — French peasant girl and national heroine called *La Pucelle d'Orléans* or "The Maid of Orleans"

Jackie Kennedy — U.S. First Lady called "La Belle Jacqueline" by the French

La-di-da — 3-word hyphenated term meaning "affectedly aristocratic in speech and manners"

Lamentations — Biblical book whose abbreviation is both La and Lam

Lanthanum — Chemical element whose symbol is La

The Last Supper — Leonardo Da Vinci's famous fresco on the wall of the refectory in Milan called *La Cène* in French

Suzanne Lenglen — French tennis player nicknamed "La Grande Suzanne"

Louis XIV — French king to whom Louise de La Vallière was mistress in the 1660s

Madame de Maintenon — Marquise called "la Belle Indienne," the mistress and 2nd wife of France's King Louis XV

The Maltese Falcon — 1930 Dashiell Hammett novel in which the statue of a rare bird is taken from Hong Kong to San Francisco aboard the ship *La Paloma*

Elizabeth Monroe — U.S. First Lady born Elizabeth Kortright and called "La Belle Américaine" by the French

Blaise Pascal — French inventor of *La Pascaline*, his 1642 mechanical adding machine

Giovanni da Verrazano — Italian who in 1524, aboard *La Dauphine*, explored the North American coast from North Carolina to Cape Breton Island for Francis I of France

S-E-X: Everything You've Ever Wanted To Know About It

According to President Clark Kerr of the University of California in a 1958 speech, the 3 major administrative problems on U.S. college campuses: "_____ for the students, _____ for the alumni, and _____ for the faculty"
Answer: "Sex (for the students), athletics (for the alumni), and parking (for the faculty)."

BEGINNING S-E-X
Sexagenarian—Person 60-69 years old
Sexagesima—Second Sunday before Lent, so named because it is 60 days before Easter
Sexcentenary—Period of 600 years
Sexdecillion—1 followed by 51 zeros in the U.S. or 96 in the U.K.
Sexennial—Happening every 6 years
Sexily—In a sexy manner
Sexism—Discrimination against people on the basis of sex
Sexless—Without the characteristics of sex, or asexual
Sexology—Science dealing with human sexual behavior
Sexploitation—Coined term designating the use of explicit sexual material to increase commercial appeal
Sexpot—Young woman who has a lot of sex appeal
Sextans—Equatorial constellation between Leo and Hydra
Sextant—Instrument navigators use to find the position of a ship, named from the Latin for "a sixth part"
Sextet(te)—Chamber music group composed of 6 people
Sextilis—Romans' name for their 6th month, later renamed for Emperor Augustus
Sextillion—1 followed by 21 zeros in the U.S. or 36 in the U.K.
Sexton—Person who maintains church property
(Anne) Sexton—Poet who committed suicide in 1974 and is known for her *All My Pretty Ones* and *Live or Die*, the 1967 Pulitzer Prize-winning collection of poems
Sextuplets—6 babies born together
Sextuplicate—To make 6 copies of a document or a set of 6 identical copies
Sexy—Sexually appealing

BEGINNING SEPARATED S-E-X
Sex and the City—TV sitcom starring Sarah Jessica Parker, Kim Cattrall, Kristin Davis, and Cynthia Nixon as Carrie, Samantha, Charlotte, and Miranda, respectively
Sex and the Single Girl—Helen Gurley Brown's 1962 best-seller
Sex appeal—Physical charm that attracts members of the opposite sex
Sex cell—Gamete
Sex change—Modification of a person's biological sex characteristics
Sex chromosome—*x* or *y*, as used in genetics
Sex crime—Rape, molestation, or other sexual abuse
Sex discrimination*—Unequal treatment of people based on their sex

*Also called *gender discrimination*

***Sex* education**—Study of the characteristics of males and females, especially as related to reproduction
***Sex* gland**—Gonad
***Sex* hormone**—Organic compound produced by a sex gland effecting the sexual features of an organism
***Sex* kitten (bomb)**—Slang for a young woman who has a good deal of sex appeal
Sex, Lies, and Videotape—1989 film starring James Spader and Andie MacDowell
***Sex*-limited**—Biological term describing the capability of phenotypic expression in one sex but not in the other
***Sex*-linked**—Biological term describing the characteristic of being transmitted by genes located in the sex chromosomes
***Sex* object**—Person viewed solely as a center of sexual attention
***Sex* ratio**—Proportion of males to females in a population
***Sex* symbol**—Informal term for a famous person considered to be representative of sexual attractiveness
***Sex* therapy**—Treatment of sexual problems

ELSEWHERE S-E-X

Bis*sex*tile year—Leap year, or year having a February 29
Fair *sex*—Women in general, now considered a pejorative term
Group *sex*—Sexual behavior involving more than 2 people at the same time
Is Sex Necessary?—James Thurber's 1929 work written with E.B. White
The Joy of Sex—Alex Comfort's 1972 book with illustrations
Middlesex—2003 Pulitzer Prize-winning novel by Jeffrey Eugenides that also names a former English county, now part of Greater London
Obligatory *sex* scene—Full meaning of the initialism OSS as used in the film industry
Safe *sex*—Sexual activity in which safeguards are used to reduce the possibility of sexually transmitted disease
Same-*sex* marriage—2 men or 2 women living together as a legally married pair
The Second Sex*—Simone de Beauvoir's 1949 essay on women's secondary status in society
Stronger *sex*—Men as a group, based on assumed physical superiority
Sus*sex*—Of Delaware's 3 counties, the one other than Kent and New Castle, or the former English county on the English Channel
24 Sus*sex* Drive—Official residence of the Prime Minister of Canada
Uni*sex*—Suitable for both sexes, as used especially in fashion
Weaker *sex*—Women as a group, based on assumed physical inferiority
Wes*sex*—Anglo-Saxon kingdom of England where Egbert was king from 802-839

*In French, *Le Deuxième Sexe*

SEXUAL TRIVIA

The Society for the Suppression of _____, the New York society formed in 1873 to guard the public against literature damaging to public morals, so named with the word designating a trivial fault, a defect, a bad habit, a wicked action, evil behavior, or prostitution
Answer: Vice.

CENSORING

Anthony Comstock* —"The Great American Bluenose" who founded the New York Society for the Suppression of Vice and whose name has since become part of the lexicon meaning "strict censorship"

Comstock Law—1873 statute that prohibits the mailing of indecent materials (even information about birth control or abortion), named for this "Great American Bluenose"

Comstockery—Strict censorship, as coined from the name of this "Bluenose"

George Bernard Shaw**—Irish playwright who coined this word for "strict censorship" after this "Bluenose" shut down his play *Mrs. Warren's Profession*, set in a brothel, in its New York debut—the ban was lifted the next day

Walt Whitman—American author whom this "Bluenose" got the Department of the Interior to fire on grounds that his book *Leaves of Grass* was obscene

Victoria Woodhull—First woman to run for U.S. President, in 1872, whom he had arrested on charges of obscenity for sending an account of adultery by the Rev. Henry Ward Beecher through the mail

Margaret Sanger—Woman whose books on birth control he got the city of New York to ban

Woodrow Wilson—President who in 1915 named this censor the U.S. Representative to the International Purity Congress in San Francisco

Watch— _____ and Ward Society, the Boston society against all forms of vice inspired by this "Bluenose"'s New York society

"Banned in Boston"—Alliterative phrase for censorship that developed from this Boston society's persistent pressuring of the city's censor to ban books from sale

Bowdlerize—To remove what is considered to be offensive material from a book or play, from the name of English editor Thomas Bowdler who published his *Family Shakespeare* in 1818

Expurgate—To remove passages or words considered objectionable from a book, play or the like

*He boasted of having destroyed "160 tons of obscene literature" and having "hounded or driven 15 people to suicide." **Shaw said of him, "Comstockery is the world's standing joke at the expense of the U.S."; Comstock called Shaw an "Irish smut dealer."

FAMOUS ACTRESS

Mae West—Actress who says to Cary Grant in 1933's *She Done Him Wrong*, "Why don't you come up sometime and see me? I'm home every evening."

Better—Word completing this actress' remark in the film *I'm No Angel*: "When I'm good, I'm very, very good; but when I'm bad, I'm _____."

Drifted—Word completing her remark in *Peel Me a Grape*: "I used to be Snow White . . . but I _____."

Evils—Word completing her alleged remark, "When I'm choosing between two _____, I always try the one I've never tried before."

Goodness—Word completing her remark in *Night After Night* in reply to the comment: "_____ what beautiful diamonds!"—"_____ had nothing to do with it, dearie."

Gun—Word completing her remark in *Peel Me a Grape*: "Is that a _____ in your pocket, or are you just glad to see me?"

Men—Word completing her remark in *I'm No Angel*: "It's not the _____ in my life that counts—it's the life in my _____."

Streets—Word completing her remark in *She Done Him Wrong*, "You're a fine woman, Lou. One of the finest women that ever walked the _____."

Wrong—Word completing her remark in *She Done Him Wrong*, "When women go _____, men go right after them."

PROPER NAMES LINKED SEXUALLY

Amazons—Mythical race of warlike women, named with the word literally meaning "breastless" since they allegedly removed their breasts to enable them to draw the bow better

Aspasia—Pericles' mistress, a Greek courtesan, considered to be beautiful, cultured, and intellectual

Bacchae (Bacchants; Maenads)—Female attendants of the mythological Bacchus or Dionysus, who drank lots of wine and took part in the wild woodland revelry that characterized his worship

Tallulah Bankhead—American actress who said, "I'm as pure as the driven slush."

Brigitte Bardot—French actress known as "The Sex Kitten" and "The Eternal Sex Goddess"

Simone de Beauvoir—French influential postwar thinker who wrote *The Second Sex*

Bess—Stevedore Crown's weak-willed mistress who becomes the "temporary" woman of Porgy, the crippled beggar in DuBose Hayward's *Porgy*

Brothers Karamazov—Russian family members known for their streak of sensuality in an 1879-80 novel by Fyodor Dostoyevsky

Camille* (Gautier)—Courtesan who falls in love with Armand Duval in Alexandre Dumas fils' play *La Dame aux camélias*

Casanova—Giovanni Jacopo _____ de Seingalt, the Italian adventurer who claimed in his memoirs to have had many love affairs and whose name is now used to designate a seducer, philanderer, or libertine

Wilt Chamberlain—NBA player known as "With the Stilt" who claimed he had sex with 20,000 women

Dick Cheney—U.S. Vice President who used the obscene F-word on the Senate floor in an exchange with Patrick Leahy (Dem.-Vt.) in 2004

Kate Chopin—American author whose *The Awakening*, an account of a married woman's growing awareness of her sexuality and extramarital love, was published in 1899 amid great controversy

Cleopatra—Egyptian queen of the Ptolemaic dynasty who used charm, beauty, and sex to get power

Stephen Crane—American author whose *Maggie: A Girl of the Streets* features a young woman who becomes a prostitute and kills herself

Rodney Dangerfield—The "I get no respect" comedian who said, "If it weren't for pickpockets, I'd have no sex life at all."

Charles Darwin—British naturalist who wrote *The Descent of Man* and *Selection in Relation to Sex* as well as *On the Origin of Species*

Don Juan—Legendary Spanish nobleman and seducer of women who appears in literature and music and is carried off to hell in various poems, plays, and operas, including a long poem by Lord Byron

(Sir John) Falstaff—Fat, cheerful, and debauched character in Shakespeare's *Henry IV: Parts I and II* and *The Merry Wives of Windsor*

*Known in America as Camille Gautier but elsewhere as Marguerite.

Fanny Hill—John Cleland's 18th-century erotic novel whose subtitle is *Memoirs of a Woman of Pleasure*

Sigmund Freud—Austrian psychiatrist whose theories emphasized sex as a major motivator in human behavior

Grand Teton—Mountain whose name means "big breast," the highest in Wyoming's Teton Range

Jezebel—Shameless, immoral wife of the biblical Ahab, who because she used cosmetics is referred to as a *painted woman* (2 Kings 9:30)

Lady Macbeth—Shakespeare character who said, "Come, you spirits / That tend on mortal thoughts, unsex me here, / And fill me from the crown to the toe top-full / Of direst cruelty!"

Gypsy Rose Lee—Famous stripper of the 1930s born Louise Rose Hovick

Lilith—In Babylonian, Jewish, and Muslim folklore, Adam's first wife, who left him because she refused to be considered his inferior, or more generally a sensual female spirit said to be a demon or vampire

Lolita—12-year-old title character who stays in motels with the middle-aged Humbert Humbert in a Vladimir Nabokov novel and whose name is now used to designate a sexy seductive adolescent girl

Lothario—Seducer of women in Nicholas Rowe's play *The Fair Penitent* whose name is used to designate a libertine or rake

Madonna—American singer known for her 1992 book *Sex*, released simultaneously with her album *Erotica*

Mary Magdalene—Woman from whom Jesus cast out 7 demons and who then followed Him the rest of His life, erroneously said to have been a prostitute

Madame de Maintenon—Mistress and second wife of France's Louis XIV

George Michael—Bushey, England, singer known for his 1987 hit "I Want Your Sex"

Wolfgang Amadeus Mozart—Austrian composer whose opera *Don Giovanni* is based on the story of the notorious Don Juan Tenorio

Nero—Roman emperor (54-68) who lived a depraved and dissolute life and ordered the deaths of many Christians

Pan—Greek god depicted as part goat, part handsome shepherd with horns, usually shown playing the syrinx, or panpipe, and known for his lewd and lustful ways

Marquise de Pompadour—Mistress of France's Louis XV

Poppaea—Mistress and later wife of Nero, who, to please her had his wife, Octavia, murdered

Elvis Presley—"Whirling dervish of sex" whose hit "Heartbreak Hotel" was released in 1956

Sally Rand—Striptease dancer born Hazel Beck who used ostrich plumes in her act and was called "Her Sexellency" and "Fan-tastic Sally"

Grigory Yefimovich Rasputin—Immoral Russian holy man known as "The Holy Satyr" and "The Debauched One" and killed in 1916 because of his influence with the Czar and Czarina

David Reuben—American author who wrote *Everything You Always Wanted to Know About Sex (But Were Afraid to Ask)*

Samuel Richardson—British author who wrote the novel *Clarissa*, in which Robert Lovelace, a womanizer, seduces and rapes the virtuous Clarissa

Mrs. Robinson—Middle-aged woman who lusts after young Ben Braddock in the film *The Graduate*

Romeo—Any passionate lover, from the name of a hero of a William Shakespeare tragedy

Roth—_____ *v. United States*, the 1957 Supreme Court case that defined obscenity and ruled that the 1st Amendment to the Constitution does not protect the publication of obscene material

Salome—Provocative dancer who performed for King Herod and, at the urging of her mother, demanded the head of John the Baptist on a platter
Satyr—Lustful mythological woodland creature, a follower of Bacchus, with pointed ears, short horns, the head and body of a man, and the legs of a goat or horse
George Bernard Shaw—Irish author noted for his "Don Juan in Hell" scene in *Man and Superman*
Sodom or Gomorrah—Any very wicked or corrupt place, from the name of the ancient cities destroyed by God (Genesis 19:1-29) because of their wickedness
Potter Stewart—Supreme Court justice who said in 1964, "I shall not today attempt further to define [pornography] . . . But I know it when I see it; and the motion picture involved in this case is not that."
Rod Stewart—English singer known for his 1978 hit "Do Ya Think I'm Sexy?"
Thaïs—Greek courtesan who was the mistress of Alexander the Great and Ptolemy I
Violetta (Valéry)—Wealthy courtesan in Paris in Verdi's opera *La Traviata*
Mae West—Actress known as "The Siren of Sex" who appeared in films such as *Peel Me a Grape*
Tom Wolfe—American author whose novel *I Am Charlotte Simmons*, set at Dupont University, includes the line: "Sex! Sex! It was in the air along with nitrogen and oxygen! The whole campus was humid with it! tumid with it!"
Zeus—Supreme mythological god who had 7 wives and many extramarital affairs and was known by the ancients for his lasciviousness
Emile Zola—French author who wrote *Nana*, a novel in which a young woman becomes a prostitute and lives a wasted existence

POTPOURRI OF SEXUAL TRIVIA
Bacchanalia*—Drunken feast, as derived from the name of the orgiastic festival in honor of the Roman god of wine
"Battle of the Sexes"—Televised 1973 tennis match in the Astrodome featuring 55-year-old Bobby Riggs who lost to Billie Jean King in 3 straight sets
Bordello/brothel—House of prostitution
Boston marriage—19th-century phrase for a long-running, intimate friendship between 2 women, usually sharing the same lodging, and alluding to a New England capital
Clara Bow—Effervescent and sexy actress known as "The It Girl" after starring as a flapper in the 1927 movie *It*, based on Elinor Glyn's 1927 novel
Chauvinism—Unreasoning belief in the supremacy of one's country, race, sex, or group, derived from the name of Nicholas Chauvin, a devoted soldier of Napoleon I
Civil Rights Act of 1964—1964 act that bans discrimination because of a person's color, race, national origin, religion, or sex
Concubine—Woman living with a man without being legally married, or in some societies, a secondary wife with an inferior rank or rights, from the word meaning "to lie with"
Concupiscence—13-letter word beginning with *C* for sexual desire or lust
Courtesan—Prostitute, especially a mistress of a king or of a man of nobility
Demimonde—French term for a class of women of low repute or the world of prostitution
Double entendre—French term for an expression with two meanings, especially when one of them is risqué
Ecdysiast—Stripteaser, as coined by H.L. Mencken in 1920 from the Greek *ecdysis*, designating the process of molting or shedding an outer layer, such as a snakeskin or the carapace of insects and crustaceans

*From Bacchus; a similar festival, the Dionysia, was held in honor of Dionysus; the adjectives *bacchanalian*, *bacchantic*, and *bacchic* mean "drunken and wildly merry"; the noun *bacchanal* means "a wild party" or "a drunken partygoer."

Harlot—Word for "a prostitute" that completes the title of William Hogarth's series of satirical engravings called *A _____ 's Progress*

"immoral"—Word completing Alexander Woollcott's statement, "All the things I really like to do are either _____, illegal, or fattening."

"It"—Word for unlimited "sex appeal" coined by author Elinor Glyn in a 1927 novel banned in Boston, and also used in the game of tag for the one who must catch the others

J—Letter of the alphabet that Terry and John Garrity used as a pseudonym in writing *The Sensuous Woman*

Julius Caesar—Shakespeare play in which Portia says to Brutus: "I grant I am a woman, but withal / A woman well reputed, Cato's daughter. / Think you I am no stronger than my sex, / Being so father'd and so husbanded?"

M—Letter of the alphabet that identifies the author of *The Sensuous Man*

Madam—Woman in charge of a house of prostitution

Massachusetts—State where Tanya McCloskey and Marcia Kadish became the nation's first same-sex couples to exchange vows legally, in 2005

Mistress—Woman who has an illicit sexual relationship with a man and is financially supported by him

Mononucleosis—Disease known as "the kissing disease"

People—Magazine known for its yearly "The Sexiest Man Alive" issue

Peyton Place—Grace Metalious' 1956 novel about small town morals, covering problems from infidelity to murder, or the 1964-1969 TV program based on it

POSSLQ—Acronym for a person of the opposite sex sharing living quarters

Rake—Word for "a dissolute, debauched man" that completes the title of William Hogarth's *A _____ 's Progress*, a series of 8 satirical engravings portraying social and moral issues

Red-hot mama—Slang phrase for a pretty, sexy, affectionate female or a sexually exciting woman

Red-light district—Area known for its brothels

Risqué—French word meaning "daring" or "suggestive" or "off-color"

Roué—French word for "a debauched person or rake," from the verb meaning "to break on the wheel"

Seven-year itch**—Phrase designating a married man or woman's tendency to stray sexually after a certain number of years, or the 1955 film starring Marilyn Monroe and Tom Ewell

Statutory rape—Crime of having sexual intercourse with someone who is under the age of consent

Syphilis—Venereal disease the English refer to as "the French disease," derived from the name of a hero of a 16th-century work whose name means "friend of swine"

Tart—Promiscuous woman, or a small jam-filled pastry shell

Title IX—Landmark legislation of 1972 that bans sex discrimination in schools whether it be in academics or athletics

Va-va-voom—Interjection beginning with *V* for an exclamation of delight, especially one related to sex

White marriage—Union between 2 people without sexual relations

X-rated—"Sexually explicit" or "obscene," as derived from movie rating system

**The film is entitled *The Seven Year Itch.*

Just "Sexual"

Russian-born author who in *Speak, Memory* said: "I reject completely the vulgar, shabby, fundamental medieval world of Freud, with its crankish quest for sexual symbols . . ."
Answer: Vladimir Nabokov.

AIDS—First worldwide sexually transmitted disease that affects the victim's disease-fighting immune system

Aphrodisiac—Word derived from the name of Aphrodite, the Greek goddess of love and beauty designating any drug, food, potion, or other agent arousing sexual desire

Asexual—Lacking the characteristics of sex or sexless

Bisexual—Having both male and female organs, or having a sexual desire for both sexes

Bondage and domination—Meaning of B & D, as used in psychology designating the use of whips, chains, etc., for sexual pleasure

Anita Bryant—Former female singer known for saying, "If homosexuality were normal, God would have made Adam and Bruce."

Casting couch—Slang for the sofa on which aspiring actresses allegedly earn their film roles by granting producers sexual favors

William Clinton—U.S. President known for saying about an alleged affair with former White House intern: "I did not have sexual relations with that woman, Ms. Lewinsky."

Clone—Living creature copied from a single cell, without sexual reproduction or meiosis

(To) come out of the closet—Expression meaning to reveal something hidden, especially a sexual preference for those of one's own sex

Date-rape—Form of sexual assault committed by someone known to the victim, often while under the influence of the sedative Rohypnol secretly administered

Denmark—Scandinavian country whose parliament, the Folketing, voted in 1999 to legalize prostitution, after more than 2 decades of tolerating the sale of sexual services

Diddy wa Diddy—Term for a legendary place of plenty, especially sexual fulfillment, as derived from the language of blues and jazz musicians

Electra complex—Daughter's abnormal fondness or sexual desire for her father and hostility toward her mother, alluding to the daughter who helped plan the murder of her mother, Clytemnestra

Eros—Freud's term for the life instinct of sexual desire, as derived from the name of the Greek god of love

Erotic—Evoking sexual desire, as derived from the name of the Greek god of love

Erotophobia—Fear of sexual love

Estrus—Period of heightened sexual activity in the female mammal during which mating may take place

Gay—Somewhat dated term for a homosexual, especially a homosexual man

Hermaphrodite—Person or living thing having both male and female reproductive organs and sexual characteristics, derived from the name of Hermes and Aphrodite's son who became joined in one body with a nymph while bathing

Heterosexual—Person who prefers sex with those of the opposite sex

Homophobia—Irrational fear or hatred of homosexuality

Homosexual—Person who has sexual desire for someone of the same sex

Incest—Sexual relations between persons too closely related to marry legally, an action prohibited by many societies

Incubus*—Evil male spirit or devil thought in medieval times to descend upon and have sexual intercourse with a human female

Ishtar/Astarte—Babylonian/Greek goddess of fertility, sexual love, maternity, and war who had numerous lovers and was Phoenicia's most important goddess

Lesbian—Homosexual female, after the island of Lesbos, Greece, home of the lyric poet Sappho, considered to be the leader of a homosexual group

Libido—Latin word for sexual drive

Lysistrata—Aristophanes play in which the heroine and title character persuades the women whose husbands are at war to refuse to have sexual contact with them until peace is made

David Mamet—Playwright who wrote *Sexual Perversity in Chicago* as well as *Glengarry Glen Ross*

Masochism—Deriving of pleasure from being mistreated in some way, after Leopold von Sacher-Masoch, an Austrian novelist whose characters enjoyed sexual pleasure accompanied by pain, just as he did

Metrosexual—Urban, usually straight man very interested in his appearance, grooming, household furnishings, the arts, and food

Kate Millett—American author of 1970's *Sexual Politics*, a work arguing that the male establishment has a need to maintain its power over women

Nymphomania—Abnormal and uncontrollable sexual drive in a woman, derived from the name of the minor female spirits who lived on Earth in classical mythology

Oedipus complex—Son's unconscious and abnormal sexual desire for his mother and hostility toward his father, alluding to the son who unknowingly killed his father and married his mother in Greek mythology

Outing**—Term beginning with *O* for the practice of disclosing the homosexual preferences of a closeted person, especially a celebrity

Peeping Tom—Someone who gets sexual pleasure from secretly watching others, after the tailor in Coventry who watched Lady Godiva ride naked, covered only by her long hair

Platonic—Word from Greek philosophy used to describe a relationship free from sexual activity

Sadism—Pleasure, especially sexual pleasure, derived from inflicting pain on another, after the Marquis de Sade, a soldier and novelist whose writings describe sexual aberrations

Sexual harassment—Inappropriate, unwelcome sexual behavior, as by an employer toward an employee, punishable under federal or state law

Sexual intercourse—Coitus or copulation

Sexually transmitted disease—Full meaning of the initialism STD, which replaced the initialism VD around 1990

Sexuality—State or quality of being sexual

Sodomy—Abnormal sexual intercourse, as derived from the name of a Biblical town

Succubus—Evil female spirit or devil thought in medieval times to descend upon and have sexual intercourse with a sleeping human male

Texas—State whose law banning sex between homosexuals the U.S. Supreme Court struck down in 2003, reversing a 1986 ruling that upheld anti-sodomy laws

Clarence Thomas—Supreme Court nominee accused by Anita Hill of having sexually harassed her when she worked for him in the early 1980s

Tiresias—Theban prophet whom an enraged Hera allegedly blinded for disagreeing with her by saying that women enjoy sexual intercourse 9 times more than men

*In 1997, Reebok mistakenly named a women's running shoe after this mythical demon. **Some use "Ining"

Leo Tolstoy—Russian author of *War and Peace* whom Theodore Roosevelt called "a sexual and moral pervert"

Trollop***—Sexually promiscuous woman, from a deviant spelling of the surname of Anthony _____, who wrote the "Barsetshire Novels"

Venereal—Transmitted through sexual intercourse, as derived from the name of Venus, the Roman goddess of love, and represented by the *V* in the initialism VD

Dr. Ruth Westheimer—German-born psychosexual therapist whose radio program "Sexually Speaking" began in 1980

Oscar Wilde—Irish-born poet and playwright sentenced for homosexual acts whose poem "The Ballad of Reading Gaol" was inspired by his imprisonment for such offenses

***His surname is Trollope.

AMERICANA

Katharine Lee Bates's song that includes the following lines: "O beautiful for spacious skies / For amber waves of grain; / For purple mountain majesties / Above the fruited plain! / America! America! / God shed His grace on thee / And crown thy good with brotherhood / From sea to shining sea!"
- Answer: "America the Beautiful."

Amerigo Vespucci—Italian-born explorer sailing for Spain and Portugal who between 1499 and 1504 made 3 confirmed trips to South America after whom German geographer Martin Waldseemüller named America
Mayflower—Only ship that brought the founding Pilgrims to this country in 1620 because the *Speedwell* was not seaworthy to make the trip
Plymouth Rock—Massachusetts boulder site where the Pilgrims are said to have landed in 1620
Thanksgiving—Annual celebration commemorating the day in 1621 when the Pilgrims celebrated a good harvest and the blessings they felt they had received
Liberty Bell—Symbol of American freedom cast in England, delivered to the U.S. in 1752, and recast in 1753 after cracking when it was first rung
Philadelphia—City in which this bell is located
Liberty Bell Center*—Building in which this bell is now located
Leviticus (25:10)—Biblical book that is the source of this bell's inscription: "Proclaim Liberty Throughout All the Land Unto All the Inhabitants Thereof"
John Marshall—Chief Justice of the U.S. during whose funeral in 1835 the bell allegedly cracked for a second time
Old State House Bell—This bell's name until abolitionists began referring to it as the Liberty Bell in 1839
Bald eagle—National symbol, adopted June 20, 1782, and featured on the Great Seal of the U.S.
Olive branch—Branch this bird clutches in its right talon, symbolizing the power to make peace and bearing 13 leaves for the 13 original colonies
Arrows—13 objects this bird is clutching in its left talon, symbolizing the power to make war
E Pluribus Unum***—Latin motto meaning "from many, one" or "out of many, one" featured on a scroll held in the beak of this bird
$1 bill—Value of the U.S. currency with the Great Seal on the reverse side
Pyramid—Stone structure with 13 steps representing the Union that also appears on this bill
- **1776**—Date at the bottom of this stone structure, in Roman numerals MDCCLXXVI
Eye of Providence—Eye enclosed in a triangle watching over this stone structure, representing the hoped for divine favor
Annuit Coeptis—Latin motto above the eye meaning "He (God) has favored our undertakings" (Vergil's *Aeneid,* Book IX, verse 625)
Novus Ordo Seclorum—Latin motto below the eye meaning "A new order of the ages" (from Virgil's fourth *Eclogue*)
- **Rose**—Official U.S. flower, adopted October 7, 1986
"The Stars and Stripes Forever"—Official national march, adopted in 1987

*Originally located in Pennsylvania's State House, later named Independence Hall; from 1976 to 2003, the bell was located in the Liberty Bell Pavilion, next to Independence Hall. **This motto, suggested in 1776, is from Horace's *Epistles* and since 1883 has been required on all U.S. coinage.

Stars and Stripes—3-word popular name for the U.S. flag
Red, white, and blue—3 colors of the U.S. flag and now used as a symbol of patriotism
Apple pie—America's most traditional wholesome dessert
Baseball—Sport considered "America's pastime"
Old Glory—2-word name for the U.S. flag given to it in 1831 by William Driver, a Massachusetts sea captain of the brig *Charles Doggett*
Navy Jack—2-word name for the blue flag with white stars that stands for the U.S. when flying on a U.S. Navy ship
Betsy Ross—Philadelphia seamstress who has been traditionally credited with having made the first American flag
June 14, 1777***—Date the flag was adopted by Congress as the official flag of the U.S.—now called Flag Day, first officially observed in 1877
13 (of each)—Number of stars and number of stripes on first U.S. flag, the stars on a blue field, the stripes alternately red and white
50—Number of stars on the current flag, one for each state
Francis Hopkinson****—Member of the Continental Congress from New Jersey now generally credited with having actually designed the first flag
Yankees—Derisive term that British soldiers used for New England troops during the Revolutionary War, possibly derived from the Dutch name Jan Kees
Yankee Doodle—Words completing the following lines of the song British troops sang making fun of the poorly dressed and untrained colonial soldiers: "____ went to town, / Riding on a pony, / Stuck a feather in his cap / And called it macaroni."
Brother Jonathan—Original personification of the U.S. and its people, from the clever Yankee in Royall Tyler's 1787 play *The Contrast*
Uncle Sam*****—Personification of the U.S. government and its citizens acquired from the nickname given to a Troy, New York, meat-packer who sometimes inspected the meat supplied to the military
Samuel Wilson—Meat-packer at Elbert Anderson's stockyard who was given this nickname in 1812 from the imprint "E.A.—U.S." stamped on pork barrels that he sometimes inspected
Harper's Weekly—Magazine that in an 1869 cartoon was the first to give whiskers to this U.S. personification
Pledge of Allegiance******—Statement of loyalty to the U.S. written in 1892
Francis Bellamy—Person who wrote this statement for publication in *The Youth's Companion* to help commemorate the 400th anniversary of Christopher Columbus' voyage to the New World
"under God"—2 words added to this statement in 1954

In 1916, Woodrow Wilson established it as an annual celebration; in 1949, President Truman signed the National Flag Day Bill. ****Most historians now agree that in 1780 he asked Congress to compensate him for his work designing the U.S. flag, the U.S. seal, and other projects, requesting payment in wine. *****He evolved from the Revolutionary War caricature Brother Jonathan; Joseph Keppler created a bewhiskered Uncle Sam in the magazine *Puck*, which he founded in 1876. ***"I pledge allegiance to the flag of the United States of America and to the Republic for which it stands, one Nation under God, indivisible, with liberty and justice for all"; "the flag of the United States of America" replaced "my flag" in 1923 in these lines.

BENJAMIN FRANKLIN

British poet who said in speaking about Benjamin Franklin: "A philosophical Quaker full of mean and thrifty maxims"—this poet wrote "Ode on a Grecian Urn"
Answer: John Keats.

Poor Richard's Almanac(k)—Almanac that Benjamin Franklin published annually from 1733 to 1758
Richard Saunders—Pseudonym under which he published this work
Boston—City he fled at age 17 in 1723 after an argument with his brother
Philadelphia—City to which he fled, later founding there America's first privately supported circulating library—it was the largest city in the colonies
The Pennsylvania Gazette—Newspaper he bought in 1729 and ran until 1766
"Join, or Die"—Caption of his newspaper cartoon featuring a disjointed snake urging the separate colonies to unite against the French and Indians—the first cartoon in America
(Deputy) postmaster (general)—Post he held beginning in 1753 to improve the poor service of the colonial system for sending mail
American Philosophical Society—Professional organization he established for scholars in 1743
University of Pennsylvania—University that developed out of The College, Academy, and Charitable School he helped found
Lightning rod—Device he invented to secure "the habitations and other buildings from mischief from thunder and lightning"
Gulf Stream—Atlantic Ocean current he became the first scientist to study
Franklin stove—Device he invented to make a sitting room twice as warm with much less fuel
Bifocals—Device he invented combining reading and distance lenses in a single frame
Glass (h)armonica—Modern day name of the instrument of tuned glasses he invented and called a glassychord
Albany, New York—State capital where he presented his Plan of Union in 1754 to unite the 13 colonies in "one general government"—this plan laid the groundwork for the 1781 Articles of Confederation
Philadelphia—City in which Franklin served as a member of the Second Continental Congress
Postmaster general—Post this body chose him for in 1775 because of his experience as a colonial postmaster
Declaration of Independence—Document he not only helped draft but also signed in 1776
Hang—Word completing his statement in signing, "We must indeed all _____ together, or assuredly we shall all _____ separately"
France—Country where he served as minister, succeeding in getting a Treaty of Alliance signed in 1778
Treaty of Paris—Treaty he signed in 1783 ending the Revolutionary War
Constitution—Document he signed in 1787, at age 81, as the oldest person there
Christ Church—Philadelphia church where Franklin was buried in 1790
✓ **Franklin Pierce**—First U.S. President named after him, the 14th
Franklin Roosevelt—2nd U.S. President named after him, the 32nd

Death and taxes—2 things he said were certain in life
God—According to his almanac, who "helps them that helps themselves"
Healthy, wealthy, and wise—Completion of his saying "Early to bed and early to rise makes a man _____, _____, and _____"
Oaks—According to his almanac, the "great" trees felled by "little strokes"
Autobiography* —His self-written account of part of his life, a manuscript he began for his son in 1771 but never completed
Turkey—Animal he wanted to use as a symbol instead of the bald eagle, arguing that it was a more "respectable bird" and "a true original native of America" while the chosen one was a "bird of bad moral character"

*In full, the *Autobiography of Benjamin Franklin*, published in 1868

POOR RICHARD'S ALMANAC

Nail—A little neglect may breed great mischief . . . for want of a _____ the shoe was lost; for want of a shoe the horse was lost; for want of a horse the rider was lost.
Penny—A _____ saved is a _____ earned.
Leak—A small _____ will sink a great ship.
Guest—After three days men grow weary, of a wench, a _____, and rainy weather.
Pound—An ounce of prevention is worth a _____ of cure.
Glass—Don't throw stones at your neighbor's, if your own windows are _____.
Eat—_____ to live, and not live to _____.
Fish—_____ and visitors stink in 3 days.
Rivals—He that falls in love with himself will have no _____.
Fasting—He that lives upon hope will die _____.
Bug—Here Skugg lies snug—As a _____ in a rug.
Heir—He's a fool that makes his doctor his _____.
Honesty—_____ is the best policy.
Lost—_____ time is never found again.
Necessity—_____ never made a good bargain.
Money—Remember that time is _____.
Otherwise—Some are weatherwise, some are _____.
Success—_____ has ruin'd many a Man.
Peace—There never was a good war or a bad _____.
Dead—Three may keep a secret, if two of them are _____.
Love—Where there's marriage without _____, there will be _____ without marriage.
Tomorrow (today)—Work as if you were to live 100 years. Pray as if you were to die _____.

DECLARATION OF INDEPENDENCE

Virginia patriot and Senator who on June 7, 1776, made the following resolution: "That these United Colonies are, and of right ought to be, free and independent states"
Answer: Richard Henry Lee.

- 1) Identify the first 7 words in the preamble of the Declaration of Independence.
  Answer: "When in the course of human events."

2) Identify the 3 most important rights enjoyed by Americans as stated by Thomas Jefferson in the Declaration of Independence: "We hold these truths to be self-evident, that all men are created equal, that they are endowed by their Creator with certain unalienable rights, that among these are _____, _____, and the _____."
Answer: Life, liberty, and the pursuit of happiness (a typographical or spelling error occurred as "unalienable" was printed instead of "inalienable").

3) Identify the 3 things the signers pledged to each other in the final lines of the Declaration of Independence.
Answer: "Our Lives, our Fortunes, and our sacred Honor."

4) Name the 5 members of the committee that drafted the Declaration of Independence.
Answer: John Adams, Benjamin Franklin, Thomas Jefferson, Robert Livingston, and Roger Sherman.

- 5) Identify the 2 future U.S. Presidents who signed the Declaration of Independence, both of whom died on July 4, 1826.
  Answer: John Adams and Thomas Jefferson.

6) Identify the 2 U.S. Presidents whose fathers signed the Declaration of Independence.
Answer: John Quincy Adams and William Henry Harrison.

(Second) Continental Congress—Congress that adopted the Declaration
July 4, 1776—Date—month, day, and year—on which it was adopted, now known as Independence Day
- **56***—Number of delegates who signed it
Caesar Rodney—Delaware's 3rd delegate who rode 80 miles to bring the colony's support for the Declaration
August 2, 1776—Date on which about 50 of the Congress's members officially signed the engrossed (done in stylish script) document
Thomas Jefferson—Its primary author, called "The Father of the Declaration of Independence"
Philadelphia—City where this document was adopted
Independence Hall—Current name of the building where this document was adopted, then called the Pennsylvania or Philadelphia State House
King George III—British king against whom the Declaration was directed
John Hancock**—Delegate who was the first to sign it, doing so in a large, bold signature

*On January 28, 1777, Mary K. Goddard's *The Maryland Journal* was the first to publish the Declaration of Independence with the names of all the signers. **The phrase *John Hancock* today designates a person's signature, especially on legal documents, an allusion to Hancock's large, bold signature.

Pennsylvania—Colony represented by Robert Morris, Benjamin Rush, and Benjamin Franklin, among others

Connecticut—Colony represented by Roger Sherman, Samuel Huntington, William Williams, and Oliver Wolcott

Georgia—Colony represented by Button Gwinnett, Lyman Hall, and George Walton

Benjamin Franklin—"Elder Statesman" who was the oldest signer of this document

Georgia—Of the original 13 colonies, the only one that did not send delegates to the First Continental Congress in 1774

National Archives—Washington, D.C., building in which the original copy of the Declaration of Independence is housed

John Hancock—President of the Continental Congress when the Declaration was adopted

Charles Carroll—Carrollton, Maryland-born last surviving signer of the Declaration, who died November 14, 1832

- **87**—Numbers of years between the Declaration of Independence and the Gettysburg Address

John Witherspoon—Scottish-born Presbyterian president of the College of New Jersey (now Princeton University) who, as a member of the Continental Congress, was the only minister to sign this document

U.S. CONSTITUTION

U.S. Senator from Kentucky who in 1850 said: "The Constitution of the United States was made not merely for the generation that then existed, but for posterity—unlimited, undefined, endless, perpetual posterity"
Answer: Henry Clay.

1) Identify the first 3 words of its preamble, which begins as follows: "____ of the United States, in Order to form a more perfect Union, . . . "
Answer: We, the people,

2) Identify the 3 words completing the following remaining part of the preamble: ". . . establish ____, insure domestic ____ provide for the common ____, promote the general Welfare, and secure the Blessings of Liberty to ourselves and our Posterity, do ordain and establish this Constitution for the United States of America."
Answer: Justice, Tranquillity, defense.

3) Identify the 5 freedoms delineated in the First Amendment.
Answer: Freedom of the press, speech, religion, right of assembly, and right to petition.

4) According to the 5th Amendment, which 3 things may a person not be deprived of without due process of law?
Answer: Life, liberty, and property.

September 17, 1787—Date the Constitution was signed
Philadelphia—City in which it was signed
7—Number of articles it contains
27—Number of amendments attached to it
Bill of Rights—Name given to the first 10 amendments ratified on December 15, 1791
James Madison—Statesman called the "Father of the Constitution"
George Washington—Besides the "Father of the Constitution," the other Constitutional Convention delegate who became a U.S. President
39*—Of the 42 delegates present, the number who signed the Constitution
Gouverneur Morris—Member who headed the committee that wrote the final draft of the Constitution and who is credited with most of its wording
National Archives—Building in Washington, D.C., where the original Constitution is displayed
New Hampshire—State whose delegates were the first to sign the Constitution
Rhode Island—State not represented at the Constitutional Convention
Georgia—State whose delegates were the last to sign the Constitution
Cato—Roman name the governor of New York used as a pseudonym in opposing ratification in New York newspapers
9—Number of states that had to ratify the Constitution before it could take effect
Delaware**—First state to ratify the Constitution, on December 7, 1787
New Hampshire—9th state to ratify it, putting it in effect on June 21, 1788
April 6, 1789—First day that Congress conducted business under the Constitution

*Elbridge Gerry, George Mason, and Edmund Randolph did not sign because they felt the Constitution gave the federal government too much power.
**Followed by Pennsylvania (December 12), New Jersey (December 18), Georgia (January 2), and Connecticut (January 9).

Rhode Island—Last state to ratify the Constitution, on May 29, 1790
Jonathan Dayton—Youngest signer of the Constitution, at age 26
George Washington—President of the Constitutional Convention
Benjamin Franklin—Oldest delegate at the Constitutional Convention and the oldest signer of the Constitution, at age 81
Annapolis (MD)—City where representatives from 5 states met in September 1786 and proposed that states appoint commissioners to meet to revise the Articles of Confederation
Virginia Plan—Plan favored by the larger states at the Constitutional Convention under which population would determine the number of state representatives in the legislature
New Jersey Plan—Plan favored by the smaller states under which all states would have an equal number of representatives
Connecticut Compromise***—State credited by name with the "Compromise" plan finally adopted giving states equal representation in the Senate and representation based on population in the House
The Federalist—Title for the book of 85 letters originally written to newspapers by 3 men to answer New York Governor George Clinton's objections and to urge New Yorkers to approve the U.S. Constitution
Publius—Pseudonym under which all but 8 of the 85 letters appeared during 1787 and 1788
Alexander Hamilton—Statesman who wrote 52 of the 85 letters
James Madison and John Jay—2 statesmen who wrote, respectively, 28 and 5 of these letters (authorship of the other 15 is not assured)

***Also called the Great Compromise

U.S. Government

Author who in *Common Sense* said, "Government, even in its best state, is but a necessary evil; in its worst state, an intolerable one"
Answer: Thomas Paine.

1) Which 3 verbs complete the following oath of office taken by a President as prescribed by Article II, section 1 of the Constitution: "I do solemnly swear (or affirm) that I will faithfully execute the office of President of the United States, and will to the best of my ability, _____, _____ and _____ the Constitution of the United States"?
Answer: "Preserve, protect and defend."

2) After repeating the presidential oath given by Robert R. Livingston of New York on the balcony of Federal Hall in New York City on April 30, 1789, which 4 words did George Washington add?
Answer: "So help me God!"

3) Name the 3 capitals of the U.S. in chronological order.
Answer: New York City (1789-1790); Philadelphia (1790-1800); and Washington, D.C. (1800 to the present).

4) Name the 3 years the inaugurations of elected U.S. Presidents were not held in Washington, D.C.
Answer: 1789 (Washington in New York City), 1793 (Washington in Philadelphia), and 1797 (John Adams in Philadelphia).

5) Name the men who were the first to head the 3 "executive departments" set up by Congress in 1789, specifically State, Treasury, and War.
Answer: Thomas Jefferson, Alexander Hamilton, and Henry Knox, respectively (John Jay, chief justice of the U.S., was acting secretary of state until Jefferson assumed the office in 1790; Edmund Randolph and Samuel Osgood served respectively as first Attorney General and first Postmaster General).

6) Identify the 3 independent branches of the U.S. government.
Answer: Executive, legislative, and judicial.

7) Give the 3 requirements to become President of the U.S. according to Article II, Section 1 of the Constitution.
Answer: A natural-born citizen, at least 35 years of age, and a resident of the U.S. for at least 14 years.

8) Give the 3 requirements to become Vice President of the U.S. according to Article II, Section 1 of the Constitution.
Answer: A natural-born citizen, at least 35 years of age, and a resident of the U.S. for at least 14 years.

9) Give the 3 requirements to become a member of the U.S. Senate. according to Article I, Section 3 of the Constitution.
Answer: 30 years of age, a citizen of the U.S. for 9 years, and a resident of the state which elects him/her.

10) Give the 3 requirements to become a member of the U.S. House of Representatives according to Article II, Section 2 of the Constitution.
Answer: 25 years of age, a citizen of the U.S. for 7 years, and a resident of the state which elects him/her.

Congress—Legislative branch, the one that has the power to declare war according to Article 1, Section 8
Bicameral—Word designating the legislative branch as a body having 2 houses, or chambers
Senate—"Upper House" of this legislative branch
House of Representatives—"Lower House" of this legislative branch
The Capitol—Domed building in which the legislative branch meets
100—Number of U.S. Senators, 2 per state
435—Number of U.S. Representatives, based on the state population
Electoral College—Group of people chosen by the voters of each state to elect the President and Vice President
538—Voting members of this "College," determined by the number of Senators, number of Representatives, plus 3 electors from the District of Columbia
270—Number of votes of this "College" required to win the presidency
6 years—Term of office for each member of the U.S. Senate—no limit on being reelected
2 years—Term of office for each member of the U.S. House—no limit on being reelected
4 years—Term of office for the President of the U.S.—can be reelected once
10 years—Maximum number of years the President of the U.S. can serve
Life—Term of office for a Supreme Court Justice—there is no retirement age
Vice President of the U.S.—Presiding officer of the Senate
President *pro tempore*—Title for the person chosen by the Senate to preside when the presiding officer is absent
Speaker of the House—Title for the chief officer of the House
Commander in chief—Title for the President as the highest ranking officer in the armed forces
State of the Union message—President's annual message to Congress to report on the state of the country and outline a program for the future
Supreme Court of the U.S.—Highest U.S. court and the only one specifically created by the Constitution
Chief justice of the U.S.—Head of the judicial branch of the U.S. who presides over this highest court
8—Number of associate justices that along with the chief justice make up this court
6—Number of members of this court prior to its increase to 9 members in 1869
October—Month in which this court's annual term starts on the first Monday
Treason and bribery—2 crimes the Constitution specifies along with "other high crimes and misdemeanors" as grounds for impeachment
2—Number of witnesses required to convict a person of treason
Rebellion and invasion—2 circumstances in which the government may suspend the *writ of habeas corpus*, which orders the police to produce the arrested person in court, thus preventing unjust imprisonment
Democratic and Republican—2 main political parties in the U.S.
Donkey and elephant—Symbols of these 2 political parties*
Chief justice of the U.S.—Official who, since Washington's time, has administered the oath of office to the President
Cabinet—Part of the executive branch consisting of the heads of federal executive departments

*The Green Party played an important role in the 2000 elections, and its symbol is the sunflower.

THE WHITE HOUSE*

Union Army general who said in 1864: "If forced to choose between the penitentiary and the White House for four years . . . I would say the penitentiary, thank you"
Answer: William T. Sherman.

Identify the 3 principal first-floor White House rooms named with colors.
Answer: Red Room, Blue Room, and Green Room.

1792—Year the White House, Washington, D.C.'s oldest public building, had its cornerstone laid on October 13
Pierre L'Enfant—French "child" who as city planner together with George Washington chose the site for the location of the White House in 1790
James Hoban—Irish-born architect who designed it
1600 Pennsylvania Avenue—White House address
132—Number of rooms in the White House
Theodore Roosevelt—President who authorized *White House* as the official title, in 1901
Rose Garden—Garden where many ceremonial events take place
John Adams—First President to live in the White House, in 1800
East Room—Largest room, where First Lady Abigail Adams dried the laundry because no outside area had been provided
President's Park—Name often used for the south lawn where trees and shrubs planted by former White House occupants are located
West Wing—Executive wing of the White House where the President's office and Cabinet Room are located
Oval Office—Office in which the President works, whose name is often used figuratively to represent the power of the President of the U.S.
Blue Room—Colorful room used as the main reception room for guests of the President
Green Room—Colorful room whose furniture is in the style of Duncan Phyfe
Red Room—Colorful room used as a parlor and furnished in the American Empire style
Thomas Jefferson—First President to make his home in the White House after being inaugurated in Washington, D.C.
1814—Year the British set fire to the White House
Gilbert Stuart—Artist whose famous portrait of George Washington was hastily loaded into a carriage before the British arrived to burn the White House
Dolley Madison—First Lady who saved this portrait of George Washington
James Madison—President who moved back into the White House in 1817 while the building was rebuilt
Octagon House—8-sided house in which this President lived while the White House was being rebuilt
Andrew Jackson—President who escaped through a window as a throng mobbed the White House following his 1829 inauguration—the people moved to the lawn when the whiskey and food were moved outside
Abraham Lincoln—President considered to be "The White House Ghost"
Harry Truman—President who lived in a nearby house while the White House underwent extensive repairs from 1948 to 1952

*Or the Executive Mansion; formerly called the President's House or the President's Palace, then the Executive Mansion.

Blair House—President's Guest House across from the White House used for distinguished state visitors where the President stayed from 1948 to 1952 as the White House was being repaired

Roosevelt Room—New name of the Fish Room, site of an aquarium and fishing mementos, renamed by Richard Nixon in 1969 to honor the 26th and 32nd Presidents

Jacqueline Kennedy—First Lady who in 1961 began restoring the White House interior to its original appearance

"THE STAR-SPANGLED BANNER"

One of the 2 songs that were in competition with "The Star-Spangled Banner" as the country's national song until 1831 when Congress resolved the issue by voting for it as the national anthem
Answer: "Hail Columbia" or "America the Beautiful."

Words completing the following lines from stanza 1:
light—"Oh! say, can you see, by the dawn's early _____,
gleaming—What so proudly we hailed at the twilight's last _____?
fight—Whose broad stripes and bright stars thro' the perilous _____
streaming—O'er the ramparts we watched, were so gallantly _____?
air—And the rockets' red glare, the bombs bursting in _____,
there—Gave proof thro' the night that our flag was still _____.
wave—Oh! say, does that star-spangled banner yet wave—
brave—O'er the land of the free and the home of the _____?"

Francis Scott Key* —Washington poet and lawyer who on September 13-14, during the War of 1812, wrote what has come to be known as the national anthem
1814—Year in which it was written on September 13-14
Fort McHenry*—Fort during whose bombardment it was written
Baltimore—City in whose bay it was written
Chesapeake Bay—Bay in which it was written
H.M.S. *Minden*—British sloop flying a truce flag aboard which this composer and Colonel John S. Skinner were being held behind the British fleet after negotiating the release of Maryland physician Dr. William Beanes**
"Defence of Fort M'Henry"—This song's original title
"To Anacreon in Heaven"—Tune to which the words of the song were first sung
"In God We Trust"—National motto adopted July 30, 1956, based on the song's 4th stanza: "Then conquer we must, when our cause is just, / And this be our motto, 'In God is our Trust.'"
Smithsonian Museum***—Museum that placed the flag on exhibit for the first time, in 1907
Woodrow Wilson—President who proclaimed "The Star-Spangled Banner" as the national anthem in 1916
Herbert Hoover—President in office when Congress confirmed this action in 1931

*A flag flies continuously over Francis Scott Key's grave at Frederick, Maryland, and over Baltimore's Fort McHenry. **The British agreed to release Beanes but kept all parties aboard until after the 25-hour bombardment; during the bombardment, the elderly Dr. Beanes, whose eyesight was failing, allegedly kept asking "Is the flag still there?" ***The flag is now on display in the Museum of American History.

STATUE OF LIBERTY

• Title of the poem inscribed on a bronze plaque originally on the interior wall of the pedestal but now in the Statue of Liberty's museum
Answer: "The New Colossus."

Words completing the following last 5 lines of the poem "The New Colossus":
poor—"Give me your tired, your ____,
free—Your huddled masses yearning to breathe ____.
shore—The wretched refuse of your teeming ____.
me—Send these, the homeless, tempest-tost to ____,
door—I lift my lamp beside the golden ____!"

Emma Lazarus—American author who wrote the poem "The New Colossus"
Mother of Exiles*—Name given to the statue in this poem
France—Country that gave the 151-foot copper statue to the U.S. on July 4, 1884, to celebrate the idea of liberty and friendship
Seine River—River where a one-fourth size model of the original statue given to France in 1885 by U.S. citizens living in Paris is located on an island
Frédéric Auguste Bartholdi—Sculptor who created this statue from an idea suggested by Edouard-René Lefebvre de Laboulaye
Liberty's face—Part of the statue modeled after the sculptor's mother, Auguste Charlotte ____
Philadelphia—City where the statue's original torch was displayed at the Centennial Exposition in 1876
Grover Cleveland**—U.S. President who dedicated the monument on October 28, 1886
"Liberty Enlightening the World"—Full English name of the statue whose French name is *La Liberté Eclairant le Monde*
Glowing torch—Object that the female figure Liberty is holding in her uplifted right arm
7—Number of spikes in her crown, representing both the number of seas and the number of continents of the world
July 4, 1776—Date on the tablet, or written document, she cradles in her left arm
Chain—Broken object representing tyranny that lies at her feet
Alexandre Gustave Eiffel—Person who constructed the supporting statue's iron framework
Liberty Island—Island in New York Harbor on which the statue is located
Bedloe's Island—Former name of this island
Joseph Pulitzer—Publisher and Hungarian immigrant whose editorials in *The World* asking for donations for the statue's pedestal raised $100,000 (in all, Americans gave $350,000)
Ellis Island—Former immigration station until 1954 that became part of the Statue of Liberty National Monument in 1965

*The beginning lines are: "Not like the brazen giant of Greek fame, / With conquering limbs astride from land to land; / Here at our sea-washed, sunset gates shall stand / A mighty woman with a torch, whose flame / Is the imprisoned lightning, and her name / Mother of Exiles. From her beacon-hand—Glows world-wide welcome; her mild eyes command / The air-bridged harbor that twin cities frame. / 'Keep ancient lands, your storied pomp!' cries she / With silent lips." **It was presented to the Minister of the U.S. in Paris, on July 4, 1884, and shipped to the U.S. in May 1885 aboard the French ship *Isère* in 350 pieces.

AMERICAN REVOLUTION, OR REVOLUTIONARY WAR IN AMERICA

Massachusetts patriot who when he first heard shots fired on April 19, 1775, said: "What a glorious morning for America!"
Answer: Samuel Adams.

LEADING TOWARD WAR
Committee of Correspondence—Informal group of colonial leaders formed in 1764 that communicated with similar groups in other colonies to mobilize public opinion against Britain
Stamp Act Congress—Body that took the first united action against an unpopular British law, in 1765 in New York, saying that only the colonial government could tax the colonists
Sons of Liberty—Secret radical patriotic organization formed to oppose this unpopular British law in 1765
Boston Massacre—March 5, 1770, street fight between soldiers and towns-people
Crispus Attucks—Black American patriot who was the first one killed in this March 5, 1770, incident
John Adams—Future U.S. President who defended the British soldiers in this March 5, 1770, incident
Redcoats—Name other than "lobsterbacks" and "bloody-backs" for the British soldiers in the colonies because they wore bright red jackets
Boston Tea Party—December 16, 1773, event when colonials dressed as Mohawk Indians dumped chests of tea into Boston Harbor to protest the British tax on tea
Samuel Adams—Boston patriot and "Penman of the Revolution" who led the resistance to all the British acts and urged colonial independence from Great Britain
Intolerable Acts—Another name for the five 1774 Coercive or Repressive Acts passed by Parliament in response to the December 16, 1773, event
Faneuil Hall—Boston site named after Peter _____ and known as the "Cradle of Liberty" because it was the scene of many protests by angry colonists before the war
Philadelphia—City where the First Continental Congress met to protest these acts, from September 5 to October 26, 1774
Tories—Name patriots used for Loyalists, that is, colonists who sympathized and remained faithful to George III and opposed the Declaration of Independence

Which 3 men gave warning of the coming of the British on April 18, 1775?
Answer: Paul Revere, William Dawes, and Dr. Samuel Prescott (all 3 started for Concord, but a British patrol forced Dawes to turn back, and Revere was captured and brought back to Lexington, where after being released, he joined Hancock and Adams as they fled; Joseph Warren had sent Revere and Dawes to Lexington on April 18, 1775, to warn Hancock and Adams of danger).

THE WAR CHRONOLOGICALLY
1775-1783—Beginning and ending years for the war

Lexington—Massachusetts town where the Revolution began on April 19, 1775
Concord—Massachusetts town in which the 2nd skirmish occurred on April 19, 1775
Minutemen—Colonial militiamen known for their readiness to fight at a moment's notice who fought the British on April 19, 1775
Fort Ticonderoga—New York fort on Lake Champlain seized by Ethan Allen and Benedict Arnold on May 10, 1775
Green Mountain Boys—Ethan Allen's Vermont militia group that participated in the capture of this fort
Continental Army—Military force the Second Continental Congress organized in June 14, 1775
George Washington—Person this Congress appointed as commander in chief of this military force on June 15, 1775
Bunker Hill*—War's first major battle, on June 17, 1775, which the colonists were winning until they ran out of ammunition
William Prescott**—Colonel who said, "Don't fire until you see the whites of their eyes!" at the June 17, 1775, battle
Olive Branch Petition—July 8, 1775, petition sent to England to ask for a cessation of hostilities—refused in August by George III
Navy—U.S. military branch the Continental Congress established on November 28, 1775
July 4, 1776—Date the Declaration of Independence was adopted
Nathan Hale—21-year-old captain who was caught spying on the British on Long Island and hanged on September 22, 1776—his final words were "I only regret that I have but one life to lose (give) for my country."
Hessians—German mercenary soldiers hired by Britain
Trenton—New Jersey town in which Washington defeated the British-mercenary garrison after crossing the Delaware on December 25-26, 1776
Princeton—New Jersey town Washington attacked and captured in a brilliant victory on January 3, 1777
Brandywine Creek—Chadds Ford, Pennsylvania, site where on September 11, 1777, Gen. Howe's forces defeated Washington's and then took Philadelphia
Freeman's Farm—New York site where Britain's John Bourgoyne's forces suffered heavy losses to Gates's forces on September 19, 1777—also known as the First Battle of Saratoga
Bemis Heights—October 7, 1777, New York site where British forces suffered great losses at the hands of Gates, Benedict Arnold, and Daniel Morgan—also known as the Second Battle of Saratoga
Saratoga—New York town where the British surrendered on October 17, 1777, marking a turning point in the war as the colonists' victory convinced France to enter the war on America's side
Conway Cabal—Failed 1777 conspiracy to remove George Washington as commander in chief of the Continental Army following defeats at Brandywine Creek and Germantown
Valley Forge—Pennsylvania site where George Washington's troops spent a difficult winter in 1777-1778
Battle of Monmouth—Last major battle of the war in the North, on June 27-28, 1778, in New Jersey
George Rogers Clark—Frontier military leader whose forces captured the 3 key settlements of Cahokia (Illinois), Kaskaskia (Illinois), and Vincennes (Indiana) in 1778-1779, leading to U.S. control of what had been British territory
John Paul Jones—Naval hero whose *Bonhomme Richard* defeated the British ship *Serapis* on September 23, 1779

*Battle was actually fought on Breed's Hill. **It also could have been Major Israel Putnam who made this famous statement.

Charleston—South Carolina port city where a 5,400-patriot force under Benjamin Lincoln surrendered on May 12, 1780, to Gen. Clinton's forces
Camden—South Carolina site where Gates' militiamen and Continentals were easily defeated by Lord Charles Cornwallis' men on August 16, 1780
Kings Mountain—South Carolina site where Cornwallis' men were surrounded and captured on October 7, 1780, a loss helping to break British military power in the South
Cowpens—South Carolina site where the patriots under Morgan defeated the British under Tarleton on January 17, 1781
Guilford Courthouse—/ North Carolina site of the March 15, 1781, battle that the British won but lost so many troops that Cornwallis decided to leave the state
Yorktown***—Virginia town where on October 19, 1781, Cornwallis surrendered to Washington
Treaty of Paris—Peace treaty on September 3, 1783, ending the war

***Cornwallis, feigning illness, sent General Charles O'Hara to surrender; O'Hara offered his sword to Comte Rochambeau, who sent him to Washington, who in turn sent him to General Benjamin Lincoln, because deputy must surrender to deputy.

WAR POTPOURRI

Old North Church—Popular name for Christ Church, the Boston site where lanterns were hung to warn patriots of a British attack—"One if by land, two if by sea"
Richard Montgomery—Brigadier general who captured Montreal in 1775 but died in the attack on Quebec
Patrick Henry—Patriot famous for his 1775 speech in which he said, "I know not what course others may take, but as for me, give me liberty or give me death!"
"Light-Horse Harry"—Nickname of Henry Lee, the cavalry leader known for his lightning raids during the war
Henry Knox—Colonel, later a secretary of war, who led his forces in bringing 60 guns and mortars from Ticonderoga to Boston in the winter of 1775-1776, forcing the British evacuation of Boston
Thomas Paine—American author whose January 19, 1776, pamphlet *Common Sense* urged the colonists toward complete independence
Richard Henry Lee—Virginian whose June 7, 1776, resolution calling for independence from Britain was adopted, leading to the Declaration of Independence
Thomas Jefferson—"Scribe of the Revolution" who was the principal drafter of the Declaration of Independence
Ben Franklin—Chairman of the Committee on Secret Correspondence to deal with Great Britain, the one who helped send French officers, soldiers, and guns to America after Saratoga and who was a representative along with John Adams and John Jay at the 1783 Paris peace conference
Thaddeus Kosciusko—Polish patriot who built fortifications to help the victory at Saratoga after arriving in 1776
Casimir Pulaski—Polish count who served as aide-de-camp at Brandywine in 1777, organized America's first cavalry unit, and died after being wounded at Savannah in 1779
Baron von Steuben—Former Prussian soldier who drilled Washington's forces while they were stationed at Valley Forge in 1777-1778 and led a division of troops at Yorktown
Marquis de Lafayette—French soldier who was wounded at Brandywine, persuaded France to send military aid to the colonies, and played a major role at Yorktown
Molly Pitcher—Heroine who carried water to troops and possibly replaced her husband as a gunner when he was felled by heat stroke at the June 1778 Battle of Monmouth—her real name is Molly Ludwig Hays

Anthony Wayne—General nicknamed "Mad Antony" because he ordered his troops to fight with empty muskets and fixed bayonets at Stony Point in 1779

Robert Morris—So-called "Financier of the Revolution" who played a major role in raising money to sustain the war effort

Francis Marion—South Carolina military leader known as the "Swamp Fox" because of his daring guerrilla raids against British and Loyalist troops

Benedict Arnold—America's most infamous traitor, stopped in 1780 from surrendering West Point to the British

John André—British major hanged as a spy in 1780 for conspiring to capture West Point

Benjamin Franklin—Statesman whose 1754 Albany Plan of Union laid the groundwork for the 1781 agreement for a permanent union of 13 states

Articles of Confederation—Agreement establishing a federal government adopted by the Second Continental Congress in 1777 and ratified by the 13 states in 1781—the first U.S. constitution

Philip Freneau—"Poet of the American Revolution" who hated all things British and in 1781 wrote the vitriolic poem "The British Prison-Ship" after serving time on one

Count Rochambeau—French lieutenant general who arrived in the U.S. in 1780 in command of about 5,500 French soldiers and joined the battle against Cornwallis in 1781

François de Grasse—French admiral whose fleet linked up with the Americans in 1781 to help force the British fleet to withdraw, thus helping trap Cornwallis at Yorktown

"World Turned Upside Down"—Song allegedly played by the British band after the defeat at Yorktown

Purple Heart—More popular name of the Badge of Military Merit George Washington instituted in 1782

Annapolis (Maryland)—City in which Washington officially resigned his commission as commander in chief of the Continental Army before Congress on December 23, 1783

Ralph Waldo Emerson—Writer who in 1836 referred to the first shot fired by the patriots as "the shot heard round the world" in his "Concord Hymn"*

Emanuel Leutze—German-American artist known for his famous 1851 painting entitled *Washington Crossing the Delaware*

*"By the rude bridge that arched the flood, / Their flag to April's breeze unfurled, / Here once the embattled farmers stood, / And fired the shot heard around the world."

WAR OF 1812

Kentucky "War Hawk" who in 1812 after a victory of the *Constitution* said: "Strike wherever we can reach the enemy, at sea and on land. But if we fail, let us fail like men, lash ourselves to our gallant tars, and expire together in one common struggle, fighting for free trade and seamen's rights!"
Answer: Henry Clay.

1) Name the 2 ships involved in the June 22, 1807, incident off Hampton Roads, Virginia, that ultimately led to the War of 1812. When the American commander refused to release several American sailors whom the British commander claimed to be deserters, the British ship fired on the American one, killing 3 Americans before impressing 4 sailors.
Answer: *Leopard* (British) and *Chesapeake* (American, captained by James Barron; 4 years later the British apologized and paid damages).

2) The American plan of attack in the War of 1812 involved 3 simultaneous invasions of Canada from which 3 locations: a city, a river near Buffalo, and, to attack Montreal, a lake?
Answer: Detroit (across the Detroit River), the Niagara River, and Lake Champlain (historians generally agree Canada would have fallen if all the efforts had been directed at Montreal).

3) A group opposed to the War of 1812—most of them Federalists—met in secret at Hartford, Connecticut, from December 15, 1814, to January 5, 1815, to discuss their opposition and to seek redress for wrongs from the Federal government. Name the 5 New England states represented by these delegates.
Answer: Connecticut, Massachusetts, Rhode Island, New Hampshire (2 counties sent delegates), and Vermont (one county sent a delegate; Federalist opposition to the war, as demonstrated by the convention, helped destroy the party).

Impressment—British government policy of forcing men from American ships into naval service, claiming the right to stop ships on the high seas and the right to remove sailors of British birth

Embargo Act—December 1807 law that forbade all ships from entering or leaving U.S. ports, passed to retaliate for the *Chesapeake-Leopard* affair—repealed in 1809

Tippecanoe—November 7, 1811, battle in Indiana Territory that came about because of the conflict between Westerners desirous of expansion and Indians supported by the British

William Henry Harrison—Governor of the Indiana Territory who led the American troops on November 7, 1811

Tenskwatawa—So-called "Shawnee Prophet" who led the Indians at the November 7, 1811, battle, and had been urging tribesmen to return to Native American methods and customs to defend Indian lands against the whites since 1806

War Hawks—Young Democratic-Republican Congressmen from Southern and Western states who advocated war against Great Britain in 1810-1812 and shouted "On to Canada!" since they wanted Canada as well

Henry Clay—Speaker of the House (1811-1814) and leader of these young Congressmen whose slogan was "Free Trade and Seamen's Rights"

James Madison* —President on June 18, 1812, when Congress declared the U.S. at war with Great Britain

Detroit —Michigan city captured by British General Sir Isaac Brock on August 16, 1812, along with American General William Hull's 2,000-man force that came across the Detroit River

Constitution —U.S. frigate commanded by Isaac Hull that defeated the *Guerrière* off Nova Scotia in a great naval victory on August 19, 1812

"Old Ironsides" —Famous nickname of this U.S. frigate so derived from its hard oak hull that was so little damaged in this war

Boston —City in which this oldest commissioned ship still afloat is docked at the Charleston Navy Yard

Queenston Heights —Battle on the Niagara River, fought on October 13, 1812, that ended the 2nd American attempt to invade Canada

Raisin River —River site of a January 22, 1813, British victory at Frenchtown (present-day Monroe, Michigan) followed by an Indian massacre of wounded Kentucky troops left behind after the British troops departed with their able-bodied prisoners

York —Capital of Upper Canada that was captured briefly and had some of its public buildings burned on April 27, 1813, in what is now the city of Toronto

James Lawrence —Captain whose dying words "Don't Give up the Ship!" on June 1, 1813, became the motto of the U.S. Navy—he was in command of the *Chesapeake* during a battle near Boston against the *Shannon*

Lake Erie** —September 10, 1813, battle in which an American commander defeated and captured the entire British fleet led by Commodore Robert Barclay

Oliver Hazard Perry —Commander who defeated the British on September 10, 1813, having boarded the *Niagara* after his flagship the *Lawrence* was disabled

William Henry Harrison —American general to whom this commander reported his September 10 victory with the famous words, "We have met the enemy and they are ours; two ships, two brigs, one schooner, and one sloop."

Thames River —River site of the October 5, 1813, Battle of Moraviantown in present-day Ontario at which the Americans defeated the retreating Redcoats fleeing from Detroit

William Henry Harrison —American general who defeated the British and Indians at the October 5, 1813, battle

Tecumseh —Shawnee leader and a brigadier general in the British Army who died at the October 5, 1813, battle, thereby ending the cooperation between the Indians and the British

Chippewa (Chippawa) —Battle of July 5, 1814, where American forces led by Gen. Winfield Scott defeated the British along the Niagara frontier near Fort Erie

Lundy's Lane —Battle of July 25, 1814, in Canada along the Niagara frontier where the British defeated the Americans in what was their last attempt to invade Canada

Bladensburg —Maryland battle on August 24, 1814, that was followed by the British capture and burning of Washington's government buildings, including the Capitol and White House

Dolley Madison —First Lady who hastily loaded a well-known portrait of President George Washington into a carriage before the British arrived to burn the White House

Gilbert Stuart —Artist who painted this well-known portrait of President Washington

Lake Champlain —New England lake where on September 11, 1814, the entire British Navy surrendered

*The War of 1812 was also called Mr. Madison's War, the Second War for American Independence, the Unnecessary War, and the War of Iniquity.
**Also called the Battle of Put-In-Bay (Ohio)

Fort McHenry—Maryland fort where the British were turned back despite their all-night bombing attack on September 13-14, 1814, at the end of which the flag was still flying

Treaty of Ghent—Treaty signed on December 24, 1814, that ended the War of 1812

Belgium—Country in which this treaty was signed

New Orleans—Louisiana battle fought on January 8, 1815, that was called the "unnecessary or needless battle" because it was fought 15 days after the treaty ending the war was signed

Andrew Jackson—American general who easily defeated the British at the January 8, 1815, battle

Jean Laffite (Lafitte)—French-born New Orleans smuggler and pirate who aided the American general in the 1815 battle

James Madison—President who pardoned this smuggler and pirate in return for his help

Barataria Bay—Bay where this pirate had his headquarters on Grand Terre Island in the Gulf of Mexico

THE ALAMO*

Greek mountain pass named in this inscription "_____ had its messenger of defeat. The Alamo had none," alluding to the defeat of a Spartan army there
Answer: Thermopylae (the Alamo is sometimes called the "Thermopylae of America")

Cradle or Shrine—Word completing "_____ of Texas Liberty," designating the Texas fortified mission called the Alamo
1836—Year of the 19th-century battle that took place at the Alamo 4 days after Texas declared her independence from Mexico
March 6—Month and ending date for this battle that began at the Alamo on February 23
Cottonwood—Type of trees surrounding the Alamo after which it was named
San Antonio—Texas city in which the Alamo is located
William Barret Travis—Lieutenant Colonel in charge of about 150 men (later 189) who on February 24 sent the message, "I shall never surrender or retreat. . . . Victory or Death" and later died there
James Bowie—Frontiersman credited with inventing a hunting knife who died there
David Crockett—Frontiersman and former congressman from Tennessee who died there
Santa Anna**—Mexican general who with about 6,000 men defeated the American forces there—he lost over 1,500 men
Sam Houston—Texan president who told the commanding officers not to defend the fort and later surprised the Mexican forces on April 21, capturing the Mexican leader and forcing him to sign a treaty recognizing the independence of Texas
Sidney Sherman—Army colonel credited with creating a famous American battle cry linked with the battle
"Remember the Alamo"—Battle cry this Army colonel is said to have created
Goliad***—Site where about 340 troops led by Colonel James W. Fannin Jr. were massacred on March 27, after being captured at the Battle of Coleto
San Jacinto—April 21 battle at which the Mexican leader was captured and the independence of Texas was established

*Built as a Roman Catholic mission and called San Antonio de Valero. **In full, Antonio López de Santa Anna ***Other mottoes were "Remember Goliad" and "Death to Santa Anna."

THE ALAMO IN FILM
John Wayne—Actor who plays Davy Crockett in the 1960 movie *The Alamo*
Richard Windmark—Actor who plays Jim Bowie in the 1960 movie
Laurence Harvey—Actor who plays Col. William Barret Travis in the 1960 movie
Billy Bob Thornton—Actor who plays Davy Crockett in the 2003 movie *The Alamo*
Jason Patric—Actor who plays Jim Bowie in the 2003 movie
Patrick Wilson—Actor who plays Col. William Barret Travis in the 2003 movie
Dennis Quaid—Actor who plays General Sam Houston in the 2003 movie

MEXICAN WAR

Doctrine advocating continued territorial expansion as the duty of the United States destined by Divine Providence, a doctrine popular in the U.S. by the time of the 1844 presidential campaign
Answer: Manifest Destiny.

1846—Year the Mexican War with the U.S. began
James K. Polk—U.S. President during this war
Texas—State whose annexation into the Union in 1845 led Mexico to break relations with the U.S.
Rio Grande—River this state claimed as its boundary with Mexico
John Slidell—Envoy who failed in an 1845 mission to Mexico to work out a deal for California and New Mexico and the western boundary of Texas at this river
Zachary Taylor—General the President sent to this river with 6,000 men, an "Army of Observation," to provoke the Mexicans into an attack
Nueces River—River 100 miles west of the site where Mexico attacked the U.S. "invaders" on April 25, 1846, leading the President to tell Congress that "Mexico has invaded our territory and shed American blood on American soil"—Congress declared war on May 13
Henry David Thoreau—Famous literary recluse arrested in 1846 and jailed in Concord for one night for refusing to pay a $1 poll tax because he believed the war an immoral advancement of slavery
Palo Alto—Name, meaning "Tall Timbers," given to the battle waged between Americans and Mexicans on a plain near the lower Rio Grande on May 8, 1846, a few days before Congress officially declared war
Brownsville*—Present-day Texas town near which both this battle and the May 9 Battle of Resaca de la Palma (or Resaca de Guerrero), took place, with U.S. forces defeating those of General Mariano Arista on both occasions
Bear Flag Revolt—June 14, 1846, revolt staged by Sacramento Valley settlers who wanted California to break away from Mexico
John Charles Frémont—American soldier and explorer in California who encouraged the American settlers to revolt against Mexican rule
Grizzly bear—Animal portrayed on the "California Republic" flag this soldier had the settlers raise after capturing Sonoma
Monterrey—Important battle fought September 21-24, 1846, in Mexico at which U.S. forces defeated the Mexicans
Santa Anna—Mexican general at the February 22-23, 1847, battle of Buena Vista defeated by the U.S. with a weakened force of 5,000 men
Vera Cruz—Port city on Mexico's east coast where a 9,000-man force made the first amphibious landing in American history on March 9, 1847, leading to its fall on March 29
Winfield Scott—U.S. general who made this amphibious landing to march on Mexico City
Cerro Gordo—Mountain pass—whose name means "big hill"—near Jalapa, where this general's forces attacked and defeated 13,000 Mexicans led by Santa Anna on April 17-18, 1847

*These victories enabled Taylor to cross the Rio Grande and occupy Matamoros and helped President Polk to induce Congress to declare war on Mexico on May 13.

Churubusco—Major victory of this general's forces on August 20, 1847, against 30,000 Mexicans after storming the fortified camp of Contreras

Chapultepec—Next-to-last battle of the Mexican War, fought by this general's forces on September 12-13, 1847

Los Niños—Mexican cadets who died at this September 12-13 battle defending the Mexican Military College, allowing the other defenders to retreat to the capital

Mexico City—Last battle of the war, fought September 13-14, 1847

National Palace—Palace in this city where a Marine cut down the Mexican flag and replaced it with the "Stars and Stripes" on September 14, 1847—the legendary "Hall(s) of Montezuma"

Abraham Lincoln—Whig representative from Illinois who in a December 1847 resolution questioned the legality of the start of the Mexican War and the "spot" where American blood was shed

Treaty of Guadalupe Hidalgo—Treaty ending the war, signed in a village near Mexico City on February 2, 1848

Nicholas Trist—U.S. negotiator who, although he had been recalled, stayed to sign the treaty that conformed to all of his original instructions

$15 million—Amount of money the U.S. paid for the territory it acquired

Mexican Cession**—Name given to this territory of 525,000 square miles comprising present-day California, Nevada, Utah, and parts of New Mexico, Arizona, Wyoming, and Colorado

Gadsden Purchase—Agreement of December 30, 1853, that enabled the South to claim a desired railroad route through what had been Mexican territory

Santa Anna—Mexican leader who agreed to the treaty

Franklin Pierce—American President who purchased for $10,000,000 the Mexican land needed for this southern railway route

Arizona and New Mexico—Two present-day U.S. states whose boundaries were expanded as part of this purchase

**Over a million square miles of new territory were added to American control during President Polk's administration from 1845 to 1849; only Jefferson had added more territory.

Spanish-American War

U.S. Secretary of State who near the end of the war said: "It has been a splendid little war"
Answer: John Hay.

Cuba—Country in which Spanish general Gen. Valeriano Weyler [y Nicolau], nicknamed "the Butcher," started an insurrection after herding farmers into concentration camps, prompting many Americans to call on the U.S. to intervene
William McKinley—U.S. President in office at the time of the war
Frederic(k) Sackrider Remington—Artist who was sent to Cuba by the New York *Journal* editor and allegedly filed the report: "Everything is quiet. There is no trouble here. There will be no war. Request to be recalled."
William Randolph Hearst—Editor of the New York *Journal* who supposedly replied to this newspaper artist: "Please remain. You furnish the pictures and I'll furnish the war."
Joseph Pulitzer—Editor of the New York *World* who also used sensationalism—called *yellow journalism*—to incite the public and attract readers
Enrique Dupuy de Lôme—Spanish minister in Washington whose private letter criticizing President McKinley was published by the *Journal* on February 9, while a U.S. ship was at anchor in the Havanna, Cuba, harbor—he resigned before he could be recalled by Spain
Maine*—U.S. ship that was sunk off Cuba's coast after being sent there to protect and evacuate Americans in case a conflict began—its sinking resulted in the loss of 260 officers and crew and its name completes the slogan: "Remember the _____! To hell with Spain!"
Havana—Harbor in which it was sunk
1898—Year this ship was sunk on February 15
112—Number of days this war lasted after being declared on April 24, retroactive to April 21
Theodore Roosevelt—Assistant secretary of the Navy who campaigned for war saying, "[The President] has no more backbone than a chocolate éclair!"
Teller Amendment—After the declaration of war against Spain on April 25, the amendment Congress adopted to grant Cubans their freedom once the Spanish were overthrown—it also stated that the U.S. would not annex Cuba
George Dewey—Commodore whom the assistant secretary of the navy sent to the Philippines in the event the war spread there
Manila Bay**—This commodore's easy May 1 victory over the Spanish fleet in the Philippines
Gridley—Name completing this commodore's statement, "You may fire when you are ready, _____," the surname of Captain Charles V. _____, commander of the flagship *Olympia* at the May 1, 1898, battle
Garcia—Name completing "Carry a message to _____," the now metaphorical May 1, 1898, order given to Lt. Major Andrew S. Rowan to get through the Spanish blockade into Cuba, deliver a message to this Cuban insurgent leader, and report back to Washington.
San Juan Hill—Hill captured along with Kettle Hill and up which Theodore Roosevelt led a charge on July 1

*No one today knows with certainty the cause of the explosion—the "yellow" journals of the time blamed it on the "enemy," but a 1975 inquiry headed by Adm. Hyman Rickover concluded the explosion was internal. **American troops arrived and captured Manila on August 13, 1898, with the help of Filipino leader Emilio Aguinaldo.

John J. Pershing—First Lieutenant, later nicknamed "Black Jack," who said after this battle: "White regiments, black regiments . . . fought shoulder to shoulder, unmindful of race or color . . . and mindful only of their common duty as Americans."

Rough Riders***—Name given to the horseless troops Teddy Roosevelt led in a charge up a hill at the July 1 battle—they were joined by the black 9th and 10th Regiments

Santiago Bay (Harbor)—July 3 battle in which ships under the direction of Rear Admiral William Sampson and Commodore Winfield S. Schley destroyed Admiral Cervera's fleet

Santiago—Cuban city that fell to General William Shafter's forces at the July 17 battle, just weeks after El Caney had fallen

Treaty of Paris—Peace treaty signed on December 10, 1898, officially ending the war and granting independence to Cuba, though the armistice had been signed on August 12, 1898—by the war's end, the U.S. had lost about 1,500 men to bullets and over 5,000 to tropical illnesses and to diseased food the troops called "embalmed beef"

Guam—Isolated Pacific island the U.S. captured from Spain during the war and then obtained through the treaty

Puerto Rico****—Caribbean island the U.S. also obtained through the treaty

Foraker Act—April 12, 1900, act establishing this Caribbean island as an unconsolidated U.S. territory

Philippines*****—Pacific island the U.S. obtained from Spain for $20 million under the terms of the treaty

***Also called "Teddy's Terrors" and "Wood's Weary Walkers" ****In 1917 the U.S. granted Puerto Ricans citizenship and more autonomy through the Jones Act; the Insular Cases, a group of Supreme Court cases between 1901 and 1904, defined the legal status of Puerto Rico. *****Filipino leader Aguinaldo, resentful that his country had not been given its freedom, began fighting Americans on February 4, 1899, and fought until captured in March 1901; the Philippine Insurrection ended by presidential proclamation on July 4, 1902, with provisions for a civil government.

U.S. PRESIDENTS

U.S. President who in 1881 said: "My God! What is there in this place [the White House] that a man should ever want to get into it?"
Answer: James A. Garfield.

PRESIDENTS AND THEIR VICE PRESIDENTS

	PRESIDENT	TERM	BIRTH STATE	PARTY	VICE PRESIDENT
1)	George Washington	1789-1797	VA	None*	John Adams
2)	John Adams	1797-1801	MA	Federalist	Thomas Jefferson
3)	Thomas Jefferson	1801-1809	VA	D-R**	Aaron Burr and George Clinton
4)	James Madison	1809-1817	VA	D-R	George Clinton (d. 1812) and Elbridge Gerry (d. 1814)
5)	James Monroe	1817-1825	VA	D-R	Daniel D. Tompkins
6)	John Quincy Adams	1825-1829	MA	D-R	John C. Calhoun
7)	Andrew Jackson	1829-1837	SC	Democratic	John C. Calhoun (resigned 1832) and Martin Van Buren
8)	Martin Van Buren	1837-1841	NY	Democratic	Richard M. Johnson
9)	William H. Harrison (d. 1841)	1841-1841	VA	Whig	John Tyler
10)	John Tyler	1841-1845	VA	Whig	
11)	James K. Polk	1845-1849	NC	Democratic	George M. Dallas
12)	Zachary Taylor (d. 1850)	1849-1850	VA	Whig	Millard Fillmore
13)	Millard Fillmore	1850-1853	NY	Whig	
14)	Franklin Pierce	1853-1857	NH	Democratic	William Rufus De Vane King (d. 1853)
15)	James Buchanan	1857-1861	PA	Democratic	John C. Breckinridge
16)	Abraham Lincoln (d. 1865)	1861-1865	KY	Republican, Union***	Hannibal Hamlin and Andrew Johnson
17)	Andrew Johnson	1865-1869	NC	Democratic, Union	
18)	Ulysses S. Grant	1869-1877	OH	Republican	Schuyler Colfax and Henry Wilson (d. 1875)
19)	Rutherford B. Hayes	1877-1881	OH	Republican	William A. Wheeler
20)	James A. Garfield (d. 1881)	1881-1881	OH	Republican	Chester A. Arthur
21)	Chester A. Arthur	1881-1885	VT	Republican	
22)	Grover Cleveland	1885-1889	NJ	Democratic	Thomas A. Hendricks (d. 1885)
23)	Benjamin Harrison	1889-1893	OH	Republican	Levi P. Morton
24)	Grover Cleveland	1893-1897	NJ	Democratic	Adlai E. Stevenson
25)	William McKinley (d. 1901)	1897-1901	OH	Republican	Garret A. Hobart (d. 1899) and Theodore Roosevelt
26)	Theodore Roosevelt	1901-1905	NY	Republican	
	Theodore Roosevelt	1905-1909			Charles W. Fairbanks
27)	William H. Taft	1909-1913	OH	Republican	James S. Sherman (d. 1912)
28)	Woodrow Wilson	1913-1921	VA	Democratic	Thomas R. Marshall
29)	Warren G. Harding (d. 1923)	1921-1923	OH	Republican	Calvin Coolidge
30)	Calvin Coolidge	1923-1925	VT	Republican	
	Calvin Coolidge	1925-1929			Charles G. Dawes
31)	Herbert C. Hoover	1929-1933	IO	Republican	Charles Curtis
32)	Franklin D. Roosevelt (d. 1945)	1933-1945	NY	Democratic	John N. Garner, Henry A. Wallace, and Harry S Truman
33)	Harry S Truman	1945-1949	MO	Democratic	
	Harry S Truman	1949-1953			Alben W. Barkley
34)	Dwight D. Eisenhower	1953-1961	TX	Republican	Richard M. Nixon
35)	John F. Kennedy (d. 1963)	1961-1963	MA	Democratic	Lyndon B. Johnson
36)	Lyndon B. Johnson	1963-1964	TX	Democratic	
	Lyndon B. Johnson	1964-1969			Hubert H. Humphrey
37)	Richard M. Nixon (resigned 1974)	1969-1974	CA	Republican	Spiro T. Agnew (resigned 1973) and Gerald R. Ford
38)	Gerald R. Ford	1974-1977	NE	Republican	Nelson A. Rockefeller
39)	James E. Carter Jr	1977-1981	GA	Democratic	Walter F. Mondale
40)	Ronald W. Reagan	1981-1989	IL	Republican	George H.W. Bush
41)	George H.W. Bush	1989-1993	MA	Republican	Dan Quayle
42)	William J. Clinton	1993-2001	AR	Democratic	Albert Gore
43)	George W. Bush	2001-	CT	Republican	Dick Cheney

*Sometimes he is listed as a Federalist for his 2nd term of office. **Democratic Republican ***The National Union Party (formed in 1864) consisted of Republicans and War Democrats.

PRESIDENTIAL NICKNAMES*

John Adams—Father of American Independence, His Rotundity, Old Sink or Swim
John Quincy Adams—John the Second, Old Man Eloquent
Chester A. Arthur—America's First Gentleman, Our Chet
James Buchanan—Bachelor President, Old Buck, Sage of Wheatland
George H.W. Bush—Liberator of Kuwait, Persian Gulf War President, Poppy
George W. Bush—Axis of Evil President, Compassionate-Conservative President, Iraqi Quagmire President
Jimmy Carter—Gentleman from Georgia, Peanut Farmer, Pious Jimmy
Grover Cleveland—Buffalo Hangman, Grover the Good
Bill Clinton—Comeback Kid, Slick Willie
Calvin Coolidge—Silent Cal, Sphinx of the Potomac
Dwight D. Eisenhower—Ike, Kansas Cyclone
Millard Fillmore—Accidental President, Last of the Whigs
Gerald R. Ford—Jerry, Mr. Clean, Mr. Nice Guy
James A. Garfield—Boatman Jim, Martyr President
Ulysses S. Grant—Hero of Appomattox, Hero of Fort Donelson, Unconditional Surrender
Warren G. Harding—Teapot Dome, Winnie, Wobbly Warren
Benjamin Harrison—Centennial President, Grandpa's Grandson
William Henry Harrison—First of the Whigs, Log Cabin and Hard-Cider Candidate, Tippecanoe
Rutherford B. Hayes—Fraud President, Old Eight to Seven
Herbert Hoover—Depression President, Great Humanitarian, Quaker Engineer
John F. Kennedy—Jack, Man of the New Frontier, That Wit in the White House
Andrew Jackson—Hero of New Orleans, Old Hickory, Sage of the Hermitage
Thomas Jefferson—Father of the Declaration of Independence, Sage of Monticello
Andrew Johnson—Man Without a Party, Tennessee Tailor
Lyndon B. Johnson—Big Daddy, Colonel Cornpone, Landslide Lyndon
Abraham Lincoln—Great Emancipator, Honest Abe, Martyr President
James Madison—Father of the Constitution, Sage of Montpelier
William McKinley—High Priest of Protective Tariffs, Wobbly Willie
James Monroe—Era of Good Feeling President, Last of the Cocked Hats
Richard M. Nixon—Gloomy Gus, Tarnished President, Tricky Dick(y)
Franklin Pierce—(Second) Dark Horse President, Handsome Frank
James K. Polk—First Dark Horse, Young Hickory
Ronald Reagan—Dutch, Great Communicator, Teflon President
Franklin D. Roosevelt—Champion of the Four Freedoms, Fireside Chatterer, New Deal Caesar
Theodore Roosevelt—Cowboy President, Hero of San Juan Hill, Rough Rider
William Howard Taft—Big Bill, Big Chief, Good Old Will
Zachary Taylor—Hero of Buena Vista, Old Rough and Ready
Harry S Truman—Fair Deal President, Man From Independence, (Little) Man From Missouri
John Tyler—Young Hickory, Young Tippecanoe
Martin Van Buren—Little Magician, Little Van, Sage of Kinderhook
George Washington—Father of His Country, Old Fox, Sage of Mount Vernon
Woodrow Wilson—The Professor in Politics, The Schoolmaster, Woody

*See many more presidential nicknames in *Campbell's High School/College Book of Lists*

PRESIDENTIAL QUOTATIONS*
(Some are alleged)

John Adams—"Thomas Jefferson still survives" (1826)

James Buchanan—"If I withdraw Anderson from Sumter, I can travel home to Wheatland by the light of my own burning effigies" (1861)

George H.W. Bush—"The Congress will push me to raise taxes, and I'll say no, and they'll push, and I'll say no, and they'll push again. And all I can say to them is read my lips: No New Taxes" (1988); "A line has been drawn in the sand" (1990)

George W. Bush—"Our grief has turned to anger, and anger to resolution. Whether we bring our enemies to justice, or bring justice to our enemies, justice will be done [following 9/11 attacks]" (2001); "Year after year Saddam Hussein has gone to elaborate lengths, spent enormous sums, taken great risks to build and keep WMD" (2003)

Jimmy Carter—"If I ever tell a lie, if I ever mislead you, if I ever betray a trust or a confidence, I want you to come and take me out of the White House" (1976)

Grover Cleveland—"If it takes the entire army and navy of the United States to deliver a postal card in Chicago, that card will be delivered" (1894)

William J. Clinton—"I feel your pain" (1992); "I am going to say this again: I did not have sexual relations with that woman, Ms. Lewinsky. I never told anybody to lie, not a single time. Never. These allegations are false and I need to go back to work for the American people" (1998)

Calvin Coolidge—"The chief business of America is business" (1925); "If you don't say anything, you won't be called on to repeat it" (1928)

Dwight D. Eisenhower—"People of Western Europe: A landing was made . . . on the coast of France by the troops of the Allied Expeditionary Force. . . . I call upon all who love freedom to stand with us now. Together we shall achieve victory" (1944); "I shall go to Korea" (1952)

Gerald R. Ford—"I am a Ford, not a Lincoln" (1973); "Our long national nightmare [Watergate scandal] is over" (1974)

Ulysses S. Grant—"No terms except an unconditional and immediate surrender can be accepted. I propose to move immediately upon your works [Fort Donelson]" (1862); "The war is over—the Rebels are our countrymen again" (1865)

Herbert Hoover—"The slogan of Progress is changing from the 'Full Dinner Pail' to the full garage" (1928)

Andrew Jackson—"By the Eternal, they [the British] shall not sleep on our soil" (1815)

Thomas Jefferson—"We hold these truths to be self-evident: that all men are created equal, that they are endowed by their Creator with certain unalienable rights, that among these are life, liberty, and the pursuit of happiness" (1776)

Andrew Johnson—"I cannot understand how he [Jefferson Davis] can be willing to hail another banner, and turn from that of his country"

Lyndon B. Johnson—"Come now, let us reason together" (1963); "This nation, this generation, in this hour has man's first chance to build a Great Society, a place where the meaning of man's life matches the marvels of man's labor. . . . This administration, here and now, declares unconditional war on poverty in America" (1964)

John F. Kennedy—"The New Frontier of which I speak is not a set of promises—it is a set of challenges. It sums up not what I intend to offer the American people, but what I intend to ask of them" (1960); "And so, my fellow Americans, ask not what your country can do for you; ask what you can do for your country" (1961)

*See many more presidential quotations in *Campbell's High School/College Book of Lists*

Abraham Lincoln—"A house divided against itself cannot stand. I believe this government cannot endure permanently half-slave and half-free" (1858); "My paramount object in this struggle is to save the Union, and is not either to save or to destroy slavery. If I could save the Union without freeing any slave, I would do it; and if I could save it by freeing all the slaves, I would do it; and if I could do it by freeing some and leaving others alone, I would also do that" (1862)

William McKinley—"I have already transmitted to Congress the report of the naval court of inquiry on the destruction of the battleship *Maine*. . . . The destruction of that noble vessel has filled the national heart with inexpressible horror" (1898)

James Monroe—"The American continents . . . are henceforth not to be considered as subjects for future colonization by any European powers" (1823)

Richard M. Nixon—"I want you all to stonewall it, let them plead the Fifth Amendment, cover up or anything else, if it'll save it, save the plan" (1973)

James K. Polk—"The cup of forbearance has been exhausted. . . . After reiterated menaces, Mexico has passed the boundary of the United States, has invaded our territory and shed American blood on American soil" (1846)

Ronald W. Reagan—"Honey, I forgot to duck [during assassination attempt]" (1981); "Mr. Gorbachev, if you seek peace, come here to this gate! Mr. Gorbachev, open this gate! Mr. Gorbachev, tear down this wall!" (1987)

Franklin D. Roosevelt—"I pledge you, I pledge myself, to a new deal for the American people" (1932); "So, first of all, let me assert my firm belief that the only thing we have to fear is fear itself—nameless, unreasoning, unjustified terror" (1933)

Theodore Roosevelt—"There is a homely adage which runs, 'Speak softly and carry a big stick; you will go far'. If the American nation will speak softly and yet build and keep at a pitch of the highest training a thoroughly efficient navy, the Monroe Doctrine will go far" (1901)

Zachary Taylor—"Tell him [Santa Anna] to go to hell. . . . General _____ never surrenders" (1847)

Harry S Truman—"Sixteen hours ago an American plane dropped one bomb on Hiroshima. . . . The force from which the sun draws its powers has been loosed against those who brought war to the Far East" (1945)

George Washington—"It is our true policy to steer clear of permanent alliances with any portion of the foreign world" (1796)

Woodrow Wilson—"It must be peace without victory. . . . Victory would mean peace forced upon the loser, a victor's terms imposed upon the vanquished. . . . Only a peace between equals can last" (1917); "The world must be made safe for democracy" (1917)

PRESIDENTIAL FIRSTS

George W. Bush—First President to receive $400,000 in salary
John Adams—First to live in the White House
Andrew Jackson—First presidential candidate to be named by a national nominating convention
William H. Taft—First in office with 48 states, in 1912 when Arizona joined the Union
Woodrow Wilson—First to earn a doctoral degree (from Johns Hopkins, in 1886)
Thomas Jefferson—First to be elected by the House of Representatives
William Henry Harrison—First to die in office (April 4, 1841)
James K. Polk—First "dark horse" presidential candidate to be elected
George Washington—First without a college education

U.S. PRESIDENTS

Martin Van Buren—First born a U.S. citizen and not a British subject
Abraham Lincoln—First to be born in the U.S. but not in the 13 original states—he was born in Kentucky
Lyndon B. Johnson—First to be sworn in on an airplane and the first sworn in by a woman
Richard M. Nixon—First to visit China
Theodore Roosevelt—First to travel outside the U.S. (to Panama)
Warren Harding—First to have a cabinet member (Albert B. Fall) convicted and sent to prison
Dwight D. Eisenhower—First Republican in the 20th century to serve 2 full terms
Calvin Coolidge—First to be sworn in by his father
Abraham Lincoln—First to be assassinated
Herbert Hoover—First born west of the Mississippi (in Iowa)
Franklin D. Roosevelt—First to take office on January 20 (1937)
Harry S Truman—First to take office during a war
Gerald R. Ford—First to serve as Vice President and President without being elected to either office
George H.W. Bush—First incumbent vice president to be elected President since Martin Van Buren in 1836
Andrew Johnson—First to be impeached (he was acquitted)
John Tyler—First Vice President to succeed to the presidency upon the death of the President
Ulysses S. Grant—First West Point graduate to become President
Chester A. Arthur—First one to walk across the Brooklyn Bridge (doing so when it was officially opened on May 24, 1883)
Ronald Reagan—First one to have been head of a union (the Screen Actors Guild)
George W. Bush—First one to attend a papal funeral, that of John Paul II in 2005

PRESIDENTIAL ONLYS, SECONDS, AND LASTS
James Madison—Only President to live temporarily in the Octagon House
John F. Kennedy—Only one to win a Pulitzer Prize (in 1956 for *Profiles in Courage*)
Jimmy Carter—Only one to have graduated from the U.S. Naval Academy
Grover Cleveland—Only one to serve 2 nonconsecutive terms
Franklin Pierce—Only President to affirm his oath rather than swear to it
Benjamin Harrison—Only one preceded and succeeded by the same man
James Buchanan—Only one to remain a bachelor
Rutherford B. Hayes—Only one to win the election by one electoral vote
James A. Garfield—Second to be assassinated
Bill Clinton—Second to be impeached (he was acquitted)
John Quincy Adams—Second to be elected by the House of Representatives
William McKinley—Last to have served in the Civil War
Zachary Taylor—Last Whig to be elected President
Millard Fillmore—Last Whig to serve as President
James Monroe—Last of the so-called "Virginia Dynasty"
James A. Garfield—Last one to be born in a log cabin
Herbert Hoover—Last "lame duck" President or the last one whose term of office ended on March 3
Woodrow Wilson—Last one listed alphabetically
Harry Truman—Only one whose temporary official residence was the Blair House
William Howard Taft—Only one to serve as both President and Chief Justice of the U.S.

MIDDLE NAMES OF PRESIDENTS

Quincy—John _____ Adams
Henry—William _____ Harrison
Knox—James _____ Polk
Simpson—Ulysses _____ Grant
Birchard—Rutherford _____ Hayes
Abram—James _____ Garfield
Alan—Chester _____ Arthur
Howard—William _____ Taft
Gamaliel—Warren _____ Harding
Clark—Herbert _____ Hoover
Delano—Franklin _____ Roosevelt
S*—Harry _____ Truman
David—Dwight _____ Eisenhower
Fitzgerald—John _____ Kennedy
Baines—Lyndon _____ Johnson
Milhous—Richard _____ Nixon
Rudolph—Gerald _____ Ford
Earl—James _____ Carter
Wilson—Ronald _____ Reagan
Herbert Walker—George _____ Bush
Jefferson—William _____ Clinton
Walker—George _____ Bush

*Even though Truman often placed a period after the S when he signed his name, technically there is no period because the S is not an abbreviation; he chose the initial so as not to show any favoritism to his grandfathers, named Anderson *Shippe* Truman and *Solomon* Young.

PRESIDENTS AND THEIR MONOGRAMS

John Quincy Adams—JQA
William Henry Harrison—WHH
James Knox Polk—JKP
Ulysses Simpson Grant*—USG
Rutherford Birchard Hayes—RBH
James Abram Garfield—JAG
Chester Alan Arthur—CAA
Stephen Grover Cleveland**—SGC
William Howard Taft—WHT
Thomas Woodrow Wilson***—TWW
Warren Gamaliel Harding—WGH
John Calvin Coolidge****—JCC
Herbert Clark Hoover—HCH
Franklin Delano Roosevelt—FDR
Harry S Truman—HST
Dwight David Eisenhower—DDE
John Fitzgerald Kennedy—JFK
Lyndon Baines Johnson—LBJ
Richard Milhous Nixon—RMN
Gerald Rudolph Ford*****—GRF
James Earl Carter—JEC
Ronald Wilson Reagan—RWR
George Herbert Walker Bush—GHWB
William Jefferson Clinton******—WJC
George Walker Bush—GWB

*He was named Hiram Ulysses Grant at birth, but not liking HUG as his initials, he changed it to Ulysses Hiram Grant, then later adopted his current name Ulysses Simpson Grant after it was accidentally changed to this when he applied for an appointment to West Point. **Cleveland dropped the name Stephen in his youth. ***Wilson dropped the name Thomas soon after he graduated from college. ****Coolidge dropped the name John after leaving college. *****Born Leslie Lynch King Jr. ******Born William Jefferson Blythe IV

PRESIDENTIAL MATRICULATIONS

1) Identify the 9 Presidents who did not attend college.
   Answer: George Washington, Andrew Jackson, Martin Van Buren, Zachary Taylor, Millard Fillmore, Abraham Lincoln, Andrew Johnson, Grover Cleveland, and Harry S Truman.

2) Identify the 5 Presidents who earned their undergraduate degrees at Harvard.
   Answer: John Adams, John Quincy Adams, Theodore Roosevelt, Franklin Roosevelt, and John Kennedy.

3) Name the Presidents who ran against each other in what came to be called the "Big Three" election of 1912 because they all had graduated from "Big Three" football powers—one from Harvard in 1880, another from Yale in 1878, and the third from Princeton in 1879.
   Answer: Theodore Roosevelt, William Howard Taft, and Woodrow Wilson, respectively.

4) Identify the 3 Presidents who graduated from William and Mary College—the 3rd, 5th, and 10th.
   Answer: Thomas Jefferson, James Monroe, and John Tyler.

U.S. PRESIDENTS 127

5) Identify the 3 Presidents who not only earned their undergraduate degrees at Yale but were also members of Skull and Bones, a secret society.
Answer: William Howard Taft, George H.W. Bush, and George W. Bush.

6) Identify the 2 Presidents who received law degrees from the Yale University Law School.
Answer: Gerald Ford and Bill Clinton.

7) At what 3 colleges did President Jimmy Carter do his undergraduate work?
Answer: Georgia Southwestern College (in Americus), Georgia Tech (in Atlanta), and the U.S. Naval Academy (in Annapolis, Maryland, from which he graduated).

8) Identify the 2 Presidents who graduated from the U.S. Military Academy.
Answer: Ulysses S. Grant and Dwight D. Eisenhower.

9) Identify the 2 Presidents who graduated from Princeton University.
Answer: James Madison and Woodrow Wilson.

OTHER PRESIDENTS AND THEIR COLLEGES

William H. Harrison—Hampden Sydney*
James K. Polk—North Carolina
Franklin Pierce—Bowdoin
James Buchanan—Dickinson
Rutherford B. Hayes—Kenyon
James A. Garfield—Williams
Chester A. Arthur—Union

Benjamin Harrison—Miami of Ohio
William McKinley—Allegheny*
Warren G. Harding—Ohio Central*
Calvin Coolidge—Amherst
Lyndon B. Johnson—Southwest Texas State
William J. Clinton—Georgetown

*Left before graduation

PRESIDENTS AND COLLEGE SPORTS

George H.W. Bush—Baseball at Yale
George W. Bush—Cheerleader at Yale
Jimmy Carter—Cross-country at the U.S. Naval Academy
Dwight D. Eisenhower—Football at the U.S. Military Academy at West Point
Gerald Ford—Football at the University of Michigan
John F. Kennedy—Swimming at Harvard
Richard Nixon—Football at Whittier College
Ronald Reagan—Football, track, and swimming at Eureka College

PRESIDENTS AND ACADEMIA

George W. Bush—First President with an M.B.A., from Harvard in 1975
Dwight Eisenhower—One who served as president of Columbia
James A. Garfield—First President to be a college president, at Western Reserve Eclectic Institute
Warren Harding—First one since the Civil War to speak in the South for the rights of blacks, doing so while accepting an honorary degree at the University of Alabama in 1921
Rutherford B. Hayes—First one whose wife had a college degree, from the Wesleyan Female College in Cincinnati
Herbert Hoover—One with an engineering degree from Stanford
Andrew Jackson—First since George Washington not to attend college—he was born in a log cabin located on the boundary between North and South Carolina

Thomas Jefferson—One known as the "Founder of the University of Virginia"
Richard Nixon—One who attended Duke University Law School, graduating in 1937
Harry S Truman—Only one in the 20th century who never attended college and the last one without a college degree
Woodrow Wilson—First one to earn a doctoral degree, from Johns Hopkins, in 1886; the first one to be president of a major university, Princeton; and the only one to teach at a women's college, Bryn Mawr

QUESTIONS ON PRESIDENTS

1) Name the 4 presidential monuments in the nation's capital.
Answer: Washington Monument, Jefferson Memorial, Lincoln Memorial, and Franklin Delano Roosevelt Memorial.

2) Five of the first 7 Presidents served 8 consecutive years in office. Name these 5.
Answer: George Washington, Thomas Jefferson, James Madison, James Monroe, and Andrew Jackson.

3) Name the 3 successive Presidents from Virginia known as the "Virginia Dynasty."
Answer: Thomas Jefferson, James Madison, and James Monroe.

4) Name the only 4 Vice Presidents to succeed to the presidency by being elected to that post and not because of the death or resignation of the President.
Answer: John Adams, Thomas Jefferson, Martin Van Buren, and George H.W. Bush.

5) Which 3 Presidents died on a July 4, two in the same year and one 5 years later?
Answer: John Adams (1826), Thomas Jefferson (1826), and James Monroe (1831; Calvin Coolidge was the only President born on a July 4).

6) Identify the 4 Whig Presidents.
Answer: William Henry Harrison, John Tyler, Zachary Taylor, and Millard Fillmore (Tyler took office upon Harrison's death, and Fillmore, upon Taylor's death; Tyler took office as a Whig even though he opposed the policies of a national bank and protective tariffs the Whigs favored).

7) Name the 3 Presidents who held office during 1841.
Answer: Martin Van Buren, William Henry Harrison, and John Tyler.

8) Name the 3 Presidents who held office during 1881.
Answer: Rutherford B. Hayes, James A. Garfield, and Chester A. Arthur.

9) Name the 4 Presidents born in Massachusetts.
Answer: John Adams, John Quincy Adams, John Kennedy, and George H.W. Bush.

10) Which 4 Presidents have been assassinated?
Answer: Abraham Lincoln (1865), James Garfield (1881), William McKinley (1901), and John Kennedy (1963).

11) Name the 4 men who assassinated these Presidents.
Answer: John Wilkes Booth (Abraham Lincoln); Charles Guiteau (James Garfield); Leon Czolgosz (William McKinley); and Lee Harvey Oswald (John Kennedy).

12) Identify the 3 cities in which the 4 Presidents were assassinated.
Answer: Washington, D.C. (Abraham Lincoln in 1865 and James Garfield in 1881); Buffalo, New York (William McKinley in 1901); and Dallas, Texas (John Kennedy in 1963).

13) Name the 4 Vice Presidents to become President upon the assassination of the President.
Answer: Andrew Johnson (Lincoln), Chester A. Arthur (Garfield), Theodore Roosevelt (McKinley), and Lyndon Johnson (Kennedy).

14) Identify the 4 Republican Presidents who died in office.
Answer: Abraham Lincoln, James A. Garfield, William McKinley, and Warren G. Harding.

15) Name the 4 Presidents to die a natural death in office.
Answer: William H. Harrison, Zachary Taylor, Warren G. Harding (as far as it can be determined; some think his wife poisoned him), and Franklin D. Roosevelt.

16) Identify the only 3 Republican Presidents to serve 2 full terms.
Answer: Ulysses S. Grant, Dwight D. Eisenhower, and Ronald Reagan.

17) Name the 5 Democratic Presidents who served at least 2 full terms.
Answer: Andrew Jackson, Grover Cleveland, Woodrow Wilson, Franklin Roosevelt (elected to 4 and served 3 full terms), and Bill Clinton.

18) From 1840 to 1960, all Presidents elected in a year ending with 0 died in office. Name these 7.
Answer: William Henry Harrison (1840); Abraham Lincoln (1860); James A. Garfield (1880); William McKinley (1900); Warren G. Harding (1920); Franklin D. Roosevelt (1940); and John F. Kennedy (1960; Ronald Reagan, elected in 1980, survived an assassination attempt).

PRESIDENTIAL/VICE PRESIDENTIAL TWOS

John C. Calhoun and Spiro Agnew—2 Vice Presidents to resign the office
Andrew Johnson and Bill Clinton—2 Presidents to be impeached, although neither was removed from office
Adams and Bush*—2 pairs of Presidents who share both a first and a last name
Andrew Jackson and William Henry Harrison—2 Presidents who, prior to their election, had won military fame during the War of 1812
Harry S Truman and Dwight Eisenhower—2 Presidents who had served in the military during WWI
Virginia and Massachusetts—2 states that fathered the first 6 Presidents
Ronald Reagan (69) and William Henry Harrison (68)—2 oldest men ever sworn in as Presidents

*John Adams and John Quincy Adams and George H.W. Bush and George W. Bush

Ronald Reagan (77) and Dwight Eisenhower (70)—2 oldest men to serve as President

James Monroe and James Madison—2 Presidents named James who served 2 full terms

John F. Kennedy and Richard M. Nixon—2 presidential candidates who took part in the first TV campaign debate

Abraham Lincoln and George Washington—2 Presidents specifically remembered on Presidents' Day because their birthdays fall in February—the 12th and 22nd, respectively

William H. Taft and John Kennedy—2 Presidents buried in Arlington National Cemetery

Thomas Jefferson and John Quincy Adams—2 Presidents elected by the House of Representatives, in 1800 and in 1824, respectively

John Adams and Thomas Jefferson—First 2 sitting Vice Presidents to become President

Warren Harding and John Kennedy—Only 2 sitting senators to become President

Thomas Jefferson and James Madison—First 2 consecutive Presidents from the same state

John Adams and John Quincy Adams—First 2 Presidents to serve just one term each

George Washington and Ulysses S. Grant—First 2 military men in U.S. history, both future Presidents, to hold the rank of full general

Martin Van Buren and John Tyler—8th and 10th Vice Presidents who became the 8th and 10th Presidents

Harry S Truman and Dwight Eisenhower—2 Presidents in office during the Korean War

Theodore Roosevelt (42) and John Kennedy (43)—2 youngest Presidents, both of whom served in the 20th century

William Henry Harrison and Benjamin Harrison—2 Presidents related as grandfather and grandson

William Henry Harrison and James A. Garfield**—2 Presidents who served the least amount of time in office

FDR and John Kennedy—2 Democratic Presidents to die in office

**Harrison, 31 days in 1841, and Garfield, 6½ months in 1881

R<small>ED</small>, W<small>HITE</small>, A<small>ND</small> B<small>LUE</small>

Word completing the phrase *to _____ red, white, and blue*, describing someone as a very patriotic American
Answer: *Bleed*.

Cheers—Word completing the line "Three _____ for the red, white, and blue" in the patriotic song "O Columbia, the Gem of the Ocean"
Chile—South American country whose blue, white, and red flag was adopted by the government of Bernardo O'Higgins
Costa Rica—Central American country whose blue, white, and red flag was designed by the country's first lady in 1848
Croatia—European country whose red, white, and blue flag was adopted in 1848, though its flag had a red star in the center as part of the Federation of Yugoslavia
Cuba—Only Communist state in the Americas whose red, white, and blue was modeled on the Stars and Stripes of the U.S.
Czech Republic—European country whose white, blue, and red stripes on its flag represent Bohemia, Moravia, and Slovakia, respectively
France—European country whose blue, white, and red flag is known as *le tricolore*, or the *tricolor*
Liberia—African country whose red, white, and blue flag with a lone star is quite similar to the U.S. flag
Luxembourg—Grand Duchy whose red, white, and blue flag was first used in 1228
Malaysia—Asian country whose red, white, and blue flag called the *Jalur Gemilang*, or "Glorious Stripes," resembles the U.S.'s but has a yellow crescent and star
Montreal Candiens—NHL team known as "*le bleu-blanc-rouge*" and "*le Tricolore*"
Nellie Melba—Australian soprano who said, "Music is not written in red, white, and blue. It is written in the heart's blood of the composer."
Netherlands—European country whose red, white, and blue flag derives from the orange, white, and blue flag of Prince William I of Orange
Norway—Scandinavian country whose flag with a cross has the red, white, and blue of the French *tricolore*
Georgia O'Keeffe—20th-century artist with a museum dedicated to her work in Santa Fe and especially known for her painting *Cow's Skull: Red, White, and Blue*
Paraguay—South American country whose red, white, and blue flag is based on the French *tricolore*
Red, White and Blue—Susan Isaacs' novel about immigrant Herschel Blaustein, Dora Schottland, and their descendants
Russia—European/Asian country whose white, blue, and red flag was adopted in 1991 and modified in 1993
Slovak Republic—European country that has white, blue, and red stripes on its flag and was part of Czechoslovakia from 1919 to 1991
Slovenia—European country whose flag with red, white, and blue stripes was based on the flag of the Duchy of Carniola
Thailand—Asian country whose red, white, and blue flag is called the *trairanga* or tricolor
United States—Country whose red, white, and blue flag was designed in 1776

Yugoslavia—European country that now consists of Serbia and Montenegro and uses the blue, white, and red flag that was the flag of the Kingdom of Serbs, Croats, and Slovenes from 1918 to 1929

RED, WHITE, OR BLUE

Red—Communist, or having to do with the former Soviet Union or any other Communist country
Blue—Sad, gloomy, cheerless, dreary
White—Symbol of purity and goodness
Blue—Great or extreme
White—Lacking color
Red—Political revolutionary
White—Spiritually pure and innocent
Blue—Union soldier
White—Harmless or lacking evil design
Red—Having a flushed color
The Blue—The sky or the sea
White—Counterrevolutionary, ultraconservative
White (space)—Blank space in printing
Red—Bloodshot, inflamed
White—Honest, decent, or trustworthy
Blue—Person representing Oxford or Cambridge in a sport
White—Color containing all the visible rays of the spectrum
Blue—Strict in morals or religion, puritanical
White—Pale, pallid, or ashen
Blue—Improper, risqué, or indecent
White—Caucasian
White—Albumen surrounding the yolk of an egg
Reds—Nickname for the Communists, or Bolsheviks, in the former Soviet Union because of the color of the national flag
(The) Blues—Low spirits, dejection, depressed unhappy feeling
Red (Army)—Army of the Soviet Union
White—Outermost ring of a target in archery
Red—Color refracted the least when a beam of white light passes obliquely from air into a glass prism
Blue—Color of the hot flame produced by a Bunsen burner

RED

1950's campaign whose slogan was "Better red than dead."
Answer: Nuclear disarmament campaign.

1-WORD REDS

Redbait—To denounce or accuse someone as being Communist, especially without any evidence
Redball (red ball)—Fast freight train
Red-blooded—Hyphenated adjective meaning "full or life"
Redbreast—An American robin
Redbreasted sapsucker—North American sapsucker found on the Pacific coast
Redbrick—Term used in Britain for any university other than Oxford and Cambridge
Redcap—Railroad or bus station porter
Redcoats—British soldiers during the Revolutionary War because they wore bright red jackets
Red-eye (redeye)—Late-night commercial flight; cheap, strong whiskey; or a railroad danger signal
Red-faced—Very embarrassed
Red-hot—Very hot, excited, or angered
(To) redline—To cancel something; to set the limit on the speed of an airplane; to deny a home mortgage to those considered poor financial risks

Redneck—Poor, white, rural Southerner, usually considered to be bigoted and intolerant, from the sunburned area of the body acquired by working in the fields in the South

(To) red-pencil—To revise as when editing

(To) redshirt—To hold back an athlete from a year of competition in order to extend his eligibility and the practice of delaying a child's entry into kindergarten, etc., for reasons of immaturity or to improve the child's school performance

Redskin—Pejorative for an American Indian, one derived from Red Indian

Redwood—Sequoia sempervirens, the world's tallest living tree, found on the U.S. West Coast

2-WORD REDS

Red admiral—Purplish-black butterfly having white spots and bright-orange or red bands

Red alert—Imminent danger warning

Red carpet—Material for royalty and other dignitaries to walk on during a formal reception

Red clay—Reddish-brown mud found on ocean bottoms

Red dog—Lowest grade of flour from milling; card game of chance using only 3 cards at a time; or to blitz the quarterback in football

Red dwarf—Faint star in the main-sequence group having cooler temperatures and lesser luminosity than the others

Red fire—Combustible compound such as salts of lithium or strontium used in fireworks

Red flag—Symbol of revolution, a sign of danger, and figuratively, anything that incites anger

Red giant—Star with great size and brightness and with a relatively low surface temperature

Red hat—Rank of cardinal in the Roman Catholic Church

Red heat—Condition of being red-hot

Red herring—Something introduced in order to draw someone's attention away from the situation at hand

Red-hot mama—Slang phrase for a pretty, sexy, affectionate female, or a sexually exciting woman

Red hots—Another name for frankfurters besides *hot dogs* and *wieners*

Red ink—Financial loss

Red light—Any danger or warning sign, such as one at an intersection

Red-light district—Area known for its brothels

Red line—Ice hockey boundary dividing the rink into 2 spheres

Red rag—Something that causes great anger

Red ribbon—Second place prize in a competition

Red shift—Movement in the light of stars toward the longer wavelength end of the spectrum, indicating movement outward at increasing speed

Red tape—Obstructive paperwork and procedures of some government departments, or something complicated

Red tide—Bloom of toxic algae that spreads on the surface of seawater

Red zone—Area between the 20-yard line and goal line on a football field, as used when the opponent's line of scrimmage is at or inside the 20-yard line

RED IDIOMS

Beet(root)—Vegetable whose name completes the simile *as red as a* _____

Bull—Animal whose name completes the simile *like a red flag to a* _____

(To) catch (nab) red-handed—To discover someone in the act of doing something illegal

(To be) in the red—In debt

Lobster*—Crustacean whose name completes the simile *as red as a* _____

*Other similes are *as red as a cherry, as red as a poppy, as red as a rose, as red as a ruby,* and *as red as blood*

Not worth a red cent**—Worthless

(To be) out of the red—Showing a profit

(To) paint the town red—To carouse or to go on a spree

Red carpet treatment—Especially good treatment or the floor covering put down during an official visit of an important or royal person

(To be) red in the face—To be embarrassed

Red letter day—A memorable day or event

Red Queen's race—Running at a very fast pace but remaining in the exact spot where you began, as derived from *Through the Looking Glass*

(To) roll out the red carpet—To treat in a royal manner

(To) see red—To be very angry

(To) see the red light—To see potential danger in the future

Thin red line—Small group of brave people that defend and refuse to surrender, as derived from the defensive line of British troops wearing scarlet uniforms in the Crimean War

(To) wave the red flag—To incite violence

**Or *to not have a red cent*

GEOGRAPHY REDS

Alabama—Tuscaloosa university whose athletic teams are called "The Crimson Tide" and "The Red Elephants"

Alhambra—Palace and fortress built in Grenada, Spain, by the Moors between 1248 and 1354, whose name means "Red or Crimson Castle"

Alpine—Red or green soft felt hat decorated with a feather, named after the Alps where Swiss guides and others wear them

Baton Rouge—U.S. state capital whose name means "Red Stick" in French

Birmingham—Alabama city in which the Statue of the Roman god Vulcan is located on Red Mountain

Boston Red Sox—Team for which Babe Ruth played in his first major league game

China—Country in which the Red River rises before flowing through Vietnam and emptying into the Gulf of Tonkin

Cincinnati Reds—Major League baseball team of the 1970s known as "The Big Red Machine"

Colgate University—Hamilton, New York, university whose athletic teams were once called "The Red Raiders" and now just the "Raiders"

Colorado—U.S. state whose Spanish name means "reddish" or "reddish-brown"

Colorado River—U.S. river whose Spanish name means the "red river"

Cornell University—Ithaca, New York, university whose athletic teams are called "The Big Red"

Detroit Red Wings—NHL team that plays its home games in the Joe Louis Arena

Eureka College—Illinois college whose athletic teams are nicknamed the "Red Devils" and from which Ronald Reagan graduated

Huntsville—Alabama city near which the Redstone Arsenal, the rocket and guided-missile center of the U.S. Army, is located

Lansing (Michigan)—Capital located at the junction of the Grand, Red Cedar, and Sycamore rivers

Louisville—Kentucky university whose athletic teams are called "The Cardinals" and "The Red Rage"

Manchester United—English soccer team nicknamed the "Red Devils" and based in Old Trafford

Manitoba—Present-day Canadian province where the Red River Rebellion took place in 1869 and 1870

Miami University—Oxford, Ohio, university whose athletic teams are called "The RedHawks"
Minnesota—State whose border with North Dakota is formed by the Red River of the North as it flows north to Canada before emptying into Lake Winnipeg
Moscow—World capital known for its Red Square
Oklahoma—State whose Indian name means "The Land of the Red Men"
Oklahoma City—2nd largest U.S. state capital in land area, whose name is derived from Indian words meaning "red people"
Paris—European capital in which Danny the Red led street riots in 1968
Red Sea* —Body of water located between NE Africa and the Arabian Peninsula that, according to the Bible, God parted to enable the Israelites to escape from Egypt; named *Mare rubrum* by the Romans
Red Stockings—Cincinnati's first professional baseball team
Redwood National Park—California national park in which the Tall Trees Grove is located
Rhode Island—U.S. state whose name is in part from the Dutch for "red"
Rhode Island Red—Breed of domestic chicken raised for its meat, named after a small Atlantic coast state
Rocky Mountains—Mountains in which the Red Deer River rises in southwest Alberta, Canada, from which it flows about 385 miles into Saskatchewan
St. John's—Jamaica, New York, university whose athletic teams are called "The Red Storm"
Texas—State in which the Red River rises and forms part of the border with Oklahoma
Texas Tech—Lubbock, Texas, university whose athletic teams are called "The Red Raiders"
Tibet—Autonomous region known for its Potala Palace, which includes the Red Palace (Potrang Marpo), a building devoted to religion
Ulaanbaatar (Ulan Bator)—Capital of Mongolia, whose name means "Red Hero"
Washington Redskins—NFL team Doug Williams quarterbacked to a Super Bowl win in 1988

*Because the Hebrew text says "sea of reeds," most scholars believe this body of water was really the marshy land well north of the Red Sea.

HOMO SAPIENS REDS

Paul N. Adair—Famous oil-well fighter nicknamed "Red" or "Texas Red"
Arnold Auerbach—Boston Celtics coach known as "Red" whose teams won 8 straight NBA titles
Barbarossa—16th-century Greek-Ottoman pirate born Khayr al-Din, known as "Redbeard"
Walter Barber—Baseball play-by-play commentator known as "Red" and "the Old Redhead"
Clara Bow—Actress known as "The It Girl" and "The Red Head"
Red Buttons—Comedian born Aaron Chwatt, known for his "Ho-Ho" song
Caryl Chessman—"Red-Light Bandit" who was executed in the gas chamber at San Quentin in 1960
Calvin Coolidge—30th U.S. President called "Red"
John Dillinger—"Public Enemy No. 1" shot and killed by FBI agents on July 22, 1934, at the Biograph movie theater in Chicago, after allegedly being betrayed by the "Lady (Woman) in Red"
Eric the Red* —Viking who colonized Greenland about A.D. 985
Frederick I—German king and Holy Roman Emperor from 1152-1190 known as "Barbarossa" or "Red Beard"
Arthur Godfrey—TV host and entertainer known as "Red" and "Old Redhead" who fired Julius LaRosa on the air

*Eric Thorvaldson or Erik Thorvaldsson

Emma Goldman—American anarchist of Jewish ancestry known as "Red Emma"

Harold Grange—"Galloping Ghost" known also as "Red" whose retired uniform number is 77

Thomas Jefferson—3rd U.S. President, called the "Red Fox"

Elton John—Middlesex, England-born singer, songwriter, pianist whose "The Red Piano" concert series has been extended through 2008 at Caesars Palace in Las Vegas

Chief Joseph—Nez Percé chief called the "Napoleon of the Indian Race" and the "Red Napoleon"

Rosa Luxemburg—Polish-born German socialist writer and revolutionary known as "Red Rosa" who helped found the German Communist Party and its newspaper, *Die Rote Fahne*, or *Red Flag*

Malcolm X—Person born Malcolm Little, who was known as "Big Red" and "Detroit Red"

Claude Pepper—Liberal Florida Democrat known as "The Red Pepper" by his political opponents

John Red Pollard—Jockey who became well known for riding the racehorse Seabiscuit

Red Cloud—Oglala Teton Sioux who said in 1870, "When you [Whites] first came we were very many, and you were very few; now you are many, and we are getting very few. And we are poor."

Red Eagle—Creek Indian also known as William Weatherford who was defeated at Horseshoe Bend

Orville Redenbacher—Popcorn guru devoted to making the perfect popcorn

Robert Redford—American actor known for his films *Butch Cassidy and the Sundance Kid* and the *Sting*

Lynn Redgrave—British actress known for her films *Georgy Girl* and *Shine*

Michael Redgrave—British actor known for his films *Importance of Being Earnest* and *The Loneliness of the Long Distance Runner*

Vanessa Redgrave—British actress known for her films *Blowup* and *Howards End*

Red Jacket—Seneca Indian called Sagoyewatha but later known by a name based on an article of clothing he was awarded for helping the British during the Revolutionary War

Pierre Auguste Renoir—French impressionist who painted *Dance at Bougival* and once said, "I want my red to sound like a bell."

Walter Reuther—President of the United Automobile Workers (UAW) from 1946 to 1970 called "The Red-Headed Kid from Wheeling"

Cardinal Richelieu—French statesman and chief minister to Louis XIII called "*l'Eminence rouge*" or "The Red Eminence" or "Red Cardinal"

Manfred von Richthofen—German WWI flying ace known as the "Red Baron" who flew a red Fokker triplane

Albert Fred Schoendienst—St. Louis 2nd baseman known as "Red"

(Richard) Red Skelton—Comedian known as the "Marcel Marceau of Television" and "America's Crown Prince," the creator of such personas as Freddie the Freeloader

Red Smith—Journalist and sports columnist in New York nicknamed "Red" with the given names Walter Wellesley

Martin Van Buren—U.S. President called the "Red Fox of Kinderhook"

Bobby Vinton—Pop singer nicknamed "The Polish Prince" whose "Roses Are Red (My Love)" was a No. 1 hit in 1962

Antonio Vivaldi—17th-18th century Italian composer and violinist nicknamed "*Il Pretre Rosso*," or "The Red Priest," and known for his 4 violin concertos called *The Four Seasons*

LITERARY REDS

Hans Christian Andersen—Danish author who wrote "The Red Shoes"
Robert Burns—Scottish poet who wrote the lines, "O, my Luve is like a red, red rose, / That's newly sprung in June."
Willa Cather—American author whose life on a ranch near Red Cloud, Nebraska, influenced her novels, especially *My Antonia,* set in that state
Tom Clancy—American author who wrote *The Hunt for Red October*, *Redstorm Rising*, and *Red Rabbit*
James Fenimore Cooper—American author who wrote *The Red Rover*, *The Redskins*, and the Leather-Stocking Tales
Stephen Crane—American author who wrote *The Red Badge of Courage*
Arthur Conan Doyle—English author who wrote the short story *The Red-Headed League*
Fern—Word completing the title of Wilson Rawls' *Where the Red _____ Grows*, a novel about Billy Colman, the boy who owns the coon dogs Old Dan and Little Ann
Fire—In Rudyard Kipling's *The Jungle Book*, that which is called "the Red Flower" and is something "every beast lives in deadly fear of"
Dashiell Hammett—"Father" of the "hard-boiled" school of detective fiction who wrote the novel *Red Harvest* before writing *The Maltese Falcon*
O. Henry—American author who wrote "The Ransom of Red Chief"
James Jones—American author who wrote *The Thin Red Line*, a novel set in WWII
Little Red Hen—Folk tale character who by herself plants wheat, harvests it, and bakes bread, then refuses to share it with those who were unwilling to help her
Little Red Riding Hood—Fairy tale heroine who goes to grandmother's house and is deceived by the wolf pretending to be her grandmother
Mao Tse-tung—Chinese leader whose sayings are found in his *Little Red Book**
Herman Melville—American author who wrote *Typee*, *Omoo*, and *Redburn*
A.A. Milne—English author who wrote *The Red House Mystery*, a detective novel, but is better known for creating Winnie-the-Pooh
Charles Perrault—French author of *Tales of My Mother Goose*, a collection which includes "Little Red Riding Hood"
Edgar Allan Poe—American author who wrote "The Masque of the Red Death" about Prince Prospero trying to isolate himself in his abbey from the plague
Puss in Boots—Red-booted fairy tale cat who through a series of clever tricks pleases the king and wins the princess's hand for his master
Red King—"Royal" person in Lewis Carroll's *Through the Looking Glass* who is asleep and is considered to be the dreaming architect of the Looking-Glass world
Red Knight—Chivalrous elderly man who is always falling off his horse and who is one of Alice's acquaintances in Carroll's *Through the Looking Glass*
Red Queen—"Royal" person in Carroll's *Through the Looking Glass* who says "Faster! Faster!" and "it takes all the running you can do, to keep in the same place"
"Red River Valley"—Theme song of 2 films based on literary works, 1940's *The Grapes of Wrath* and 1943's *The Ox-Bow Incident*
The Red Tent—Anita Diamant's bestseller that retells the story of Jacob and Leah's daughter Dinah as found in Genesis 34
Rose Red—Snow White's sister in a Brothers Grimm tale and a mansion in a Stephen King teleplay
Jean-Paul Sartre—French existentialist whose *Les Mains sales* was produced on Broadway under the title *Red Gloves*

*Or *Quotations from Chairman Mao Zedong*

Dorothy Sayers—English detective novelist who wrote *The Five Red Herrings* in 1931
Sir Walter Scott—Scottish author who wrote the novel *Redgauntlet* as one of the Waverly Novels
Edmund Spenser—English poet whose Book I of *The Faerie Queene* features the Red Cross Knight, a symbol of holiness, who slays a dragon and marries Princess Una
John Steinbeck—American author who wrote "The Red Pony"
Stendhal—Pseudonym of the French author who wrote *The Red and the Black*, or *le Rouge et le noir*
Robert Louis Stevenson—Scottish author who created the red-headed Scottish government agent Colin Roy Campbell, called the "Red Fox of Glenure," in the novel *Kidnapped*
August Strindberg—Swedish writer whose novel *The Red Room* satirized the Stockholm art world

POTPOURRI OF REDS IN THE ANSWER
American Red Cross—Full name of the ARC
Big Red—Wrigley's artificially flavored cinnamon gum
"Big Red"—Nickname of the racehorses Man o'War and Secretariat
Big Red One—3-word name given to the American Army's famous first division in France in WWI, the oldest continuously serving division
Code Red—British boy band, a cherry-flavored Mountain Dew soft drink, or an unofficial military order to rough up a problem soldier
Fire engine red—Strong dark red frequently used on emergency vehicles
The Little Red-Headed Girl—Object of Charlie Brown's affection in the comic strips
Red Alert—Warning signal alerting Starfleet personnel to report to duty stations in the Star Trek universe, Homeland Security's highest level of vigilance, or Peter George's 1958 book about nuclear war on which Stanley Kubrick based his film, *Dr. Strangelove*
The Red Arrows—RAF's or the Royal Air Force's aerobatic team
The Red Balloon—1956 French film without dialogue about a small boy and an object that befriends him
Red Book—Industry standard for an audio CD established so that one can be played on any CD player
Redbook Magazine—Informational magazine directed at married women in their 30s
Red Brigades—Leftist terrorist organization that kidnapped Aldo Moro, a former Italian premier, in 1978 and killed him after holding him hostage
Red Bull—Austrian-made energy drink
Red Chamber—Senate in the Canadian Parliament
Red China—People's Republic of China, with reference to its Communist government
Red Crescent—Muslim organization equivalent to the Red Cross
Red Cross—American organization founded by Clara Barton after the international one had been founded by Jean Henri Dunant
Red Dye No. 3—Food coloring believed to cause thyroid cancer in rats that the FDA finally banned in 1990
Redeye missile—Backpacked surface-to-air missile with an infrared eye
Red eye—Conjunctivitis caused by a virus infection
✓ ***Red Eye***—Wes Craven's 2005 suspense film starring Rachel McAdams and Cillian Murphy
Red Guards—Young Chinese Communists aligned with Mao who were leaders of the 1966-1967 Chinese cultural revolution
Red Hat Society—Sue Ellen Cooper's organization dedicated to the idea that turning 50 can be fun and adventurous

Red Hot Chili Peppers—Los Angeles-based, rap-style rock foursome whose *Blood Sugar Sex Magik* was a bestseller in 1991

Red Hot Peppers—Jelly Roll Morton's band from 1926 to 1930

Red Letter Agent—Atlanta band known for its 2005 album *Burn the Good Ones Down*

Red Mass—Roman Catholic rite celebrated in honor of the Holy Ghost

Red ribbon—Colorful symbol on the 29-cent stamp issued to mark World AIDS Day in 1993

"Red River Valley"—Title of the song with the lines: "Come and sit by my side if you love me, / Do not hasten to bid me adieu, / But remember the _____ Valley / And the girl that has loved you so true."

Red rose—Emblem of the British House of Lancaster

Red Rover—Children's game in which players form 2 lines or chains facing each other and a player from one team as called by the other team tries to break that team's chain, also known as Octopus Tag

Red Ryder—"America's famous fighting Cowboy" who rode "from out of the Far West" with his Navajo Indian sidekick Little Beaver in a comic strip created by Fred Harman

Reds—1981 film depicting the Russian Revolution starring Warren Beatty as John Reed, a radical journalist

"Red Scare"—Fear of communism that swept through the U.S. following WWI and again from the late 1940s through the mid-1950s

Red schoolhouse—Building that became symbolic of education in the U.S.

Red Shirts—Giuseppe Garibaldi's famous volunteer troops with whose help he conquered the Kingdom of the Two Sicilies for the Kingdom of Italy

The Red Shoes—1948 film based on a Hans Christian Anderson's tale about magic footwear

Red Stripe—Jamaican lager-style beer whose logo is a bold, diagonal stripe

The Red Violin—François Girard's fictional film about an immortal musical instrument that is varnished with the blood of the instrument maker's wife and child and brings great suffering to each of its subsequent owners

Red Zone—Old Spice's body spray or soft solid antiperspirant and deodorant

POTPOURRI OF REDS OTHERWISE

Alice in Wonderland—Disney film featuring the song "Painting the Roses Red"

Bullfighting—Sport in which a matador makes passes at an animal with a *muleta*, or red cloth or cape draped over a stick

Captain America—Superhero whose principal WWII enemy is a spy-leader known as the Red Skull

Captain Marvel—Superhero nicknamed "The Big Red Cheese"

Cartier—French jewelry house that packages jewelry and watches in red, heart-colored boxes that are overwrapped in white paper

A Christmas Story—1983 film in which Ralphie Parker asks for and receives a Red Ryder BB gun that he calls the "Holy Grail of Christmas Gifts"

Erythrocyte—Red blood cell, red cell, or red corpuscle

France—Country whose revolutionary patriots used a *bonnet rouge* or red cap of liberty

(West) Germany—Country whose Baader-Meinhof Gang terrorist group calls itself the Red Army Faction

Howard Hawks—Director of the 1948 film *Red River* starring John Wayne

Ice hockey—Sport in which a red light is used to indicate a goal

Iditarod—Annual Trail Sled Dog Race for which the Red Lantern Award is a prize presented to the last musher to finish

Jupiter—Planet whose huge whirlwind, 20,000-25,000 miles long by 8,000 miles wide and first spotted in 1664, is known as "The Great Red Spot"

Khmer Rouge—"Red Cambodians," the Communists who ruled the country from 1975 to 1979

Mars—"The Red Planet," named after the Roman god of war

Mobil—Gasoline company whose trademark is the Flying Red Horse named Pegasus

Moulin Rouge—1889 dance hall in the Montmartre section of Paris whose English name is the "Red Mill"

Evelyn Nesbit—"The Girl in the Red Velvet Swing" whose husband Harry Thaw killed her lover, architect Stanford White

Northern Spy—Yellowish-red winter apple

Republican—Party of the candidate the "red" states voted for in the 2000 and 2004 U.S. presidential elections

Rouge—One point in Canadian football or the French word for "red" for a cosmetic used to add color to the cheeks

Rouge et noir—Gambling game known by the French phrase for "red and black"

Rubella—German measles, as named from *rubellus*, meaning "reddish"

Rubeola—Measles, as named from *rubeus*, meaning "red"

Rubric—In early manuscripts, decorative writing printed in red, and a direction, as in a prayer manual, for conducting a religious service

Ruby—Clear, deep-red variety of corundum, derived from *rubeus*, meaning "red"

Rudolph—Red-nosed reindeer who "Had a very shiny nose / And if you ever saw it / You would even say it glows"

Salvation Army—Charity organization whose red kettles were banned from Target stores in 2004 but made more than ever that year

Snoopy—Beagle who periodically fights his archenemy, the Red Baron, in Charles Schulz's *Peanuts* comic strip

Soccer—Sport in which a referee holds up a red card when a player is ejected

Thor—Red-haired and bearded Norse god of thunder and lightning

Time—Weekly news magazine founded in 1923 and known for its signature red border—it's only change was a black border to show mourning for the 9/11 attacks

Tour de France—Annual French bicycle race whose last rider to finish is given the Red Lantern (Lanterne rouge) Award

UB40—English Reggae group known for 1988's "Red Red Wine"

Warning—Word completing the sailor's saying: "Red sky at morning, Sailor (shepherd) take _____, / Red sky at night, Sailor's (shepherd's) delight."

WHITE

U.S. President who said, "There will be no whitewash in the White House" in referring to the Watergate scandal
Answer: Richard Nixon.

1-WORD WHITES
White-bread—Hyphenated adjective describing something as bland or conventional or characteristic of the middle class
Whitecap—Wave with foam at its crest
White-hot—Glowing white with heat, or zealous
White-livered—Cowardly
Whiteout—Condition in the polar regions in which everything is snow-covered and becomes a solid mass of reflected light
White-Out—Quick-drying fluid used to correct a mistake typed on paper
Whitesmith—Person who does finishing work, such as polishing, on iron
Whitewall—Pneumatic tire
Whitewash—Effort to hide a flaw or a failure; to soundly defeat an opponent; white liquid that is made of lime, powdered chalk, and water
White-water—Pertaining to frothy water or to an activity such as rafting taking place on a river with rapids
Whitey—Slang term of contempt for white people

2-WORD WHITES
White backlash—Antagonistic reaction by whites to black demands for equality
White belt—Lowest order in judo
White book—Official publication of a national government
White chip—Something of minimal value, such as the disk used for the least amount of money in poker
White collar—Professional or office wage earner whose work generally does not involve manual labor
White dwarf—Star of low luminosity that is nearing the end of its life
White elephant—Burdensome possession hard to maintain or sell and of little use to its owner
White flag—Cloth raised to signal a truce or surrender
White flight—Movement of white people from the city to the suburbs
White goods—Large household appliances or household linens
White hat—In information technology, person who is ethically opposed to computer system abuse
White heat—Temperature at which material glows hot, or intense emotion
White hole—Hypothetical area in outer space from which energy and stars and other celestial matter emerge
White hope—Something or someone expected to be a success, such as a white boxer
White knight—Person who rescues a business from a hostile raider and prevents an unwanted takeover
White knuckle—Tensely nervous or apprehensive, from the appearance of a hand clenched in fear

White lie—Untruth supposedly told for good reasons
White lightning (mule)—Slang for homemade whiskey
White list—People or things considered worthy of approval
White magic—Incantation practiced for positive instead of negative purposes
White marriage—Union between 2 people without sexual relations
White matter—Whitish nerve tissue of the brain and spinal cord
White night—Sleepless evening
White noise—Sound heard when the whole range of audible frequencies is produced at the same time, or sound that masks other sounds
White paper—Government publication establishing the official position on a particular subject
White room—Specialized area that has been sterilized and pressurized for use in laboratory work or manufacturing
White sale—Special offering of towels, bed linens, and similar items
White slave—Woman who is forced into prostitution, especially when taken abroad
White smoke—Outward mark of a decision having been reached behind closed doors, as in the election of a pope
White squire—Investor sympathetic to management who holds lots of stock in a company subject to a takeover
White supremacy—Repression and exploitation of minorities by whites based on the idea of racial superiority
White tie—Men's formal evening dress
White trash—Slang for poor white people or hillbillies
White whale—Beluga
Whited sepulchre—Hypocrite, according to Matthew 23:27

WHITE IDIOMS
(To) bleed someone white—To take all a person's money
Great white hope—Something or someone expected to be a success, especially a white boxer considered capable of winning the heavyweight championship
(To) show the white feather—To act in a cowardly manner
(To) show the white flag—To surrender
White as a sheet—Having lost facial color from fright
White as (new fallen) snow—Totally white, without blemish
White collar crime—Crime, such as fraud, committed by someone in business or government
White man's burden—The supposed duty of whites to manage the affairs of the underdeveloped colored races, as derived from the title of a Rudyard Kipling poem

GEOGRAPHY WHITES
Albania—European country named from the Latin *albus*, for "white," because the land was covered with snow—it calls itself Shqipëri(a), meaning "eagles' land"
Arkansas/Missouri—2 states through which the 690-mile-long White River flows toward the Mississippi River
Barents Sea—Sea of which the White Sea of Northwest Russia is an inlet
Belarus*—Country named from the Russian for "white Russia," alluding to the white garments worn as the national costume

*Also Belorussia and Byelorussia

Casablanca—Moroccan city whose name means "white house" in Spanish
Chicago—City whose White City was erected for the 1893 World's Columbian Exposition
Cornell University—Ithaca, New York, university whose first president was Andrew Dickson White
Dover—English town on the Strait of _____ famous for its white cliffs made of chalk
England—Country whose poetic name is Albion, meaning "mountain land" or "white land"
Helsinki—Finnish capital called the "White City of the North"
Japan—Country in which Shirasagijo, or "White Heron," Castle is located near Osaka
Lebanon—Middle Eastern country named from the Aramaic word *laban* or *libnan*, meaning "white," referring to its snow-covered mountains or its limestone rock
London—City in which the Whitechapel district murders began on August 31, 1888, by Jack the Ripper
Maine—State that is the site of Colby College in Waterville whose athletic teams are called the "White Mules"
Mauna Kea—Dormant Hawaiian volcano whose name in English is "White Mountain"
Mt. Blanc—France's highest peak whose name in English is "White Mountain"
Nebraska/South Dakota—2 states through which the 325-mile-long White River flows toward the Missouri River
New Hampshire—"The White Mountain State" so called because of its Appalachian mountain range called the White Mountains
New Mexico—State in which the White Sands Missile Range and White Sands National Monument are located west of Alamogordo
South Carolina—State whose flag features a white palmetto tree in the center and a white crescent moon in the upper left corner
Tibet—Autonomous region in which the Potala Palace includes the White Palace (Potrang Karpo), a building devoted to government
Warm Springs—Georgia town where President Roosevelt died at his Little White House
Whitechapel—East End London district, immediately to the east of the Tower of London
Whitefriars—Central London district near the Thames, formerly the site of a Carmelite monastery
Whitehall—Wide London thoroughfare between Trafalgar Square and the Houses of Parliament; former royal palace in Westminster, destroyed by fire in 1698; or the British government
Whitehorse—Capital of Canada's Yukon Territory
White House—Structure located at 1600 Pennsylvania Avenue, or the executive branch of the U.S. government
White Nile—River flowing northward to Khartoum, where it joins the Blue Nile
White Plains—Present-day suburb of New York City where an October 28, 1776, battle was fought
White Sox—Major League baseball team in Chicago
White Sulphur Springs—West Virginia city where The Greenbrier health resort hotel is located
White Tower—Name given to the central keep, or donjon, of the Tower of London because of its limestone—it is the oldest of these buildings and was built by William the Conqueror
White Volta—River of Burkina Faso and Ghana

HOMO SAPIENS-RELATED WHITES

Spiro T. Agnew—Vice President who resigned whose enemies called him both "The White Knight" and "Nixon's Nixon"

Anne (Queen Anne's lace)*—British queen for whom a lacy white wild flower, also called "Wild Carrot," is allegedly named

Mel Blanc—Actor who is the voice of such cartoon characters as Porky Pig, Bugs Bunny, and Daffy Duck, and whose surname means "White" in English

Calamity Jane—Woman born Martha Jane Cannary who was sometimes called "the White Devil of the Yellowstone"

George Armstrong Custer—"Boy General" whom the Indians called the "White Chief with Yellow Hair"

Edward C. Ford—New York Yankee southpaw pitcher known as "Whitey"

Ulysses S. Grant—U.S. President whose Missouri estate, White Haven, was made a historic site in 1989

Robert Ranke Graves—English author who wrote the non-fiction work *The White Goddess: a Historical Grammar of Poetic Myth* about the alleged Muse of poetry

Horace Greeley—Newspaperman known as "Old White Hat" who lost the 1872 presidential election to Ulysses Grant

Sonja Henie—Norwegian ice skater known as "The Girl in White"

Jasper Johns—Artist whose painting *White Flag* sold for $7 million in 1988, setting a record for the highest price ever for a work by a living artist

Chief Joseph—Leader of the Nez Percé Indians who defeated U.S. troops in 1877 at White Bird Canyon

Ku Klux Klan—Organization of whites in the South sometimes called the "White League," founded in 1865 and known for committing violent acts against blacks following the Civil War

Mary Stuart (Mary Queen of Scots)—Queen beheaded in 1587 who was called "The White Queen" after wearing white instead of black following the murder of her husband, Lord Darnley

Greg Norman—Australian golfer known as the "Great White Shark"

William Prescott**—Revolutionary War colonel who said, "Don't fire until you see the whites of their eyes."

Bobby Riggs—U.S. tennis champion, later tennis hustler, nicknamed "The White Mohammed Ali"

Theodore Roosevelt—U.S. President known as the "Great White Chief"

George Segal—20th-century sculptor known for his white plaster sculptures cast from living models of people going about what he calls "the magic of everyday life"

Mae West—Actress known for the remark in the film *Peel Me a Grape*: "I used to be Snow White . . . but I drifted"

White Russians***—Members of a faction that fought against the Bolsheviks in a Russian civil war

*Possibly after Saint Anne, mother of the Virgin Mary and patron saint of lacemakers. **Also attributed to Israel Putnam. ***Or Byelorussians or Belorussians.

LITERARY/ENTERTAINMENT WHITES

The Adventures of Tom Sawyer—Mark Twain novel that includes the line, "Tom appeared on the sidewalk with a bucket of whitewash and a long-handled brush"

Banbury Cross—Place to which one rides "a cockhorse / To see a fine lady upon a white horse" in a nursery rhyme

Mikhail Baryshnikov—Russian dancer who helped found the White Oak Dance Project, a touring ballet company

The Beatles—English rock group known for their *White Album*

Bianca—Katharina's pretty, younger sister in Shakespeare's *The Taming of the Shrew* whose name means "white" in Italian

Blanche DuBois—Tennessee Williams character in *A Streetcar Named Desire* whose French name means "white of the woods" in English

Carrie White—Adolescent girl with a very religious mother in a 1974 Stephen King horror novel

William Wilkie Collins—English novelist who wrote *The Woman in White* in 1860 and is often called the first English author of true detective and mystery novels

Dante—Italian author of *The Divine Comedy* who called himself "The White Flower," one influenced by the sun

Joan Didion—American author whose *The White Album* is about California

Arthur Conan Doyle—English author who wrote the historical novel *The White Company*

Great White Hope—1970 film starring James Earl Jones as Jack Johnson, the first black heavyweight champion

Ernest Hemingway—American author who wrote the short story "Hills Like White Elephants"

Holiday Inn—1942 film starring Frank Sinatra in which Irving Berlin's song "White Christmas" won an Oscar for Best Song

P.D. James—English author born Phyllis Dorothy James White

Rudyard Kipling—British author who wrote the poem "The White Man's Burden"

C.S. Lewis—British author in whose *The Lion, the Witch and the Wardrobe* the White Witch, called the Queen of Narnia, is eventually defeated

Little Tom(my) Tucker—Nursery rhyme character who "Sings for his supper / What shall he eat? / White bread and butter"

Jack London—American author who wrote *White Fang*, a novel about a dog

Mary—Character with a lamb whose "fleece was white as snow" according to Sarah Josepha Hale

Herman Melville—American author who wrote *White Jacket*, a novel subtitled *or, The World in a Man-of-War*

Moby-Dick—Melville novel in which Ahab says, "It's a white whale. Skin your eyes for him."

Perry White—Editor of the Daily Planet in stories about Superman

Snow White—Fairy tale character poisoned by her wicked stepmother and awakened by a prince who later marries her

Snow White and the Seven Dwarfs—Disney film that includes the lines: "Mirror, mirror on the wall, Who is the fairest one of all?"

Tarzan—Edgar Rice Burroughs character whose name in ape language means "white skin"

"The Ugly Duckling"—Hans Christian Andersen story in which an animal becomes a lovely white swan

Uncle Tom—Black whose behavior toward whites is considered as humiliating or servile, from the name of the black slave who is devoted to his white master in a Harriet Beecher Stowe novel

"White Christmas"—Bing Crosby's all time best-selling song written by Irving Berlin

White Christmas—1954 film starring Bing Crosby, Danny Kaye, and Rosemary Clooney

The White Cliffs of Dover—1944 film starring Irene Dunne and set in WWII with a flashback to WWI

White Dog—1982 film starring Kristy McNichol about a dog trained to attack and kill blacks

White Heat—1949 film starring James Cagney as gangster Cody Jarrett
White King—"Royal" person who sends all of his horses and all of his men to help Humpty Dumpty in Carroll's *Through the Looking Glass*
White Knight—Chivalrous elderly character who rescues Alice from the Red Knight in Carroll's *Through the Looking Glass* and like him, is always falling off his horse
White Men Can't Jump—1992 sports comedy film starring Wesley Snipes and Woody Harrelson
White Queen—"Royal" person in a perpetual dither in Carroll's *Through the Looking Glass*
White Rabbit—Agitated animal with pink eyes who is always in a hurry and disappears down a hole in Carroll's *Alice's Adventures in Wonderland*
"White Rabbit"—Grace Slick and Jefferson Airplane's hit that opens with the line, "One pill makes you larger, and one pill makes you small"
The White Stripes—Band known for its albums *Elephant* and *Get Behind Me Satan*
Andrew Lloyd-Webber—British composer for the musical *The Woman in White*, a work freely adapted from Wilkie Collins's thriller of the same name

POTPOURRI OF WHITES IN THE ANSWER
Bobwhite—American quail with a grayish body
Chinese white—Slang for pure or nearly pure heroin
Great White Father—3-word Indian name for the President of the United States (frequently used facetiously now for someone considered to be important)
(Great) White Fleet—U.S. fleet of 16 battleships sent by President Roosevelt on a successful 14-month goodwill world cruise in 1907
Great white shark—Species of shark considered to be the most dangerous to humans
Great White Way—Well-lit theatre district along Broadway in New York City
Mrs. White—Character in the game of *Clue*
White admiral—Nymphalid butterfly
White Anglo-Saxon Protestant—Full name of the acronym WASP
White Castle—Oldest hamburger fast food chain in the U.S., known for its square burgers called "slyders" and, since 2003, its slogan "What You Crave"
White Diamonds—Elizabeth Taylor perfume launched in 1991
White elephant—Animal once considered sacred in Siam
White Flash—Tex Ritter's horse in the movies
White hat—Hero in early western silent movies, as designated by an article of clothing he wore
White Lotus (Society)—Leafy floating plant, or the Buddhist cult founded in China that started an uprising in 1796 during the Ch'ing dynasty
White meat—Breast portion of a chicken or turkey
White Owl—Cigar brand
White Russian—Drink of vodka, kahlua, and light cream or milk
White slavery—Prostitution
White Star Line—British firm that along with Cunard dominated transatlantic passenger service until about 1900
White Surrey—Richard III's favorite horse
White Way Motel—New York City hotel at Times Square where the 1938 Marx Brothers film *Room Service* is set
Whitewater—Clintons' real estate venture investigated by a special prosecutor in the 1990s

WHITE

Whitey—Rutherford B. Hayes' horse, or Zachary Taylor's favorite horse, or Hoot Gibson's horse in the movies

POTPOURRI OF WHITES OTHERWISE

Africa—"Dark Continent" also called the "White Man's Grave"
Ajax—Household cleaner said to clean like "a White Tornado"
Albedo—Word from the Latin *albus*, meaning "white," used in astronomy for the reflecting power of a planet expressed as a power of reflected light to the total amount falling on the surface
Albino—Person with white skin, whitish hair, and pink eyes
Album—Word from the Latin *albus*, meaning "white," for a book with blank pages for mounting pictures, etc.
Albumen—White part of an egg
Asbestosis—Medical condition known as "white lung"
Béchamel—Creamy, white sauce named after Louis de _____, Louis XIV's chef who created it
Carrara—Italian city famous for the white marble quarried by Michelangelo
Carte blanche—French for "white card" for freedom to do as one pleases
Cotton—Dominant Southern crop before the Civil War called "white gold"
Emily Dickinson—New England poet who by 1870 was dressing only in white and seeing very few visitors
Edelweiss—Plant whose name means "noble white" in German
52—Number of white keys on a standard piano keyboard
Fiona/Fionn—Celtic female or male name meaning "white" or "fair"
Gaspar (Caspar)—Of the 3 Magi, the one whose name means "the white one"
Henry IV (of Navarre)—French king known for saying to rally his cavalry, "Let my white panache be your rallying point"
Io—Mistress whom Zeus changed into a white cow to conceal her from Hera
Kaolin (kaolinite)—Fine white clay used especially in making ceramics
Laban—Biblical Jacob's father-in-law whose name means "white"
Leukocyte—White blood cell, white cell, or white corpuscle
Mann Act—Official name for the so-called "white slave traffic act" of 1910, prohibiting interstate transport of women for "immoral purposes"
Platinum—Silver-white, metallic element named from the Spanish word for "silver" and known as "white gold" among miners
Pork—Meat advertised as "the other white meat"
Prism—Wedge-shaped glass that breaks white light into the colors of the spectrum
Queen Mary—Luxury ocean liner now moored in Long Beach, California, said to be haunted by a mysterious woman in white
Sclera—Technical term for the white of the eye
Taj Mahal*—White marble mausoleum built in Agra, India, by Shah Jahan in memory of his wife Mumtaz Mahal
Teflon—Waxy white solid called the "slickest solid on Earth" and used to coat cookware
Termite—Insect known as a "white ant"
Toque**—White hat traditionally worn by chefs and used as a symbol of ranking in Michelin Guide's to restaurants
Tuberculosis—Medical condition known as the "white plague"

*Taj is a corruption of *Mumtaz*. **Short for *toque blanche*

Whitsunday—Pentecost, so named from the white ceremonial robes worn by candidates for baptism on this day
Whittier—Surname of American poet James Greenleaf _____ whose name means "a harness maker, dresser of white leather"
Wyoming—U.S. state whose flag features a white bison

"WHITE" PEOPLE

Margaret Bourke-White—Photo-journalist and one of the original staff photographers at *Fortune*, *Life*, and *Time* magazines—she was the first female war correspondent
Micklewhite—Surname of Maurice Joseph _____, better known as Michael Caine
Barry White—Singer known as "Dr. Love" whose signature song is "Can't Get Enough of Your Love, Babe"
Betty White—Actress who starred on TV's *The Golden Girls*
Bill White—First baseman who became baseball's first black president, in the National League in 1989
Byron Raymond White—All-American halfback nicknamed "Whizzer" who served as justice of the U.S. Supreme Court from 1962 to 1993
Charles White—Black American artist known for his series of charcoal drawings entitled *J'Accuse* and *Homage to Langston Hughes*
Dan White—San Francisco supervisor who assassinated Mayor George Moscone and Supervisor Harvey Milk in 1978
Edward Douglas White—9th chief justice of the U.S. Supreme Court, from 1910 to 1921
Edward H. White—First American astronaut to make a spacewalk, on June 3, 1965
E(lwyn) B(rooks) White—American author who wrote *Stuart Little* and *Charlotte's Web*
Gilbert White—"Father of British naturalists" who wrote *The Natural History of Selborne*
Jaleel White—Actor who played Steve Urkel on *Family Matters*
"Jo Jo" White—Alliterative name by which Joseph Henry White of the Boston Celtics' is known
Patrick White—Australian who won the Nobel Prize in literature in 1973
Pearl (Fay) White—Movie actress who appears in the film series *The Perils of Pauline*
Peregrine White—First English child born in New England, on the *Mayflower* in Cape Cod Bay in 1620
Ryan White—Indiana youngster who contracted AIDS from a blood transfusion and died April 8, 1990
Stanford White—Architect who designed the first Madison Square Garden and during an affair with Evelyn Nesbit was shot to death by her husband Harry Thaw
T(erence) H(anbury) White—English author who wrote *The Once and Future King*
T(heodore) H(arold) White—American journalist whose *The Making of the President, 1960* won the 1961 Pulitzer Prize
Vanna White—Famous letter-turner on TV's *Wheel of Fortune*
William Allen White—Kansas newspaper owner of the *Emporia Gazette* who won the Pulitzer Prize for editing in 1923
George Whitefield—18th-century Anglican preacher and evangelist who helped touch off the Great Awakening religious revival in the U.S.
Alfred North Whitehead—British mathematician who with Bertrand Russell wrote *Principia Mathematica*
Paul Whiteman—Bandleader called the "King of Jazz" and "Pops" who conducted the 1924 premiere of *Rhapsody in Blue*

BLUE

Irish-born British poet and dramatist who wrote the lines: "I never saw a man who looked / With such a wistful eye / Upon that little tent of blue / Which prisoners call the sky," doing so in *The Ballad of Reading Gaol*
Answer: Oscar Wilde.

1-WORD BLUES
Bluebill—Any of various American ducks
Bluebird—Small North American songbird
Bluebonnet—Flat, blue woolen cap formerly worn in Scotland or a blue flower common in the southwest U.S.
Bluebrick—Term used in Britain for prestigious universities like Oxford and Cambridge
Blue-chip—Something valuable
Blue-chip (stock)—High-priced stock with an excellent earnings record
Bluecoat—Policeman, or a Union soldier during the Civil War
Blue-collar—Label used to describe a person who wears work clothes and performs manual labor
Bluegrass—American folk music originating in Kentucky characterized by rapid notes and improvisation and the use of stringed instruments such as the guitar, banjo, and fiddle
Bluejacket—U.S. Navy enlisted person
Blueline—In printing, a final proof made on photosensitive paper from negatives
Bluenose—Puritanical person, or a Nova Scotian
(To) blue-pencil—To edit
Blueprint—Photographic reproduction, as of architectural plans, or a detailed plan for doing anything
Blue-ribbon—Deemed to be the most outstanding of its kind, or said of a jury chosen especially because of its expertise
Blues—Form of jazz with slow tempo and melancholy words that developed from black folk music, especially work songs and spirituals
Blue-sky—Visionary, or having no value
Bluet—Small plant of the madder family whose name is derived from the French word *bleu*
Bluestocking—Learned, bookish woman
True-blue—Very loyal

2-WORD BLUES
Baby blue—Soft, light blue
Baby blue-eyes—Native California wildflower
Bas bleu—French word for a bluestocking, or learned, bookish woman
Blue baby—Infant born with cyanosis
Blue blood—Person descended from nobility, a translation of the Spanish *sangre azul*
Blue Book—Official government report or registry; student examination book; or listing of socially prominent people
Blue Cross—Nonprofit health insurance organization aligned with Blue Shield
Blue devils—Delirium tremens, or a feeling of depression
Blue-eyed boy—Derogatory term for someone who is highly favored by an employer or important person

Blue flu—Planned joint absence from work claiming illness, as used by police and others as a means of protest
Blue funk—Depressed state of mind, usually temporary, or in a state of panic
Blue language—Profanity
Blue law—Strict puritanical ordinance that regulates Sunday activity
Blue moon—2nd full astronomical event of the month, which rarely occurs but did so in 1990, 1993, 1996, and 1999
Blue murder—Something very difficult or disastrous
Blue peter—Signal flag with a white square in the center used by a merchant ship showing it is ready to sail
Blue-plate special—Inexpensive meal served in a restaurant
Blue ribbon—First place prize in a competition
Blue shift—Movement in the light of stars toward the shorter wavelength end of the spectrum, indicating movement inward, that is, toward the Earth, or the motion of galaxies toward the Earth, like Andromeda
Blue-sky (law)—Law that regulates the sale of stocks and bonds in order to protect the public from being deceived
Blue slip—Policy of allowing a single Senator to secretly block a nomination from leaving committee for a vote by failing to return the approval form provided by the Majority Leader
Blue streak—Way of talking with an endless stream of chatter, or anything considered to be very fast

BLUE IDIOMS
(To) be black and blue—To be badly bruised
Between the devil and the deep blue sea—Between 2 equally dangerous or difficult choices
Blue around the gills—Hung over, as derived from the color of one's complexion
Blue dahlia—Something hopeless or unattainable, as derived from a flower impossible to cultivate in a blue color
Blue in the face—Exhausted from great effort, especially after having talked a lot without accomplishing anything
(To) feel blue—To feel sad or depressed
(To) get away with blue murder—To do something reprehensible without suffering any consequences
(To) have the blues—To feel depressed or sad
(To) hoist the blue peter—To alert others that a merchant ship is ready to sail
Into the blue—Into a distant future, or where one has gone if out of sight, especially when vanishing suddenly without leaving a clue
Once in a blue moon—Very seldom
(Bolt) out of (from) the blue—Unexpected event that strikes suddenly
(To) scream (yell) blue murder—To shout loudly and with emotion
(To) sing the blues—To bemoan one's situation, or to be despondent
Sky—3-letter word completing the simile *as blue as the* _____
(To) talk a blue streak—To talk a lot and do so rapidly
What in blue blazes—Exclamation questioning rash or extreme behavior, referring to the burning of brimstone

FINE ARTS/MUSIC BLUES

Béla Bartók—Hungarian composer known for his 1911 opera *Duke Bluebeard's Castle*
"Blue Flame"—Theme song of Woody Herman's orchestra
Blue Man Group—Group whose performances feature 3 bald and blue characters and whose debut album in 1999, *Audio*, was nominated for a Grammy
Blue Öyster Cult—Long Island hard-rock group known for "(Don't Fear) The Reaper" and "Burnin' For You"
(The) Blue Rider—Expressionist art movement founded by Wassily Kandinsky and Franz Marc before WWI and in Germany known as *Der blaue Reiter*
"Blue-Tail Fly"—19th-century song featuring a black slave and having the refrain "Jimmy crack corn, and I don't care; / My master's gone away."
Blue Velvet—Bobby Vinton's 1963 album with the singles "Blue on Blue" and "Blue Moon"
The Blues Brothers—1980 film starring John Belushi and Dan Akyrod as musicians Joliet Jake and Elwood Blues
David Bowie—Singer born David Robert Jones known for "Blue Jean"
Mary Cassatt—American artist known for her impressionist paintings of women and children, such as *Little Girl in a Blue Armchair*
Chartres Cathedral—Famous Gothic cathedral in France known for its 2 bell towers and the blue glass in its huge stained-glass windows
Bing Crosby—Singer and film actor known for the 1931 song "Where the Blue of the Night"
Delft—Blue-and-white glazed pottery, as named after a city in the Netherlands
Neil Diamond—Gem of a singer known for his No. 1 1972 hit "Song Sung Blue"
Fats Domino—R&B singer known for "My Blue Heaven," "Blueberry Hill," and "Blue Monday"
Thomas Gainsborough—British artist known for the painting *The Blue Boy*
George Gershwin—American composer known for *Rhapsody in Blue*
W.C. Handy—Composer nicknamed "W.C." and "Father of the Blues" and known for "St. Louis Blues" and "Beale Street Blues"
Irene—1919 hit musical with the song "Alice Blue Gown"
Elton John—Middlesex, England, singer known for his 1982 "Blue Eyes"
B.B. King—Rock and Roll Hall of Fame inductee known as the "King of the Blues" and the "Blues Boy"
Lady Sings the Blues—1972 film in which Diana Ross plays Billie Holiday
The Marcels—R&B vocal group from Pittsburgh known for their 1961 hit "Blue Moon"
Henri Matisse—French fauvist leader who painted *The Blue Nude*
Jacques Offenbach—German-born French composer known for his 1866 operetta *Barbe-Blue* based on the Bluebeard theme
Carl Perkins—"Rockabilly King" who wrote and recorded "Blue Suede Shoes" in 1956
Pablo Picasso—Spanish-born painter who helped originate Cubism and is known for his "Blue Period"
Elvis Presley—"Whirling dervish of sex" whose "Blue Suede Shoes" was released in 1956
Gertrude Rainey—Blues singer from Columbus, Georgia, born Gertrude Pridgett, known as "Ma" and the "Mother of the Blues"
Rhythm and blues—Full meaning of R & B in music
LeAnn Rimes—Jackson, Mississippi, singer known for her 1996 "Blue"
Frank Sinatra—Singer known as "Ol' Blue Eyes"
Bessie Smith—Vocalist known as the "Empress of the Blues"
Johann Strauss Jr.—Austrian "Waltz King" who composed "On the Beautiful, Blue Danube"
"U.S. Air Force Song"—Song that includes the line "Off we go, into the wild blue yonder"

Paul Whiteman—Musician who in 1924 conducted the first performance of George Gershwin's "A Rhapsody in Blue"
The Wizard of Oz—1939 film featuring the song lines: "Somewhere over the rainbow / Bluebirds fly. / Birds fly over the rainbow— / Why then, oh why can't I?"
"**Zip-A-Dee-Doo-Dah**"—Title of the Disney song in the film *Song of the South* that mentions "Mister Bluebird on My Shoulder"

GEOGRAPHY BLUES
Australia—Country whose Blue Mountains National Park is located in New South Wales
Bluebonnet—State flower of Texas
Blue Nile—River flowing from northwest Ethiopia to Sudan
Blue point—Small oyster, usually eaten raw, named after a Long Island location where beds of such oysters originated
Blue Ridge Mountains—Easternmost range of the Appalachian Mountains extending from Pennsylvania to Georgia
Blue Ridge Parkway—Scenic drive parkway linking Virginia's Shenandoah National Park with North Carolina's Great Smoky Mountains National Park
Capri—Southern Italian island in the Bay of Naples, famous for its Blue Grotto
Chile—South American country where Torres del Paine National Park, called the Blue Towers, is located
Columbus—NHL team named the Blue Jackets
Connecticut—State nicknamed the "Blue Law State"
Delaware—State nicknamed the "Blue Hen State" whose state bird is the Blue Hen and whose athletic teams at the university in Newark are the "Fightin' Blue Hens"
France—Country in which a string cheese with a bluish mold was originally made at Roquefort
Frankfort—U.S. state capital nicknamed the "Bluegrass Capital"
Houston—Texas city in which the Bluebonnet Bowl was once played
Indigo—Reddish blue, after a dyestuff first produced from plants in India
Iran—Middle Eastern country known for its Blue Mosque in Tabriz
Jamaica—Caribbean country where the Blue Mountains rise to 7,402 feet at Blue Mountain Peak
Kentucky—State known as the "Bluegrass State"
Lexington—Kentucky city known as "The Bluegrass Capital" because of the grass eaten by its thoroughbreds
Minnesota—State known as the "Land of Sky-Blue Waters"
New Mexico—State whose Blue Hole Lake is sacred to the Pueblo Indians of Taos
Nova Scotia—Canadian province whose inhabitants are known as Blue Noses
Oregon/Washington—2 western states in which the Blue Mountains are located
Prussian blue—Dark blue as named after the historic region of Europe including what is now Germany where it was made accidentally by a Berlin color-maker trying to make red
St. Louis—NHL team named the Blues
Stilton—Blue-veined cheese named after a village in England
Tennessee—State in which spelunkers discovered the huge Blue Springs Cave underneath the farmland of the Cumberland Plateau
Toronto—American League baseball team in Canada named the Blue Jays
Tuareg—"Blue Men of the Desert," the Arabic word for a member of the largest group of Berber people of the West and Central Sahara, so called because of their indigo-dyed robes, which leave such a color on their skin

Turkey—Asian-European country whose Blue Mosque is also known as the Sultan Ahmet Mosque
West Virginia—State whose city of Bluefield is in a coal-mining region of the Appalachian Mountains

LITERARY/ENTERTAINMENT BLUES

Babe—Paul Bunyan's giant blue ox
James Baldwin—Black American who wrote the short story "Sonny's Blues" and the play *Blues for Mister Charlie*
Becky Thatcher—"Lovely little blue-eyed creature with yellow hair" in *The Adventures of Tom Sawyer*
Bluebeard*—Fairy tale character who keeps the remains of 6 previous wives in a room and forbids his present wife to enter that room in Charles Perrault's *Tales of Mother Goose*
Bluebeard's castle—2-word term for a dangerous place alluding to a fairy tale character who murdered 6 wives there in Perrault's *Tales of Mother Goose*
The Blue Angel—1930 film starring Marlene Dietrich as Lola Frohlich
Blue caterpillar—Animal that smokes a hookah and sits on a mushroom in *Alice's Adventures in Wonderland*
Blue's Clues—Nickelodeon TV show featuring Blue, a dog that uses paw prints as symbols
The Blue Dahlia—1946 film starring Veronica Lake as Joyce Harwood
Blue Fairy—Good imaginary being who changes Pinocchio from a puppet into a real boy
Blue Hawaii—1962 Elvis Presley film with Joan Blackman set in the 50th U.S. state
Blue jay—Kind of bird that tries to fill a house with acorns in a yarn by Mark Twain
The Blue Lagoon—1980 film starring Brooke Shields and Christopher Atkins
The Blue Max—1966 film from the point of view of Kaiser Wilhelm II's aerial aces in WWI
Blue Meanies—Music-hating bad guys led by the evil Chief Blue _____ who attack Pepperland in the Beatles' 1968 cartoon movie *Yellow Submarine*
Blue Skies—1946 film starring Bing Crosby and Fred Astaire
Blue Sky—1994 film for which Jessica Lange won a Best Actress Oscar
Blue Thunder—1983 film starring Roy Scheider about a state-of-the-art helicopter
Blue Velvet—1986 David Lynch film starring Kyle MacLachlan and Isabella Rossellini
Casablanca—Film in which Signor Ferrari, as played by Sydney Greenstreet, owns the Blue Parrot café
Raymond Chandler—American author who wrote the screenplay *The Blue Dahlia* and the novel *The Big Sleep*
Stephen Crane—American author who wrote the short stories "The Blue Hotel" and "The Open Boat"
Eugene Field—Poet who wrote "Little Boy Blue"
Hill Street Blues—1981-1987 TV police drama starring Daniel J. Travanti as Capt. Frank Furillo
Langston Hughes—Poet who wrote *The Weary Blues*
Little Boy Blue—Nursery rhyme character who is "under the haystack, fast asleep"
John D. MacDonald—American author who wrote *The Deep Blue Good-By*
Maurice Maeterlinck—Belgian dramatist who wrote *The Blue Bird*
Minerva—Mythological goddess of wisdom Homer called the "Blue-eyed Maid"
Molière—French dramatist whose comedy *The Blue-Stockings* was published in 1672 as *Les Femmes savantes*, sometimes translated as *The Learned Ladies*

*Based on the French baron and marshal named Gilles de Rais or Gilles de Retz, a man noted for his cruelty.

Toni Morrison—American Nobel Prize winner in literature who wrote *The Bluest Eye*
N.Y.P.D. Blue—TV show from 1993-2005 starring Dennis Franz as Det. Andy Sipowicz
Scott O'Dell—American author who wrote *Island of the Blue Dolphins*
Charles Perrault—French creator of the fairy tale about Bluebeard
A Patch of Blue—1965 film starring Shelley Winters in an Oscar-winning performance
Dr. Seuss—American author who wrote *One Fish Two Fish Red Fish Blue Fish*
Neil Simon—Playwright who wrote *Biloxi Blues*
Smurfs—Blue creatures who live in mushrooms or toadstools and are 3 apples high
Travis McGee—John D. MacDonald character who first appears in *The Deep Blue Good-By*
Varsity Blues—1999 film with James Van Der Beek playing a high school quarterback in Texas

POTPOURRI OF BLUES IN THE ANSWER
Alice blue—Light blue with a hint of gray, named for Teddy Roosevelt's daughter, since it was her favorite color and the color of her eyes
Vida Blue—Oakland pitcher who was 24-8 in 1971
Blue Angels—U.S. Navy's precision flying team based in Pensacola, Florida, and known for its famous diamond formation
Bluebacks—Confederate paper money during the Civil War, as named to distinguish it from the Union greenbacks
Bluebeard—Any man today who marries women and then murders them
Blue Bird—Animal that symbolizes happiness
Bluebird—Land-speed vehicle and jet-powered boat in which Donald Campbell set speed records in both in 1964
Blue box—Electronic device rigged to prevent telephone equipment from recording long-distance charges
Blue crab—Seafood with a greenish-brown shell that gets its name from its blue legs
Blue Eagle—Symbol of the National Recovery Administration, the agency created in 1933 to enforce codes of fair practices in business and industry
Bluefin tuna—Largest tuna, one with a high fat content and bright red meat
Blue glow—Lethal dose of radiation, such as that emitted in 1964 in a Los Alamos laboratory
Blue Grass Boys—Bill Monroe's band that included Lester Flatt and Earl Scruggs
Blue-green algae—Common name for cynobacteria
Blue helmet*—Member of the United Nations military force
BlueHippo—Bad-credit computer financing company
Blue jeans—Heavy blue denim trousers created by Levis
Blue Lodge—Basic organization of Freemasonry
Bluenose—Famous Canadian fishing schooner that won numerous races and whose image appears on the Canadian dime
Blue Nun—Liebfraulich wine having a religious person depicted on its label
Blue racer—Long, bluish, fast-moving snake of North America
Blue Ribbon—In Great Britain, the badge of the Order of the Garter, the highest honor of British knighthood
Bluetooth—Danish king, Harald _____, who united the country and encouraged the spread of Christianity there about 950 or a wireless technology used for connecting mobile phones and other electronic devices, developed by Swedish mobile phone giant Ericsson

*The line established anywhere by U.N. forces is known as the Blue Line.

Blue vitriol—Poisonous, crystalline compound of copper and sulfuric acid used in making germicides and batteries, also called cooper sulfate and cupric sulfate
Blue whale—Largest animal ever; heaviest marine mammal
Blue-winged teal—Small duck of North America
Bonnie Blue—Eugenie Victoria Butler's nickname in Margaret Mitchell's *Gone With the Wind*
"Bonnie Blue Flag"—National anthem of the Confederacy
Cerulean blue—Sky-blue, or azure
Cobalt blue—Dark-blue pigment that is a mixture of the element with the atomic number 27 and aluminum oxides
Cordon bleu—Master chef, or a person highly competent in a field—French for "blue ribbon"
Code Blue—Medical alert calling for emergency procedures to revive a patient in cardiac arrest
Dodger blue—Color blood Tommy Lasorda, former Los Angeles manager, says he still bleeds
JetBlue—Low cost airline started by David Neeleman in 1999
Midnight blue—Dark blue, formerly called Prussian blue in the Crayola line
Navy blue—Very dark, purplish blue, from the color of British naval uniforms
Russian (British) blue—Domestic cat, named after a European country
Sacrebleu**—French interjection meaning "good God!"
Tiffany Blue—Company whose traditional blue box is used to wrap a customer's purchase of a $100 bracelet or $100,000 square-cut diamond engagement ring—usually tied in white satin
Venetian blue—Strong blue to greenish blue whose name is derived from the name of Venice
**Words similar in meaning are *morbleu* and *parbleu*.

POTPOURRI OF BLUES OTHERWISE
Antelope—Now extinct African animal also known as a bluebuck
Base—Classification for any compound that turns red litmus paper blue
Boise State—Idaho college whose football team plays its home games on a blue field called Smurf Turf
Benjamin Franklin Butler—Draconian Union governor during the Civil War called the "Beast Ben" and the "Bluebeard of New Orleans"
Chronic bronchitis—Medical condition known as a "blue bloater"
Anthony Comstock—"The Great American Bluenose" who founded the New York Society for the Suppression of Vice and whose name now refers to "strict censorship"
Cookie Monster—Blue "googly-eyed" character on *Sesame Street* who in 2005 began advocating eating healthy
Creighton University—Omaha, Nebraska, university whose athletic teams are nicknamed the "Blue Jays"
Democratic—Party of the candidate the "blue" states voted for in the 2000 and 2004 U.S. presidential elections
De Paul University—Chicago university whose athletic teams are nicknamed the "Blue Demons"
Duke University—Durham, North Carolina, university whose athletic teams are nicknamed the "Blue Devils"
Hockey—Sport in which there are blue lines parallel to each goal line
Hope Diamond—Large blue diamond, one of the world's largest, now on display at the Smithsonian's Museum of Natural History
IBM—Corporation known as "Big Blue" whose BlueGene/L with a top speed of 92 teraflops was the world's top supercomputer in 2005

Thomas "Stonewall" Jackson—Civil War general known as "Old Blue Light" because of his alleged religious prejudice

Jesse James—Missouri bank robber called the "Robin Hood of the Little Blue"

Johns Hopkins University—Baltimore, Maryland, university whose athletic teams are nicknamed the "Blue Jays"

Lapis lazuli—Azure-blue, opaque semiprecious stone

Manitoba—Canadian province in which the CFL team in Winnipeg is called the Blue Bombers

Monday—Day of the week designated as "Blue" because it is considered a depressing day

Montgomery—Alabama city in which the Blue-Gray game was held from 1938 to 2001

Policemen—Group of service personnel referred to as the "thin blue line" and the "Men" or "Boys in Blue"

Emily Post—Manners expert who published her *Etiquette: The Blue Book of Social Usage* in 1922

Prussic acid—Another name for hydrocyanic acid, so called because it was first obtained from a dark blue solid substance with a coppery luster

Siamese cat—Variety of cat that includes the blue point, the red point, and the chocolate point

Sixpence—Word completing the wedding rhyme: "Something old, something new, / Something borrowed, something blue, / And a lucky ____ for her shoe"

South Korea—Country whose presidential house called the Blue House is located in Seoul

Touareg*—Volkswagen SUV whose name is derived from an Arabic word for a Berber people of the Sahara, so called because of their indigo-dyed robes, which leave such a color on their skin

Turquoise—Greenish-blue gem whose name means *Turkish stone*

UFOs—Flying objects the U.S. Air Force's program Project Blue Book investigated from 1952 to 1969

Union soldiers—Civil War soldiers called the "Boys in Blue" and "Blue Bellies"

USA Today—U.S. newspaper whose news section features the color blue in its masthead

Viagra—Pfizer's "little blue pill" used to correct ED, or erectile dysfunction

Noah Webster—U.S. lexicographer whose 1783 *American Spelling Book* was called the "Blue-backed Speller"

Wellesley—Massachusetts college for women whose athletic teams are called "The Blue"

*The name of the tribe is Tuareg.

U.S. COLLEGES AND UNIVERSITIES

British novelist who in *Nightmare Abbey* said: "He was sent, as usual, to a public school, where a little learning was painfully beaten into him, and from thence to the university, where it was carefully taken out of him"—his surname designates both "a vain strutting person" and "any male peafowl with brightly colored plumage"
Answer: Thomas Love Peacock.

1) Name the 8 Ivy League schools, so named by Caswell Adams of the *New York Journal American* because of the ivy-colored walls of these institutions.
Answer: Brown, Columbia, Cornell, Dartmouth, Harvard, University of Pennsylvania, Princeton, and Yale.

2) Name in chronological order of their founding the 5 oldest universities in the United States.
Answer: Harvard (1636), William & Mary (1693), Yale (1701), Princeton (1746), and Columbia (1754, originally King's College; the other 4 colonial colleges founded by royal decree are the University of Pennsylvania, 1755, though it began as a charity school in 1740; Brown, in 1764; Rutgers in 1766; and Dartmouth, in 1769).

3) What 3 colleges are historically nicknamed "The Big 3"?
Answer: Harvard, Princeton, and Yale.

4) What 3 New England colleges are historically called "The Little 3"?
Answer: Amherst, Williams, and Wesleyan.

5) What colleges are called "The 7 Sisters"?
Answer: Barnard (affiliated with Columbia), Bryn Mawr, Mount Holyoke, Radcliffe (merged with Harvard), Smith, Vassar (now coed), and Wellesley.

6) Name the first 5 state colleges chartered by state legislatures.
Answer: Georgia (the oldest—chartered in 1785, but not established until 1801); North Carolina (chartered in 1789, and the first state university to hold classes, in 1795); Vermont (chartered in 1791); South Carolina (chartered in 1801); and Ohio (chartered in 1804).

IVY LEAGUE SCHOOLS: THEIR NICKNAMES AND LOCATIONS

Brown University—Bruins, Bears—Providence, RI
Columbia University—Lions—New York, NY
Cornell University—Big Red—Ithaca, NY
Dartmouth College—Big Green—Hanover, NH
Harvard University—Crimson—Cambridge, MA
Pennsylvania, University of—Quakers, Red and Blue—Philadelphia
Princeton University—Tigers—Princeton, NJ
Yale University—Bulldogs, Elis—New Haven, CT

MAJOR COLLEGES/STATE UNIVERSITIES: THEIR NICKNAMES AND LOCATIONS
(Listed alphabetically by state)

Alabama, University of—Crimson Tide, Red Elephants—University (Tuscaloosa)
Auburn University—Plainsmen, Tigers, War Eagles—Auburn, AL

Alaska-Anchorage—Seawolves—Anchorage
Arizona, University of—Wildcats—Tucson
Arizona State University—Sun Devils—Tempe
Arkansas, University of—Razorbacks, Hogs—Fayetteville
California, University of (UCLA)—Bruins—Los Angeles
Southern California, University of (USC)—Trojans—Los Angeles
Stanford University—Cardinal—Stanford, CA
Colorado, University of—Buffaloes, Buffs—Boulder
Colorado State University—Rams—Fort Collins
Connecticut, University of—Huskies—Storrs
Delaware, University of—Fightin' Blue Hens—Newark
Florida, University of—Gators—Gainesville
Florida State University—Seminoles—Tallahassee
Miami, University of—Hurricanes—Coral Gables, FL
Georgia, University of—Bulldogs—Athens
Georgia Tech University—Yellow Jackets, Rambling Wreck—Atlanta
Hawaii, University of—Warriors—Honolulu
Idaho, University of—Vandals—Moscow
Illinois, University of (Urbana-Champaign)—Fighting Illini—Urbana-Champaign
Indiana University—Fightin' Hoosiers—Bloomington
Notre Dame, University of—Fighting Irish—Notre Dame (South Bend), IN
Purdue University—Boilermakers—West Lafayette, IN
Iowa, University of—Hawkeyes—Iowa City
Iowa State University—Cyclones—Ames
Kansas, University of—Jayhawks—Lawrence
Kansas State University—Wildcats—Manhattan
Kentucky, University of—Wildcats—Lexington
Louisville, University of—Cardinals, Red Rage—Louisville, KY
Louisiana State University—Fighting Tigers—Baton Rouge
Maine, University of—Black Bears—Orono
Maryland, University of—Terrapins, Terps—College Park
Boston College—Eagles—Chestnut Hill, MA
Massachusetts, University of—Minutemen—Amherst
Michigan, University of—Wolverines—Ann Arbor
Michigan State University—Spartans—East Lansing
Minnesota, University of—Golden Gophers—Minneapolis
Mississippi, University of—Rebels, Ole Miss—Oxford*
Mississippi State University—Bulldogs—Mississippi State**

Missouri, University of—Tigers—Columbia
Montana, University of—Grizzlies—Missoula
Nebraska, University of—Cornhuskers—Lincoln
Nevada, University of—Rebels—Las Vegas
New Hampshire, University of—Wildcats—Durham
Rutgers University—Scarlet Knights—New Brunswick, NJ
New Mexico, University of—Lobos—Albuquerque
New Mexico State University—Aggies—Las Cruces
Syracuse University—The Orange—Syracuse, NY
Duke University—Blue Devils—Durham, NC
North Carolina, University of—Tar Heels—Chapel Hill
North Carolina State University—Wolfpack—Raleigh
North Dakota, University of—Fighting Sioux—Grand Forks
Cincinnati, University of—Bearcats—Cincinnati, OH
Ohio State University—Buckeyes—Columbus
Oklahoma, University of—Sooners—Norman
Oklahoma State University—Cowboys—Stillwater
Oregon, University of—Ducks—Eugene
Oregon State University—Beavers—Corvallis
Penn State University—Nittany Lions—University Park, in State College, PA
Pittsburgh, University of—Panthers—Pittsburgh, PA
Villanova University—Wildcats—Villanova, PA
Rhode Island, University of—Rams—Kingston
Providence University—Friars—Providence, RI
Clemson University—Tigers—Clemson, SC
South Carolina, University of—Fighting Gamecocks—Columbia
South Dakota, University of—Coyotes—Vermillion
Tennessee, University of—Volunteers, Vols—Knoxville
Vanderbilt University—Commodores—Nashville, TN
Texas, University of—Longhorns—Austin
Texas A&M University—Aggies—College Station
Utah, University of—Utes—Salt Lake City
Utah State University—Aggies—Logan
Vermont, University of—Catamounts—Burlington
Virginia, University of—Cavaliers, Wahoos—Charlottesville
Virginia Tech—Hokies, Gobblers—Blacksburg
Washington, University of—Huskies—Seattle
Washington State University—(Fighting) Cougars—Pullman
West Virginia University—Mountaineers—Morgantown
Marquette University—Golden Eagles—Milwaukee, WI
Wisconsin, University of—Badgers—Madison
Wyoming, University of—Cowboys—Laramie

*Sometimes listed as University. **Sometimes listed as Starkville.

Aviation

U.S. actor and director who said: "There are only two emotions in a plane: boredom and terror"—he is known for his 1941 film *Citizen Kane*
Answer: Orson Welles.

AIRCRAFT RELATED
Aerodynamics—Branch of dynamics dealing with the forces exerted by air on objects in motion and used as the basis for airplane design
Aeronautics—Science or art of designing, making, and operating aircraft
Ailerons—Hinged sections along the trailing edge of the wing, one on each side, which provide control of the plane
Amphibian—Plane that can land and take off on both land and water
AWACS—Acronym for the Air Force's Airborne Warning and Control System aircraft with a radar dome to detect aircraft and missiles
Biplane—Aircraft with 2 pairs of wings, one above the other
Dead reckoning—2-word term for a method of finding the position of an aircraft or ship without astronomical observations, as by using compass readings and other previously recorded data
Delta (wing)—Fighter plane with swept-back or triangular wings to provide great speed
Dogfight—Air battle between fighter planes
Drone—Pilotless plane guided by an electronic device
Fuselage—Body of a plane
Glider—Sailplane, or one that does not have an engine
Global—Word represented by *G* in GPS, designating the worldwide navigation or positioning system using radio signals from satellites
Reconnaissance—Any aircraft outfitted with cameras or electronic devices for use in surveillance or collecting information
Rudder—Movable piece attached to an aircraft's stabilizer and used to control direction to the left or right
Supersonic—Adjective describing an aircraft that can fly faster than sound travels, as in the name _____ *transport plane*, or SST
Throttle—Device that controls the engine's speed and power
Ultralight—Very light aircraft that have one seat and a single engine
Vertical—Adjective represented by the *V* in V/STOL, for _____/Short Take-Off and Landing, designating a plane designed for a short runway

AIRCRAFT/PILOTS (Listed chronologically)
Daedalus—Father who with his son Icarus escaped from the Labyrinth using wings of feather and wax in Greek mythology
Leonardo da Vinci—Italian inventor whose design for a flying machine, called an ornithopter, had wings projected to flap like those of a bird
Montgolfier—Surname of French brothers Jacques Etienne and Joseph Michael who made the balloon in which 2 Frenchman flew in 1783
Wright—Surname of brothers Orville and Wilbur whose heavier-than-air and engine-powered plane made the world's first flight in 1903 in North Carolina

Flyer — Heavier-than-air plane these brothers flew at Kitty Hawk, North Carolina, in 1903

Louis Blériot — Frenchman who, aboard the Blériot XI, became the first to fly across the English Channel, in 1909

Igor Sikorsky — Russian inventor who in 1913 built and flew the first 4-engine plane, the *Russky Vitaz* ("Russian Knight")

Sopwith — English WWI plane known as a "camel" and flown by Snoopy (his doghouse) in *Peanuts*

Manfred von Richthofen — German WWI flying ace known as the "Red Baron" who was shot down in his red Fokker triplane over the Somme Canal, near Amiens, France

Roy Brown — Canadian air ace who became famous for downing the "Red Baron" in WWI in his Sopwith Camel

Lafayette Escadrille — Group of volunteer American pilots organized in 1916 who flew with the French Aviation Service and claimed to have shot down about 200 German aircraft

Antoine de Saint-Exupéry — French aviator who wrote *Night Flight* in 1931 and died during a reconnaissance flight in the Mediterranean in 1944

Richard Evelyn Byrd — U.S. explorer who flew as navigator with pilot Floyd Bennett in the *Josephine Ford* on what was allegedly the first flight over the North Pole, on May 9, 1926

Billy Mitchell — U.S. aviator who was court-martialled in 1926 for insubordination for having criticized the military for its incompetence regarding air capability

Charles A. Lindbergh — U.S. pilot who made the first solo nonstop transatlantic flight, in 1927

Spirit of Saint Louis — Ryan monoplane this American flew in 1927 on his 33½-hour trip from New York to Paris

Floyd Bennett — Plane that Richard Evelyn Byrd was piloting on November 29, 1929, when he became the become the first to fly over the South Pole

Amelia Earhart — First woman to fly alone across the Atlantic, in 1932, from Harbour Grace, Newfoundland, to Londonderry, Northern Ireland — she disappeared in the Pacific in 1937 without a trace

Wiley Post* — American who made the first solo around-the-world flight, in 1933, in a Lockheed Vega nicknamed *Winnie Mae* — he died in a plane crash in Alaska in 1935 along with Will Rogers

"Wrong Way" — Name by which Douglas Corrigan became known in 1938 for flying his monoplane *Lizzy* from Brooklyn to Dublin, Ireland, rather than to California, his announced destination

MIG — Russian fighter plane developed in 1940 and named for designers and engineers Artem Mi(koyan) and Mikhail I. G(urevich)

Zero — Japanese WWII fighter plane whose name designates a sight setting for a range in gunnery though it can mean "without measurable value"

Mustang — U.S. WWII plane named for a small wild horse of the American southwest

Jimmy Doolittle — Aviator who set a world speed record in 1932 but is better known as the American general who led the famous bombing raid on Tokyo on April 18, 1942

Messerschmitt — German Me 262 model that was the first jet combat plane flying missions over Europe in 1944 and 1945

Enola Gay* — Plane piloted by Colonel Paul Warfield Tibbets on the August 6, 1945, bombing mission over Hiroshima

Bock's Car* — Plane piloted by Major Charles W. Sweeney on the August 9, 1945, bombing mission over Nagasaki

Charles "Chuck" Yeager — Pilot who on October 14, 1947, became the first to fly faster than the speed of sound, aboard his Bell X-1 plane over California's Mojave Desert

*Post took more than 7 days and stopped numerous times. ** *The Great Artiste*, a B-29 observation plane, accompanied this plane on its mission.

"Glamorous Glennis"—Nickname of the Bell X-1 plane Yeager flew on October 14, 1947

Hercules—Mythology-based name of Howard Hughes' 8-engine, 200-ton wooden flying boat that flew on November 2, 1947, for its first and only time

"Spruce Goose"—Nickname of Howard Hughes' 200-ton wooden flying boat

B-52s—Type of airplanes first flown in 1952 and used by the U.S. in Vietnam, Kuwait, Afghanistan, and Iraq to carpet-bomb an area

Boeing 707—First U.S. production jet airliner, built in 1954-1955 by a company founded by William E. _____ in 1916

U-2—Espionage plane Francis Gary Powers was flying over Russia when he was shot down on May 1, 1960, on the eve of a scheduled summit meeting

Mirage—French fighter plane whose name designates "an optical illusion in the desert"

Blackbird—U.S. SR-71 reconnaissance plane that set a New York to London speed record in 1974 of 1 hour 54 minutes, flying at over 2,000 mph

Gossamer Condor—77-pound aircraft built by Paul MacCready that was powered by pilot, Bryan Allen, in 1977 over a one-mile course in California to win the $95,000 Kremer Prize for human-powered aircraft

Gossamer Albatross—First human-powered aircraft to cross the English Channel, peddled by Bryan Allen, on June 12, 1979

Concorde—Supersonic transport plane built by Britain and France that began passenger service in 1983 and ceased flying in 2003

Voyager—Plane piloted by Dick Rutan and Jeana Yeager on their non-stop, unrefueled round-the-world flight December 14-23, 1986

B-2—U.S. plane developed in 1988 using stealth technology designed to evade detection by radar and known as the "flying wing"

Double Eagle II—First balloon to cross the Atlantic Ocean successfully, in 1978, piloted by Ben Abruzzo, Maxie Anderson, and Larry Newman

Bertrand Piccard—Swiss doctor who with a British pilot completed the first circumnavigation of the world in a hot-air balloon, doing so in 1999 in the *Breitling Orbiter 3*—they left Switzerland and landed in Mauritania 19 days later

Brian Jones—British pilot who with a Swiss doctor completed the first circumnavigation of the world in a hot-air balloon, in the *Breitling Orbiter 3*

Steve Fossett—American adventurer who in 2002 became the first person to fly a balloon solo around the world, finally succeeding on his 6th attempt, in his 140-foot-tall *Spirit of Freedom*

SpaceShipOne—Spaceship that made history's first privately financed manned spaceflight on June 21, 2004, piloted by Mike Melvill***

Globalflyer—Plane American adventurer Steve Fossett piloted to become the first to make a solo non-stop flight around the world without refueling, in 2005

Air Force I—Plane in which the President of the U.S. flies

Air Force II—Plane in which the Vice President of the U.S. flies

***He became the first to have "commercial astronaut wings," having qualified as an astronaut by flying beyond the 50-mile line, and did reach an altitude of 62 miles, the point at which weightlessness is experienced.

No Fear Of Flying Here

U.S. pilot who said: "Of course I realized there was a measure of danger. Obviously I faced the possibility of not returning when first I considered going. Once faced and settled there really wasn't any good reason to refer to it," as recorded in her autobiography *Last Flight*, published posthumously by her husband
Answer: Amelia Earhart.

U.S. AIRPORTS

Atlanta, Georgia—Hartsfield-Jackson International
Anchorage, Alaska—Ted Stevens International
Austin, Texas—Bergstrom International
Baltimore, Maryland—Baltimore-Washington International Thurgood Marshall Airport
Barrow, Alaska—Wiley Post-Will Rogers Memorial Airport
Boston, Massachusetts—Logan International
Burbank, California—Bob Hope Airport
Charleston, West Virginia—Chuck Yeager Airport
Charlotte, North Carolina—Douglas International
Chicago, Illinois—Midway Airport
Chicago, Illinois—O'Hare International
Cleveland, Ohio—Hopkins International
Columbus, Ohio—Eddie Rickenbacker International
Dallas, Texas—Love Field
Grand Rapids, Michigan—Gerald Ford International
Houston, Texas—George Bush Intercontinental
Houston, Texas—William P. Hobby Airport
Jackson, Mississippi—Jackson-Evers International
Las Vegas, Nevada—McCarran International
Milwaukee, Wisconsin—General Mitchell Field
New Orleans, Louisiana—Louis Armstrong International
New York, New York—John F. Kennedy International
New York, New York—La Guardia International
Oklahoma City, Oklahoma—Will Rogers World Airport
Phoenix, Arizona—Sky Harbor International
Richmond, Virginia—Richard E. Byrd Airport
Saint Louis, Missouri—Lambert International
San Diego, California—Lindbergh International
San Juan, Puerto Rico—San Muñoz Marin International
Santa Ana, California—John Wayne Airport
Virginia (serving D.C.)—Dulles International
Washington, D.C.—Ronald Reagan National

WORLD AIRPORTS

Amsterdam, Netherlands—Schiphol International
Bologna, Italy—Guglielmo Marconi International
Kolkata (Calcutta), India—Dum Dum International
Caracas, Venezuela—Simón Bolívar International
Casablanca, Morocco—Mohammed V Airport
Cologne, Germany—Konrad Adenauer International
Dakar, Senegal—Léopold Sédar Senghor Airport
Havana, Cuba—José Martí International
Krakow, Poland—John Paul II/Balice International
Istanbul, Turkey—Atatürk International
Liverpool, England—John Lennon Airport*
London, England—Gatwick International
London, England—Heathrow International
Lyon, France—Saint Exupéry International
Madrid, Spain—Barajas International
Manila, Philippines—Ninoy Aquino International
Mexico City, Mexico—Benito Juárez International
Montreal, Canada—Pierre Elliott Trudeau International
Moscow, Russia—Sheremetyevo International
Nairobi, Kenya—Jomo Kenyatta International
New Delhi, India—Indira Gandhi International
Ottawa, Canada—Macdonald-Cartier International
Paris, France—Charles de Gaulle International
Paris, France—Orly International
Pisa, Italy—Galileo Galilei International
Rio de Janeiro—Antonio Carlos Johim International
Riyadh, Saudi Arabia—King Khaled International
Rome, Italy—Leonardo da Vinci International
St. Maarten, Netherlands Antilles—Princess Juliana International
Seoul, South Korea—Kimpo International
Taipei, Taiwan—Chiang Kai Shek International
Tel Aviv, Israel—Ben-Gurion Airport

*The airport's slogan is "Above us only a sky," a phrase from Lennon's song "Imagine."

Tokyo, Japan—Haneda International**
Tokyo, Japan—Narita International***
*Also called Tokyo International ***Also called New Tokyo International

Toronto, Canada—Lester Pearson International
Venice, Italy—Marco Polo Airport

COUNTRIES AND THEIR AIRLINES

Australia—Airlines of Tasmania
Australia—Qantas Airways
Austria—Tyrolean Airways
Bahrain—Gulf Air
Brazil—Varig
Belgium—SN Brussels Airlines
Belgium—Virgin Express
Bulgaria—Air Sofia
Cambodia—Angkor Airlines
Cambodia—Kampuchea Airlines
Cambodia—Royal Khmer Airlines
Canada—Labrador Airways
Canada—Northwest Territorial Airways
China (Hong Kong)—Cathay Pacific Airways
China (Hong Kong)—Dragonair
China—Shanghai Airlines
Colombia—Avianca
Ecuador—Ecuatoriana
Finland—Finnair
Germany—Deutsche BA
Germany—Lufthansa
Great Britain (Gibraltar)—GB Airways
Greece—Olympic Airways
Indonesia—Garuda*

Ireland—Aer Lingus
Ireland—Ryanair
Isle of Man—Manx Airlines
Israel—El Al
Italy—Alitalia
Japan—All Nippon Airways
Japan—JAL
Japan—Nippon Cargo Airlines
Latvia—Riga Airlines
Luxembourg—Luxair
Netherlands—KLM
Netherlands Antilles—Air Aruba
New Zealand—Mount Cook Airlines
Russia—Aeroflot
South Africa—Theron Airways
Spain—Iberia
Sweden—SAS (Scandinavia Airlines)
Thailand—Bangkok Airways
Tunisia—Tunis Air
Turkey—Istanbul Airways
United Arab Emirates—Emirates
United Kingdom—Britannia Airways
Venezuela—Avensa
Virgin Island—Air St. Thomas

*In Hindu folklore, phoenix-like bird that is part eagle and part man with a white face, red wings, and a golden body.

U.S. AIRPORT CODES (Listed alphabetically by the code)

Albuquerque, NM—ABQ
Anchorage, AK—ANC
Atlanta, GA—ATL
Austin, TX—AUS
Birmingham, AL—BHM
Boston, MA—BOS
Baton Rouge, LA—BTR
Burbank, CA—BUR
Baltimore, MD—BWI
Cleveland, OH—CLE
Columbus, GA—CSG
Cincinnati, OH—CVG
Daytona Beach, FL—DAB
Washington, DC (Reagan National)—DCA
Denver, CO—DEN
Dallas/Fort Worth, TX—DFW
Detroit, MI—DTW
El Paso, TX—ELP
Newark, NJ—EWR
Green Bay, WI—GRB
Honolulu, HI—HNL

Houston, TX (Hobby)—HOU
Huntsville, AL—HSV
Washington, DC (Dulles)—IAD
Houston, TX (Bush)—IAH
Indianapolis, IN—IND
Jacksonville, FL—JAX
New York, NY (Kennedy)—JFK
Las Vegas, NV—LAS
Los Angeles, CA—LAX
Lexington, KY—LEX
New York, NY (La Guardia)—LGA
Little Rock, AR—LIT
Chicago, IL (Midway)—MDW
Montgomery, AL—MGM
Miami, FL—MIA
Milwaukee, WI—MKE
Minneapolis/St. Paul, MN—MSP
New Orleans, LA—MSY
Oakland, CA—OAK
Oklahoma City, OK—OKC
Chicago, IL (O'Hare)—ORD

Philadelphia, PA—PHL
Phoenix, AZ—PHX
Pittsburgh, PA—PIT
Raleigh/Durham, NC—RDU
Reno, NV—RNO
San Diego, CA—SAN

San Antonio, TX—SAT
San Francisco, CA—SFO
Salt Lake City, UT—SLC
St. Louis, MO—STL
Tampa/St. Petersburg, FL—TPA
Tucson, AZ—TUS

WORLD AIRPORT CODES (Listed alphabetically by the code)

Acapulco, Mexico—ACA, in Latin America
Amsterdam, Netherlands—AMS, in Europe
Barcelona, Spain—BCN, in Europe
Bangkok, Thailand—BKK, in Asia
Bogotá, Colombia—BOG, in South America
Brussels, Belgium—BRU, in Europe
Budapest, Hungary—BUD, in Europe
Canberra—CBR, in Australia
Kalkota (Calcutta) India—CCU, in Asia
Paris, France (Charles de Gaulle)—CDG, in Europe
Copenhagen, Denmark—CPH, in Europe
Cape Town, South Africa—CPT, in Africa
Dublin, Ireland—DUB, in Europe
Entebbe, Uganda—EBB, in Africa
Florence, Italy—FLR, in Europe
Rio de Janeiro, Brazil—GIG, in South America
Geneva, Switzerland—GVA, in Europe
Istanbul, Turkey—IST, in Europe and Asia
London, U.K. (Gatwick)—LGW, in Europe
London, U.K. (Heathrow)—LHR, in Europe
Madrid, Spain—MAD, in Europe
Marseille, France—MRS, in Europe
Montevideo, Uruguay—MVD, in South America
Tokyo, Japan (Narita)—NRT, in Asia
Paris, France (Orly)—ORY, in Europe
Beijing, China—PEK, in China
Rotterdam, Netherlands—RTM, in Europe
St. Thomas, U.S. Virgin Islands—STT, in the Caribbean
Tel Aviv, Israel—TLV, in Asia
Toronto, Ontario—YYZ, in Canada
Zurich, Switzerland—ZRH, in Europe

SHIPS, BOATS, SUBS

British author who in *The Wind in the Willows* said: "There is nothing—absolutely nothing—half so much worth doing as simply messing about in boats"
Answer: Kenneth Grahame.

1) Identify the 3 ships of Christopher Columbus in his first voyage to the New World in 1492.
Answer: *Niña*, *Pinta*, and *Santa María* (his flagship).

2) Which 3 ships of the London Company, part of the Virginia Company, brought settlers to Jamestown on May 24, 1607?
Answer: The *Discovery*, the *Godspeed* (*Goodspeed*), and the *Susan* (*Sarah*) *Constant*.

3) Identify the 3 ships English explorer Henry Hudson used for the 4 voyages he made from 1607 to 1611, exploring for both the English and the Dutch.
Answer: *Hopewell*, *Half Moon*, and *Discovery*.

4) Identify the 2 ships involved in the June 22, 1807, impressment incident off Hampton Roads, Virginia, that ultimately led to the War of 1812—the British ship fired on the American ship, killing 3, and then dragged 4 "deserters" away.
Answer: *Leopard* (British) and *Chesapeake* (American).

5) Identify both the British ship aboard which Confederate diplomats James M. Mason and John Slidell left Havana for Britain and France and the American ship that stopped it in open waters on November 8, 1861, by command of Captain Charles Wilkes, who was acting without orders from Washington.
Answer: R.M.S. *Trent* and U.S.S. *San Jacinto*.

6) Identify the 2 ironclad ships that fought off the coast of Virginia on March 9, 1862, at the Battle of Hampton Roads.
Answer: U.S.S. *Monitor* and C.S.S. *Virginia* (or *Merrimack*).

7) Identify both the Confederate ship commanded by Raphael Semmes that was defeated off the coast of France in 1864, ending its destructive threat, and the Union ship commanded by John A. Winslow that defeated it.
Answer: C.S.S. *Alabama* and U.S.S. *Kearsarge*.

8) Identify the 8 U.S. battleships that were among the 86 naval vessels present in Pearl Harbor at the time of the Japanese attack on December 7, 1941.
Answer: U.S.S. *Arizona* (sunk), U.S.S. *California* (sunk), U.S.S. *Nevada* (sunk), U.S.S. *Maryland*, U.S.S. *Oklahoma*, U.S.S. *Pennsylvania*, U.S.S. *Tennessee*, and the U.S.S. *West Virginia* (the U.S.S. *Utah*, an old target battleship, was also sunk).

9) Identify both the Italian ocean liner and the Swedish ship that collided in heavy fog on July 25, 1956, off Nantucket Island, Massachusetts, with over 50 lives lost.
Answer: *Andrea Doria* and *Stockholm*.

VESSELS/COMMANDERS (Listed chronologically from 15th-18th century)

John Cabot—Italian navigator who, aboard the *Matthew* sailing for Henry VII of England in 1497-1498, made the first recorded landfall on the North American mainland since Norse explorers landed there in the 11th-12th century

Victoria—Ferdinand Magellan's ship that finished the first circumnavigation of the globe in 1522 following his death in 1521—his flagship the *Trinidad* had sprung a leak

Giovanni da Verrazano—Italian who explored the North American coast from North Carolina to Cape Breton Island for Francis I of France aboard *La Dauphine* in 1524

Golden Hind—New name Sir Francis Drake gave to his flagship the *Pelican*, aboard which he became the first Englishman to circumnavigate the globe from 1577-1580

Half Moon—Henry Hudson's ship during his 3rd voyage in 1609-1610 sailing for the Dutch East India Company when he explored today's Hudson River, a trip on which Holland based its claims to land in North America

Discovery—Ship on which Henry Hudson sailed in search of the Northwest Passage in 1610 and from which he was set adrift in 1611 when the crew mutinied

Mayflower—Boat that brought the Pilgrims to America from Plymouth, England, landing on December 21, 1620, near Plymouth Rock, Massachusetts

Arbella—Flagship of the Puritan expedition aboard which John Winthrop, the English-born Puritan governor of the Massachusetts Bay Colony, came to America in 1630

(Sieur de) La Salle—French explorer who in 1679 became the first European to cross the Great Lakes, aboard *Le Griffon*, and in 1682, as the first European to navigate the Mississippi to its mouth at the Gulf of Mexico, named the Mississippi Valley region Louisiana after Louis XIV

Queen Anne's Revenge—Flagship British pirate Blackbeard, or Edward Teach, used in terrorizing the Carolina and Virginia coasts in 1717 and 1718

Endeavour—Ship on which Captain James Cook completed his first circumnavigation of the world from 1768 to 1771

Rhode Island—Present-day state off which the H.M.S. *Gaspée*, a British revenue ship was burned on June 9-10, 1772, by American colonists after running aground in Narragansett Bay while chasing the *Hannah*

Privateers—Privately owned ships the Continental Congress authorized to attack enemy vessels in 1775, shortly after it created the Continental Navy

Turtle—First effective submarine, built by David Bushnell in 1775—its first 2 attempts to sink a ship were unsuccessful

Bonhomme Richard—John Paul Jones's ship aboard which he made his "Sir, I have not yet begun to fight" statement on September 23, 1779

Serapis—British ship named for the protector of sailors, a Greco-Egyptian deity, and to whose captain John Paul Jones was speaking on September 23, 1779

Columbia—First American ship to circumnavigate the globe, departing from Boston on September 30, 1787, under the command of Captain Robert Gray, and returning in 1790

HMS Bounty—Ship aboard which Fletcher Christian led the April 28, 1789, mutiny that set Captain William Bligh adrift to survive what turned out to be a 48-day voyage of over 3,600 miles

U.S.S. *Constitution*—Oldest U.S. Navy ship still in commission, launched in 1797, nicknamed "Old Ironsides," and now located in a Boston harbor

U.S.S. *Constellation*—Second frigate ever built for the U.S. Navy, launched on September 7, 1797, and broken up in 1854 to make a 22-gun *sloop-of-war*, which in turn was restored to its pre-1850 appearance in the early 1960s and is now berthed in the Baltimore harbor, making it the last Civil War vessel still afloat

SHIPS, BOATS, SUBS

VESSELS/COMMANDERS (Listed chronologically in 19th century)

Nautilus—Robert Fulton's copper-covered submarine, built in 1801

Victory—Horatio Nelson's flagship at the Battle of Trafalgar, in 1805

Clermont—More popular name of *The North River Steamboat*, the 1807 boat invented by Robert Fulton that was the first practical and financially successful steamboat

Chesapeake—Ship in a naval duel with the H.M.S. *Shannon* off the coast of Canada, on June 1, 1813, aboard which Captain James Lawrence uttered his famous last words, "Don't give up the ship"

Lawrence*—Oliver Hazard Perry's flagship at the Battle of Lake Erie on September 10, 1813, on which he had hoisted a 9-foot standard bearing the words DON'T GIVE UP THE SHIP

Savannah—First American-built steam-powered ship to cross the Atlantic, in 1819

H.M.S. *Beagle*—Ship on which Charles Darwin was the chief naturalist from 1831 to 1836

Amistad—Slave ship aboard which African slaves led by Cinque revolted in 1839, took over the ship off the coast of Cuba, but were then seized and brought to the U.S. for trial

John Tyler—President who narrowly escaped death aboard the U.S.S. *Princeton* in the explosion of its naval gun on February 28, 1844

Matthew C. Perry—Commodore who aboard his flagship the U.S.S. *Mississippi* made his 1852-1854 voyage to open Japan to American trade

Flying Cloud—Clipper ship that set the speed record for an 89-day trip from New York to San Francisco in 1851 (the *Andrew Jackson* set a new speed record in 1859-1860)

Monitor**—Civil War ship built by Swedish engineer John Ericsson and known as "a cheese box on a raft" or "Ericsson's Folly"

Hartford—David G. Farragut's flagship during the Civil War

H.L. Hunley***—Confederate sub that was the first sub to sink an enemy vessel in battle—the Union ship the USS *Housatonic* on February 17, 1864

Sultana—Mississippi riverboat that exploded on April 27, 1865, killing more than 1,500 Union soldiers formerly held as Confederate prisoners in what was the worst steamboat disaster in U.S. history

Cutty Sark****—Clipper ship built in 1869 for Captain John Willis for the China tea trade, now preserved at Greenwich on the Thames in London

Mary (Marie) Celeste—American "Ghost ship" bound from New York for Genoa found abandoned in the North Atlantic in 1872 with the captain, his family, and 8 crew members missing

H.M.S. *Challenger*—Royal Society of London's ship that was the first to circumnavigate the world's oceans for scientific reasons, doing so from 1872 to 1876

Statue of Liberty—Copper sculpture from France that was shipped to the U.S. aboard the *Isère* in 1885

Maine—U.S. battleship that exploded on February 15, 1898, in the Havana Cuba, harbor with over 260 lives lost

Olympia—George Dewey's flagship during the Spanish-American War

*Perry defeated the British fleet by abandoning his ship, rowing to the *Niagara*, and boarding it. **In 2002, its turret was raised from the Atlantic Ocean off Hatteras, North Carolina, where it sank during a storm in 1862. ***The *Hunley* was raised from the Charleston, South Carolina, harbor in 2002. ****Its figurehead is a bare-breasted woman in flowing garments with outstretched arms and a mare's tail in her hand.

VESSELS/COMMANDERS (Listed chronologically in 20th-21st century)

Potempkin—Russian battleship aboard which a mutiny occurred in 1905

Roald Amundsen—Norwegian explorer whose ship the *Gjoa* completed the first trip through the Northwest Passage, in 1906

Great White Fleet—Name given to the U.S. fleet of 16 battleships sent by President Roosevelt on a successful 14-month goodwill world cruise in 1907

Roald Amundsen—Norwegian explorer who traveled to the Ross Ice Shelf aboard the *Fram* and from there became the first to reach the South Pole on December 14, 1911

Titanic—Ship that struck an iceberg and sank in the North Atlantic on April 15, 1912, with more than 1,490 lives lost

Carpathia—Cunard liner that came from 58 miles away to be the first to rescue 705 survivors of the ship that sank on April 15, 1912

U-boats—Shortened name for the German *Unterseeboote*, the submarines that terrorized the seas by waging unrestricted warfare on Allied ships during WWI

Wolf packs—Groups in which German submarines hunted

Lusitania—Ship that was sunk by a German submarine off the coast of Ireland on May 7, 1915, with over 1,195 lives lost

Henry Ford—American automobile maker who chartered the Scandinavian liner *Oscar II* as the Peace Ship to Europe in 1915 in an unsuccessful attempt to find a diplomatic end to WWI

Queen Mary—Luxury ocean liner of the Cunard Line that first set sail in 1936 and is now moored in Long Beach, California, as a museum, restaurant, and hotel

Panay—U.S. gunboat bombed by Japan in 1937 on the Yangtze (Chang Kiang) River in China

Graf Spee—German battle cruiser damaged by 3 British ships on December 12, 1939, and then scuttled by its captain in Montevideo, Uruguay

Bismarck—Germany's largest WWII battleship, which was severely damaged by British ships and either sunk by them or scuttled by its crew on May 27, 1941

Reuben James—Destroyer that was the U.S.'s first warship to be sunk in WWII when torpedoed off Iceland by Germany on October 31, 1941

U.S.S. *Arizona*—Sunken U.S. battleship over whose hull prayers are said and a moment of silence is observed each anniversary of the Japanese attack on Pearl Harbor on December 7, 1941

U.S.S. *Yorktown*—Aircraft carrier, nicknamed "The Fighting Lady," that was sunk at the 1942 Battle of Midway

U.S.S. *Juneau*—U.S. ship aboard which 5 sons of the Sullivan family from Waterloo, Iowa, were killed on November 13, 1942, at the Battle of Guadalcanal

U.S.S. *Enterprise*—Aircraft carrier nicknamed "Big E" and "The Old Lady" that fought in nearly every major WWII sea battle

PT-109—John Kennedy's "patrol torpedo" boat that was rammed by the Japanese destroyer *Amagiri* in 1943 in the Solomon Islands

U.S.S. *Missouri*—Battleship nicknamed "Mighty Mo" on which General Douglas MacArthur on September 2, 1945, conducted formal ceremonies in Tokyo Bay marking the end of the war with Japan

Kon-Tiki—Norwegian Thor Heyerdahl's balsa wood boat on which he sailed from Peru to Polynesia in 1947 to prove that Polynesia could have been settled by South American Indians

Hercules*—Howard Hughes's 8-engine, 200-ton wooden flying boat nicknamed the "Spruce Goose" that flew on November 2, 1947, for its first and only time

Calypso—Oceanographic research ship Jacques Cousteau began using in 1951

*This flying boat is now located at the Evergreen Aviation Museum in McMinnville, Oregon.

Britannia—British royal family yacht named for the female personification of the British Empire, or the empire that "ruled the waves," and launched in 1953—it was decommissioned in 1997 and is permanently moored in Edinburgh

U.S.S. *Nautilus* —World's first nuclear-powered submarine, launched on January 21, 1954, and named in honor of the submarine built by inventor Robert Fulton in 1800—it was the first ship to cross under the North Pole from Atlantic to Pacific, in 1958

Mayflower II—Ship that duplicated in June 1957 the Pilgrim's original voyage across the Atlantic in 1620

Savannah—Vessel commissioned on July 21, 1959, as the U.S.'s first nuclear merchant ship—its maiden voyage was on August 22, 1962, from Yorktown, Virginia, to Savannah, Georgia

U.S.S. *Triton*—U.S. Nuclear-powered submarine that completed the first underwater circumnavigation of the globe on May 10, 1960

U.S.S. *Enterprise*—Ship launched on September 24, 1960, at Newport News, Virginia, as the world's largest ship and the first nuclear-powered aircraft carrier

U.S.S. *Thresher*—U.S. nuclear submarine that sank in the North Atlantic on April 10, 1963, leaving 129 dead

Gypsy Moth IV—Boat used by British sailor Francis Chichester on his 226-day one-stop circumnavigation of the world in 1966-1967

U.S.S. *Liberty*—U.S. Navy communications ship that was bombed and blasted by Israeli jets, killing 34 crewmen, on June 8, 1967, in international waters during the Six-Day War

U.S.S. *Pueblo*—U.S. intelligence ship commanded by Lloyd M. Bucher that was seized by North Korea on January 23, 1968—its crew of 83 were all released on December 23

Glomar Challenger—400-foot-long drilling ship used for the DSDP, or Deep Sea Drilling Project, a scientific study of the ocean bottom begun in 1968

U.S.S. *Scorpion*—U.S. nuclear submarine that sank on May 22, 1968, near the Azores with 99 dead

Queen Elizabeth 2—QE2, the Transatlantic flagship of the Cunard Line that first set sail in 1969

U.S.S. *Hornet*—Recovery ship that rescued the *Apollo 11* astronauts after they splashed down in the Pacific on July 24, 1969

Atlantis—Woods Hole Oceanographic Institution's research ship that began studying the Gulf Stream in the 1970s and has the distinction of having a space shuttle named for it

Ra II—Papyrus-reed and rope raft on which Thor Heyerdahl sailed across the Atlantic from Morocco to Barbados in 57 days in 1970, proving that the Egyptians could have done the same thing

U.S.S. *Mayagüez*—U.S. merchant ship seized in Cambodia's Gulf of Siam on May 11-12, 1975—its crew of 39 was freed on May 14 but 15 U.S. soldiers died in the rescue operation

Edmund Fitzgerald—Freighter that sank in Lake Superior in a November 10, 1975, gale made legendary by Gordon Lightfoot's song

St. Brendan—Celtic abbot and missionary whose currach, a sailing ship, was replicated to re-create his alleged journey from Ireland to North America in the 6th century A.D., in 1976

Amoco Cadiz—Ship that ran aground in 1978 off the coast of Brittany, France, spilling 68.7 gallons of oil

Achille Lauro—Cruise ship on which American passenger Leon Klinghoffer was killed in a hijacking by Palestinians led by Abu Abbas in 1985

Rainbow Warrior—Greenpeace environmental protest ship sunk in the Aukland, New Zealand, harbor by French Secret Service agents on July 10, 1985—the newest Greenpeace ship bears the same name

Exxon Valdez—Tanker that ran aground in Prince William Sound in Alaska, spilling 11 million gallons of oil on March 24, 1989

Thursday's Child—Clipper ship that in 1989 set a new record for the 14,500 mile trip around Cape Horn, beating the old record by 8 days

Henson—U.S. Navy's oceanographic survey ship named for Matthew _____, the black Arctic explorer who accompanied Robert E. Peary on his 1909 trek to the North Pole

U.S.S. *Cole*—U.S. Navy destroyer damaged by a terrorist attack using a small boat packed with explosives on October 12, 2000, in the Port of Aden, Yemen, killing 17 U.S. sailors

Queen Mary 2—Ship that set sail in 2004 as the world's largest, longest, widest, tallest, and most expensive passenger ship, the QM2, commissioned by Britain's Cunard Lines

SAINTS

American author whose *Devil's Dictionary* lists the following: "*Saint*, n. a dead sinner revised and edited"
Answer: Ambrose Bierce.

1) Name the 3 patron saints of England, Scotland, and Ireland, represented by 3 crosses on the United Kingdom's flag, the Union Jack.
Answer: St. George (red cross on a white ground), St. Andrew (diagonal white cross on a blue ground), St. Patrick (diagonal red cross on a white ground).

2) Name the 3 saints whose voices French maiden Joan of Arc said she heard.
Answer: St. (Archangel) Michael, St. Margaret, and St. Catherine.

3) Identify the expression including the names of 2 saints meaning "to take from one undertaking or person to pay another."
Answer: To rob Peter to pay Paul.

MALE SAINTS
St. Albertus Magnus—13th-century German-born Christian theologian, philosopher, and scientist whose writings influenced his most famous pupil, St. Thomas Aquinas
St. Ambrose—Bishop of Milan whose sermons and holiness inspired St. Augustine to convert to Christianity
St. Andrew—First of the 12 Apostles, martyred in Greece by being crucified on an X-shaped cross
St. Anthony of Egypt—Founder of Christian monasticism and the "Patriarch of Monks" who spent most of his life as a hermit in the Egyptian desert
St. Anthony of Padua—13th-century Lisbon-born Franciscan friar considered a great teacher and miracle worker
St. Augustine—Bishop of Hippo in Africa who wrote the *Confessions* and *The City of God*
St. Bartholomew—One of the 12 Apostles and missionary to Ethiopia, considered to have been martyred by having his skin stripped off and beheaded
St. Thomas (à) Becket—Archbishop of Canterbury murdered by knights of King Henry II in 1170
St. Benedict (of Nursia)—Italian who was the father of Christian monasticism in the West, the founder of the Benedictine monastery at Monte Cassino, Italy
St. Bonaventure—Medieval Italian theologian known as the "Seraphic Doctor" who was minister general of the Franciscan order
St. Boniface—English-born Christian missionary known as the "Apostle of Germany"
St. Brendan—Celtic abbot and missionary who some believe was the first discoverer of America in the 6th century A.D.
St. Cyril—Greek missionary who converted Slavs to Christianity in the 9th century, the saint for whom the Russian alphabet is named
St. John Fisher—Roman Catholic bishop of Rochester, England, who was beheaded in 1535 for saying that Henry VIII was not the supreme head of the church in England

St. Francis of Assisi—Founder of the Franciscan order of the Roman Catholic Church in 1209, said to have been the first ever to receive the *stigmata* while praying

St. George—Legendary figure and favorite of the Crusaders who was said to have slain a dragon with his lance to save the king's daughter—his symbol was a red cross on a white ground

St. James—Early Christian church leader called "the Just" for his strict observance of the law, sometimes called the "brother" of Jesus

St. James the Great(er)—First apostle to be martyred, by King Agrippa I, according to Acts 12:2; by tradition, his body was taken to Santiago de Compostela, Spain, where his bones were interred, now a pilgrimage shrine

St. Isaac Jogues—Jesuit martyr of North America killed by Mohawk Indians in 1646 while preaching among the Hurons

St. John (the Apostle)—The "Beloved Disciple" honored as the patron saint of Asia Minor, said to have been martyred by being boiled in oil—he is also referred to as the Evangelist or the Divine

St. John the Baptist—Prophet who prepared the way for the coming of the Lord and was arrested by Herod Antipas and beheaded at Salome's request

St. Joseph—Husband of Mary, Jesus' mother, said to have been a carpenter

St. Justin the Martyr—Christian *apologist* who defended Christians from false accusations and was martyred along with 6 other Christians about 165

St. Ignatius Loyola—Founder of the Society of Jesus in 1540, the Roman Catholic religious order also called the Jesuits

St. Luke—"Beloved Physician" and friend of St. Paul who, according to tradition, painted the first Madonna picture—he is the only artist ever canonized

St. Michael—Of the 4 archangels in Jewish and Christian scriptures, the one who is said to be a great warrior and Israel's guardian

St. Thomas More—Statesman beheaded in 1535 by Henry VIII for refusing to accept him as head of the English church and declared a saint in 1935, the subject of Robert Bolt's biography *A Man for All Seasons*

St. John N. Neumann—Philadelphia bishop from 1852 to 1860 who was the first male U.S. citizen to be recognized as a saint by the Roman Catholic Church, in 1977

St. Nicholas—Saint whose feast day is December 6 and who is the inspiration for Santa Claus, a derivative of his Dutch name *Sinterklaas*

St. Paul—"Apostle to the Gentiles" who was born Saul and converted to Christianity following a vision on the road to Damascus, and possibly beheaded on June 29, about A.D. 64 or 67

St. Peter*—"Prince of the Apostles," also called the "Apostle to the Jews," who was the first bishop of Antioch and the first bishop of Rome, and is said to be buried under the basilica in Vatican City

St. Sebastian—Early Christian martyr tied to a tree and shot with arrows by Roman troops, later clubbed to death having survived the arrows

St. Stephen—First Christian martyr, having been stoned to death by a mob outside Jerusalem after the crucifixion

St. Stephen I—First king of Hungary who served from 1000 to 1038

St. Swithin**—English bishop who died in 862 and is associated with the rhyme about July 15 and the weather and is called the "master of the rain"

*Peter was originally named Simon and is sometimes called Simon Peter. **"St. Swithin's Day if thou dost rain, / For forty days it will remain; / St. Swithin's Day if thou be fair, / For forty days 'twill rain na mair."

St. Thomas—Apostle called Didymus, meaning "The Twin" in Greek, who needed physical proof of Jesus' resurrection

St. Thomas Aquinas—13th-century Italian theologian and philosopher, often called the "Angelic Doctor," whose greatest work, the *Summa Theologica*, is his attempt to prove the existence of God

St. Valentine—Name for either of 2 early Christian martyrs beheaded in Rome on February 14

St. Vincent de Paul—17th-century French founder of the present-day Sisters of Charity and the Congregation of the Mission, a preaching and teaching order

St. Vladimir***—Grand Prince of Kiev from 980 to 1015 who became a Christian about 989 and converted many Russians to Christianity

St. Wenceslas—Bohemian prince killed in 929 and made famous in the 19th-century Christmas carol "Good King _____"

St. Francis Xavier—16th-century Spanish-French Jesuit missionary known as the "Apostle of the Indies"

***Or Vladimir I or Vladimir the Great

FEMALE SAINTS

St. Anne—Wife of St. Joachim and mother of the Virgin Mary

St. Bernadette*—French girl in Lourdes, France, to whom the Virgin Mary is said to have appeared 18 times in 1858, saying "I am the Immaculate Conception"

St. Frances Xavier (Mother) Cabrini—First U.S. citizen to be canonized, in 1946, the Italian native who established the Missionary Sisters of the Sacred Heart in 1880

St. Catherine—4th-century virgin in Alexandria tortured on a wheel and beheaded after the bonds strapping her down snapped

St. Catherine—Siena, Italy, mystic who served the poor and helped bring about the return of the pope from Avignon to Rome

Mother Katherine Mary Drexel—Former Philadelphia socialite, who used her inheritance to found the Sisters of the Blessed Sacrament in 1891 and Xavier University in New Orleans in 1915, and became in 2000 the 3rd American woman and the 4th U.S. citizen canonized

St. Elizabeth—Mother of John the Baptist and wife of Zechariah

St. Helena—Constantine the Great's mother traditionally credited with the finding of the true cross of Christ

St. Mary**—Mother of Jesus

St. Rose of Lima—First person born in the Western Hemisphere to be canonized, in 1671

St. Elizabeth (Mother) Seton—First American-born Roman Catholic saint, canonized in 1975—she founded the Sisters of Charity of St. Vincent de Paul in Emmitsburg, Maryland, in 1813

St. Edith Stein—Nun with the first name Edith killed in the gas chambers of Auschwitz and canonized by Pope John Paul II in 1998, making her the first Jewish-born saint of the modern era

St. T(h)eresa (of Avila)—Spanish nun who restored the Carmelite order to the original austerity of its rule—in 1970, she became the first woman elevated to the position of Doctor of the Church

Ste. Thérèse (of Lisieux)—French Carmelite nun known as the "Little Flower of Jesus" whose 1898 autobiography *Story of a Soul* became popular after her death

*Born Bernadette Soubirous **The mother of Jesus is also known as the Virgin Mary, the Blessed Virgin Mary, or the Blessed Virgin.

St. Ursula—Legendary British maiden whom Huns slaughtered about 451 at Cologne along with 11,000 virgins accompanying her after a pilgrimage to Rome—there were probably only about 10 women with her on the journey

MALE PATRON SAINTS
St. Albertus Magnus—Patron saint of students of the natural sciences
St. Andrew—Patron saint of fishermen, Greece, Russia, and Scotland
St. Anthony (of Padua)—Patron saint of Portugal, the poor, and lost articles
St. Bartholomew—Patron saint of tanners and leatherworkers
St. Boniface—Patron saint of Germany
St. Christopher—Patron saint of travel consultants and travelers—according to legend, he carried across a river a child who later revealed he was Christ
St. Columba—Patron saint of Scotland—an Irish monk who settled on Scotland's west coast and began to covert Picts to Christianity in 563
Sts. Cosmas/Damian—Patron saints of doctors, pharmacists, and surgeons
Sts. Crispin/Crispian(us)—Brothers who are patron saints of shoemakers and leatherworkers
St. David—Patron saint of Wales—only Welsh saint to be canonized
St. Denis*—Patron saint of France
St. Fiacre—Patron saint of cab drivers, gardeners, and venereal disease sufferers
St. Francis of Assisi—Patron saint of Italy, animals, ecology, merchants, and the environment—portrayed in art by Giotto as preaching to the birds
St. Francis de Sales—Patron saint of authors, journalists, writers
St. Gabriel (the Archangel)—Patron saint of telephone, telegraph, radio, and postal workers
St. George—Patron saint of England and of the Order of the Garter
St. Gonzaga—Italian Jesuit who is the patron saint of teenagers
St. Gregory (the Great)—Patron saint of musicians—a chant bears his name
St. Hippolytus—Patron saint of horses and prison officers
St. James—Patron saint of Spain
St. Jerome—Patron saint of scholars, librarians, and translators—he is the preparer of the *Vulgate*
St. Isaac Jogues—Patron saint of North America
St. John (the Apostle)—The "Beloved Disciple," the patron saint of Asia Minor
St. John of God—Patron saint of hospitals, nurses, and the sick
St. Joseph—Patron saint of carpenters, Belgium, Canada, and China
St. Jude—Patron saint of hopeless causes or desperate situations
St. Luke—Patron saint of artists and physicians
St. Mark—Patron saint of Venice
St. Matthew—Patron saint of accountants, bankers, bookkeepers, and tax collectors
St. Thomas More—Patron saint of politicians (as of 2000 by Pope Paul II) and attorneys
St. Nicholas—Patron saint of children, sailors, bakers, merchants, and Greece and Russia
St. Olaf (Olav II)—King and patron saint of Norway
St. Patrick**—Patron saint of Ireland—he allegedly drove the snakes out of the country and used the shamrock, a 3-leafed clover, to explain the Trinity
St. Paul—Patron saint of preachers, the Lay Apostolate, tentmakers, Malta, and Greece
St. Peter—"Prince of the Apostles" and patron saint of fishermen and of Rome and popes
St. Sebastian—Patron saint of athletes and archers

*St. Martin of Tours is also the patron saint of France. **St. Bridget, also called St. Bride, is also the patron saint of Ireland.

St. Stanislas—Patron saint of Poland and the city of Krawków
St. Stephen—Patron saint of Hungary
St. Thomas (the Apostle)—Patron saint of masons and architects
St. Thomas Aquinas—Patron saint of students and Catholic schools
St. Valentine**—Patron saint of lovers
St. Vitus—Patron saint of comedians and those with chorea
St. Wenceslas—Patron saint of the Czech Republic and Bohemia
St. Francis Xavier—Patron saint of all missions and of Japan
***Raphael is also the patron saint of lovers.

FEMALE PATRON SAINTS

St. Agnes—Patron saint of young virgins for having refused to renounce her faith and marry the prefect's son, for which she was executed—she is the subject of a John Keats poem and is honored on January 21
St. Anne—Patron saint of women in childbirth and of Canada
St. Anne(-de-Beaupré)—Patron saint of married women, childless couples, and sailors
St. Frances Xavier Cabrini—Patron saint of immigrants
St. Catherine—Patron saint of wheelrights, philosophers, and scholars
St. Catherine of Siena—Patron saint of Italy
St. Cecilia—Patron saint of music, traditionally said to have invented the organ, and patron saint of the blind, because she was blind
Ste. Geneviève—Patron saint of Paris, who helped save the city from an attack by Attila the Hun and for whom Paris's Pantheon was originally named
St. Joan of Arc—Patron saint of soldiers and of France
St. Lucy—Patron saint of sore eyes, sore throats, and epidemic diseases
St. Mary Magdalene—Patron saint of penitents—she is the woman out of whom Jesus "cast seven devils"
Our Lady of Guadalupe—Patron saint of Mexico and of the Americas
St. Rose of Lima—Patron saint of Peru and of all of South America
St. T(h)eresa—Patron saint of Spain
St. Veronica*—Patron saint of portraitists and photographers
*This woman of Jerusalem allegedly wiped Jesus' face with a cloth on His way to Calvary, leaving an exact likeness on the cloth.

Sinners (A.K.A. Notorious Homo Sapiens)

Fall River, Massachusetts, woman acquitted in 1893 of killing her father and stepmother with an ax as described in the rhyme "_____ took an ax / And gave her mother forty whacks; / When she saw what she had done; / She gave her father forty-one"
Answer: Lizzie Borden.

JAMES BUTLER HICKOK
"Wild Bill"—Famous nickname of this frontier army scout, peace officer, and gambler
George A. Custer—Lieutenant colonel and famous Indian fighter in charge of the army's Seventh Cavalry for whom Hickok scouted in 1867
Abilene*—Kansas city where Hickok served as marshal from 1869 to 1871, a job from which he was fired after accidentally killing his deputy
"Buffalo Bill" Cody—Person with the given names William Frederick with whose Wild West Show Hickok toured in 1872 and 1873, showing off his great marksmanship
"Dead man's hand"**—Poker phrase meaning "holding 2 (black) aces and 2 (black) eights," the hand Hickok was holding when he was murdered on August 2, 1876
Jack McCall—Person who murdered Hickok
Deadwood—City in the Dakota Territory where Hickok was killed at Mann's Saloon Number 10
Calamity Jane—Woman born Martha Jane Cannary with whom Hickok was linked—she dressed like a man and was sometimes called "the White Devil of the Yellowstone"
*Starting in 1872, Texas drovers took their cattle to Wichita and Ellsworth instead of Abilene. **He was also holding the nine of diamonds.

WILLIAM H. BONNEY*
"Billy the Kid"—Nickname of this famous outlaw said to have killed as many as 21 people
Pat Garrett—Sheriff who shot him
New Mexico—Territory in which he was shot and killed on July 15 and then buried
1881—Year he was killed, the same President Garfield was assassinated
*His original name may have been Henry McCarty.

OCTOBER 26, 1881, GUNFIGHT
Earp*—Surname of brothers Morgan, Virgil (the town marshal), and Wyatt (his deputy), who were involved in the famous 1881 gunfight
(John "Doc") Holliday—Surname of "Doc," the dentist who was involved in the fight on the side of these brothers
Clanton or McLaury**—Surname of either set of opposing brothers in this fight
Tombstone, Arizona—City and state in which this fight took place
O.K. Corral—Specific site on the corner of Fourth and Allen Streets where this fight took place and whose name is now used for "the site of a showdown"
*James, another of the Earps, was not involved in the fight. **Also spelled McLowery or McLowry

MISSOURI OUTLAWS
Jesse James—Former Confederate guerrilla who in 1866 formed a Missouri bank-and-train-robbing gang with his brother Frank and several cousins and became known as the "Robin Hood of the Missouri" and "Robin Hood of the Little Blue"

Youngers—Surname of their cousins, brothers Jim, Bob, and Cole, who teamed with these brothers in 1866

Pinkerton—Detective agency responsible for throwing into the home of this outlaw leader's mother a smoke bomb that exploded in the fireplace killing a stepbrother

J.B. Howard—Pseudonym this outlaw adopted, while his brother Frank took the name B.J. Woodson

Bob Ford—Gang member who killed this outlaw leader on April 3, 1882, shooting him from behind to collect a reward, thus becoming known as the "dirty little coward who shot Mr. _____"

SALOONKEEPER AND JUDGE

Judge Roy Bean—West Texas frontier judge, saloon-keeper, and justice of the peace who ruled by one law book and a 6-shooter and boasted that he was the only "Law West of the Pecos"

"(Texas) Hanging Judge"*—Frontier judge's nickname alluding to his execution of a number of people

Langtry—Name he gave his town of Vinegaroon in 1882 in honor of an English actress

Lillie Langtry—Full name of the English actress he honored with the renaming of Vinegaroon

Jersey Lily—Saloon named in her honor where he held court at the bar

*He allegedly said, "Hang 'em first, try 'em later" but never hanged that many people (Judge Isaac C. Parker of Fort Smith, Arkansas, also called "The Hanging Judge," was known for saying when he pronounced death sentences: "I do not desire to hang you men, but it's the law" and "Ain't no law west of St. Louis, ain't no God west of Fort Smith"—the sign on his gallows read: "The Gates of Hell," and his court was known as the "Court of the Damned" since about 80 death sentences out of 160 were carried out in his 21 years on the bench).

COLLEGE CRIME

Loeb—Surname of Richard, one of the 2 wealthy college students who kidnapped and killed a 14-year-old neighbor in 1924 to commit "the perfect murder"—both were sentenced to prison for life plus 99 years, and he was murdered there in 1936

Leopold Jr.—Surname of Nathan, his partner in the crime who was paroled in 1958

Chicago—City in which this killing took place

Bobbie Franks—Boy whom they killed

Clarence Darrow—Lawyer who defended them, saving them from the death penalty

Carl Sandburg—Pulitzer Prize-winning poet and historian who pleaded Nathan's case during the 4th parole hearing

1920s NEW ENGLAND MURDER CASE

Nicola Sacco—Italian-born shoemaker and anarchist who died in the electric chair August 23, 1927, after being convicted of murdering a paymaster and his guard in a robbery on April 15, 1920

Bartolomeo Vanzetti—Italian fish peddler and anarchist convicted along with him and also executed August 23, 1927

Massachusetts—State where this crime netting $16,000 took place, in South Braintree

Shoe factory—Type of factory in which this incident occurred

"(Braintree) Martyrs"*—Completion of the 2-word nickname "Braintree _____" given the pair by those who believed in their innocence

Boston**—City whose first Italian-American mayor declared in 1997 that these two men did not receive a fair trial

*The case was a *cause célèbre* because many believed there was insufficient evidence and that they were convicted because of their radical beliefs.
**In the same year, Massachusetts Governor Michael Dukakis declared that "any stigma and disgrace should be forever removed from their names."

Upton Sinclair—Muckraking author of *The Jungle* who based his 1928 novel *Boston* on this case

Maxwell Anderson—Playwright whose verse dramas *Gods of the Lightning* and *Winterset* are based on this case

Edna St. Vincent Millay—Poetess whose essay "Fear" pleads the case of these 2 Italians and whose poem "Justice Denied in Massachusetts" was inspired by their convictions

Ben Shahn—American artist known for his series of 23 pictures painted to protest the 1927 execution of these men

Katherine Anne Porter—Author of *Ship of Fools* who in 1977 published her recollections of the trial in her book *Never-Ending Wrong*

FAMOUS KIDNAPPING

Charles A. Lindbergh—Famous aviator whose 20-month-old child was kidnapped on March 1, 1932

Anne Morrow Lindbergh—Wife of this aviator

New Jersey—State in which this kidnapping took place near Hopewell

Bruno Richard Hauptmann—German immigrant and carpenter charged with the kidnapping and murder of the child in 1934 after some of the $50,000 ransom money was found in his house—he was convicted of the crime and executed in 1936

"Lindbergh law"—Popular name for the Federal Kidnapping Statute passed by Congress in 1932 to make kidnapping a federal offense if the victim is taken across state lines or if the mails are used to demand ransom

Col. H. Norman Schwarzkopf—Superintendent of the state police who investigated the kidnapping—he was the father of the general who led the coalition forces in the Persian Gulf War

CARYL CHESSMAN

Folsom Prison—California prison from which he was on parole in 1948 when his crime spree began

"Red-Light Bandit"—His nickname, as derived from the device he used as a symbol of authority in approaching people parked in lonely spots so that he could rob and then, in some cases, sexually assault the women involved

"Little Lindbergh" law—California law providing for the death penalty in cases of kidnapping "with bodily harm" under which he was convicted even though he did not kill anyone or hold anyone for ransom

Cell 2455—His death row cell number that became the title of one of his 4 best-selling books

Edmund G. Brown—California governor, strongly opposed to capital punishment, who said he could not save Chessman

San Quentin—California prison in which he was executed in the gas chamber in 1960

FAMOUS ESPIONAGE CASE

Rosenberg*—Surname of the husband and wife convicted in 1951 for conspiracy to commit espionage for the Soviet Union and executed in the electric chair June 19, 1953—they were the first U.S. citizens ever executed under the Espionage Act of 1917 for wartime spying

Julius and Ethel—Their first names

*Their lawyer said they were "victims of political hysteria" and claimed their sentence was due to "extraneous political considerations having no legitimate or legal connection with the crime charged against them"; the U.S. was not at war with the Soviet Union at the time of the alleged offenses.

William O. Douglas—Long-serving associate justice of the U.S. Supreme Court whose stay of execution granted in 1953 was reversed by the full court

Sing Sing—New York prison where this execution took place

Los Alamos—Top-secret New Mexico laboratory where the wife's brother, David Greenglass**, was working on the Manhattan Project when she allegedly asked him in 1944 to provide information about the atomic bomb project

E.L. Doctorow—American author of *The Book of Daniel*, a 1971 novel loosely based on the case

**He was a convicted spy and admitted in 2001 that he had falsely implicated his sister in order to protect his wife and children.

1968 TRIAL

Chicago 7—Name designating the group of Rennie Davis, David Dellinger, John Froines, Tom Hayden, Abbie Hoffman, Jerry Rubin, and Lee Weiner, most of whom were sentenced to 5 years in prison plus a $5,000 fine for inciting riots, though all convictions were overturned

Bobby Seale—So-called eighth member of this group who was bound and gagged for his disruptions at the start of the trial and sentenced later to 4 years in prison

Chicago—City in which these alleged riots took place in 1968

Democratic National Convention—Event in this city at which they allegedly incited riots

Richard Daley—Mayor of this city who had resolved not to have anti-Viet Nam War protests mar this event

William Kunstler—This group's lawyer who was aided by Leonard Weinglass

Julius J. Hoffman—Judge at their trial when it began in September 1969

CULT SUICIDE

Guyana—South American country in which a cult leader allegedly presided over the murder-suicide of over 900 people on November 19, 1978

People's Temple—Completion of _____ Full Gospel Church, this cult's name

Rev. Jim Jones—Protestant clergyman who had moved his California-based group to South America and ordered the mass suicide/murder using a cyanide-laced drink

Jonestown—Commune in which this suicide took place after cult leaders killed U.S. Congressman Leo Ryan and 3 journalists investigating allegations of abuse

San Francisco—California city from which he had moved his group to avoid government scrutiny

MURDERER

Norman Mailer—Author whose 1979 Pulitzer Prize-winning book *The Executioner's Song* documents the story of a murderer condemned to death for killing a motel manager

Gary Gilmore—Murderer who is the subject of this book

Utah—State in which he was executed in 1977, 5 years after the death penalty had been reinstated in *Furman v. Georgia*

Firing squad—Manner in which he was executed after saying, "Let's do it"

CULT TRAGEDY

Waco, Texas—City and state in which a heavily-armed religious cult's compound was destroyed in a fire on April 19, 1993, killing about 82 people, following a 51-day stand-off with federal law enforcement officers

Ranch Apocalypse—Compound or "ranch" named after the Jewish and Christian writings depicting symbolically the ultimate destruction of evil and triumph of good
Branch Davidian—Name of this cult
David Koresh—Cult leader who is considered to have started the fire himself or given orders to do so—an investigation by former U.S. Senator John Danforth cleared the FBI of starting the fire
Vernon Howell—Birth name of this leader who at times claimed to be Jesus Christ
ATF—Initialism for the federal Bureau of Alcohol, Tobacco, and Firearms that raided the compound in February to search for weapons, losing 4 members in a gun battle
Janet Reno—U.S. attorney general who after a 51-day standoff authorized the use of force by the FBI

TERRORIST ATTACK
Alfred P. Murrah—Federal building destroyed by a truck bomb on April 19, 1995, killing 168 people
Oklahoma City—City in which this bombing occurred
Timothy McVeigh—Person convicted and executed in 2001 for setting this bomb
Terre Haute—"High ground" Indiana city in which he was executed
Terry Nichols—Person convicted as an accomplice in this bombing and now serving a life term in prison

9/11/2001
World Trade Center—New York City twin tower building totally destroyed when airplanes hijacked out of Boston's Logan Airport by terrorists crashed into them, resulting in about 2,900 total casualties
Pentagon—Department of Defense building in Arlington, Virginia, severely damaged on the same date by planes hijacked out of Dulles
Pennsylvania—State in which another plane crashed, hijacked out of Newark, probably brought down by the actions of the passengers
Let's roll!—32-year-old businessman Todd Beamer's 2-word exclamation of command to several other passengers aboard United Airlines Flight 93 as they began the takeover of their highjacked plane, causing it to crash in a field
Saudi Arabian—Nationality of most of the 19 terrorists on these planes
Osama Bin Laden—Terrorist considered responsible for the attacks
al-Qaeda (al-Quaida)—This terrorist's organization in Arabic whose English meaning is "The Base"
Afghanistan—Landlocked Asian country where the suspected millionaire terrorist was believed to have been given refuge and the one attacked by the U.S. and Britain on October 7, 2001
Taliban—Extremist Islamic militia who controlled this country and formed an alliance with this leader
"God Bless the USA"—Lee Greenwood's song recorded in 1983 to honor Vietnam veterans that became very popular again following the September 11 terrorist attacks

POTPOURRI OF CRIME (Listed alphabetically)
Aldrich Ames—CIA official who sold U.S. secrets to the KGB from 1985 to 1994, betraying at least 30 agents, 10 of whom were executed by the Soviets—he was sentenced to life in prison without parole

David Berkowitz—"Son of Sam" serial murderer sentenced in 1978 for the 1977 murders of 6 people in New York City, mostly young girls or couples in parked cars—he was also known as the .44 Caliber Killer

Ted Bundy—Serial killer who took the lives of at least 23 pretty, young women across the country from 1974 to 1978—he was executed in Florida in 1989

Gary Carlton—Columbus, Georgia, stocking strangler who killed 7 elderly women from 1970 to 1978

D.B. Cooper—Northwest Orient 727 Airlines Flight 305 hijacker who on November 24, 1971, parachuted from the plane with $200,000 and was never apprehended

Jeffrey Dahmer—Milwaukee man found guilty in 1992 of killing 17 people and eating them

Albert H. DeSalvo—"Boston Strangler" who killed 13 women from 1962 to 1964

John Wayne Gacy—Chicago building contractor who sometimes posed as Pogo the Clown and killed 33 boys from 1972 to 1978—he was executed in 1994

Great Brinks Robbery—1950 robbery of $2.7 million in Boston pulled off by an 11-member gang—all members of this "crime of the century" were later arrested

Great Train Robbery—1963 robbery of $7.3 million in England pulled off by a gang of 20 or more—one of the members, Ronnie Biggs, asked to come home from Brazil in 2001

Robert Philip Hanssen—25-year FBI veteran arrested in 2001 on charges of having been a spy for Russia for more than 15 years—he was sentenced to life in prison without parole

H.H. Holmes—Serial killer of the 1880s and '90s, born Herman Webster Mudgett and known as a chemist, who admitted killing about 27 people in his Chicago hotel designed to look like a castle but serving as a torture chamber, though he may have killed 200 or more—he was hanged in 1896

Jack the Ripper—Unidentified 19th-century English murderer who in 1888 brutally murdered 6 prostitutes in the Whitechapel area of London and whose crimes were never solved

Theodore (Ted) Kaczynski—"Unabomber" sentenced in 1998 to 4 life terms in prison plus 30 years for a series of mail-bombings that killed 3 people during an 18-year period

Kansas (in Wichita)—State where the "BTK Strangler"—for bind, torture, and kill—struck again in 2004, after not having been heard from since his 1986 killings—he was captured in 2005

Los Angeles—California city where the unknown Southside Slayer has killed up to 20 prostitutes since the mid-1980s

Dr. Jeffrey MacDonald—Green Beret doctor convicted of killing his family in 1970 at Ft. Bragg although he claimed a group of drug-crazed hippies did it, chanting "Acid is groovy. Kill the pigs"

John Lee Malvo—Of the 2 snipers convicted of capital murder for killing 10 people and terrorizing the Washington, D.C., Virginia, Maryland area in 2002, the one who got life in prison

Charles Manson—Cult leader who directed a group of young women to kill 7 people, including actress Sharon Tate, in 1969 in Los Angeles, and write the words "HELTER SKELTER" and "DEATH TO PIGS" in blood on the walls of the home

Massachusetts—State in which the unknown New Bedford Strangler killed 9 prostitutes in 1988, dumping his victims alongside the highway

John Allen Muhammad—Of the 2 snipers convicted of capital murder for killing 10 people and terrorizing the Washington, D.C., Virginia, Maryland area in 2002, the one who got the death penalty

Philadelphia—Pennsylvania city in which the unknown Frankford Slasher killed as many as 9 prostitutes from 1985 to 1990

Jonathan Pollard—U.S. Navy intelligence officer who was caught in 1985 for spying for Israel, the only person in U.S. history to get a life sentence spying for an American ally

Charles Ponzi—Italian swindler in America who in 1919-1920 offered people a 50% return on their money after 3 months for investing in international postal-union reply coupons in what was essentially a pyramid scheme

O.J. Simpson—Former NFL running back who was acquitted of the murder of his former wife Nicole and her friend Ronald Goldman in 1994 in Los Angeles, though he was later held liable for their deaths in civil court, with the plaintiffs being awarded $8.5 million in compensation

Richard Speck—Murderer of 8 student nurses in a Chicago dormitory in 1966

Charles Starkweather—19-year-old from Nebraska who in the late 1950s went on a killing spree with his girl friend Caril Ann Fugate and was executed in 1959—the killing spree served as the basis for the movie *Natural Born Killers*

Robert Franklin Stroud—"Birdman of Alcatraz" who killed a man in Alaska in 1908, then killed a guard in Leavenworth in 1916, became famous as a bird expert, then was transferred to Alcatraz

Dick Turpin—English highwayman and horse thief who was captured and hanged in 1739

The Walkers—Retired Navy officer and members of his family arrested in 1985 and charged with spying for the Soviet Union

Washington—State where Gary Leon Ridgeway, the "Green River Killer," killed many women, mostly prostitutes, from 1982 to 1998, dumping them along the Green River—in 2003, he pleaded guilty to 48 murders

Charles Whitman—Ex-Marine sniper who shot and killed 16 people and wounded 31 others from atop the 27-story University of Texas tower, in Austin, Texas, in 1966

Wayne Williams—Man who was convicted of 2 counts of murdering young black boys in Atlanta from 1979 to 1981 and linked to 22 of the other 25 such murders during that time

Aileen Wuornos—Woman played by Charlize Theron in the movie *Monster* who admitted killing 7 men in Florida—she was executed in 2002

Zodiac Killer—Unknown man blamed for at least 6 murders in San Francisco in 1968 and 1969 and referred to by a nickname based on the letters and cryptograms he sent to newspapers—his story inspired the movie *Dirty Harry*

THESPIANS AND OTHER ENTERTAINERS

English film director who allegedly said, "Actors are cattle" and clarified it by saying, "Actors should be treated like cattle"
Answer: Alfred Hitchcock.

1) Name the 4 films—in 1933, 1967, 1968, and 1981—for which Katharine Hepburn won an Oscar as Best Actress.
   Answer: *Morning Glory*, *Guess Who's Coming to Dinner*, *The Lion in Winter*, and *On Golden Pond*, respectively (she was nominated for 12 Academy Awards).

2) Identify the 3 films—in 1936, 1938, and 1940—for which Walter Brennan won Best Supporting Actor Oscars.
   Answer: *Come and Get It*, *Kentucky*, and *The Westerner*, respectively.

3) Identify the 3 films—in 1975, 1983, and 1997—for which Jack Nicholson won 2 Best Actor Oscars and a Best Supporting Actor Oscar.
   Answer: *One Flew Over the Cuckoo's Nest* (Best Actor), *Terms of Endearment* (Best Supporting Actor), and *As Good As It Gets* (Best Actor).

4) Identify the 3 films—in 1944, 1956, and 1974—for which Ingrid Bergman won 2 Best Actress Oscars and a Best Supporting Actress Oscar.
   Answer: *Gaslight* (Best Actress), *Anastasia* (Best Actress), and *Murder on the Orient Express* (Best Supporting Actress).

5) Name the 5 actors who, as of 2005, have played James Bond in the series of films based on Ian Fleming's novels, excluding the spy film spoof *Casino Royale*, in which David Niven plays Bond.
   Answer: Sean Connery (6 films), George Lazenby (1 film), Roger Moore (7 films), Timothy Dalton (2 films), and Pierce Brosnan (4 films).

6) Identify the 4 most famous of the acting Barrymore family, 3 of whom appear together in the film *Rasputin and the Empress* and the other in *E.T.—The Extra-Terrestrial*.
   Answer: Lionel, Ethel, and John, and Drew, respectively.

7) Identify the 4 Oscar winners for Best Supporting Actress from 1978 to 1981 with the initials M.S.
   Answer: Maggie Smith (*California Suite*), Meryl Streep (*Kramer v. Kramer*), Mary Steenburgern (*Melvin and Howard*), and Maureen Stapleton (*Reds*), respectively.

8) Identify the 3 most famous of the acting Redgrave family, who appear in *The Importance of Being Ernest*, *Blow-Up*, and *Georgy Girl*, respectively.
   Answer: Sir Michael, Vanessa, and Lynn.

9) Identify the 3 most famous of the acting Fonda family, the father and daughter who co-star in *On Golden Pond* and the son known for his role in *Easy Rider*.
Answer: Henry, Jane, and Peter, respectively (Bridget Fonda, the daughter of Peter, made her movie debut in *Aria* and stars in *It Could Happen To You*).

10) Name the only 3 films in which James Dean stars.
Answer: *East of Eden*, *Rebel Without a Cause*, and *Giant*.

11) Name the 3 Stooges.
Answer: Larry (Fine), Moe (Howard), and Curly (Howard; accept Shemp Howard, another brother who replaced Curly; Joe Besser replaced Shemp; Joe DeRita later replaced Joe Besser).

MULTIPLE OSCAR-WINNING PERFORMANCES (Listed alphabetically by actor)
On the Waterfront and *The Godfather*—2 films—in 1954 and 1972—for which **Marlon Brando** won Best Actor Oscars
Hannah and Her Sisters and *The Cider House Rules*—2 films—in 1986 and 1999—for which **Michael Caine** won Best Supporting Actor Oscars
Dangerous and *Jezebel*—2 films—in 1935 and 1938—for which **Bette Davis** won Best Actress Oscars
To Each His Own and *The Heiress*—2 films—in 1946 and 1949—for which **Olivia de Havilland** won Best Actress Oscars
The Godfather, Part II and *Raging Bull*—2 films—in 1974 and 1980—for which **Robert De Niro** won Oscars as Best Supporting Actor and Best Actor, respectively
Hud and *Being There*—2 films—in 1963 and 1979—for which **Melvyn Douglas** won Best Supporting Actor Oscars
Norma Rae and *Places in the Heart*—2 films—in 1979 and 1984—for which **Sally Field** won Best Actress Oscars
Klute and *Coming Home*—2 films—in 1971 and 1978—for which **Jane Fonda** won Best Actress Oscars
The Accused and *The Silence of the Lambs*—2 films—in 1988 and 1991—for which **Jodie Foster** won Best Actress Oscars
The French Connection and *Unforgiven*—2 films—in 1971 and 1992—for which **Gene Hackman** won Oscars as Best Actor and Best Supporting Actor, respectively
Philadelphia and *Forrest Gump*—2 films—in 1993 and 1994*—for which **Tom Hanks** won Best Actor Oscars
The Sin of Madelon Claudet and *Airport*—2 films—in 1931-1932 and 1970—for which **Helen Hayes** won Oscars as Best Actress and Best Supporting Actress, respectively
Kramer vs. Kramer and *Rain Man*—2 films—in 1979 and 1988—for which **Dustin Hoffman** won Best Actor Oscars
Women in Love and *A Touch of Class*—2 films—in 1970 and 1973—for which **Glenda Jackson** won Best Actress Oscars
Tootsie and *Blue Sky*—2 films—in 1982 and 1994—for which **Jessica Lange** won Oscars as Best Supporting Actress and Best Actress, respectively
Gone with the Wind and *A Streetcar Named Desire*—2 films—in 1939 and 1951—for which **Vivien Leigh** won Best Actress Oscars
Mister Roberts and *Save the Tiger*—2 films—in 1955 and 1973—for which **Jack Lemmon** won Oscars as Best Supporting Actor and Best Actor, respectively

*Consecutive-year winners; Katharine Hepburn did it as well, in 1967 and 1968.

Dr. Jekyll and Mr. Hyde **and** ***The Best Years of Our Life***—2 films—in 1931-32 and 1946—for which **Fredric March** won Best Actor Oscars

Viva Zapata! **and** ***Lust for Life***—2 films—in 1952 and 1956—for which **Anthony Quinn** won Best Supporting Actor Oscars

The Great Ziegfeld **and** ***The Good Earth***—2 films—in 1936 and 1937*—for which **Luise Rainer** won Best Actress Oscars

All the President's Men **and** ***Julia***—2 films—in 1976 and 1977*—for which **Jason Robards** won Best Supporting Actor Oscars

The Prime of Miss Jean Brodie **and** ***California Suite***—2 films—in 1969 and 1978—for which **Maggie Smith** won Oscars as Best Actress and Best Supporting Actress, respectively

The Usual Suspects **and** ***American Beauty***—2 films—in 1995 and 1999—for which **Kevin Spacey** won Oscars as Best Supporting Actor and Best Actor, respectively

Kramer vs. Kramer **and** ***Sophie's Choice***—2 films—in 1979 and 1982—for which **Meryl Streep** won Oscars as Best Supporting Actress and Best Actress, respectively

Boys Don't Cry **and** ***Million Dollar Baby***—2 films—in 1999 and 2005—for which **Hilary Swank** won Best Actress Oscars

Butterfield 8 **and** ***Who's Afraid of Virginia Woolf?***—2 films—in 1960 and 1966—for which **Elizabeth Taylor** won Best Actress Oscars

Captains Courageous **and** ***Boys Town***—2 films—in 1937 and 1938*—for which **Spencer Tracy** won Best Actor Oscars

Spartacus **and** ***Topkapi***—2 films—in 1960 and 1964—for which **Peter Ustinov** won Best Supporting Actor Oscars

Glory **and** ***Training Day***—2 films—in 1989 and 2001—for which **Denzel Washington** won Oscars as Best Supporting Actor and Best Actor, respectively

Hannah and Her Sisters **and** ***Bullets over Broadway***—2 films—in 1986 and 1994—for which **Dianne Wiest** won Oscars as Best Supporting Actress

The Diary of Anne Frank **and** ***A Patch of Blue***—2 films—in 1959 and 1965—for which **Shelley Winters** won Oscars as Best Supporting Actress

*Consecutive-year winners; Katharine Hepburn did it as well, in 1967 and 1968.

ACADEMY AWARD WINNERS

BEST ACTOR

1927-28—Emil Jannings (*The Way of All Flesh, The Last Command*)
1928-29—Warner Baxter (*In Old Arizona*)
1929-30—George Arliss (*Disraeli*)
1930-31—Lionel Barrymore (*A Free Soul*)
1931-32—Fredric March (*Dr. Jekyll and Mr. Hyde*), Wallace Beery (*The Champ*)
1932-33—Charles Laughton (*The Private Life of Henry VIII*)
1934—Clark Gable (*It Happened One Night*)
1935—Victor McLaglen (*The Informer*)
1936—Paul Muni (*The Story of Louis Pasteur*)
1937—Spencer Tracy (*Captains Courageous*)
1938—Spencer Tracy (*Boys Town*)
1939—Robert Donat (*Goodbye, Mr. Chips*)
1940—James Stewart (*The Philadelphia Story*)
1941—Gary Cooper (*Sergeant York*)
1942—James Cagney (*Yankee Doodle Dandy*)
1943—Paul Lukas (*Watch on the Rhine*)
1944—Bing Crosby (*Going My Way*)
1945—Ray Milland (*The Lost Weekend*)
1946—Fredric March (*The Best Years of Our Lives*)
1947—Ronald Colman (*A Double Life*)
1948—Laurence Olivier (*Hamlet*)
1949—Broderick Crawford (*All the King's Men*)
1950—José Ferrer (*Cyrano de Bergerac*)
1951—Humphrey Bogart (*The African Queen*)
1952—Gary Cooper (*High Noon*)
1953—William Holden (*Stalag 17*)
1954—Marlon Brando (*On the Waterfront*)
1955—Ernest Borgnine (*Marty*)
1956—Yul Brynner (*The King and I*)
1957—Alec Guinness (*The Bridge on the River Kwai*)
1958—David Niven (*Separate Tables*)
1959—Charlton Heston (*Ben-Hur*)
1960—Burt Lancaster (*Elmer Gantry*)
1661—Maximilian Schell (*Judgment at Nuremberg*)
1962—Gregory Peck (*To Kill a Mockingbird*)

1963—Sidney Poitier (*Lilies of the Field*)
1964—Rex Harrison (*My Fair Lady*)
1965—Lee Marvin (*Cat Ballou*)
1966—Paul Scofield (*A Man for All Seasons*)
1967—Rod Steiger (*In the Heat of the Night*)
1968—Cliff Robertson (*Charly*)
1969—John Wayne (*True Grit*)
1970—George C. Scott (*Patton*)
1971—Gene Hackman (*The French Connection*)
1972—Marion Brando (*The Godfather*)
1973—Jack Lemmon (*Save the Tiger*)
1974—Art Carney (*Harry and Tonto*)
1975—Jack Nicholson (*One Flew Over the Cuckoo's Nest*)
1976—Peter Finch (*Network*)
1977—Richard Dreyfuss (*The Goodbye Girl*)
1978—Jon Voight (*Coming Home*)
1979—Dustin Hoffman (*Kramer vs Kramer*)
1980—Robert De Niro (*Raging Bull*)
1981—Henry Fonda (*On Golden Pond*)
1982—Ben Kingsley (*Gandhi*)
1983—Robert Duvall (*Tender Mercies*)
1984—F. Murray Abraham (*Amadeus*)
1985—William Hurt (*Kiss of the Spider Woman*)
1986—Paul Newman (*The Color of Money*)
1987—Michael Douglas (*Wall Street*)
1988—Dustin Hoffman (*Rain Man*)
1989—Daniel Day-Lewis (*My Left Foot*)
1990—Jeremy Irons (*Reversal of Fortune*)
1991—Anthony Hopkins (*The Silence of the Lambs*)
1992—Al Pacino (*Scent of a Woman*)
1993—Tom Hanks (*Philadelphia*)
1994—Tom Hanks (*Forrest Gump*)
1995—Nicolas Cage (*Leaving Las Vegas*)
1996—Geoffrey Rush (*Shine*)
1997—Jack Nicholson (*As Good As It Gets*)
1998—Roberto Benigni (*Life Is Beautiful*)
1999—Kevin Spacey (*American Beauty*)
2000—Russell Crowe (*Gladiator*)
2001—Denzel Washington (*Training Day*)
2002—Adrien Brody (*The Pianist*)
2003—Sean Penn (*Mystic River*)
2004—Jamie Foxx (*Ray*)

BEST ACTRESS

1927-28—Janet Gaynor (*Seventh Heaven, Street Angel, Sunrise*)
1928-29—Mary Pickford (*Coquette*)
1929-30—Norma Shearer (*The Divorcee*)
1930-31—Marie Dressler (*Min and Bill*)
1931-32—Helen Hayes (*The Sin of Madelon Claudet*)
1932-33—Katharine Hepburn (*Morning Glory*)
1934—Claudette Colbert (*It Happened One Night*)
1935—Bette Davis (*Dangerous*)
1936—Luise Rainer (*The Great Ziegfeld*)
1937—Luise Rainer (*The Good Earth*)
1938—Bette Davis (*Jezebel*)
1939—Vivien Leigh (*Gone with the Wind*)
1940—Ginger Rogers (*Kitty Foyle*)
1941—Joan Fontaine (*Suspicion*)
1942—Greer Garson (*Mrs. Miniver*)
1943—Jennifer Jones (*The Song of Bernadette*)
1944—Ingrid Bergman (*Gaslight*)
1945—Joan Crawford (*Mildred Pierce*)
1946—Olivia de Havilland (*To Each His Own*)
1947—Loretta Young (*The Farmer's Daughter*)
1948—Jane Wyman (*Johnny Belinda*)
1949—Olivia de Havilland (*The Heiress*)
1950—Judy Holliday (*Born Yesterday*)
1951—Vivien Leigh (*A Streetcar Named Desire*)
1952—Shirley Booth (*Come Back, Little Sheba*)
1953—Audrey Hepburn (*Roman Holiday*)
1954—Grace Kelly (*The Country Girl*)
1955—Anna Magnani (*The Rose Tattoo*)
1956—Ingrid Bergman (*Anastasia*)
1957—Joanne Woodward (*The Three Faces of Eve*)
1958—Susan Hayward (*I Want to Live!*)
1959—Simone Signoret (*Room at the Top*)
1960—Elizabeth Taylor (*Butterfield 8*)
1961—Sophia Loren (*Two Women*)
1962—Anne Bancroft (*The Miracle Worker*)
1963—Patricia Neal (*Hud*)
1964—Julie Andrews (*Mary Poppins*)
1965—Julie Christie (*Darling*)
1966—Elizabeth Taylor (*Who's Afraid of Virginia Woolf?*)
1967—Katharine Hepburn (*Guess Who's Coming to Dinner*)
1968—Katharine Hepburn (*The Lion in Winter*) and Barbra Streisand (*Funny Girl*)
1969—Maggie Smith (*The Prime of Miss Jean Brodie*)
1970—Glenda Jackson (*Women in Love*)
1971—Jane Fonda (*Klute*)
1972—Liza Minnelli (*Cabaret*)
1973—Glenda Jackson (*A Touch of Class*)
1974—Ellen Burstyn (*Alice Doesn't Live Here Anymore*)
1975—Louise Fletcher (*One Flew Over the Cuckoo's Nest*)
1976—Faye Dunaway (*Network*)
1977—Diane Keaton (*Annie Hall*)
1978—Jane Fonda (*Coming Home*)
1979—Sally Field (*Norma Rae*)
1980—Sissy Spacek (*Coal Miner's Daughter*)
1981—Katharine Hepburn (*On Golden Pond*)
1982—Meryl Streep (*Sophie's Choice*)
1983—Shirley McClain (*Terms of Endearment*)
1984—Sally Field (*Places in the Heart*)
1985—Geraldine Page (*The Trip to Bountiful*)
1986—Marlee Martin (*Children of a Lesser God*)
1987—Cher (*Moonstruck*)
1988—Jodie Foster (*The Accused*)
1989—Jessica Tandy (*Driving Miss Daisy*)
1990—Kathy Bates (*Misery*)
1991—Jodie Foster (*The Silence of the Lambs*)
1992—Emma Thompson (*Howards End*)
1993—Holly Hunter (*The Piano*)
1994—Jessica Lange (*Blue Sky*)
1995—Susan Sarandon (*Dead Man Walking*)
1996—Frances McDormand (*Fargo*)
1997—Helen Hunt (*As Good As it Gets*)
1998—Gwyneth Paltrow (*Shakespeare in Love*)
1999—Hilary Swank (*Boys Don't Cry*)
2000—Julia Roberts (*Erin Brockovich*)

2001—Halle Berry (*Monster's Ball*)
2002—Nicole Kidman (*The Hours*)
2003—Charlize Theron (*Monster*)
2004—Hilary Swank (*Million Dollar Baby*)

BEST PICTURE

1927-28—*Wings*
1928-29—*The Broadway Melody*
1929-30—*All Quiet on the Western Front*
1930-31—*Cimarron*
1931-32—*Grand Hotel*
1932-33—*Cavalcade*
1934—*It Happened One Night*
1935—*Mutiny on the Bounty*
1936—*The Great Ziegfeld*
1937—*The Life of Emile Zola*
1938—*You Can't Take It with You*
1939—*Gone with the Wind*
1940—*Rebecca*
1941—*How Green Was My Valley*
1942—*Mrs. Miniver*
1943—*Casablanca*
1944—*Going My Way*
1945—*The Lost Weekend*
1946—*The Best Years of Our Lives*
1947—*Gentleman's Agreement*
1948—*Hamlet*
1949—*All the King's Men*
1950—*All About Eve*
1951—*An American in Paris*
1952—*The Greatest Show on Earth*
1953—*From Here to Eternity*
1954—*On the Waterfront*
1955—*Marty*
1956—*Around the World in 80 Days*
1957—*The Bridge on the River Kwai*
1958—*Gigi*
1959—*Ben-Hur*
1960—*The Apartment*
1661—*West Side Story*
1962—*Lawrence of Arabia*
1963—*Tom Jones*
1964—*My Fair Lady*
1965—*The Sound of Music*
1966—*A Man for All Seasons*
1967—*In the Heat of the Night*
1968—*Oliver!*
1969—*Midnight Cowboy*
1970—*Patton*
1971—*The French Connection*
1972—*The Godfather*
1973—*The Sting*
1974—*The Godfather, Part II*
1975—*One Flew Over the Cuckoo's Nest*
1976—*Rocky*
1977—*Annie Hall*
1978—*The Deer Hunter*
1979—*Kramer vs. Kramer*
1980—*Ordinary People*
1981—*Chariots of Fire*
1982—*Gandhi*
1983—*Terms of Endearment*
1984—*Amadeus*
1985—*Out of Africa*
1986—*Platoon*
1987—*The Last Emperor*
1988—*Rain Man*
1989—*Driving Miss Daisy*
1990—*Dances with Wolves*
1991—*The Silence of the Lambs*
1992—*Unforgiven*
1993—*Schindler's List*
1994—*Forrest Gump*
1995—*Braveheart*
1996—*The English Patient*
1997—*Titanic*
1998—*Shakespeare in Love*
1999—*American Beauty*
2000—*Gladiator*
2001—*A Beautiful Mind*
2002—*Chicago*
2003—*The Lord of the Rings*
2004—*Million Dollar Baby*

NICKNAMES OF ENTERTAINERS

Fred Allen—King of the Quick Quip
Steve Allen—Steverino
Roscoe Arbuckle—Fatty, Prince of Whales
Gene Autry—America's Favorite Cowboy, Oklahoma's Yodeling Cowboy, The Singing Cowboy
Lauren Bacall—Bogie's Baby, The Look, The Windmill
Josephine Baker—La Bakhair, The Black Pearl, La Perle Noire
Lucille Ball—First Lady of Television
Tallulah Bankhead—Darling of the Gods, Tallu

Theda Bara—Original Glamour Girl, Queen of the Vampires, The Vamp
Brigitte Bardot—Bad Little Bad Girl, Eternal Sex Goddess, The Sex Kitten
P.T. Barnum—Prince of Humbugs, Prince of Showmen
Ethyl Barrymore—First Lady of the American Theatre
John Blythe Barrymore—The Great Profile
Lionel Barrymore—Hollywood's Grand Old Man
Jack Benny—Cheapest Man in the World
Edgar Bergen—Noel Coward of Ventriloquists, The Perfect Stooge
Milton Berle—Mr. Saturday Night, Mr. Television, Thief of Bad Gags, Uncle Milty
Mel Blanc—Man of a Thousand Voices
Humphrey Bogart—Bogie (Bogey)
Raymond Wallace Bolger—Mr. Rubberlegs
Edwin Booth—Prince of Players
Clara Bow—The It Girl, The Red Head
Walter Brennan—King of the Character Actors
Carol Burnett—Hot Lips
Eddie Cantor—Banjo-Eyes, Pop-Eyes
Judy Carne—Sock-It-To-Me Girl
Johnny Carson—Great Carsoni, King of Late Night TV, Prince of Darkness
Lon Chaney—Man of a Thousand Faces
Carol Channing—First Lady of Musical Comedy
Charlie Chaplin—Chapu-rin, Charlot, Little Tramp, Twentieth-Century Moses
Sidney Chayefsky—Paddy
Dick Clark—World's Oldest Living Teenager
George Michael Cohan—King of Broadway, Man Who Owned Broadway, Mr. Broadway, Prince of the American Theatre, Yankee Doodle Dandy
Gary Cooper—The It Boy
Sammy Davis—Smokey, World's Greatest Entertainer
James Dean—Father of Rock Culture
Bo Derek—The Perfect 10
Marie Dressler—Grand Old Lady of the Movies, Queen Marie of Hollywood, Old Trouper
Isadora Duncan—First of the Modern Women
Irene Dunne—First Lady of Hollywood
Jimmy Durante—Ragtime Jimmy, The Schnozz, Schnozzola
Elvira—Mistress of the Dark
Dale Evans—Queen of the Cowgirls, Queen of the West
Douglas Fairbanks Sr.—Fourth Musketeer
Lola Falana—First Lady of Las Vegas
Stepin Fetchit—White Man's Negro
Jane Fonda—Hanoi Jane, Non-Stop Activist
John Ford—Boss, Coach, Pappy
Clark Gable—The King, King of Hollywood
Greta Garbo—The Face
Judy Garland—Lady Lazarus, Little Dorothy Lost, Triple Threat Girl
Edward Richard Gibson—Hoot
John Gilbert—Great Lover, Great Squeaky Lover
Dorothy Gish—Miss Apprehension
Lillian Gish—Carrots, First Lady of the Silent Screen, Iron Horse, Miss Lillian

Jackie Gleason—The Fat One, The Great One, Mr. Saturday Night
George Gobel—Lonesome George
Arthur Godfrey—Huck Finn of Radio, Old Redhead, Red, Red Head
Betty Grable—The Legs, Number One Pin Up Girl, The Red Head, The Shape, Soldier's Inspiration, Undisputed Queen of the Movies
D(avid) Lewelyn W(ark) Griffith—American Shakespeare, Father of the Film Industry, God of Hollywood
Oliver Hardy—Babe
Jean Harlow—Blonde Bombshell, Original Platinum Blond
Helen Hayes—First Lady of the American Stage, First Lady of the American Theatre
Rita Hayworth—Love Goddess
Margaux Hemingway—Fabulous Babe
Alfred Hitchcock—Portly Master of the Involuntary Scream, Master of Suspense
Dustin Hoffman—Little Big Man, Midnight Cowboy
Bob Hope—Ski Nose
Lena Horne—Queen of Broadway
Harry Houdini—Handcuff King, Monarch of Leg Shackles
Georgie Jessel—Boy Monologuist, Toastmaster General of the U.S.A.
Al Jolson—Jolie, The Immortal Jolson
George S. Kaufman—Gloomy Dean of Broadway
Buster Keaton—Great Stone Face
Emmett Kelly—Weary Millie
Dorothy Kilgallen—Voice of Broadway
Veronica Lake—Peekaboo Girl
Dorothy Lamour—Paratrooper Pet, Sarong Girl, Sweetheart of the Foxholes
Jay Leno—Prince of Late Night Television
David Letterman—Prince of Late Night Television
Richard Lewis—King of Angst
Liberace—Mr. Showmanship
Jeannette MacDonald—The Iron Butterfly
Jayne Mansfield—Blond Bombshell
Dean Martin—Dino, Ol' Red Eyes
Victor Mature—Hollywood's Number One Glamour Boy, The Hunk
Louis B. Mayer—King of Hollywood
Marie McDonald—The Body
George Emmette McFarland—Spanky
Burgess Meredith—Bugs, Buzz
David Merrick—Barnum of Broadway Producers
Yvette Mimieux—Hollywood's Little Princess
Tom Mix—America's Favorite Cowboy, World Champion Cowboy
John Moschitta Jr.—Mighty Mouth
Paul Muni—Man of Many Faces
Wayne Newton—King of Las Vegas, Midnight Idol, Mr. Excitement, Mr. Las Vegas
John Ringling North—Greatest Showman Since Barnum
Kim Novak—Hollywood's Melancholy Blonde
Annie Oakley—America's Sweetheart, Little Sure Shot
Maureen O'Hara—Queen of the Swash Bucklers, Queen of Technicolor
Minnie Pearl—Queen of Country Corn

Sam Peckinpah—Bloody Sam, Master of Violence
Mary Pickford—America's Sweetheart, Girl with the Curl, Queen of the Movies
Molly Picon—Sweetheart of Second Avenue
ZaSu Pitts—Girl with the Ginger Snap Name
Sidney Poitier—Jackie Robinson of Film
Elvis Presley—E, Elvis the Pelvis, Father of Rock 'N' Roll, The King
Sally Rand—Fan-tastic Sally, Her Sexellency
Basil Rathbone—Man with the Finest Sneer in the Movies
Burt Reynolds—The Frog Prince
Don Rickles—Master of Insult Comedy, Merchant of Venom, Mr. Warmth
Bill (b. Luther) Robinson—Bojangles, King of the Tap Dancers, King of Tapology
Roy Rogers—King of the Cowboys, Top Boots-and-Saddle Star
Billy Rose—Basement Barnum, Midget Maestro of Broadway
Abe Saperstein—Barnum of Basketball
Arnold Schwarzenegger—Austrian Oak
Randolph Scott—Gentleman from Virginia
Mack Sennett—King of Comedy
Norma Shearer—First Lady of the Screen
Ann Sheridan—The Oomph Girl
Red Skelton—Marcel Marceau of Television
James Stewart—Grand Old Man of the Aw Shucks School
Ed Sullivan—Great Stone Face, Unsmiling Irishman
Shirley Temple—Eighth Wonder of the World, Little Goldilocks
Irving Grant Thalberg—Boy Producer, Boy Wonder
Evelyn Nesbit Thaw—Girl in the Red Velvet Swing
Marlo Thomas—Miss Independent, Princess of Situation Comedy, That Girl
Michael Todd—America's Greatest Showman, New Ziegfeld
Spencer Tracy—Old Bucko
Lana Turner—Sweater Girl
Rudolph Valentino—Great Lover, The Sheik
Rudy Vallee—The Crooner, Vagabond Lover
John Wayne—The Duke
Jack Webb—Sergeant Joe Friday
Orson Welles—Boy Genius, Boy Wonder
Mae West—Baby Vamp, Diamond Lil, Screen's Bad Girl, Siren of Sex, Siren of the Screen
Pearl White—Queen of the Silent Serials
Esther Williams—Queen of the Surf
Ed Wynn—Perfect Fool
Loretta Young—The Iron Butterfly, The Steel Butterfly
Henny Youngman—King of the One-Liners
Darryl Francis Zanuck—The Chief
Flo(renz) Ziegfeld, Jr.—Lorenzo the Magnificent of the Stage, Ziggy

PSEUDONYMS/REAL NAMES

Edie Adams—Elizabeth Edith Enke
Anouk Aimée—Françoise Sorya Dreyfus
Eddie Albert—Edward Albert Heimberger
Alan Alda—Alphonso D'Abruzzo
Jane Alexander—Jane Quigley
Jason Alexander—Jay Scott Greenspan
Fred Allen—John Florence Sullivan
Tim Allen—Timothy Allen Dick

Thespians and Other Entertainers

Woody Allen—Allen Stewart Konigsberg
June Allyson—Ella Geisman
Don Ameche—Dominic Felix Amici
Famous Amos—Wally Amos
Andre the Giant—Andre Roussimoff
Julie Andrews—Julia Elizabeth Wells
Ann-Margret—Ann-Margret Olsson
Marc Anthony—Marco Antonio Muniz
Fiona Apple—Fiona Apple McAfee Maggart
Eve Arden—Eunice Quedens
India.Arie—India Arie Sampson
James Arness—James Aurness
Beatrice Arthur—Bernice Frankel
Jean Arthur—Gladys Georgianna Greene
Ashanti—Ashanti Douglas
Fred Astaire—Frederick Austerlitz
Mary Astor—Lucille Vasconcellos Langhanke
Frankie Avalon—Francis Thomas Avallone
Charles Aznavour—Shahnour Varenagh Aznavurjan
Babyface—Kenneth Edmonds
Lauren Bacall—Betty Joan Perske
Erykah Badu—Erica Wright
Barbara Bain—Millie Fogel
Alec Baldwin—Alexander Rae Baldwin III
Anne Bancroft—Anna Maria Louisa Italiano
Theda Bara/ Theodosia Burr Goodman
Brigitte Bardot—Camille Javal
Rona Barrett—Rona Burstein
Gene Barry—Eugene Klass
Ethel Barrymore—Ethel Mae Blythe
John Barrymore—John Blythe
Lionel Barrymore—Lionel Blythe
Orson Bean—Dallas Frederick Burrows
Beck—Beck Hansen
Pat Benatar—Patricia Andrzejewski
Tony Bennett—Antonio Dominick Benedetto
Jack Benny—Benjamin Kubelsky
Robby Benson—Robert Segal
Polly Bergen—Nellie Paulina Burgin
Busby Berkeley—William Berkeley Enos
Milton Berle—Milton Berlinger
Irving Berlin—Israel Baline
Sarah Bernhardt—Henriette-Rosine Bernard
Joey Bishop—Joseph Gottlieb
Bjork—Björk Gudmundsdottir
Robert Blake—Michael Gubitosi
Blondie—Deborah Ann Harry
Michael Bolton—Michael Bolotin
Jon Bon Jovi—John Francis Bongiovi
Bono—Paul Hewson
Shirley Booth—Thelma Booth Ford

Victor Borge—Borge Rosenbaum
Ernest Borgnine—Ermes Borgnino
David Bowie—David Robert Jones
Boy George—George Alan O'Dowd
Brandy—Brandy Norwood
Fanny Brice—Fanny Borach
Beau Bridges—Lloyd Vernet Bridges III
James Brolin—James Bruderlin
Charles Bronson—Charles Buchinsky
Albert Brooks—Albert Einstein
Mel Brooks—Melvin Kaminsky
Joyce Brothers—Joyce Diane Bauer
Lenny Bruce—Leonard Alfred Schneider
Yul Brynner—Taidje Khan Jr.
George Burns—Nathan Birnbaum
Ellen Burstyn—Edna Rae Gilhooley
Richard Burton—Richard Walter Jenkins Jr.
Red Buttons—Aaron Chwatt
Nicolas Cage—Nicholas Coppola
Michael Caine—Maurice Joseph Micklewhite
Dyan Cannon—Samille Diane Friesen
Eddie Cantor—Edward Israel Iskowitz
Kate Capshaw—Kathleen Sue Nail
Diahann Carroll—Carol Diahann Johnson
Carrot Top—Scott Thompson
Hopalong Cassidy—William Boyd
Jackie Chan—Kong-Sang Chan
Stockard Channing—Susan Antonia Williams Stockard
Cyd Charisse—Tula Ellice Finklea
Ray Charles—Ray Charles Robinson
Charo—Maria Rosario Pilar Martinez Molina Baeza
J.C. Chasez—Joshua Scott Chasez
Chubby Checker—Ernest Evans
Cher—Cherilyn Sarkisian La Piere
Chuck D.—Charles Ridenhour
Eric Clapton—Eric Clapp
Patsy Cline—Virginia Patterson Hensley
Lee J. Cobb—Leo Jacoby
Claudette Colbert—Claudette Lily Chauchoin
Nat King Cole—Nathaniel Adams Coles
Mike Connors—Krekor Ohanian
Robert Conrad—Conrad Robert Falk
Coolio—Artis Ivey Jr.
Alice Cooper—Vincent Damon Furnier
David Copperfield—David Kotkin
Howard Cosell—Howard William Cohen
Elvis Costello—Declan Patrick McManus
Lou Costello—Louis Francis Cristillo
Peter Coyote—Peter Cohon
Joan Crawford—Lucille Fay LeSueur
Michael Crawford—Michael Dumble-Smith

Peter Criss—Peter Criscoula
David Crosby—David Van Cortland
Tom Cruise—Thomas Cruise Mopother IV
Tony Curtis—Bernard Schwartz
Vic Damone—Vito Farinola
Rodney Dangerfield—Jacob Cohen
Bobby Darin—Robert Walden Cassotto
Doris Day—Doris von Kappelhoff
Yvonne De Carlo—Peggy Yvonne Middleton
Kiki Dee—Pauline Mathews
Ruby Dee—Ruby Ann Wallace
Sandra Dee—Alexandra Zuck
Mos Def—Dante Terrell Smith
Catherine Deneuve—Catherine Dorleac
John Denver—Henry John Deutschendorf Jr.
Bo Derek—Mary Cathleen Collins
Angie Dickinson—Angeline Brown
Bo Diddley—Otha Ellas Bates (McDaniel)
Phyllis Diller—Phyllis Driver
Jeane Dixon—Jeane Pinckert
Troy Donahue—Merle Johnson Jr.
Donovan—Donovan Leitch
Diana Dors—Diana Mary Fluck
Kirk Douglas—Issur Danielovitch Demsky
Mike Douglas—Michael Delaney Dowd Jr.
Dr. Dre—Andre Young
Bob Dylan—Robert Zimmerman
Sheena Easton—Sheena Shirley Orr
Barbara Eden—Barbara Huffman
Carmen Electra—Tara Leigh Patrick
Jenna Elfman—Jennifer Mary Butala
"Mama" Cass Elliot—Ellen Naomi Cohen
Elvira—Cassandra Peterson
Eminem—Marshall Mathers III
Enya—Eithne Ní Bhraonáin
Gloria Estefan—Gloria Maria Fajardo
Dale Evans—Frances Octavia Smith
Linda Evans—Linda Evanstad
Eve—Eve Jihan Jeffers
Dame Enda Everage—Barry Humphries
Fabian—Fabian Forte
Fabio—Fabio Lanzoni
Douglas Fairbanks—Douglas Elton Ulman
Morgan Fairchild—Patsy McClenny
Jamie Farr—Jameel Joseph Farah
Stepin Fetchit—Lincoln Theodore Perry
W.C. Fields—William Claude Dukenfield
50 Cent—Curtis Jackson
Fannie Flagg—Patricia Neal
Rhonda Fleming—Marilyn Louis
Joan Fontaine—Joan de Havilland
*Her surname is Gerber.

John Ford—Sean Aloysius O'Fearna
John Forsythe—John Freund
Jamie Foxx—Eric Bishop
Redd Foxx—John Elroy Sanford
Connie Francis—Concetta Franconero
Dennis Franz—Dennis Schlachta
Zsa Zsa Gabor—Sári Gabor
Greta Garbo—Greta Louissa Gustafsson
Andy Garcia—Andres Arturo Garcia-Menendez
Judy Garland—Frances Gumm
James Garner—James Scott B(a)umgarner
Crystal Gayle—Brenda Gail Webb
Janet Gaynor—Laura Gainor
Mitzi Gaynor*—Francesca Marlene von Gerber
Estelle Getty—Estelle Scher
Bobbie Gentry—Roberta Streeter
Kathie Lee Gifford—Kathie Lee Epstein
John Gilbert—John Pringle
Lillian Gish—Lillian de Guiche
Paulette Goddard—Marion Levy
Whoopi Goldberg—Caryn Elaine Johnson
Samuel Goldwyn—Schmuel Gelbfisz
Elliott Gould—Elliott Goldstein
Stewart Granger—James Stewart
Cary Grant—Archibald Leach
Lee Grant—Lyova Haskell Rosenthal
Peter Graves—Peter Aurness
Macy Gray—Natalie McIntyre
Joel Grey—Joel Katz
Charles Grodin—Charles Grodinsky
Robert Guillaume—Robert Williams
Buddy Hackett—Leonard Hacker
Monty Hall—Monte Halparin
M.C. Hammer—Stanley Kirk Burrell
Jean Harlow—Harlean Carpenter
Rex Harrison—Reginald Carey
Laurence Harvey—Larushka Mischa Skikne
June Havoc—Ellen Evangeline Hovick
Helen Hayes—Helen Hayes Brown
Susan Hayward—Edythe Marrener
Rita Hayworth—Margarita Cansino
Audrey Hepburn—Edda Hepburn-Ruston
Pee-Wee Herman/Paul Reubens—Paul Rubenfeld
Barbara Hershey—Barbara Herzstein
Charlton Heston—John Charles Carter
Faith Hill—Audrey Faith Perry
William Holden—William Franklin Beedle Jr.
Billie Holiday—Eleanora Fagan

Judy Holliday—Judith Tuvim
Hedda Hopper—Elda Furry
John Houseman—Jacques Haussmann
Leslie Howard—Leslie Stainer
Rock Hudson—Roy Harold Scherer Jr. (Fitzgerald)
Engelbert Humperdinck—Arnold Dorsey
Kim Hunter—Janet Cole
Tab Hunter—Andrew Klem (Gelien)
Mary Beth Hurt—Mary Beth Supinger
Betty Hutton—Elizabeth June Thornburg
Ice Cube—O'Shea Jackson
Ice-T—Tracy Morrow
Billy Idol—William Michael Broad
Iman—Iman Abdulmajid
Burl Ives—Burle Icle Ivanhoe
Etta James—Jamesetta Hawkins
Rick James—James Johnson
David Janssen—David Meyer
Jay-Z—Shawn Carter
Jazzie B.—Beresford Romeo
Joan Jett—Joan Marie Larkin
Jewel—Jewel Kilcher
Ann Jillian—Ann Jura Nauseda
Robert Joffrey—Abdullah Jaffa Bey Khan
Elton John—Reginald Kenneth Dwight
Don Johnson—Don Wayne
Angelina Jolie—Angelina Jolie Voight
Al Jolson—Asa Yoelson
Jennifer Jones—Phyllis Lee Isley
Tom Jones—Thomas Jones Woodward
Wynonna Judd—Christina Calire Ciminella
Boris Karloff—William Henry Pratt
Danny Kaye—David Daniel Kaminski
Diane Keaton—Diane Hall
Michael Keaton—Michael Douglas
Kenny G—Kenneth Gorelick
Alicia Keys—Alicia Augello Cook
Chaka Khan—Yvette Marie Stevens
Kid Rock—Robert James Ritchie
B.B. King—Riley B. King
Carole King—Carole Klein
Ben Kingsley—Krishna Bhanji (Banji)
Nastassja Kinski—Nastassja Nakszynski
Ted Knight—Tadeus Wladyslaw Konopka
The Amazing Kreskin—George Joseph Kresge
Patty LaBelle—Patricia Louise Holt
Cheryl Ladd—Cheryl Stoppelmoor
Diane Ladd—Rose Diane Lanier
Veronica Lake—Constance Ockleman
Hedy Lamarr—Hedwig Eva Maria Kiesler
Dorothy Lamour—Mary Leta Dorothy Slaton
Ann Landers—Esther Pauline Friedman
Michael Landon—Eugene Orowitz
Frankie Lane—Frankie LoVecchio
Mario Lanza—Alfred Arnold Cocozza
Queen Latifah—Dana Elaine Owens
Stan Laurel—Arthur Stanley Jefferson
Ralph Lauren—Ralph Lipschitz (Lifshitz)
Piper Laurie—Rosetta Jacobs
Carol Lawrence—Carol Maria Laraia
Steve Lawrence—Sidney Leibowitz
Heath Ledger—Heathcliff Andrew Ledger
Brenda Lee—Brenda Mae Tarpley
Bruce Lee—Lee Jun Fan
Gypsy Rose Lee—Rose Louise Hovick
Michelle Lee—Michelle Dusiak
Peggy Lee—Norma Deloris Jean Egstrom
Pinky Lee—Pincus Leff
Spike Lee—Shelton Jackson Lee
Tommy Lee—Thomas Lee Bass
Janet Leigh—Jeannette Helen Morrison
Jennifer Jason Leigh—Jennifer Lee Morrow
Vivien Leigh—Vivian Mary Hartley
Téa Leoni—Elizabeth Téa Pantaleoni
Huey Lewis—Hugh Cregg
Jerry Lewis—Joseph Levitch
Shari Lewis—Shari Hurwitz
Jet Li—Li Lian-jie
(Lil) Bow Wow—Shad Gregory Moss
Lil' Kim—Kimberly Denise Jones
Hal Linden—Hal Lipshitz
Little Eva—Eva Narcissus Boyd
Little Richard—Richard Wayne Penniman
L.L. Cool J—James Todd Smith
Carole Lombard—Jane Alice Peters
Sophia Loren—Sofia Scicolone
Peter Lorre—László Löwenstein
Tina Louise—Tina Blacker
Courtney Love—Love Michelle Harrison
Myrna Loy—Myrna Williams
Ludacris—Christopher Bridges
Bela Lugosi—Bela Blasko
Loretta Lynn—Loretta Webb
Moms Mabley—Loretta Mary Aitken
Bernie Mac—Bernard Jeffrey McCullough
Shirley MacLaine—Shirley McLean Beaty
Gavin MacLeod—Allan See
Elle MacPherson—Eleanor Gow
Madonna—Madonna Louise Veronica Ciccone
Marjorie Main—Mary Tomlinson
Lee Majors—Harvey Lee Yeary II
Karl Malden—Mladen Sekulovich
Dorothy Malone—Dorothy Eloise Maloney

Barry Manilow—Barry Alan Pincus
Jayne Mansfield—Vera Jayne Palmer
Marilyn Manson—Brian Hugh Warner
Marcel Marceau—Marcel Mangel
Fredric March—Frederick McIntyre Bickel
Penny Marshall—Carole Penelope Masciarelli
Peter Marshall—Pierre LaCock
Dean Martin—Dino Crocetti
Ricky Martin—Enrique José Martin Morales
Tony Martin—Alvin Morris
Jackie Mason—Jacob Moshe Maza
Master P—Percy Miller
Walter Matthau—Walter Matuschanskavasky
Elaine May—Elaine Berlin
Audrey Meadows—Audrey Cotter
Jayne Meadows—Jayne Cotter
Meat Loaf—Marvin Lee Aday
Ethel Merman—Ethel Zimmerman
George Michael—Georgios Kyriacos Panayiotou
Vera Miles—Vera May Ralston
Ray Milland—Reginald Truscott-Jones
Ann Miller—Lucille Ann Collier
Joni Mitchell—Roberta Joan Anderson
Moby—Richard Melville Hall
Marilyn Monroe—Norma Jean Mortenson (Baker)
Yves Montand—Ivo Livi
Demi Moore—Demetria Gene Guynes
Juliane Moore—Julie Anne Smith
Terry Moore—Helen Koford
Rita Moreno—Rosita Dolores Alverio
Harry Morgan—Harry Bratsburg
Paul Muni—Muni Weisenfreund
Pola Negri—Barbara Appolonia Chalupiec
Nelly—Cornell Haynes Jr.
Julie Newmar—Julia Chalane Newmeyer
Mike Nichols—Michael Igor Peschkowsky
Chuck Norris—Carlos Ray
Notorious B.I.G.—Christopher Wallace
Merle Oberon—Estelle Merle O'Brien Thompson
Hugh O'Brian—Hugh Charles Krampe
Billy Ocean—Leslie Sebastian Charles
Maureen O'Hara—Maureen Fitzsimons
O.D.B.**—Russell Jones
Tony Orlando—Michael Anthony Orlando Cassavitis
Patti Page—Clara Ann Fowler
Debra Paget—Debralee Griffin
Janis Paige—Donna Mae Tjaden
Jack Palance—Vladimir Palanuik
Lilli Palmer—Lillie Marie Peiser

Irene Papas—Irene Lelekou
Louella Parsons—Louella Rose Oettinger
Les Paul—Lester Polfuss
Johnny Paycheck—Donald Lytle
Minnie Pearl—Sarah Ophelia Cannon
Luke Perry—Coy Luther Perry III
Bernadette Peters—Bernadette Lazzaro
Lou Diamond Phillips—Lou Upchurch
Michelle Phillips—Holly Michelle Gilliam
Joaquin Phoenix—Joaquin Rafael Bottom
River Phoenix—River Jude Bottom
Slim Pickens—Louis Bert Lindley
Mary Pickford—Gladys Smith
Pink—Alecia Moore
Jane Powell—Suzanne Lorraine Bruce
Stephanie Powers—Stefdnia Zofija Federkiewicz
Paula Prentiss—Paula Ragusa
Priscilla Presley—Priscilla Wagner Beaulieu
Kelly Preston—Kelly Smith
Prince—Prince Rogers Nelson
Puff Daddy—Sean John Combs
George Raft—George Ranft
Ma Rainey—Gertrude Pridgett
Sally Rand—Helen Gould Beck
Tony Randall—Leonard Rousenberg
Martha Raye—Margaret Theresa Yvonne Reed
Nancy Reagan—Anne Frances Robbins
Donna Reed—Donna Mullenger
Della Reese—Delloreese Patricia Early
Busta Rhymes—Trevor Smith Jr.
Joan Rivers—Joan Sandra Molinsky
Edward G. Robinson—Emmanuel Goldenberg
The Rock—Dwayne Douglas Johnson
Ginger Rogers—Virginia McMath
Roy Rogers—Leonard Franklin Slye
Mickey Rooney—Joe Yule Jr.
Axl Rose—William Bailey
Billy Rose—William Samuel Rosenberg
Johnny Rotten—John Lydon
Ja Rule—Jeffrey Atkins
Lillian Russell—Helen Louise Leonard
Theresa Russell—Theresa Paup
Jeri Ryan—Jeri Lynn Zimmerman
Meg Ryan—Margaret Hyra
Winona Ryder—Winona Laura Horowitz
Sade—Helen Folasade Adu
Jill St. John—Jill Oppenheim
Soupy Sales—Milton Hines (Supman)
Susan Sarandon—Susan Abigail Tomaling
Romy Schneider—Rosemarie Albach-Retty
Randolph Scott—Randolph Crane

**Also known as Ol' Dirty Bastard

Seal—Sealhenry Samuel
Mack Sennett—Michael Sinnott
Jane Seymour—Joyce Penelope Frankenberg
Shaggy—Orville Richard Burrell
Shakira—Shakira Mebarak Ripoll
Omar Sharif—Michael Shalhoub
Charlie Sheen—Carlos Irwin Estevez
Martin Sheen—Ramon Estevez
Sheila E.—Sheila Escovedo
Judith Sheindlin—Judy Blum
Talia Shire—Talia Rose Coppola
Simone Signoret—Simone-Henriette Kaminker
Beverly Sills—Belle Silverman
Jay Silverheels—Harold Jay Smith
Phil Silvers—Phil Silversmith
Nina Simone—Eunice Wayman
Sinbad—David Adkins
Sisqo—Mark Andrews
Christian Slater—Christian Michael Hawkins
Grace Slick—Grace Barnett Wing
Anna Nicole Smith—Vicky Lynn Hogan
Snoop Dogg—Cordozar "Calvin" Broadus
Elke Sommer—Elke Schletz
Ann Sothern—Harriette Lake
David Soul—David Richard Solberg
Kevin Spacey—Kevin Spacey Fowler
Robert Stack—Robert Modini
Barbara Stanwyck—Ruby Stevens
Jean Stapleton—Jeanne Murray
Ringo Starr—Richard Starkey
Cat Stevens***—Stephen Georgiou
Connie Stevens—Concetta Ann Ingolia
Inger Stevens—Inger Stensland
Jon Stewart—Jonathan Stuart Leibowitz
Sting—Gordon Matthew Sumner
Sly Stone—Sylvester Stewart
Gale Storm—Josephine Owaissa Cottle
Donna Summer—LaDonna Andrea Gaines
Mr. T—Lawrence Tureaud
Robert Taylor—Spangler Arlington Brugh
Danny Thomas—Muzyad Yakhoob
Jonathan Taylor Thomas—Jonathan Taylor Weiss

Tiffany—Tiffany Renee Darwisch
Tiny Tim—Herbert Buckingham Khaury
Michael Todd—Avrom Hirsch Goldbogen
Rip Torn—Elmore Rual Torn
Randy Travis—Randy Traywick
Claire Trevor—Claire Wemlinger
Sophie Tucker—Sophia Kalish
Janine Turner—Janine Gauntt
Tina Turner—Anna Mae Bullock
Conway Twitty—Harold Lloyd Jenkins
Usher—Usher Raymond IV
Rudolph Valentino—Rodolpho d'Antonguolla****
Frankie Valli—Frank Castelluccio
Abigail Van Buren—(Dear Abby) Pauline Esther Friedman
Jean-Claude Van Damme—Jean-Claude Van Varenberg
Mamie van Doren—Joan Lucille Olander
Vanilla Ice—Robert Van Winkle
Vendela—Vendela Maria Kirsebom
Sid Vicious—John Simon Ritchie
Muddy Waters—McKinley Morganfield
John Wayne—Marion Michael Morrison
Charlie Weaver—Cliff Arquette
Clifton Webb—Webb Parmellee Hollenbeck
Raquel Welch—Raquel Tejada
Kitty Wells—Ellen Muriel Deason
Adam West—William West Anderson
Vanna White—Vanna Marie Rosich
Gene Wilder—Jerome Silberman
Shelly Winters—Shirley Schrift
Wolfman Jack—Robert Weston Smith
Stevie Wonder—Steveland Morris Hardaway
Natalie Wood—Natalia Zakharenko
Jane Wyman—Sarah Jane Fulks
Tammy Wynette—Virginia Wynette Pugh
Yanni—Yanni Chrysomalis
Susannah York—Susannah Yolande Fletcher
Gig Young—Byron Elsworth Barr
Loretta Young—Gretchen Michaela Young

***He later adopted the Muslim name Yusuf Islam. ****In full, Guglielmi de Valentina d'Antonguolla, Rodolpho Alfonso Raffaelo Pierre Fillbert

LANGUAGE/ALPHABET

Holy Roman Emperor from 1500 to 1558 who said, "I speak Spanish to God, Italian to women, French to men, and German to my horse"
Answer: Charles V.

1) What name is given to the family of languages divided as Albanian, Armenian, Baltic, Slavic (or Balto-Slavic), Celtic, Germanic, Greek, Indo-Aryan, Iranian (or Indo-Iranian), and Romance.
Answer: Indo-European family.

2) Identify the 6 languages used by the U.N. when conducting official business.
Answer: Arabic, Chinese, English, French, Russian, and Spanish.

3) Identify the 6 languages spoken by the most people.
Answer: Northern Chinese (Mandarin or *putonghua*), English, Hindi (Urdu), Spanish, Arabic, and Bengali (in order from the most to the least; as "first language" speakers: Chinese, Hindi, English, Spanish, Bengali, and Arabic).

4) Identify the branch of the Indo-European language family consisting of languages derived from the Latin spoken by the common people in what is known as Latin Europe.
Answer: Romance languages.

5) Identify the 5 Romance language spoken the most often.
Answer: Spanish, Portuguese, French, Italian, and Romanian (listed in order from the most often to the least often).

6) Identify the 4 official languages of Interpol.
Answer: French, English, Spanish, and Arabic.

7) Identify the 3 official languages of Switzerland.
Answer: German, French, and Italian (the country has 4 national languages, the 3 official ones plus Romansh or Romansch, a language closely related to Latin).

8) Identify the 3 writing systems used in the Egyptian priests' decree commemorating the crowning of Ptolemy V Epiphanes, king of Egypt from 203 to 181 B.C., and carved on the Rosetta Stone in 196 B.C.
Answer: (Egyptian) hieroglyphics, demotic (the popular language of Egypt at the time), and Greek.

9) Identify the 2 groups of Romance dialects that developed in France in the 900s, named after the word for "yes" in each group.
Answer: Langue d'oc and langue d'oïl (the former was spoken south of the Loire River and the latter north of that river; most famous dialect of the langue d'oc was Provençal, the language used by troubadours).

Afrikaans—South Africa's official language developed from 17th-century Dutch
Amharic—Official language of Ethiopia
Arabic—Classical literary language of the Koran
Aramaic—Language spoke by Jesus and His Disciples
Baltic—Branch of the Indo-European family of languages divided into Latvian and Lithuanian
Basque—Language unrelated to others and spoken by people in the western Pyrenees of Spain and France
Bengali (Bangla)—Indo-Aryan language that is the official language of Bangladesh
Cajun—Dialect of French spoken by the descendants of French Acadians
Cantonese—Principal variety of Chinese spoken in Southern China around Guangzhou (formerly Canton), Hong Kong, and Macau—also called *Yue*
Castilian—Standard form of Spanish spoken in Castile, Spain
Catalan—Romance language closely related to Provençal and spoken mainly in Catalonia
Celtic—Branch of the Indo-European family of languages divided into Irish (Gaelic), Welsh, Scots (Gaelic), and Manx (sometimes Breton is included)
Coptic—Language of the Copts, derived from ancient Egyptian
Creole—French language spoken in Louisiana
English—World's most widely spoken language, one that has a larger vocabulary than any other language at more than 600,000 words
Farsi—Persian language spoken officially in Iran
Flemish—West Germanic language closely related to Dutch and spoken in Flanders
Gaelic—Celtic language of the Scottish Highlands
German—Language technically called *New High* _____, whose "higher" form is spoken in the mountains and "lower" one, in the lowlands
Germanic—Branch of the Indo-European family of languages divided primarily into Danish, Dutch, English, German, and Scandinavian
Greek—Language in which the New Testament was written
Hebrew—Semitic language with 22 letters in which most of the Old Testament was written, as well as the Dead Sea Scrolls, the language of the Jewish people
Hindi—India's main language, now designated the official one
Iranian—Branch of the Indo-European family of languages divided into Pashto and Persian
Joual—French dialect spoken in Canada
Khmer—Official language of Kampuchea or Cambodia
Korean—Language whose 24-letter alphabet, called *hangul*, is considered to have been the first phonetic alphabet in East Asia—about half of all its words come from Chinese
Latin—Indo-European language spoken by the ancient Romans, the ancestor of the modern Romance languages
Latvian—Baltic language also known as Lettish
Magyar—Hungary's official language, that of its main ethnic group
Mandarin—Most widely spoken of the Chinese languages
Portuguese—Brazil's official language
Punjabi—Indo-Aryan language spoken in the Punjab region in India and Pakistan
Romany—Indo-Aryan language of the Gypsies
Sanskrit—Classical literary language of Hinduism, dating to the 4th century B.C.
Semitic—Family of languages that includes Aramaic, Hebrew, and Arabic
Swahili—Bantu language that is Tanzania's official language and Kenya and Uganda's national one

Tagalog—Malay-based language spoken largely in Manila that is the basis for Filipino
Urdu—Indo-Aryan language of Pakistan and northern India similar to Hindi
Yiddish—Language spoken by Jews of Eastern and Central Europe that combines German dialects with Hebrew and other languages

MULTIPLE LANGUAGES
South Africa—Country with 11 official languages, including English, Venda, Xhosa, Swazi, Zulu, North Sesotho, South Sesotho, and *scamto*, a street slang mixing all 11 of them
Hebrew and Aramaic—2 languages in which the Talmud is written
Pashtu and Dari—2 official languages of Afghanistan
Dutch and French—2 official languages of Belgium
English and French—2 official languages of Canada
Greek and Turkish—2 official languages of Cyprus
Finnish and Swedish—2 official languages of Finland
Hindi and English—2 official languages of India
English and Irish (Gaelic)—2 official languages of Ireland
Hebrew and Arabic—2 official languages of Israel
Malagasy and French—2 official languages of Madagascar
Filipino and English—2 official languages of the Philippines
Sinhala and Tamil—2 official languages of Sri Lanka
English and Welsh—2 official languages of Wales
English and French—2 official languages of the World Court or the International Court of Justice

LANGUAGE POTPOURRI
Alpha and beta—2 Greek letters from which the word alphabet comes
American Sign Language—Full meaning of the initialism ASL
Arabic—Semitic language whose dialects include Gulf, Levantine, Maghrebi, Saudi, and Sudanese
Braille—System of writing and printing for the blind
Chinese—Only major language that has no alphabetical system of writing, using about 50,000 characters instead
Cuneiform—Wedge-shaped writing invented by the Sumerians—its name comes from the Latin word *cuneus*
Cyrillic—Slavic alphabet attributed to St. Cyril and still used in Russia, Bulgaria, and other Slavic countries
Ebonics—Form of Black English as recognized in 1997 by the Oakland School Board for use as a starting point to teach standard English
English—Belize's official language
English as a second language—Full meaning of the initialism ESL
Esperanto—International language whose name means "one who hopes," devised by Polish physician Dr. L.L. Zamenhof in 1887
Etymology—Study of the origin and development of words
Thomas Gallaudet—U.S. philanthropist who brought the system of sign language to this country and after whom a Washington, D.C., university for the deaf is named
Graffiti—Unauthorized writings and drawings on a wall or other public surface
Greek—Word completing the saying *It's _____ to me*, meaning "I cannot understand it"

Hieroglyphics—System of ancient Egyptian writing in which figures or objects were used to represent words or sounds
Interlingua—International language developed for scientific and medical writing
Jargon*—Specialized language used by a particular group
Kenya—African country whose official language is English and whose national language is Swahili
Lingua franca—2-word Latin term, literally meaning "Frankish language," designating both a hybrid language of Italian, Spanish, French, Greek, Arabic, and Turkish, and any language, especially a hybrid one, used for communication between people speaking different languages
• **Linguistics**—Word beginning with *L* for the scientific study of language
Morse code—System of sending messages using short (dit) and long (dah) sounds or dots and dashes
Neologism—Newly-coined word or expression
Philology—Scientific study of language, as named from the Greek for "love of speech"
Phoenicians—Seagoing traders and navigators whose alphabet became the basis of the Greek alphabet
Pictograph(y)—Picture-writing used before the development of the alphabet
Pidgin—Any simplified language with limited grammar and vocabulary as used by non-native speakers
Pidgin English—Simplified form of English used by East Asian and South Pacific people when speaking to foreigners
Roman—Upright style in which our 26-letter alphabet is most commonly printed
Rune—Any of the characters inscribed by the Germanic people of Europe on wood, stone, or elsewhere, named from a word meaning "secret"
Semantics—Scientific study of the meaning of words
Semaphore—System of signals for sending messages using flags, one in each hand
Sequoya(h)—Indian who invented a system for writing the Cherokee language
Sign language—Communication by means of bodily movements, especially by the hands by deaf people
Vernacular—Native language or dialect of a country
*Other similar terms are *argot*, *shoptalk*, and *slang*

INTERNATIONAL PHONETIC ALPHABET*

Alpha—A, Greek letter call sign for the international space station once called *Freedom*
Bravo—B, interjection for "well done," used to praise a performer
Charlie—C, name completing _____ Chaplin, the English filmmaker and actor, often called "the funniest man in the world"
Delta—D, letter of the Greek alphabet
Echo—E, mountain nymph punished by Hera who left her able only to repeat the words of others
Foxtrot—F, dance for couples in 4/4 time or a slow horse gait
Golf—G, sport in which one plays 18
Hotel—H, commercial establishment that provides lodging
India—I, country that is the world's most populous democracy
Juliet—J, Shakespearean title character

*As listed in the *U.S. Department of Defense Dictionary of Military Terms*; the system is sometimes called the NATO Phonetic Alphabet and replaces an earlier system using Able, Baker, Charlie, Dog, Easy, Fox, George, How, Item, Jig, King, Love, Mike, Nan, Oboe, Peter, Queen, Roger, Sugar, Tare, Uncle, Victor, William, X Ray, Yoke, Zebra.

Kilo—K, combining form meaning 1,000
Lima—L, South American capital
Mike—M, informal term for an instrument that amplifies sound
November—N, month of the year that was the 9th month of the ancient Roman year
Oscar—O, Academy Award presentation
Papa—P, alliterative word for a father
Quebec—Q, Canadian province
Romeo—R, Shakespearean title character
Sierra—S, Spanish word for "saw" designating a range of hills
Tango—T, South American dance for couples
Uniform—U, adjective for "always the same"
Victor—V, winner in a battle
Whiskey—W, strong, intoxicating liquor made from grain
X Ray—X, band of electromagnetic radiation invented by Wilhelm Konrad Roentgen
Yankee—Y, person born or living in New England
Zulu—Z, African tribe living in South Africa

GREEK ALPHABET

William Shakespeare play in which Casca says, "For mine own part, it was Greek to me"
Answer: *Julius Caesar.*

Alpha	Zeta	Lambda	Pi	Phi
Beta	Eta	Mu	Rho	Chi
Gamma	Theta	Nu	Sigma	Psi
Delta	Iota	Xi	Tau	Omega
Epsilon	Kappa	Omicron	Upsilon	

1) Identify the 5 letters that correspond with the 5 vowels—A, E, I, O, U—in the English language.
Answer: Alpha, Epsilon, Iota, Omicron, and Upsilon.

2) Identify the 5 letters ending in the letter *I*.
Answer: Xi, pi, phi, chi, psi.

3) Identify the 3 letters ending in the letter *U*.
Answer: Mu, nu, tau.

4) Identify the 3 types of interferons, proteins produced by cells in the body to fight viral infections.
Answer: Alpha, beta, and gamma.

5) Which phrase meaning "everything," "the most important part," or "the beginning and the end" comes from the first and last letters of the Greek alphabet and is used in the Bible?
Answer: The alpha and omega (from Revelation: 1:8: "I am Alpha and Omega, the beginning and the ending, saith the Lord").

6) Identify the 2 letters, one for dentistry and the other for *odont* or tooth, on the insignia adopted by the American Dental Association in 1965 as its official emblem, which also includes a serpent coiled about a staff and 32 leaves and 20 berries, representing the permanent and temporary teeth.
Answer: Delta and omicron (the design features a lilac background, the official academic color of dentistry; the letter *O*, in gold; and the letter *D* in black).

7) Identify the Aldous Huxley novel in which the D.H.C. shows his new students ". . . how the fertilized ova went back to the incubators; where the Alphas and Betas remained until definitely bottled; while the Gammas, Deltas and Epsilons were brought out again, after only thirty-six hours."
Answer: *Brave New World.*

1-WORD ANSWERS
24—Number of letters in the Greek alphabet

Alpha—Beginning of anything and the name for the brightest star in each constellation
Beta* —Trademark for an electronic system for recording and playing back videocassettes
Delta—Letter whose shape is a geometric figure
Gamma—Microgram or a unit of magnetic intensity equal to 10^{-5}
Beta—Second brightest star in each constellation
Alpha—First in a series of related items, as in chemistry and physics
Delta—Tract of flat land, usually triangular, formed by deposits of soil and sand at the mouth of a large river
Beta—Second in a series of related items, as in chemistry and physics
Mu—Mythical lost continent, allegedly having disappeared into the Atlantic about the same time as Atlantis
Delta—U.S. airline
Iota—Very small quantity
Epsilon—Very small quantity, close to zero, as used in math
Tau—Cross in the shape of the letter *T*—also called St. Anthony's cross
Upsilon—Any of a group of short-lived particles having a mass about 10 times greater than that of a proton
Psi—Psychic phenomena or paranormal abilities in parapsychology
Lambda** —Uncharged hyperon that decays rapidly into a nucleon and a pion
Epsilon—Lowest and least intelligent caste in Huxley's *Brave New World*
Pi—Letter whose symbol is used to designate the ratio of the circumference of a circle to its diameter
Omega—Watch brand advertised as "the last word in technology"
Alpha—Original name of the International Space Station, one rejected by Russia
Tau—Largest of the Manua Islands in American Samoa
Epsilon—Empty string in computer science
Omega—Last of any series
Lambda—Letter adopted as a symbol by the gay liberation movement
Sigma (7)—Mercury program spacecraft aboard which Walter M. Schirra circled the earth 6 times on October 3, 1962
Chi—Vital force said to be intrinsic in all things in Taoism
Theta—Plane angle in geometry
Upsilon—Letter from which 4 letters of the Latin alphabet arose—*U, V, W,* and *Y*
Phi (or tau)—Golden ratio, 1.618
Iota—Word completing the idiom *not one* _____, meaning "not even the smallest amount"
Pi—Letter representing the number 3.14159265
Upsilon—Letter associated with the hyoid or U-shaped bone at the base of the human tongue
Omega—One of the founding fathers of the Time Lords of the planet Gallifrey on the TV series *Doctor Who*

*In full, Betamax **Lambda particle or lambda hyperon

2-WORD ANSWERS

Alpha Dog—2005 film based on the life of Jesse James Hollywood, a young drug dealer on the FBI's most wanted list
Alpha male*—Strongest person, especially the dominant animal in a pack of wolves or baboons
Omega male—Weakest person, especially the most submissive animal in a pack of wolves or baboons

*Or female; a *beta male* is one subservient to an alpha male.

Greek Alphabet

Beta testing—Software still in a testing phase
Delta wing—Fighter plane with swept-back or triangular wings to provide great speed
Gamma ray—Electromagnetic radiation having a wave-length of 10^{-9} centimeters or less
Delta Queen—Sternwheel riverboat, a National Historic Landmark, touring up and down the Mississippi built in 1926
Delta Force—Highly-trained U.S. Army assault team that can be quickly sent to rescue hostages or fight terrorism
Delta Blues—Emotional style of music along the lower Mississippi, as played by guitarists such as Charley Patton and Robert Johnson
Gamma globulin—Protein fraction of blood serum that contains the most antibodies
Alpha Centauri—Brightest star in the constellation Centaurus, 3rd brightest in the sky, and the 2nd nearest star to our sun
The Delta—Low-lying region in NW Mississippi, extending eastward from the Mississippi River
The Omega Man—1971 film starring Charlton Heston as the last-man-on-Earth
Omega Syndrome—1986 film in which a character tracks down his daughter's abductors
Alpha particle—Positively charged particle consisting of 2 protons and 2 neutrons that becomes an atom of helium by the acquisition of 2 electrons
"Delta Dawn"—Helen Reddy's 1973 hit about "women's liberation"
Six Sigma—Highest level of corporate efficiency, a label coined by Motorola's Bill Smith in 1985
Alpha blocker—Any of a class of drugs used to dilate the blood vessels
Beta blocker—Any of a class of drugs used to control heartbeat and treat hypertension, migraine, and angina
Delta Burke—Actress who played Suzanne Sugarbaker on TV's *Designing Women*

GREEK-LETTER SOCIETIES

Phi—_____ *Beta Kappa**, America's oldest scholastic honorary society, founded at the College of William and Mary in Williamsburg, Virginia, in 1776
Kappa—_____ *Alpha* Society, the oldest ongoing general fraternity, founded at Union College in 1825
Theta—_____ *Xi*, the first professional fraternity and the only social fraternity founded during the Civil War, at Rensselaer Polytechnic Institute in 1864
Phi—_____ *Delta Phi*, the oldest ongoing professional fraternity, founded at the University of Michigan for law students in 1869
Kappa—_____ *Alpha Theta*, the first Greek-letter society for women, founded at DePauw University in Indiana in 1870
Sigma—_____ *Xi*, an honorary scientific society, founded at Cornell University in 1886
Alpha—_____ *Phi Alpha*, the nation's oldest and largest black fraternity, founded at Cornell University in 1906
Phi—_____ *Delta Kappa*, the professional association for educators, founded at Indiana University in 1906
Zeta—_____ *Phi Beta*, a black sorority, founded at Howard University in 1920 with encouragement from members of Phi Beta Sigma
Kappa—_____ *Mu*, the national college mathematics honor society
Lambda—_____ *Delta Lambda*, a national lesbian sorority
Delta—_____ *Lambda Phi*, a national gay fraternity, founded in 1986 in Washington, D.C.

*Its Greek motto *Philosophia biou kubernetes* means "the love of wisdom is the helmsman of live."

POTPOURRI OF COMPLETIONS

Delta—_____ *Clipper Experimental Advanced*, the small, reusable rocket capable of taking off and landing vertically, tested in 1996 in New Mexico

Nu—U _____, the 3-time Burmese prime minister, the last time from 1960-1962

Beta—_____ *carotene*, a yellowish form of carotene found in dark green and yellow fruits

Omega—_____*-3 fatty acid*, a polyunsaturated fatty acid found in fish or fish oil

Alpha—_____ *cells*, cells in both the pancreas that produce glucagon and in the anterior pituitary

Xi—____ Jiang, the South China river flowing from the Yunnan province to the South China Sea

Sigma—_____ *factor*, the protein that stimulates the synthesis of chains of RNA

Sigma—_____ *Octantis*, the South polar star in the constellation Octans

Lambda—_____ *point*, the temperature below which liquid helium becomes a superfluid

Delta—_____ *Wedding*, Eudora Welty's first full-length novel

Chi—Ho ____ Minh City, formerly Saigon

Zeta—Catherine _____-Jones, the actress who married Michael Douglas

Delta—*The* _____ *of Venus*, Anaïs Nin's erotic 1977 work

Lambda—_____ *virus* that infects the bacterium E. coli

Letters From A To Z

French poet whose 1870 poem "Voyelles" includes the lines: "*A noir, E blanc, I rouge, U vert, O bleu: voyelles, / Je dirais quelque jour vos naissances latentes . . .* " (translated as "Black A, white E, red I, green U, blue O: vowels, / Someday I shall tell you of your latent births"), the author of "Le Bateau ivre" ("The Drunken Boat")
Answer: Arthur Rimbaud.

1) Which 3 letters are often used to designate the basic facts or principles of a given subject?
Answer: ABC (as in *the ABC of*).

2) Identify the letters designating the time from after midnight to before noon and from after noon to before midnight.
Answer: a.m. (*ante meridiem*) and p.m. (*post meridiem*).

3) What is the Latin-based initialism for a violent state of nervousness and confusion resulting from acute alcoholism and characterized by sweating, restlessness, delusions, and hallucinations when the drinker abstains or withdraws from drinking?
Answer: DT's (from the Latin *delirium tremens*, literally "trembling delirium").

4) Give the Latin name represented by the monogram E.R. as used to designate either England's King Edward or Queen Elizabeth.
Answer: Eduardus Rex or Elizabeth Regina.

5) Which letters complete the title of *The _____ College Bowl*, the quiz show that premiered on Sunday afternoon, January 4, 1959, on CBS with Allen Ludden as host?
Answer: G.E. (for General Electric).

6) Doctors often refer to a specific part of the anatomy as the G.I. tract. What does G.I. stand for?
Answer: Gastrointestinal.

7) Which 4-letter word for "wharf" is sometimes pronounced like a letter of the alphabet?
Answer: Quay (pronounced kā or kē).

8) Identify the 5-letter British word for "a line or file of persons or vehicles waiting their turn" that is pronounced the same even if the last 4 letters are removed—it also designates a long pigtail such as that worn by early Chinese immigrants to the U.S.
Answer: Queue (pronounced as *Q*; the word *cue* meaning "a reminder," as in *cue* card for a performer, is pronounced the same way).

9) Identify the 2 letters that have for centuries served as the conventional symbol for a medical prescription or a medical appliance.
Answer: Rx (normally written with a slant across the leg of the letter *R*—derived from the Latin word *recipe*, or its imperative, *recipere*, meaning "take this").

10) Which 2 letters designate the elite semi-military unit of the Nazi party used as Hitler's personal guard and a special security force in charge of concentration camps?
Answer: SS (Troops or Corps; SS stands for the German word *Schutzstaffel*, meaning "defense squadron").

11) Which 2 letters are used in slang talk for sunshine?
Answer: UV(s; for ultraviolet light or rays).

12) Identify the 2 letters of the alphabet that designate a betrayal or a double-cross.
Answer: XX.

13) Identify the author who created *The Gashlycrumb Tinies*, a macabre alphabet book in which *A* stands for "Amy who fell down the stairs."
Answer: Edward Gorey.

14) According to many scholars, which book was written in part by unknown authors designated by the letters J, E, D, P, and R?
Answer: The Bible.

15) Identify the 2 one-letter words that are among the 10 most frequently used words in written English.
Answer: A and I.

16) Identify the letters representing the first 5 tones or notes in the scale of C major.
Answer: C, D, E, F, and G.

LETTERS A-H

A*—Nathaniel Hawthorne's "scarlet letter"
* **E**—Vowel not used in Ernest Vincent Wright's 50,000-word novel *Gadsby*, written in 1939
B—First letter that stands alone as the symbol of a chemical element
A—Letter designating the highest in quality or the first in a series
e—Number used as the base of the system of natural logarithms, approximately 2.71828
c**—Letter under which the hooklike mark called a cedilla is placed, as in some French words such as the one for "boy"
B—Of the single-letter blood types, the one found least frequently in the U.S. population
C—Grade or mark indicating average work in school
* **A**—Second most common blood type worldwide
E—Only letter standing alone on the back of a $1 bill, on the ribbon in the eagle's beak
c—Symbol for the speed of light in physics
g (G)—Symbol for acceleration due to gravity on Earth, equal to about 9.8 meters per second per second, or the letter representing the gravitational constant
C—Roman numeral for one hundred
E—Letter at the top of an optometrist's chart
F—Musical key in which the majority of horns in American cars beep
B—Letter completing Dorothy Parker's sardonic comment about Katharine Hepburn's performance in *The Lake*: "She runs the gamut of emotions all the way from A to ___."

---
*A means "adulteress." **As in *garçon*, meaning "boy"

Letters from A-Z

C—Slang term for one hundred dollars or a $100 bill
D***—Letter by which Franz Peter Schubert's works are catalogued in *Thematic Catalogue of All His Works in Chronological Order*
E (from Ecstasy)—Street name of MDMA, an illegal drug capable of producing hallucinations
G—Slang term for $1,000
c. (from *circa*)—Abbreviation from the Latin for "about" or "approximately," especially as used in dates
e—Italian word for "and"
c./C****—Abbreviation from the Latin for "hundredweight" or "one hundred"
C (for Colorado)—Large red letter encompassing a golden disk on the flag of a U.S. state
F—Generally the lowest or failing grade in school
C—Letter completing Luciano Pavarotti's nickname, "King of the High ____'s"
E—Elvis Presley's nickname
G—Letter completing the title of Johann Sebastian Bach's *Air on the* ____ *String*, Suite No. 3 in D Major, with the violinist playing on the lowest of the violin's 4 strings
B—7th tone or note in the ascending scale of C-major
F*****—Letter opposite P on a 2-letter grading scale
B—Letter completing ____-*team* for the school team below the Varsity level
a/à—Italian or French word meaning "in, to, at, with, for" in such phrases as ___ *cappella* or ___ *deux*
D—Traditionally the lowest passing grade in school
C (from *cum*)—Pharmaceutical symbol for "with," as derived from the Latin for "with"
D—Letter that completes the name of the seafood restaurant chain Captain ____'s
E—Most commonly used letter in the English language
H—German term for the note B natural
D—Roman numeral for the number 500
E—Letter designating Bruce Springsteen's ____ Street Band
C—Letter completing the phrase "gentleman's ____," meaning "a satisfactory ranking" such as one given to college students of high social standing who do not work diligently
D—Letter completing the title of Mark Chesnutt's 1994 hit "Goin' Through the Big ____"
h—Symbol for Planck's constant
D (from *Dominus*)—Abbreviation from the Latin for "God"

***For Otto Erich Deutsch ****From *centium* or *centum* *****In a pass/fail system

LETTERS I-P

J—Tenth letter of the alphabet
K—Symbol used in baseball for a strikeout
I—Roman numeral for the number one
K—Chemical symbol for potassium
i—Imaginary number that is the positive square root of negative one
O—Cirque du Soleil water extravaganza at the Bellagio in Las Vegas—its name is a take off on the French word *eau* for "water"
L—Roman numeral for the number fifty
K—Letter completing the title of J.M. Coetzee's 1983 novel *Life and Times of Michael* ____
L—An extension at a right angle to one end of a building
O—Written symbol for a hug, usually placed at the bottom of a letter

J—Last letter added to the modern English alphabet
N—Letter completing _____: *A Romantic Mystery*, a Louis Edwards novel about Aimee DuBois, a New Orleans journalist tracking the story of a murdered black teen
K—In computer technology, the number 1,024
L—Symbol for a British pound when used with a line drawn through it
J—Letter of the alphabet that Terry and John Garrity used as a pseudonym in writing *The Sensuous Woman*
K*—Letter by which Mozart's works are catalogued
L**—An elevated railroad
K—As of the 1999 season, letter marked on Wilson NFL game balls to be used only for kick-offs, punting, and place kick situations
O—Letter completing the title of James Thurber's 1957 children's fantasy *The Wonderful _____*
L—Letter completing the title of Scott Turow's first book, *One _____*, a critical account of his first year at Harvard Law School
I—Most frequently used word in conversational English
K—Letter completing the name of Frank Kafka's persecuted antagonist Joseph _____, in *The Castle* or *Das Schloss*
I—One-letter word Teddy Roosevelt was the only President not to use in an inaugural speech
M/N—Printing term for an em dash or for an en dash, or half an em dash
L—Roman numeral for fifty
O—Letter completing the line from Shakespeare's *The Tempest*: "_____ brave new world / That has such people in't!"
I—Letter designating the ego in metaphysics
k***—Symbol for the prefix for one thousand, especially in the metric system
I—Masculine plural form of the article "the" in Italian
J—Letter completing the title of Rosenberg and Bloom's *The Book of _____*, a work alleging that one of the earliest writers of the Bible was a woman
L—Letter completing the title of *The _____ Word*, Showtime's lesbian series
M—Spymaster and James Bond's supervisor in His/Her Majesty's Secret Service
J—Letter completing the name of T.S. Eliot's fictional antihero, _____ Alfred Prufrock
O—Most common blood type worldwide
M—Roman numeral for one thousand
m (meter)—In linear measure, 39.3701 inches
N—Chess notation for the knight
O—Letter meaning "descendant of," as used in Irish surnames
M—Letter of the alphabet that identifies the author of *The Sensuous Man*
O—Oprah Winfrey's magazine that debuted in 2000
M—Pseudonym of British pop musician Robin Scott, known for his 1979 "Pop Muzik"
K—Letter completing Circle _____ International, a service organization of Kiwanis International for college students
O—Interjection used as the first word of "America the Beautiful"
M—13th letter of our alphabet
O—Letter that completes the title of The Cars' 1979 hit album *Candy-___*
O (SpaghettiOs)—Letter added to the word spaghetti for a pasta dish created by the Campbell Soup Company in 1965

*By Ludwig von Köchel **For *el*, short for *elevated* ***From the French *kilo-*, for 1,000

LETTERS FROM A-Z

L/K** —Either of the 2 letters by which Domenico Scarlatti's works are catalogued
M*** —Letter of the alphabet formed by 5 of the brightest stars in the constellation Cassiopeia

****By Longo or by Kirkpatrick *****Or W

LETTERS Q-Z

X—Letter designating an experimental aircraft in the U.S. armed forces
Y—Only letter commonly used as both a vowel and a consonant
R—Letter known as the *dog's letter*, especially when pronounced with a trill
X—Letter designating Christ
S—Harry Truman's middle initial, which doesn't represent a name and technically doesn't have a period
Z—Hero of the computer-animated film *Antz* whose voice is provided by Woody Allen
X—Letter used with a number to designate the power of magnification of optical instruments
W—Chemical symbol for the element tungsten
X—Letter that diplomat George F. Kennan used as a pseudonym to write an epoch-defining essay during the Cold War
Q—British Secret Service code letter for Major Boothroyd, the weapons and research officer in James Bond films
X—Letter completing the expression _____ *marks the spot*, meaning "this is the place where something is located"
W—Letter identifying a hotel chain owned by Starwood with locations in New York City, Mexico City, and Seoul
V—Roman numeral for the number five
X—Written symbol for a kiss, usually placed at the bottom of a letter
R—Letter named in the common sense guideline that oysters should be eaten only during months with a(n) _____ in their names
R—Symbol for the universal gas constant
V—Letter formerly used interchangeably with *U* both as a vowel and as a consonant, now used only as a consonant
X—Roman numeral for ten
y—Spanish word for "and" as in *cuatro _____ medio*
W—Only letter of the alphabet with a 3-syllable pronunciation
V—Inverted shape designated by a chevron, an insignia worn on the sleeve of a noncommissioned military officer for example
Z—Letter completing Iroc _____, the super-sporty 1980s Camaro
X—Letter designated by a saltire, a bearing in heraldry like a Saint Andrew cross
Z—Slashing mark made by Zorro on his victims
V—Shape of the formation used by geese when they fly long distances
R—Backwards letter featured in the name of Toys _____ Us
S* —Letter by which Johann Sebastian Bach's works are catalogued
X—Letter completing _____-*rated*, meaning "vulgar or obscene"
Y** —Letter that sounds the same as the interrogative adverb meaning "for what reason"
T—Letter NASA uses for liftoff in its countdown, as in _____ Minus Eight, _____ Minus Seven, _____, etc.

*From Wolfgang Schmieder; the designation BWV, which sometimes replaces the S, is the abbreviation for *Bach-Werke-Verzeichnis*, the short title of Schmieder's *Thematish-systematisches Verzeichnis der musikalischen Werke von Johann Sebastian Bach*, a thematic catalog of the works of J.S. Bach. **It sounds the same as *why*, which does, however, have 2 pronunciations: hwī and wī.

X***—Letter used in cartoons to mark bottles designating booze
R (for Rwanda)—Letter on the former flag of the African country whose capital is Kigali
Z—Letter completing the name of Nissan's Datsun 240-___ sports car
X—Letter completing ___-factor, for an unknown or unnamed person, thing, or factor, or an unknown quantity, especially in algebra
Q—Letter completing Susie-___, designating a kind of shuffling dance step of the 1930s, or the title of Dale Hawkins' 1957 song
Z—Letter representing a buzzing sound
R—Initial on the high school sweater of comic strip character Archie Andrews
W—Letter formed when President George Bush, the 43rd, raises 3 fingers
V****—Letter formed by Winston Churchill's fingers, symbolizing British determination and perseverance during WWII
Q—Nickname of California's prison called San Quentin
X—Letter considered a legal signature for anyone who cannot write his name
T—Letter used as the short name for the Boston subway system, as in "The ___," short for MBTA, the Massachusetts Bay Transportation Authority, which runs it
S—Letter that begins the most words in English
X—Letter that begins the fewest words in English
X—Letter used to indicate choice, as on a ballot or exam, or an incorrect answer, as on a test
Q—Sir Arthur Thomas Quiller's pseudonym that British author Helene Hanff uses in the title of her book ___'s Legacy, telling about her self-education during the Great Depression when he was her favorite author
z—Letter completing the phrase "catch (cop) some ___'s," meaning to take a nap" or "to sleep"
X—One-letter title of INXS' 1990 album that includes "Suicide Blonde" and "Disappear"
W—Letter originally known as a "double u"
X—Letter used in math as the first of a set of unknown quantities, or a variable, or an abscissa
V—Vulcan salute on *Star Trek* signifying "Live long and prosper"
x—Abbreviation for "extra"
Q—Letter completing FDR's WWII code name, Admiral ___
V.—Thomas Pynchon's 1963 novel whose title refers to a mysterious woman
X—Informal name for a $10 bill
Y*****—Letter emblazoned horizontally on South Africa's new flag—it is sometimes used to name an intersection at which 2 roads merge to become one
W—Large-size fashion magazine published by Fairchild Publications
Z—Letter completing *Liza With a* ___, the title of Liza Minnelli's 1973 TV special for which Bob Fosse won an Emmy Award
V—Informal name for a $5 bill
x—Letter designating "captures" in chess
Z—Least-used letter in printed English
X—Letter used to indicate multiplications and dimensions
Z—Title of the 1969 Oscar-winning foreign film directed by Constantin Costa-Gavras starring Yves Montand as a political leader who is assassinated
X—Person or thing unknown or not revealed

***The more X's, the more powerful the booze. ****V for Victory *****It symbolizes yes.

COMMON 2-LETTER ABBREVIATIONS

1) Identify the small pellet of shot fired from an air gun.
Answer: BB.

2) Identify the 2-letter title of Johnny Hart's comic strip set in a prehistoric age.
Answer: *B.C.*

3) Identify the Australian hard-rock band known for its albums *Back in Black*, *Dirty Deeds Done Dirt Cheap*, and *The Razors Edge*.
Answer: AC/DC.

4) Identify the most popular model railroad scale.
Answer: HO (most popular scale after HO is *N*).

5) Which 2-letter abbreviation, thought by a number of word authorities to have come from the nickname of Martin Van Buren derived from the name of his birthplace, means "all right" or "correct"? Others believe it came from the pronunciation of *all correct* as *oll correct* and misspelled as *oll* (*orl*) *korrect*.
Answer: O.K. (Van Buren was nicknamed "Old Kinderhook," in reference to his birthplace, Kinderhook, New York).

6) Which 2 letters complete the name _____ *Flyers* designating popular tennis shoes of the 1950s?
Answer: P.F. (for Posture Foundation).

7) Which 2 letters are used to identify the guerrilla force sent by Hanoi to overthrow the government of South Vietnam from 1954 to 1975?
Answer: VC (for Viet Cong or Vietcong; U.S. troops' call name for them was "Victor Charlie," the names for *V* and *C* on the phonetic alphabet).

8) Which prefix meaning "out of," "beyond," or "away from" is also colloquially used to designate a former spouse and is pronounced as a single letter of the alphabet?
Answer: Ex (pronounced as *X*).

NOTE: Quiz from left to right on these
AA—Alcoholics Anonymous
AB/BA—Bachelor of Arts
AC/DC—Alternating current; direct current
AI—Artificial Intelligence; artificial insemination
AM/FM—Amplitude modulation; frequency modulation
AP—Associated Press; advanced placement
AV—Authorized Version; audio-visual
B.C.—Before Christ*
BS/B.Sc.—Bachelor of Science
CB (radio)—Citizens band
CB (U.S. Navy)—Construction Battalion**
CD as in CD/ROM—Compact disk (with read-only memory)
CD (banking)—Certificate of deposit
C.E. (period)—Christian, or Common, Era
CO—Commanding officer; conscientious objector
c/o—(In) care of
D.A. (law)—District Attorney
DD (degree)—Doctor of Divinity
DI (military)—Drill instructor

*B.C.E. is Before the Christian, or Common, Era. **Alteration of *cee bee*; *Seabee*, derived from these initials, designates a member of this unit.

DJ—Disc (disk) jockey
Ed.—Edition; editor; edited
ER; OR (hospital)—Emergency room; operating room
EU—European Union
FF.—Folios (page numbers); following (pages); fortissimo
FY—Fiscal year
G.I. (military)—Government issue
GP (physician)—General practitioner
GQ (publication)—*Gentlemen's Quarterly*
I.D.—Identification
IH—International Harvester (now Navistar)
IQ—Intelligence quotient
IV—Intravenous(ly)
JD (degree)—*Juris Doctor* (doctor of laws)
JD—Justice Department; juvenile delinquent
JV (sports)—Junior varsity
KO—Knock out
KP—Kitchen police
L.C.—Library of Congress
LD—Learning disability; lethal dose
M.A. (degree)—Master of Arts
MC (host)—Emcee
M.D.—*Medicinae Doctor* (Doctor of Medicine)
MI (armed forces)—Military intelligence
M.O. (law)—Method of operation, from *modus operandi*
MP—Military police; Member of Parliament; Mounted Police
MS (degree)—Master of science
MX as in MX missile—Missile experimental

N.P.—Notary public; nurse practitioner
OD (drug)—Overdose
OJ—Orange juice
PA (system)—Public-address system
PC—Personal computer; politically correct
P.E. (class)—Physical education
PG (movies)—Parental Guidance
PI—Private investigator
pj's—Pajamas
PT (treatment)—Physical therapy
PT (as in *PT-109****)—P(atrol) T(orpedo) boat
PX—Post Exchange
QT (as in *on the QT*)—Quiet; secretly
R.C.—Red Cross; Roman Catholic; remote control
R.D. (mail)—Rural delivery
RN—Registered Nurse; Royal Navy
RR—Railroad; Rural Route; Right Reverend
RV—Recreational vehicle; Revised Version
SI—*Système International (d'Unités)* or International System (of Units)
SJ—Society of Jesus
SS (sailing)—Steamship
TB—Tuberculosis
TD (sports)—Touchdown
TM—Transcendental meditation; trademark
U.K.—United Kingdom
U.N.—United Nations
VD—Venereal disease
VW—Volkswagen

*** *PT-109* was JFK's boat.

Alpha-Numerically

When a computer program sorts alpha-numerically, in which 2 ways does it sort?
Answer: By letters and by numerals.

BEGINNING WITH A LETTER
A-one (A-1)*—Colloquial term for "first-class," originally designating a ship whose hull was in excellent condition
A.1. (A-1)—Steak sauce made by Nabisco
A1A—Highway that runs along the beaches of Florida's east coast
A1C—Abbreviation for airman first class
AuH$_2$O = 1964—Bumper strip slogan advocating Barry Goldwater for President in 1964
B$_2$—Current designation of a vitamin called riboflavin, formerly called Vitamin G
B-2—U.S. stealth bombers, planes designed to be almost invisible to radar
B-25—U.S. twin-engine plane of the type used by James Doolittle for the Tokyo Raid in April 1942—planes of this type were named "Mitchell" in honor of General Billy Mitchell
B-52—Stratofotress, or a long-range, heavy bomber
B-52's, The—Athens, Georgia, band known for its 1989 album *Cosmic Thing*
C2 (Cola)—Coca-Cola's midcalorie cola designed to appeal to calorie-counting, carb-conscious consumers
C-5 (Galaxy)—America's largest cargo aircraft
E = mc^2**—Alfred Einstein's famous mass-energy theorem
F2F—Informal Internet abbreviation meaning "face to face"
F-5 (F5)—Designation for the most destructive type of tornado on a wind-damage scale named for its creator, T. Theodore Fujita
G-8 (G8)—Group of 8 industrial nations whose leaders meet annually to discuss economic policy
H$_2$O—Chemical formula for water
J-14—Magazine just for teens
K2—World's 2nd highest mountain, also called Mt. Godwin-Austen
K2—Nickname of football player Kellen Winslow
K-9 (K9) corps—Police dog unit
K-12—Designation for primary through secondary education in the U.S.
M1 (money)***—Economic term for "currency in circulation plus demand deposits"
M-1 (M1)****—Another name for the semiautomatic Garand rifle that served as the official rifle of the U.S. Army from 1936 to 1960
MI5—British equivalent of the FBI
R2-D2/C-3PO—Luke Skywalker's 2 droids in the film *Star Wars*
U2 (music)—Irish group with Bono as lead singer known for their 1987 hit "With or Without You"
U2 (U-2; plane)—Francis Gary Powers' reconnaissance plane shot down over the Soviet Union on May 1, 1960
V-1—Buzz bomb or a German pulsejet flying bomb during WWII—also called a *doodlebug*
V-2—Long-range liquid-propellant rocket developed at Peenemünde, Germany, between 1938 and 1942 (from *Vergeltungswaffe*, meaning "retaliation weapon")

*Or A number 1 **E is the energy in ergs, m is the mass of the matter in grams, and c is the speed of light in centimeters per second (c^2 = 9 * 10^{20}).
***M2 is currency in circulation plus demand deposits plus money market deposit accounts; M3 is currency in circulation plus demand deposits plus money market deposit accounts plus large time deposits at depository institutions. ****The Army now uses the M16.

V-6 or V-8—Internal combustion engine with 6 or 8 cylinders that takes its name partly from its shape

V8—Campbell Soup Company's 100% vegetable juice

W-2—Form filed with the SSA showing workers' yearly wages and taxes withheld

W3—Another way of designating the WWW, or the World Wide Web

W-4—Form filed with the SSA indicating employee withholding allowance

X-15—Rocket plane piloted by Robert H. White that in 1962 soared over 50 miles above the Earth

✓**Y2K problem*****—Common way of referring to the 2000 software bug arising from computer codes that couldn't comprehend dates beyond 1999
***** *Y2K* stands for "year 2000."

BEGINNING WITH A NUMERAL

Triple A—Colloquial name of the American Automobile Association

3 B's of classical music—Phrase designating Bach, Beethoven, and Brahms

3 B's of rock music*—Phrase designating the Beatles, the Beach Boys, and the Bee Gees

3-D (Three-D)—Kind of movie designed to produce an effect of multiple dimensions when special glasses are worn

3M—Popular name for the Minnesota Mining and Manufacturing Company, which produces Scotch tape and other products

3 R's (three R's)—Basic elements of learning: Readin', 'Ritin', and 'Rithmetic

4 C's**—Those factors denoting the value of a diamond

4F (4-F)—Selective Service classification for those who are physically, mentally, or morally unfit for military service

4-H—Youth program whose aim is to improve the "head, heart, hands, and health"

4 Y—Classification Bob Hope suggested for himself during WWII, with the *Y* designating "yellow"

Five C's (half a G)—Slang term for $500

Five W's***—Key questions of news reporting

7X—Designation for Coca-Cola's secret formula

10K (for 10 kilometers)—6.2 mile road race

10X—Designation for the most finely sifted powdered sugar

27A—Wimpole Street address of Professor Henry Higgins in the film *My Fair Lady*

110A—Piccadilly street address of the elegant and sophisticated detective Lord Peter Wimsey, a character created by Dorothy Leigh Sayers

221B—Sherlock Holmes's Baker Street address

*These names could vary, e.g., the Beatles, Byrds, Buffalo Springfield. **They are clarity, color, cut, and carat weight. ***The "Who; What; When; Where; and Why"

DIACRITICAL MARKS: UMLAUTS AND TILDES

Word beginning with *D* that, like the word *umlaut*, names the diacritical mark used over the 2nd of two vowels or a final vowel to indicate that it has a separate pronunciation
Answer: Diaeresis (dieresis; the *umlaut* specifically designates a change in a vowel sound, or a *vowel mutation*; a dot or other small mark used as a diacritic, as in an umlaut, is called a *tittle*).

UMLAUTS
Aëdes aegypti—Mosquito whose bite causes yellow fever
Aïda—Giuseppe Verdi opera featuring Radames, an Egyptian officer
Atatürk—Name meaning "father of the Turks" given to Mustafa Kemal, the founder and first president of modern Turkey in 1923
Zoë Baird—President Clinton's first choice for attorney general before he selected Kimba Wood and then Janet Reno
Blue Öyster Cult—Long Island rock group, the first such group to use an umlaut, known for their "(Don't Fear) The Reaper"
Heinrich Böll—1972 German Nobel Prize winner in literature who wrote *The Lost Honor of Katharina Blum* and *Group Portrait with Lady*
Boötes—Constellation whose name, derived from the Greek word for "ox driver," also means Herdsman or Huntsman
Björn Borg—Swedish winner of Wimbledon from 1976 through 1980
Anne Brontë—English author who wrote *Agnes Grey* and *The Tenant of Wildfell Hall*
Charlotte Brontë—English author who wrote *Jane Eyre*
Emily Brontë—English author who wrote *Wuthering Heights*
Brünn(e)hilde—Queen in Wagner's *Nibelungenlied* who is won as a bride by Gunther
Citroën—Car and auto company named after Frenchman André-Gustave _____, who founded it in 1919
Danke schön—German for "many thanks"
Doppelgänger—German word for the supposed ghostly double of a living person
Albrecht Dürer—15th-16th century German painter and engraver known for his *Madonna and Child* and for his woodcuts of the *Apocalypse*
Düsseldorf—Industrial German city on the Rhine where poet Heinrich Heine was born
Fräulein—German title for "Miss" and word for an unmarried woman
Führer—German word for leader, especially one acting like a tyrant, used as the title assumed by Hitler of Nazi Germany in 1934
Kurt Gödel—Austrian-born American mathematician and logician whose incompleteness theorem was published in 1931
Die Götterdämmerung—Richard Wagner opera named with the German word for "twilight of the gods," or what is called Ragnarok in Norse mythology, designating a time when Valhalla is enveloped in flames and the gods are destroyed
Günter Grass—1999 German Nobel Prize winner in literature who wrote *The Tin Drum* and *Dog Years*
Häagen Dazs—American ice cream company Reuben Mattus created in 1961 with just 3 flavors—vanilla, chocolate, and coffee—and sold to the Pillsbury Company in 1983

Dag Hammarskjöld—U.N. secretary general awarded the Nobel Peace Prize posthumously in 1961
Héloïse—Pierre Abélard's student who becomes his lover and later his wife
Louis Vuitton Moët Hennessy—Full name of LVMH, the French luxury goods conglomerate
Joyeux Noël—French for "Merry Christmas!"
Königsberg—Former name of Kaliningrad or the name completing _____ Bridge Problem, the topological problem of finding the route that will cross each of the 7 bridges in a [Prussian] city just once and return to the starting point
René-Théophile-Hyacinthe Laënnec—French physician called the "Father of Chest Medicine" and the "Father of the Stethoscope"
Laocoön—Priest of Troy in Greek mythology who, with his 2 sons, is killed by sea serpents after he warns the Trojans against bringing the Wooden Horse inside
USS *Mayagüez* —U.S. merchant ship seized by Cambodia in 1975
Möbius strip—Topological object described as a surface formed by twisting one side of a rectangular region 180° and attaching it to the opposite side
Mötley Crüe—Los Angeles hardrock band known for its "Dr. Feelgood"
Naïve—Lacking sophistication, or childlike
Naïveté—State of being uncritical, or simplicity
Anaïs Nin—French-American writer known for her published personal diaries
Pasiphaë—Minos' wife, the Queen of Crete, who had a lustful union with the great white bull of Poseidon and gave birth to the Minotaur
Peenemünde—German town where the long-range liquid-propellant V-2 rocket was developed between 1938 and 1942
Phaëthon—Apollo (Helios) and Clymene's son who lost control of the sun chariot and was killed by Zeus
Phaëton—19th-century light, 4-wheeled carriage or an early gasoline automobile called a touring car
Ole Rölvaag—Norwegian-American author who wrote *Giants in the Earth*
Camille Saint-Saëns—French composer of *The Carnival of the Animals* (*Le Carnaval des Animaux*) and *Phaëton*, a symphonic poem
Arnold Schönberg—Austrian musician who revolutionized modern music by establishing the 12-tone technique of serial music
Gerhard Schröder—Politician elected chancellor of Germany in 1998
Madame de Staël—French-Swiss literary salon leader born Anne Louise Germaine Necker
Süleyman—Ottoman sultan from 1520 to 1566 known as "The Magnificent"
Tannhäuser—13th-century German knight and *minnesinger* whose adventures are the subject of an 1845 opera by Richard Wagner
Thaïs—Greek courtesan who was the mistress of Alexander the Great and Ptolemy I
Tiranë (Tirana)—Capital of Albania
Über alles—German for "above all else," from the German national anthem "Deutschland _____," translated as "Germany Over All"
Übermensch—German for "Superman" as in the philosophy of Nietzsche, as a superior, controlling human
Völsunga Saga—Icelandic "Saga of the Volsungs," which gives a version of the story told in the *Nibelungenlied* and was used as one of the sources for Wagner's *Ring* tetralogy
Martin Waldseemüller—German mapmaker who in 1507 after reading Amerigo Vespucci's descriptions of the New World named it "America" after him
Die Walküre—Richard Wagner's opera about the Valkyrie Brünnhilde

Die Zauberflöte—German title of Mozart's *The Magic Flute*

TILDES
Vasco Núñez de Balboa—Spanish explorer who was the first European to discover the Pacific Ocean's east coast, in 1513, near Panama, and named it the South Sea
Luis Buñuel—Spanish film director who made the surrealist film *Un chien andalou* with Salvador Dali
Cabaña—Spanish word for "hut" for a beach shelter or a pool's bathhouse
Álvar Núñez Cabeza de Vaca—Spaniard and first European to explore present-day Texas and the Southwest from 1526 to 1534—his name means "cow's head"
Caraqueño/Caraqueña—Spanish for a resident of Caracas, Venezuela
Cien Años de Soledad—Gabriel García Márquez' book known in English as *One Hundred Years of Solitude*
Doña—Spanish word used as a title of respect for a lady
Falange Española—Fascist political party that supported Francisco Franco's Nationalists during the Spanish Civil War—its name comes from a Greek military formation and means "Spanish Phalanx"
Generation Ñ **or ñ**—Magazine for young Latinos who differentiate themselves from Generation X-ers
Hasta mañana—Spanish words for "see you tomorrow!"
La Isla Española—Name meaning "The Spanish Island" that Columbus gave to present day Hispaniola
Madrileño—Spanish for a resident of Madrid, Spain
Malacañang Palace—Manila home of the president of the Philippines
Mañana—Spanish word for "tomorrow"
Doña Marina—Female slave better known as La Malinche, a speaker of both Maya and Nahuatl (or Aztec), who became Cortés's translator and mistress
Niña—Christopher Columbus's ship on his first voyage to the New World whose name means "little girl"
La Niña—Spanish for "the little girl," naming the "cold water event" that is the reversal of the conditions caused by El Niño, the phenomenon causing the warming of waters
El Niño—Warm current of equatorial water that periodically appears off the coast of South America and causes water temperature to rise, resulting in atmospheric changes—it bears the Spanish name for "the boy child" or "Christ child" since it occurs at Christmas time
(Federico) Peña—First Hispanic to hold the posts of secretary of energy and secretary of transportation, the Clinton administration official whose surname is the Spanish word for "rock"
Piñata—Clay figure filled with candy and small gifts and hung from the ceiling for blindfolded children to attempt to break with a stick on certain Latin American holidays
Porteños—Spanish for a resident of the port of Buenos Aires, Argentina
São Paulo—Brazilian city that is the largest in South America
São Tomé—Capital of São Tomé and Príncipe
São Tomé and Príncipe—Island country in the Gulf of Guinea off western Africa
Señor/Señora—Spanish for "Mr." and "Mrs."
Señorita—Spanish for "Miss" or "young lady"
Vicuña—Smallest member of the camel family, the wild, wool-bearing animal of the Andes to which the alpaca, llama, and guanaco are related
Zuñi Indians—Indian tribe that lives in northwestern New Mexico near Arizona

EPONYMS
(Words Derived from the Names of People)

William Shakespeare play in which a female character says, "What's in a name? That which we call a rose / By any other name would smell as sweet"
Answer: *Romeo and Juliet.*

ARTICLES OF CLOTHING AND GROOMING
Bertha—Woman's wide lace collar, after Charlemagne's mother, a woman known for her modesty
Bloomers—Women's loose trousers gathered at the knee, formerly worn under a short skirt, after Amelia Jenks _____, the woman who advocated this new style of dress for women
Bowler—Hard derby hat, after John _____, a London hat manufacturer
Chesterfield—Single-breasted topcoat with concealed buttons, after Philip Dormer Stanhope, the fourth Earl of _____, because he advocated such a style
Derby—Stiff felt hat, after Edward Stanley, the 12th Earl of _____, the founder of the famed English race for 3-year-olds
Eisenhower jacket—Waist-length, olive-drab military-style jacket, after Dwight _____, the American general who wore such a jacket during WWII
Fedora—Man's soft felt hat with a curved brim, after a character wore it in a Victorien Sardou play
Frangipani—Perfume made from the flower of the red jasmine, after Muzio _____, an Italian marquis who supposedly invented it
Georgette—Thin, silk, crinkled crepe used to make dresses, after Madame _____ de la Plante, a Parisian designer
Gobelin—Kind of tapestry, after the factory and dye works of the _____ family in Paris where it was made
Leotard—Skintight, one-piece garment worn by acrobats, after Jules _____, a French aerialist
Levi's (levis)—Reinforced, blue denim work pants, after _____ Strauss and Company, the manufacturer
Mackintosh*—Waterproof raincoat, after Charles _____, a Scottish inventor
Mae West—Inflatable life jacket, after Mae _____, an American actress known for her shapely figure
Marcel—Hair curling method to get regular waves, after _____ Grateau, a French hairdresser
Plimsoll—Tennis shoe or sneaker, after Samuel _____, a British shipper from its resemblance to a set of lines on a ship
Prince Albert coat—Man's long, double-breasted coat, after Prince _____, Queen Victoria's consort
Sideburns—Man's facial hair in front of the ears, after Ambrose Burnside, a Union general who wore such a style
Stetson—Broad-brimmed hat, or "ten-gallon hat," after John B. _____, an American hat manufacturer
Tattersall—Fabric pattern of thin lines of dark colors forming squares on a light background, after a sporting enterprise and horse market in London opened by Richard

---
*His name is spelled *Macintosh*.

Vandyke beard—Closely trimmed, pointed beard, after Flemish artist Anthony _____, who sported this style as did those he painted

Wellington—Boot extending to the top of the knee, after Arthur Wellesley, the first Duke of _____

FOODS

Bartlett pear—Large, juicy yellow pear, after Enoch _____, who introduced and distributed it

Béchamel (sauce)—Basic white sauce to which egg yolk, lemon juice, and sometimes parsley are added, after Louis de _____, Louis XIV's chef who created it

Beef Stroganoff—Sliced beef fillet sautéed and mixed with onions, mushrooms, sour cream, and herbs, after Count Sergei _____, a Russian official and gourmet

Bibb lettuce—Small, dark-green variety of lettuce, after Jack _____, a Kentucky horticulturalist who developed it

Bing cherry—Dark-red variety of sweet cherry, after a Chinese man who developed it

Caesar salad—Tossed salad of greens, cheese, croutons, eggs, and anchovies, with a dressing of olive oil, lemon juice, and garlic, possibly after _____ Gardinini, a chef in Mexico who created it

Clementine—Tangerine with orange-red skin, possibly after Père Clément, a French missionary in Africa

Eggs benedict—Poached eggs and broiled ham on an English muffin, possibly after E.C. _____, a customer at Delmonico's Restaurant in New York City

Filbert—Edible hazelnut, after Saint Philibert, because the nuts ripen near his feast day, August 20

Graham cracker—Crisp, slightly sweet rectangular cracker made with whole wheat flower, after Sylvester _____, an American dietary reformer

Julienne—Clear broth garnished with vegetables cut into strips, or any meat or vegetable cut into thin strips, possibly after a French chef who prepared the dish

Loganberry—Red, tart berry, after James H. _____, an American horticulturist who developed it

Macadamia nut—Edible nut from Queensland, after John Macadam, the Scottish chemist in Australia who developed it

McIntosh apple—Bright, red apple, after John _____, a Canadian farmer who accidentally discovered the variety

Melba toast—Thinly sliced crisp toast, in honor of Dame Nellie _____, an Australian soprano

Mulligan stew—Stew made with bits of assorted meat and vegetables, after an Irishman

Oysters Rockefeller—Oysters cooked with spinach, broiled in rock salt, and served on the half shell, after an American family whose name signifies wealth

Praline—Confection made of almonds or pecans in boiled brown sugar or maple sugar, after Count du Plessis-Praslin, a French army officer whose chef made it

Salisbury steak—Ground beef patty mixed with eggs, milk, onions, and various seasonings, after James Henry _____, an American physician

Sandwich—Slices of bread with a filling between them, after John Montagu, the 4th Earl of _____, who ordered one made enabling him to stay at the gambling table

Tetrazzini—Dish in which veal, chicken, or other meat is diced, combined with pasta, mushrooms, and cream sauce, then topped with Parmesan cheese and browned in the oven, in honor of Luisa _____, an Italian operatic soprano

AWARDS

Bancroft Prize—Annual prize awarded by Columbia University for exceptional merit and distinction in American History and Diplomacy, after George _____, the American historian, diplomat, and teacher known for his 10-volume *History of the United States*

Booker Prize—Annual award for a work of fiction by a living British, Irish, or Commonwealth author, after the British food-distribution company _____ PLC

Caldecott Medal—Annual award given for the most distinguished picture book for children, after Randolph _____, an English illustrator of children's books

Clio—Statuette awarded annually for notable achievement in radio and TV advertising and in the design industry, after the Greek muse of history

Coretta Scott King Award—Literary award for African-American children authors designed to commemorate the life and works of Dr. Martin Luther King Jr. and to honor his wife, _____ King

Cy Young Award—Annual award presented to the best pitcher in Major League Baseball, after Cy _____, the winningest pitcher in history with 511 wins

Davis Cup—Annual silver bowl trophy awarded to the nation that wins the world's men's tennis championship, after Dwight F. _____, an American tennis player

Edgar—Statuette awarded annually for notable achievement in mystery writing, after Edgar Allan Poe

Fulbright—Scholarship program for the exchange of students between the U.S. and other countries, after Arkansas senator J. William _____

Hugo Awards—Awards for excellence in the field of science fiction and fantasy, after _____ Greensback, a magazine editor who founded *Amazing Stories*

Lombardi Trophy—Trophy awarded annually to the winning team in the National Football League, after Vince _____, the coach whose Green Bay Packers won the first 2 Super Bowls

Newbery Medal—Annual award given to the American author of the most distinguished contribution to children's literature, after John _____, an English publisher and bookseller

Nobel Prize—International award given in the fields of physics, chemistry, physiology or medicine, literature, peace, and economics, after Alfred _____, the Swedish inventor of dynamite who provided for these awards

O. Henry Award—Yearly prizes presented to the writer of the best American short stories, after the author born William Sydney Porter

Oscar—Statuette awarded by the Academy of Motion Picture Arts and Sciences for achievement in motion pictures, from an Academy employee's remark in 1931 saying of the statuette: "He reminds me of my Uncle _____."

Pulitzer Prize—Annual prize presented by Columbia University for outstanding work in journalism, literature, and music, after Joseph _____, a U.S. newspaper owner

Reuben—Prize awarded annually for notable achievement in cartoon artistry, after Rube [Reuben Lucius] Goldberg

Spingarn Medal—Gold medal awarded annually by the NAACP to the black who has reached a high level of achievement in his or her field, after Joel Elias _____, a white leader who served as NAACP chairman

Stanley Cup—Trophy awarded annually to the winning team in the National Hockey League, after Baron _____ of Preston, the governor general of Canada

Sullivan Award—Annual award presented to the top amateur athlete by the AAU, after James E. _____, the founder of this organization

Tony—Award made annually by the American Theatre Wing for achievement in the theatre, after the nickname for theatrical figure Antoinette Perry

GIMME AN A-A

Word coined from the names of the letters *A*, *B*, *C*, and *D* to designate a person who studies or teaches the alphabet
Answer: Abecedarian [A-B-C-DARE ee uhn] (something arranged in an *abecedarian* manner is arranged in alphabetical order; an *abecedarium* is a primer for teaching the alphabet).

HOMO SAPIENS A-A
Abigail Adams—Wife of one U.S. President and mother of another
Alice Adams—1935 film based on a Booth Tarkington novel starring Katharine Hepburn as the title character
Ansel Adams—Photographer known for his black-and-white landscapes of the American West
Alfred Adler—Austrian who founded the school of individual psychology and believed that the feeling of inferiority is the basic human problem
Ado Annie—Character in *Oklahoma!* who sings "I Can't Say No"
Andre Agassi—American who became only the 5th man to win all 4 major tennis championships, completing the slam in 1999 when he won the French Open
Alvin Ailey—Black choreographer who formed his own troupe in 1958 and is considered to be the first modern dancer to choreograph for a ballet company
Anouk Aimée—French actress playing a young widow who falls in love in the 1966 film *A Man and a Woman*
Amy Alcott—American golfer who won 29 events on the LPGA tour, including 5 major championships
Alan Alda—Actor who played Hawkeye Pierce on TV's *M*A*S*H*
Alan Ameche—Back who scored the winning touchdown in the 1958 overtime game between the Baltimore Colts and the New York Giants
Albert Anastasia—Gang leader and murderer known as "The Boss" and the "Lord High Executioner of Murder, Inc."
Annie Allen—Gwendolyn Brooks's Pulitzer Prize-winning story in verse about the experiences of a black girl growing up in America during WWII
Anthony Adverse—Hervey Allen's 1933 historical romance set in the Napoleonic era
Anne Archer—Actress starring as Michael Douglas' wife in the 1987 film *Fatal Attraction*
Archie Andrews—Red-headed comic strip teenager at Riverdale High School
Alan Arkin—Actor starring as Yossarian in *Catch-22* and as a deaf-mute in *The Heart Is a Lonely Hunter*
Arnie's Army—Nickname of golfer Arnold Palmer's followers
Arthur Ashe—First black male to win the U.S. championship, the Davis Cup, the Australian Open, and Wimbledon
Armand Assante—Actor who appeared in the films *Q & A*; *I, the Jury*; and *Fatal Instinct*; and starred as Odysseus on TV's *The Odyssey*
Amedeo Avogadro—Italian physicist who postulated that the number of molecules in one mole of any gas is the same as the number in a mole of any other gas

POTPOURRI OF A-A
Above-average—Adjective meaning "surpassing that which is normal" or "exceptional"

Absalom, Absalom!—William Faulkner novel in which 3 narrators tell the story of Thomas Sutpen, the central character
Academy Award—Annual achievement presentation, or Oscar, presented by the Academy of Motion Picture Arts and Sciences
Acetic acid—Pungent, colorless liquid responsible for the characteristic taste and odor of vinegar
Ack-ack—Antiaircraft fire
Acute accent—Mark used to indicate the quality of the sound of a vowel, as in the French word *été*, meaning "summer"
Adam's ale—Another name for water
Adam's apple—Projection of the larynx at the front of the neck, more prominent in men than in women
Addis Ababa—Capital of Ethiopia
Affirmative action—Program aimed at correcting the effects of discrimination in the employment of blacks, women, and other designated groups
Air age—Period in human history marked by the use of aircraft in war and in peace
Air alert—Signal for getting aircraft aloft in response to an attack
Al-Anon—Worldwide group of the families and friends of alcoholics
Albert Alligator—Pogo's gator friend in the comics who lives in the Okefenokee Swamp
Alcoholics Anonymous—Worldwide organization of men and women who help each other solve their drinking problems
All-Aboard!—Call initially used to signal passengers to get on a boat and now more commonly used as a train conductor's call
All-American—Title awarded to a college athlete selected as one of the best players in the U.S.
American Airlines—World's largest airline, headquartered in Fort Worth, Texas
Amino acid—Any of a group of organic compounds known as the "building blocks of proteins"
Anaheim Angels*—American League baseball team in California from 1996 until early 2005, when it adopted a new name
"Anchors Aweigh"—Official song of the U.S. Navy
Anchors Aweigh—1945 musical starring Frank Sinatra and Gene Kelly
Angela's Ashes—Frank McCourt's memoir about his family's journey from the U.S. back to their native Ireland in the 1930s
Ann Arbor—City where the University of Michigan is located
Anxiety attack—Intense worry or panic
"Arf, Arf"—Favorite expression of Little Orphan Annie's dog Sandy
Ascorbic acid—Water-soluble vitamin also called Vitamin C
Augustan Age—Golden period of Roman literature, from 27 B.C. to A.D. 14
Aurora australis—Latin phrase for the southern lights
Australian Alps—Chain of mountain ranges in the Land Down Under in the Great Dividing Range
Author! Author!—1982 film starring Al Pacino as a playwright whose wife, played by Tuesday Weld, leaves him with 5 children
Avenging Angel—Title of Hugh Small's biography of Florence Nightingale, or John Wilkes Booth's nickname, "South's _____," for having killed Abraham Lincoln
The Avenging Angel—1995 film starring Tom Berenger as a member of the Mormon Church militia

*As of early 2005, team became the Los Angeles Angels of Anaheim

"**Aye, aye (Sir)**"—Nautical term meaning "I understand and will obey," used in response to a command
Aye-aye—Arboreal, nocturnal primate of Madagascar

ATHLETES AND A-A NICKNAMES
Primo Carnera—Boxer known as the "Ambling Alp"
Don Hutson—Green Bay Packer known as the "Alabama Antelope" and the "First Super End"
Joe Louis (born Barrow)—Boxer known as the "Alabama Assassin"
Archie Moore—Boxer known as "Ageless Archie"
Margaret Court Smith—Tennis player known as the "Amazin' Amazon"

Gimme A *B-B*

Flashy jewelry, usually of a very gaudy nature
Answer: Bling bling.

HOMO SAPIENS B-B
Barbara Babcock—Actress who played Grace Gardner on TV's *Hill Street Blues*
Barbara Bach—Ringo Starr's wife who starred as Maj. Anya Amasova in *The Spy Who Loved Me*
Burt Bacharach—Composer who teamed with Hal David on 1969's "Raindrops Keep Fallin' on My Head"
Backstreet Boys—Pop vocal group and known for 1997's "Quit Playing Games (With My Heart)" and 1999's *Millennium*
Barbara Bain—Actress who played Cinnamon Carter on TV's *Mission: Impossible*
Bobby Baker—Vice President Lyndon Johnson's wheeler-dealer aide from Texas associated with underworld figures and accused of influence peddling
Benjamin Banneker—Black scientist who helped Major Ellicott survey the territory of Washington, D.C.
Brigitte Bardot—French actress starring in the 1956 film *And God Created Woman*
Bobby Bare—Country singer of the '60s, '70s, and '80s known for such hits as "Four Strong Winds," "Marie Laveau," and "New Cut Road"
Bob Barker—Host of *The Price Is Right* who celebrated his 5,000th show in 1998
Béla Bartók—Hungarian composer and collector of folk music known for his *Mikrokosmos* and *Concerto for Orchestra*
Bernard Baruch—American businessman and unpaid adviser to every President from Wilson to Eisenhower who said, "Let us not be deceived—we are today in the midst of a cold war."
Birch Bayh—U.S. senator from Indiana from 1963 to 1981
Battling Bob—Nickname of Robert La Follette, the political leader and reformer who served as Wisconsin governor and from 1906 to 1925 as U.S. senator
Brian Boru—Irish king from 1002 to 1014, who spent his time fighting the Danes and the Norse
Beach Boys—California group whose *Endless Summer* was a No. 1 album in 1974
Bob Beamon—Olympian who set a world long jump record in Mexico City in 1968 at 29 feet 2½ inches, breaking the previous record by nearly 22 inches
Beastie Boys—New York rap trio whose hits include "(You Gotta) Fight For Your Right (To Party!)"
Boris Becker—German tennis player who won Wimbledon at age 17
Bonnie Bedelia—Actress starring as Bruce Willis's wife Holly in the *Die Hard* films
Brendan Behan—Irish author noted for his satire whose *Borstal Boy* is an autobiographical account of his 3 years in a reformatory
Bix Beiderbecke—American jazz cornet player, pianist, and composer whose most famous composition recorded for the piano is *In a Mist*—he is the first important white jazz artist
Barbara Bel Geddes—Actress who played Miss Ellie on TV's *Dallas*
Bert Bell—Second commissioner of the NFL, from 1946 to 1959

Bea Benadaret—Actress who starred as Kate Bradley on TV's *Petticoat Junction*
Bruce Beresford—Director of the films *Crimes of the Heart* and *Driving Miss Daisy*
Busby Berkeley—Choreographer known for the film *42nd Street* and the Broadway musical *Kiki*
Bernardo Bertolucci—Italian director and screenwriter of 1972's *Last Tango in Paris* and 1987's Oscar-winning *The Last Emperor*
Benazir Bhutto—Pakistan prime minister who was the first woman to head an elected government in an Islamic nation
Big Bear—Boxer Sonny Liston's nickname
Big Bill—Nickname of William Howard Taft
Barbara Billingsley—Actress who played June Cleaver on TV's *Leave It to Beaver*
Brad Bird—Animator who created fashion maven Edna "E." Mode, is known for the 1999 film *The Iron Giant*, and won an Oscar for the 2004 film *The Incredibles*
Bill Bixby—Actor who played Dr. David (Bruce) Banner on TV's *The Incredible Hulk*
Black Bart—Stagecoach robber, born Charles E. Boles (a.k.a. Bolton), who never robbed a passenger and was captured in 1883
Bonnie Blair—Speedskater who became the first American woman to win 5 Olympic gold medals
Billy Blanks—Guru of the Tae Bo workout program
Bill Blass—Indiana-born fashion designer of women's clothes who won 8 Coty Awards
Bleacher Bums—Nickname of the Chicago Cubs fans in the cheap seats at Wrigley Field
Budd Boetticher—Director of *Cimarron Kid* and *East of Sumatra*
Brian Boitano—American figure skater who won 2 world titles plus the 1988 Winter Olympic gold medal
Barry Bonds—7-time NL MVP—1990, 1992, 1993, 2001, 2002, 2003, 2004—and the first player ever to reach the 500 level in both home runs and stolen bases in major league baseball
Björn Borg—Men's Wimbledon champion for 5 successive years and a 6-time French Open champion
Barbara Bosson—Actress who played Fay Furillo on TV's *Hill Street Blues*
Braxton Bragg—Confederate general defeated in the 1863 Chattanooga Campaign
Boston Brahmins—Wealthy, educated, elite, conservative, upper-class 19th-century New Englanders, so named by Oliver Wendell Holmes after the highest priestly caste in Hinduism
Barry Bostwick—Actor in *The Rocky Horror Picture Show* who starred as Mayor Randall Winston on TV's *Spin City*
Boutros Boutros-Ghali—U.N. secretary general from Egypt who succeeded Javier Pérez de Cuéllar, serving from 1992 to 1996
Bobby Bowden—Florida State football coach who set the new record for wins in major college football with 351 wins at the end of the 2004 season
Bruce Boxleitner—Actor who played Lee Stetson on TV's *Scarecrow and Mrs. King*
Belle Boyd—Confederate spy in the Shenandoah Valley who was captured on her way to England carrying letters from Jefferson Davis and later became a prominent actress
Ben Bradlee—*Washington Post* editor when it cracked the Watergate scandal
Bill Bradley—3-time All-American forward at Princeton, Rhodes scholar, New York Knicks player, New Jersey Democratic senator, and 2000 presidential candidate
Benjamin Bratt—Actor of Peruvian descent who played Det. Curtis on TV's *Law & Order*
Berke Breathed—Creator of the comic strip *Bloom County*

Bertolt Brecht—German playwright who with Kurt Weill wrote the satirical musical *The Threepenny Opera*
Beau Bridges—Actor starring in *Norma Rae* and *The Fabulous Baker Boys*
Benjamin Britten—British composer famous for his operas including *Peter Grimes* and *Billy Budd*
Bronx Bombers—Nickname of the New York Yankees
Bronx Bull—Boxer Jacob La Motta's nickname
Blair Brown—Actress who played Molly Dodd on TV's *The Days and Nights of Molly Dodd*
Bobby Brown—Singer with the hit "My Prerogative" in 1989 who married Whitney Houston
Beau Brummell—Any elegant dandy or fop, derived from the name of an Englishman famous for his fashionable dress and manners
Bill Buckner—Boston Red Sox player with 2,715 hits but remembered for missing a ground ball in the 1986 World Series
Buffalo Bill—Nickname of horseman and sharpshooter William F. Cody
Billie Burke—Actress starring as the Good Witch, Glinda, in *The Wizard of Oz*
Brooke Burke—Hostess on *E!*'s *Wild On* and frequent *Playboy* poser
Barbara Bush—Wife of one U.S. President and mother of another
Brett Butler—Actress who starred as Grace Kelly on TV's *Grace Under Fire*

GEOGRAPHY B-B
Back Bay—Fashionable residential area of Boston, Massachusetts, consisting mostly of filled-in land reclaimed from mud flats
Baden-Baden—Famous spa town in the northwest corner of the Black Forest in Germany
Baffin Bay—Ice-clogged arm of the North Atlantic between Greenland and Canada
Bergen-Belsen—Nazi concentration camp site in northern German
Bermuda Bowl—World bridge championship held on a self-governing British colony in the Atlantic Ocean
Big Bend—National park in western Texas, so named by the U-turn the Rio Grande makes, or the epithet for the triangular-shaped region of southwest Texas formed by this river
Big Black—River rising in north-central Mississippi and flowing about 330 miles to the Mississippi River near Vicksburg
Big Blue—River rising in southeast Nebraska and flowing about 300 miles to the Kansas River
Biscayne Bay—Narrow inlet of the Atlantic in southeast Florida
(Halona) Blowhole Beach—Oahu, Hawaii, location where the love scene between Burt Lancaster and Deborah Kerr was partially filmed for the 1953 movie *From Here to Eternity*
Bondi Beach—Australian surfing site on the Pacific coast of New South Wales where the 2000 Olympic volleyball competition was played
Bora Bora—French Polynesian island in the Leeward group of the South Pacific's Society Islands
Borscht (Borsch) Belt—Informal term designating New York's resort hotels in the Catskills so named by entertainers because of their Jewish cuisine featuring a Russian beet soup
Boston Bruins—NHL team located in the New England "Hub of the Universe"
Botany Bay—Inlet of the Tasman Sea near Sydney, Australia, named by Captain James Cook for its extensive plant life
Brooklyn Bridge—Structure designed by John Roebling that was called the "eighth wonder of the world" when it was opened in 1883

Buffalo Bills—NFL team located in a city at the head of the Niagara River at the eastern end of Lake Erie

Buzzards Bay—Atlantic Ocean inlet in Massachusetts connected with Caper Cod Bay by a canal

LITERARY/FILM/TV/MUSIC B-B

"Baby Baby"—Amy Grant's 1991 hit inspired by her 6-week-old child Millie—from the album *Heart in Motion*

Baby Boom—1987 film starring Diane Keaton as a hard-working career woman whose life is interrupted by the unexpected arrival of a child

"Backstage Babble"—Song from Cole Porter's Broadway musical *Applause*

Bada Bing Club—Strip joint Tony Soprano owned on TV's *The Sopranos*

"Bad Boys"—Theme song for TV's *Cops* that reached No. 8 on *Billboard's* top pop singles chart in 1993—written by Ian Lewis and performed by Inner Circle

Balki Bartokomous—Character Bronson Pinchot played on TV's *Perfect Strangers*

Bamm Bamm—Rubbles' son, "the world's strongest boy," on the TV cartoon series *The Flintstones*

"(The) Barefoot Boy"—John Greenleaf Whittier poem or the words that complete its lines "Blessings on thee, little man, / _____ with cheek of tan!"

(*The*) *Bartered Bride*—Bedrich Smetana's 1866 opera about a woman who has to marry a man she has never seen

Bas bleu—French for "a bluestocking" or "an intellectual woman"

Batman Begins—2005 film exploring the origins of "The Dark Knight" and starring Christian Bale

"Beep Beep"—Only 2 words the Road Runner utters in the cartoons

Beetle Bailey—Mort Walker comic strip Army private whose eyes are never shown

Benjamin Braddock—Dustin Hoffman's character in the film *The Graduate*

Benjamin Bunny—Peter Rabbit's thrill-seeking cousin

Best boy—Main assistant to the gaffer or grip on a film crew

Betty Boop—Sexy animated cartoon star in the 1920s and 1930s with big eyes, a squeaky voice, and prominent breasts who made her first appearance in *Dizzy Dishes*

Big band—Ensemble of 10 or more musicians playing jazz and popular dance music or dance music as played by the orchestras of the Swing Era of the 1930s and 1940s

Big Bird—Sesame Street's 8-foot-2-inch tall yellow character whose birthday is March 20

Big Boned—Descriptive term South Park character Cartman uses for himself in arguing that he is not fat, just _____

Big Bopper—Nickname and stage name of singer J.P. Richardson who was killed in a plane crash with Buddy Holly and Ritchie Valens

Big Brother—Figure representing an authoritarian government that invades individual privacy, from George Orwell's *1984*

Bikini Bottom—Underwater lair of SpongeBob SquarePants and his best friend, Patrick

Bilbo Baggins—Hero of J.R.R. Tolkien's novel *The Hobbit, or There and Back Again*

Bill Bittinger—Unlikable character Dabney Coleman played on the TV sitcom *Buffalo Bill*

Bill Bones—*Treasure Island* seaman, a retired captain, who dies of fright when the pirates bring him his death warning

Billy Bathgate—E.L. Doctorow novel or 1991 gangster film starring Loren Dean as the title character

Billy Batson—Radio station broadcaster who is transformed into Captain Marvel, "the world's mightiest mortal"

Billy Budd—Herman Melville novella about a sailor hanged by Captain Vere for the slaying of John Claggart

Biloxi Blues—Second play in Neil Simon's loosely autobiographical trilogy

Bionic Bunny—TV superhero who in real life is Wilbur, an ordinary rabbit

Black Bart—Black sheriff played by Cleavon Little in the all-white town of Rock Ridge in the 1974 film *Blazing Saddles*

Black Beauty—Horse that narrates Anna Sewell's novel protesting cruelty to horses or the name of the Green Hornet's car

Black Boy—Richard Wright's 1945 autobiographical work subtitled *A Record of Childhood and Youth*

Blonde Bombshell—Jean Harlow's famous nickname

Blondie Boopadoop—Maiden name of the flapper who married comic strip character Dagwood Bumstead

(*The*) *Blue Boy*—Thomas Gainsborough painting done to prove that a blue painting need not be dull

(*The*) *Blues Brothers*—1980 film starring John Belushi and Dan Aykroyd as Jake and Elwood

Bonnie Blue—Eugenie Victoria Butler's name in Margaret Mitchell's *Gone With the Wind*

Boo Boo—Little bear who is the best friend of cartoon character Yogi Bear

Book burning—Destruction of writings considered politically or socially objectionable, used as a means of censorship

Boris Badenov—Spy from Pottsylvania and arch-enemy of Rocky and Bullwinkle in the cartoons

Borstal Boy—Irish author Brendan Behan's autobiographical account of his imprisonment for trying to carry explosives into Great Britain for the IRA

Bosom Buddies—Song from the Broadway musical *Mame* about close friends or the 1980s sitcom starring Peter Scolari and Tom Hanks

Boston Blackie—Jack Boyle-created detective featured on 1950s TV drama starring Kent Taylor as an "enemy of those who make him an enemy, friend of those who have no friend"

Boston Brahmins—Epithet given to Cambridge, Massachusetts, poets in the 1830s, especially Longfellow, Holmes, and Lowell, a name taken from the highest caste of the Hindu religion

Bowery Boys—Teenagers featured in a series of films in the 1940s and 1950s and also known as the Dead End Kids, the Little Tough Guys, and the East Side Kids

(*The*) *Brady Bunch*—TV sitcom about a widow with 3 daughters who married a widower with 3 sons

Brer (Br'er) Rabbit—Animal created by Joel Chandler Harris in his *Uncle Remus* stories

Brom Bones—Nickname of Abraham Van Brunt, Ichabod's rival for the hand of Katrina Van Tassel in Washington Irving's "The Legend of Sleepy Hollow"

Bronco Billy—1980 film starring Clint Eastwood as the owner of a Wild West show

(*The*) *Bronco Buster*—Frederic Remington's famous bronze sculpture featuring a cowboy atop a bucking horse

Buffalo Bill—TV sitcom set in New York starring Dabney Coleman

Bugs Bunny—Warner Brothers' cartoon rabbit known for saying, "Ah . . . what's up, Doc?"

Burger Barn—Fast food restaurant where Alexander Bumstead works in the comic strip *Blondie*

(*The*) *Burning Bed*—1984 TV film starring Farrah Fawcett as the wife of an abusive husband

Buster Brown—R.F. Outcault's well-dressed comic strip character and his dog Tige who later were adopted by a shoe company as mascots since they lived in a shoe
Buzz Buzzard—Woody Woodpecker's nemesis in cartoons

HOMO SAPIENS-RELATED B-B
Baby Blues—Rick Kirkman and Jerry Scott's comic strip about raising babies and children
Baby boom/bust—Sudden increase in a population's birthrate or a sudden decline in the birthrate
Baby boomer—Person born during the U.S. population explosion between 1946 and 1965
Baby box—B.F. Skinner's controlled environmental chamber for infants
Baby buggy—Small carriage used to wheel an infant about, or a perambulator
Baby bunting—Infant's warm, hooded outer garment or blanket closed at the bottom
Bafana Bafana—South Africa's national soccer team, named from a Zulu word meaning "The Boys"
Ball boy—Youngster who retrieves tennis balls that have gone out of play
Beach bum—Chronic loafer along the seashore
Beltway Bandit—Former government employee turned consultant and working for a firm feeding at the government trough in the suburbs near the Beltway around Washington, D.C., or the firm itself providing goods and services to the government
Big Ben—Nickname of both Pittsburgh Steelers Roethlisberger and Detroit Pistons center Wallace
Black belt—Person who has achieved the highest rank in a martial art or the sash that symbolizes this rank
Black book—Pocket-size book listing available female companions or a list of people to be punished or restricted from jobs or other opportunities
Blindman's bluff (buff)—Game in which a blindfolded person attempts to catch and identify another person
Blood bath—Massacre, or the killing of a large number of people
Blood brother—Person bound to another by the ceremony of having mixed his blood with that of the other
Blue baby—Infant born with cyanosis
Blue Bird*—Member of the youngest group of Camp Fire Girls or the words completing the phrase ____ *of happiness*, meaning "elusive happiness"
Blue blood—An aristocrat or member of a socially prominent family
B'nai Brith—Jewish fraternal society founded in New York City in 1843 and named with the Hebrew for "Song of the Covenant"
Boomerang baby—Slang for a young person who leaves home only to return there to live with his or her parents
Bra burner—Slang for a woman with militant feminist opinions
Brady Bill—Legislation named after Ronald Reagan's former aide that restricts or limits the purchase of handguns or other lethal weapons
Brooks Brothers—New York City department store at 44th and Madison known for its conservative men's wear
Brown belt—Person who has achieved the martial art prize awarded to the rank just below the highest one or the sash that symbolizes this rank
Bucket brigade—Line of people fighting a fire by passing pails of water from one to the other
Buddy-Buddy—Slang describing great outward friendship

*Camp Fire Girls is now Camp Fire USA, as the group is coed, and the name Blue Bird has been changed to Starflight.

Bug Boy—Jockey apprentice who gets a weight allowance when riding
Bully boy—Violent person or a hired thug
Bunsen burner—Small laboratory gas burner that produces a hot, blue flame named after a German chemist

POTPOURRI OF B-B

Baby Bell—Nickname given to any of the regional telephone companies originally part of AT&T or Ma Bell before the breakup
Baby's breath—Any of several plants of the genus *gypsophila*, with small, delicate, white or pink flowers
✓ **Bachelor's button**—Plant with round flower heads, especially the cornflower and knapweed
Back burner—Reduced priority, or a place of secondary importance
Bada bing (bada boom)—Exclamation from mob culture emphasizing that something will happen with little effort and as predicted
Bad blood—Phrase for a feeling of mutual enmity, or a 1975 Neil Sedaka hit
Bail bond—Security offered or deposited to ensure a defendant's appearance at trial
Bailey Bridge—Portable prefabricated steel structure designed to carry heavy loads in WWII, named after British engineer Donald Coleman _____
Baily's beads—Brilliant spots of sunlight shining through valleys on the rim of the moon during a total eclipse of the sun
✓ **Balance beam**—Long, narrow wooden rail used in gymnastics
Ball bearing—Object used to reduce friction in machinery and in wheels and axles
Bare bones—Slang for the "basic elements of something, without any frills"
✓ **Bargain(-)basement**—Very low-priced, as derived from a department store level where relatively inexpensive goods are sold
Barn burner—Slang for a noteworthy event, such as a high-scoring game, in allusion to a fable of a Dutchman who burned down his barn to rid it of rats
Beach buggy—Recreational vehicle with wide tires, used for driving on the sand
Bean ball—Pitch aimed at a batter's head in baseball
Beanie Baby—Popular beanbag stuffed toy collectible of the 1990s and later
Beecher's Bibles—Nickname for the Sharps rifles used in "Bloody Kansas" in the 1850s because they were more effective than debate in changing pro-slavery opinions, named after a Brooklyn clergyman
Beer belly—Slang term for "a protruding abdomen," especially from excessive alcohol consumption
Beetle-brained—Having a very hard head, derived from *betl*, meaning "hammer"
Beetle-browed—Having overhanging eyebrows, derived from *betl*, meaning "hammer"
Belmont Breeze—Belmont horse race's official drink made of Seagram's 7, sherry, orange juice, cranberry juice, lemon juice, simple syrup, 7UP, and club soda
Beta blocker—Any of a class of drugs used to control heartbeat and treat hypertension, migraine, and angina
Black Betsy—Babe Ruth's 44-ounce baseball bat and "Shoeless Joe" Jackson's bat
Blankety-blank—Slang for cursed or damned, used in much the same way as asterisks or dashes are used to mark a space where a curse word has been omitted in print
Blood bank—Place where whole blood or blood plasma is kept for future use
Bible Belt—Area in the South where fundamentalist Christian beliefs prevail
Big Bang (theory)—Theory that the universe originated in a violent explosion of a hot, dense mass of matter, or a single cataclysmic event creating spectacular change

Big Ben—Great bell in the Parliament clock tower in London or the tower itself
Big Bertha—Nickname of the large, long-range German cannon of WWI made by Krupp
Big Blue—Nickname for IBM or the International Business Machines corporation
Big Board—Listing of the securities that are bought and sold on the New York Stock Exchange or the New York Stock Exchange itself
Big Book—*Alcoholics Anonymous* text, as known by those within AA
Big Boxes—Large retail stores, especially when they become vacant and leave an empty shell
Big brass—Highest level business executives, originally a military term
Big Brown—Nickname of UPS, or the United Parcel Service
Big bucks—Slang term for "a huge amount of money"
Big Business—Largest corporations, regarded collectively, as opposed to small individually or family-owned ones
Billy Beer—Alcoholic product once promoted by President Jimmy Carter's brother
Black bag job—Secret illegal break-in by a government agency, in allusion to a burglar's satchel of tools
Black bear—Large North American animal whose Latin name is *Euarctos* or *Ursus americanus*
Black bears—Nickname of the athletic teams at the University of Maine
Black belt—Area of rich, fertile soil, especially in Alabama and Mississippi as well as an area with a large population of African-Americans
Black bile—Of the 4 humors of the body, the one the ancient Greeks believed cause melancholy
Black box—Aircraft's self-contained electronic device to record flight data that is colored orange
Blue Bonnet—Brand of margarine
Blue book—Official government report, an examination booklet, or a listing of socially prominent people
Body bag—Rubberized container sealed with a zipper used for carrying a dead person
Body blow—Hard hit knocking a person down, or a serious setback or disappointment
Boeuf bourguignon—French term for the dish consisting of seasoned cubes of beef cooked in red wine together with onions, mushrooms, and bacon
Bomb burst—Signature maneuver of the Thunderbirds, the U.S. Air Force's demonstrative flying team
Bonnie Blue (flag)—South Carolina's succession flag
Boo-boo—Baby talk for "a foolish mistake" or "a minor bruise"
Boogie Board—Brand name of a bodyboard, or a piece of foam used like a surfboard but mainly ridden lying down
Boola Boola—Yale University's fight song or noisy support for one's college team
Boom box—Large, loud portable radio, or in slang, a ghetto blaster
Brain Bus—Winnebago motor home the Clue Crew uses to travel the country for TV's *Jeopardy!*
Brown bagging—Practice of carrying one's own alcoholic beverage into a restaurant when the law prevents alcohol from being sold there or the practice of taking one's lunch to work
Brown Bess—Nickname for an 18th-century British army flintlock musket
Brown betty—Baked apple dessert made with butter, spices, sugar, and bread crumbs
Bucking bronco—Unbroken horse of the U.S. plains known for throwing rodeo riders and depicted on the license plate of the state of Wyoming

Bucky Beaver—Rodent used in Ipana toothpaste commercials in the 1950s
Bulletin board—Wall area on which notices are placed or a computer system for airing information to be shared
Bumble Bee—Company known for its canned tuna, salmon, sardines, and now Omega 3&6 Fish Oil Supplements
Burning bush—Shrub out of which an angel appeared to the biblical Moses in a flame of fire or a plant with brilliant red flowers, berries, or leaves
Bush baby—Nocturnal primate with a long, bushy tail living in a tropical African forest
BuzzBee—Honey Nut Cheerios cartoon mascot that wears white shoes
Buzz bomb—Colloquial term for a robotic explosive device used by Germany against England in WWII
Bye-bye—Baby talk for going to bed or to sleep, or an interjection of farewell

ATHLETES AND B-B NICKNAMES
Terry Bradshaw—Pittsburgh quarterback known as the "Blond Bomber" and "Ozark Ike"
Lou Brock—St. Louis Cardinal player known as the "Base Burglar"
Brooklyn Dodgers—Baseball team known as the "Beloved Bums" and "Dem Bums"
Orlando Cepeda—Baseball player known as the "Baby Bull"
Bob Feller—Indian pitcher known as "Bullet Bob" and "Rapid Robert"
Bernie Geoffrion—Montreal Canadiens player known as "Boom Boom"
Bob (Robert Lee) Hayes—Olympian and NFL player known as "Bullet Bob" and the "World's Fastest Human"
Ben Hogan—Golfer known as "Bantam Ben" and "Blazing Ben"
Bobby Layne—Detroit Lions quarterback known as the "Blonde Bomber"
Joe Louis (born Barrow)—Boxer known as the "Black Beauty," the "Brown Bomber," and the "Dark Destroyer"
Ray Mancini—Boxer known as "Boom Boom"
Rocky Marciano*—Boxer known as the "Brockton Blockbuster" and the "Brockton Bull"
Jesse Owens—4-time Olympic gold-medalist known as the "Brown Bombshell" and the "Buckeye Bullet"
Bill Tilden—Tennis player known as "Big Bill"
Bob Turley—Oriole pitcher known as "Bullet Bob"
*Born Rocco Francis Marchegiano

GIMME A C-C

Slang for any modern convenience that contributes to a person's physical well-being, such as food, clothing, and shelter
Answer: Creature comfort.

HOMO SAPIENS C-C
Cab Calloway—Jazz musician and big band leader known as the Hi-De-Ho Man and featured in the 1980 movie *The Blues Brothers*
Clarence Campbell—NHL president from 1946 to 1977
Claudia Cardinale—Actress starring in the films *The Professionals* and the *Pink Panther*
Charisma Carpenter—Actress starring as Cordelia Chase on the WB series *Angel*
Charles Carroll—Last surviving signer of the Declaration of Independence, from Carrollton, Maryland, the only Catholic to sign this document
Carlos Castaneda—Cultural anthropologist who published *The Teachings of Don Juan: A Yaqui Way of Knowledge* in 1968
"Coco" Channel—20th-century Parisian couturière known for her short skirts, tailored suits, and perfumes
Carol Channing—Actress who starred in the musical comedies *Gentlemen Prefer Blondes* and *Hello Dolly!*
Charlie Chaplin—Actor who created the character "The Little Tramp"
Cyd Charisse—Actress and dancer starring in 1957's *Silk Stockings*
Charlie Chase—Lorianne Crook's partner on TV's The Nashville Network
Chevy Chase—Actor starring in *Caddyshack*, *Fletch*, and *Three Amigos*
Cesar Chavez—Labor organizer who headed the United Farm Workers of America from 1966 until 1993
Chubby Checker—Pseudonym of Ernest Evans, who is credited with popularizing the dance The Twist with his 1960 song of the same name
Claire Chennault—Army aviation pioneer who headed the volunteer group called the Flying Tigers and served as an adviser to Chiang Kai-shek
Caryl Chessman—Convicted sex offender known as the "Red Light Bandit" who was executed on May 2, 1960
Connie Chung—Journalist who joined Dan Rather as co-anchor of the CBS *Evening News* from 1993 to 1995
Charlotte Church—Welsh prodigy whose first album, *Voice of an Angel*, went platinum, making her at age 13 the youngest artist ever to reach No. 1 on the American classical chart
Craig Claiborne—Chef who served as food editor of the *New York Times* from 1957 to 1988
Champ Clark—Kentuckian who served as Speaker of the U.S. House of Representatives from 1911 to 1919
Cassius Clay—Boxer Muhammad Ali's name at birth
Chelsea Clinton—Presidential daughter who graduated from Stanford University
Clue Crew—Cheryl Farrell, Sofia Lidskog, Jimmy McGuire, and Sarah Whitcomb on *Jeopardy!*
Charles Coburn—Actor who in 1943 won a Best Supporting Actor Oscar for *The More the Merrier*
Claudette Colbert—Actress who in 1934 won a Best Actress Oscar for her *It Happened One Night*

Charles Collingwood—Edward R. Murrow's replacement as host of TV's *Person to Person* from 1959 to 1961
Carlo Collodi—Pseudonym of Carlo Lorenzini, the Italian author who wrote *The Adventures of Pinocchio*
Charles Colson—President Nixon's chief counsel who spent time in prison for his involvement in the Watergate scandal and later founded his Prison Fellowship organization
Chris Columbus—Director of *Home Alone*, *Mrs. Doubtfire*, and 2 of the Harry Potter films
Christopher Columbus—Explorer who "sailed the ocean blue in 1492"
Charlie Comiskey—Chicago White Sox owner from 1901 to 1931, known as "The Old Roman"
Chuck Connors—Actor who starred as Lucas McCain on the TV series *The Rifleman*
Conway Cabal—Failed 1777 conspiracy to remove George Washington as commander in chief of the Continental Army following defeats at Brandywine Creek and Germantown
Calvin Coolidge—President who succeeded Warren Harding
Chuck Cooper*—First black to be drafted by an NBA team, for the Boston Celtics on April 25, 1950
Charlotte Corday—Woman who stabbed Jean Paul Marat to death in his bathtub during the French Revolution's Reign of Terror in 1793
Charles Cornwallis—British general and Lord who surrendered his troops at Yorktown, Virginia, on October 19, 1781
Charles Coughlin—Roman Catholic priest in Michigan turned demagogue whose weekly radio program denounced FDR's New Deal and other policies
Clint Courtney—Major league catcher known as "Scrap Iron"
Courteney Cox—Actress who played Lauren Miller on TV's *Family Ties* and Monica Geller Bing on *Friends*
Clarence Crabbe—Gold-medal winner of the 400-meter freestyle at the 1932 Olympics nicknamed "Buster" and later the actor who played Tarzan in film
Cindy Crawford—Supermodel who married Richard Gere and then Rande Gerber and debuted in the 1995 film *Fair Game*
Charles Crocker—One of the Big Four magnates who built the Central Pacific Railroad
Christopher Cross—Singer whose 1980 album with the singles "Ride Like the Wind" and "Sailing" won a Grammy for Album of the Year
Cameron Crowe—Director of *Jerry Maguire* and *Almost Famous*
Countée Cullen—Harlem Renaissance poet and novelist who wrote *Copper Sun* and *One Way to Heaven*
Charles Curtis—Herbert Hoover's Vice President

*Nat "Sweetwater" Clifton" was the first black to sign an NBA contract, and Earl Lloyd was the first black to enter an NBA game, on October 31, 1950, one day before the other two.

GEOGRAPHY C-C

Calaveras County—California region named in the title of Mark Twain's story "The Celebrated Jumping Frog of _____," about a frog named Dan'l Webster
California condor—Largest flying land bird in North America
Canterbury Cathedral—Building in which Archbishop Thomas à Becket was killed in 1170
Cape Canaveral—Florida site from which NASA launched its manned space exploration programs until 1964 when they were moved to Merritt Island
Cape Cod—Hook-shaped peninsula projecting from the southern coast of Massachusetts
Cape Cod—Type of rectangular house with a steep gabled roof, originating in Massachusetts
Carlsbad Caverns—Chain of huge underground limestone caves in southeastern New Mexico

Carson City—Only U.S. state capital to fit this category
Century City—Planned city in West Los Angeles bordering Beverly Hills and called a "city within a city"—its first building was completed in 1963
Champagne Castle—South Africa's highest point, a peak in the Drakensberg mountain range whose name loosely suggests "a bubbly chateau"
Charing Cross—Area adjoining Trafalgar Square from which road distances from London are often measured and where King Edward I placed a memorial to his wife, Eleanor of Castile
Checkpoint Charlie—Most famous border crossing point along the Berlin Wall, which divided West Berlin from East Berlin from 1961 to 1990
Chevy Chase—Washington, D.C., residential suburb located in Maryland that shares its name with a well known comic actor
Chicago Cubs—National League baseball team in the "Windy City"
Cleveland Cavaliers—NBA team located in a city on the southern shore of Lake Erie
Columbus Crew—MLS team located in the capital of Ohio
Corpus Christi—Texas city on the Gulf of Mexico whose name means "the Body of Christ"
Crescent City—Nickname given to New Orleans, Louisiana, because its French Quarter lies along a giant curve in the Mississippi River
Crown colony—Any of Britain's distant territories directly under the control of the home government of London
Crystal Cathedral—Famous glass church built in Garden Grove, California
Culver City—City in Los Angeles County that is the home of MGM Studios, NPR, and Sony Pictures Entertainment

LITERARY/FILM/TV/MUSIC C-C

Cabot Cove—Town on the coast of Maine where TV's *Murder, She Wrote* was set
Calico cat—Animal that got into a terrible spat with a gingham dog in Eugene Field's poem "The Duel"
Can-Can—Cole Porter Broadway musical that includes the songs "C'est Magnifique" and "I Love Paris" or a lively dance, originally performed in Paris dance halls
Candace Compson—Only daughter of Jason and Caroline in William Faulkner's *The Sound and the Fury*
Candid Camera—Long-running humorous TV show produced and hosted by Allen Funt
Caped Crusader—Batman's nickname
Captains Courageous—Rudyard Kipling's 1897 novel about the sea or a 1937 film starring Spencer Tracy and based on the novel
"Cathy's Clown"—The Everly Brothers 1960 hit
Cat's Cradle—Kurt Vonnegut novel in which an eccentric invents a crystal called ice-nine, which freezes anything it touches
Charlie Chan—Fictional Chinese detective on Honolulu's police force in works by Earl Derr Biggers
Chee-Chee—Monkey in Hugh Lofting's *The Story of Dr. Dolittle*
Cheshire Cat—Constantly grinning animal in Lewis Carroll's *Alice's Adventures in Wonderland* that sometimes leaves just its grin behind
Chitty Chitty—Words completing the title of Ian Fleming's 1964 novel _____ *Bang Bang* about a flying car, made into a 1968 movie
Chris Cagney—Detective played by Sharon Gless on TV's *Cagney & Lacey*
"(A) Christmas Carol"—Charles Dickens' story featuring Ebenezer Scrooge

Cimarron City —TV western set in the 1890s that starred George Montgomery as Matthew Rockford
Cinnamon Carter —Role Barbara Bain played on TV's *Mission: Impossible*
Cliff Clavin —Character John Ratzenberger played on TV's *Cheers*
Cloud-cuckooland —Ideal city suspended between heaven and earth in Aristophanes' comedy *The Birds* —its name has come to mean "a place of fantasy" or "foolish behavior"
Cold Case —TV drama about crimes that have never been solved, starring Kathryn Morris as Lilly Rush
Conspicuous consumption —Thorstein Veblen's phrase designating showy excess intended to impress others with one's wealth—from *The Theory of the Leisure Class*
Corrina, Corrina —1994 film starring Whoopi Goldberg as a maid working for Ray Liotta playing a Jewish jingle writer
The Cotton Club —1984 film starring Richard Gere as Dixie Dwyer and Gregory Hines as Sandman Williams
Credence Clearwater (Revival) —California rock group _____ Revival whose 1969 hits include "Proud Mary," "Bad Moon Rising," and "Down on the Corner"
Criss Cross —1949 film starring Burt Lancaster as an honest armored-car guard
Cross Creek —Marjorie Kinnan Rawlings' memoirs about a trip in the Florida backwoods or the 1983 film based on her work starring Mary Steenburgen
Culture Club —British pop group whose "Karma Chameleon" was a 1984 hit

POTPOURRI OF C-C
Cabin cruiser —Motorboat with sleeping, cooking, and other living facilities
Cable car —Type of streetcar pulled up a steeply inclined street, as in San Francisco
Ca-ca —Child's slang term for excrement or feces
Calling card —Engraved card bearing one's full name
Candy cane —Striped stick of Christmas candy whose curved top resembles a walking stick
Cavalry charge —Military assault by soldiers on horseback, especially against Indians on the western frontier
Carbon copy —Replica, or any person or thing that closely resembles another
Card-carrying —Slang for holding membership in a particular group, as in the Communist Party
Card catalog —Library's collection of files containing data arranged alphabetically, now widely replaced by computer databases
Cash cow —Slang for a regular and reliable source of income or profit
Cash crop —Produce grown to be sold rather than simply consumed, as on a farm
Cassiopeia's Chair —*W*-shaped design formed by the 5 brightest stars in the constellation between Andromeda and Cepheus
Casting couch —Slang for the sofa on which aspiring actresses allegedly earn their roles by granting producers sexual favors
Catalytic converter —Automobile device used to convert exhaust gases into a harmless product with the goal of reducing air pollution
Cat's cradle —Children's game played with string
Cattle call —Show business audition for extras
Cause célèbre —French for "a celebrated legal case" or "a situation attracting great attention"
Cave canem —Latin phrase meaning "beware the dog"
Central Casting —Company formed in 1926 to provide extras to film producers, or a movie studio department responsible for hiring actors, especially for nonstarring roles

Cerebral cortex—Furrowed outer layer of gray matter covering the cerebrum of the brain
Cha-cha—Rhythmic ballroom dance of Latin American origin
Chi-chi—Slang for extremely chic or conspicuously stylish
Chicken colonel—Slang for a full colonel in the military
Children's Crusade—Failed 1212 campaign in which thousands of French and German youngsters set out to end the Muslim domination of the Holy Land
Chinaman's chance—No chance at all, from the plight of certain poor immigrants who, despite having worked hard to build railroads, had little chance of making a fortune in America
Chin-chin—Chitchat, or a toast to someone's health, from the Chinese *qing-qing*, meaning "please-please"
Chinese checkers—Game using marbles of different colors on a board with holes patterned in a 6-pointed star
Choo-choo—Child's term for "a railroad train"
Chop-chop—Pidgin English for "quickly"
Chow chow—Breed of dog of Chinese origin having a blue-black tongue, or a slang term for food or mealtime
Christian Coalition—Religious organization founded by Pat Robertson in 1989
Chump change—Slang for a relatively small or trivial amount of money
Class consciousness—Awareness of rank in the social order, especially on an economic level
Clean-cut—Neat and trim or sharply defined
Clear-cut—Clear and obvious, or a tract of land that has had all of its trees cut down
Close call—Narrow escape from injury or death
Closing costs—Fees associated with the completion of a real estate transaction
Cloud chamber—Large vessel that makes the path of electrically charged subatomic particles visible
Coca-Cola—Drink invented in the late 19th century by Dr. John S. Pemberton, whose apothecary is located in Columbus, Georgia, the city in which he is buried
Coffin corner—Area near the sideline where punts are kicked out of bounds near the opponent's goal line in football
Coin collecting—Hobby that numismatists engage in
Cold call—Telephone contact or visit made to a prospect without any advance notice
Cold cash—Money on hand or money paid in full when business is transacted
Cold comfort—Very limited sympathy
Cold cut—Slice of cooked or smoked meat served without being heated
(To) come clean—To confess, or to tell the truth
Common carrier—Person or company in the business of transporting the public, goods, or messages for a fee
Common Cause—Citizens' lobby for political and social reform founded by John Gardner, who served as secretary of health, education, and welfare from 1965 to 1969
Community chest—Private fund collected in a city to support local social agencies
Compassionate conservative—Phrase used by George W. Bush as a slogan to allegedly show that he is a politician who cares
Complimentary close—Part of a letter that by convention immediately precedes the signature, as "Cordially" or Sincerely yours"
Concentration camp—Internment site where political enemies and prisoners of war are kept or any situation characterized by very cruel conditions

Conference call—Consultation by telephone among 3 or more persons in different locations

Continental Congress—Either of the 2 conventions of delegates of the American colonies convened in 1774 and 1775 to seek unity against British parliamentary acts

Cookie(-)cutter—Device for making shaped forms or an informal term describing something unoriginal or a plan done according to a predetermined idea

Core curriculum—Course of study considered essential and made mandatory for all school students

Coronation Chair*—Throne in the chapel of Edward the Confessor in Westminster Abbey built to hold the Stone of Scone, or Stone of Destiny, upon which all but 2 English kings were crowned

Corpus callosum—Transverse band of nerve fibers that connect the brain's cerebral hemispheres, named from the Latin for "callous body"

Corpus Christi—Festival whose name means "the Body of Christ" celebrated after Trinity Sunday, in honor of the Eucharist

Cotton candy—Spun sugar

Country club—Private organization for social and sports activities, such as tennis and golf

Country cousin—Colloquial for a rural person unfamiliar with city life and bewildered by it

Cover charge—Fixed cost for entering a nightclub or restaurant

Cow college—Slang for an agricultural school, or a small, rural college

Crayola Crayons—Brand in whose first box in 1903 were 8 colors and sold for a nickel and that has had as many as 120 colors in its biggest box

Creeping crud—Tiredness or discomfort suggesting the onset of flu or another contagious disease being passed around

Creepy-crawly—Slang for a crawling insect considered frightening

Crew cut—Closely cropped haircut, so called because rowers adopted the style

Crisis Center—Headquarters from which emergency disaster relief is controlled or that gives support to people with personal problems

Crop circle—Geometric design on a flattened area in a field at one time said to be the work of creatures from outer space and now attributed to pranksters

Cruise control—Motor vehicle device for maintaining a constant speed

Curtain call—Appearance of performers on stage at the end of a play to acknowledge the applause of the audience

*Also called King Edward's Chair

ATHLETES AND C-C NICKNAMES

Don Budge—Tennis player known as the "California Comet"

Orlando Cepeda—Baseball player known as "Cha-Cha"

Charlie Justice—"Tarheel" and Washington Redskins player known as "Choo Choo"

Mickey Mantle—New York Yankee known as the "Commerce Comet"

Shirley Muldowney—Female race driver known as "Cha Cha" and the "Queen of the Drag Strip"

Juan Rodriguez—Golfer known as "Chi Chi" and the "Clown Prince of Golf"

Gimme A D-D

Batman and Robin's nickname as a pair
Answer: Dynamic Duo.

HOMO SAPIENS D-D
Dorothy Dandridge—First black actress to receive an Oscar nomination as Best Actress (for *Carmen Jones*), in 1954—Halle Berry starred in a 1999 HBO film about her
Darryl Dawkins—First basketball player to go straight from high school to the NBA, nicknamed "Chocolate Thunder," "Mr. Earthquake," and "Dr. Jam"
Dennis Day—Irish tenor who became a regular on *The Jack Benny Show*
Doris Day—Singer and actress known for her signature song "Que Sera Sera" and her films *The Pajama Game*, *Pillow Talk*, and *That Touch of Mink*
Dorothy Day—Roman Catholic journalist and social worker who with Peter Maurin founded the Catholic Worker Movement and newspaper in 1933
Daniel Day-Lewis—Actor who won a Best Actor Oscar playing Irish-born artist and writer Christy Brown in 1989's *My Left Foot*
Dizzy Dean—30-game winner, 1934 MVP for the world champion Cardinals, and sports commentator known for saying, "The runner slud into third."
Dave DeBusschere—New York Knicks forward known as "Big D"
"Dede Dinah"—Frankie Avalon's first hit song, in 1958
Daniel Defoe—British author who wrote *Moll Flanders* and *Robinson Crusoe*
Dana Delany—Actress who played Nurse Colleen McMurphy on TV's *China Beach*
Dino De Laurentiis—Producer of the films *War and Peace*, *King Kong*, and *Ragtime*
Don DeLillo—Author who wrote the novels *Americana*, *White Noise*, and *Underworld* the last of which begins in 1951 at the Brooklyn Dodgers-New York Giants playoff game
Dolores Del Rio—Actress starring in *Flying Down to Rio* and *Journey Into Fear*
Dom Deluise—Actor starring in *Cannonball Run*, *Smokey and the Bandit II*, and *Robin Hood: Men in Tights*
Danny DeVito—Actor starring in *Romancing the Stone*, *Tin Men*, and *Twins*
Denis Diderot—Materialist thinker of the French Enlightenment and originator of the *Encyclopédie*
Dom DiMaggio—Boston Red Sox outfielder known as the "Little Professor"
David Dinkins—First black mayor of New York City
Dorothea Dix—Prison reform leader who was head of the U.S. Army's nurses in the Civil War
Dr. Death—Nickname of Jack Kevorkian, the Michigan doctor who helped many people end their lives
Diana Dors—Actress born Diana Mary Fluck known for *Deep End* and *I Married a Woman*
David Doyle—Actor who played John Bosley on TV's *Charlie's Angels*
Daryl Dragon—Real name of The Captain of the pop duo Captain & Tennille
Dr. Dre—Rap artist born Andre Young
Don Drysdale—Dodger pitcher who won the Cy Young Award in 1962 and had a record 6 straight shutouts in 1968
David Duchovny—Actor who starred as Fox Mulder on TV's *The X-Files*
David Duke—Former national grand wizard of the Knights of the Ku Klux Klan who ran unsuccessfully for governor of Louisiana, U.S. senator, and President

Doris Duke—Billionaire heiress of a tobacco baron played by Lauren Bacall in a 1999 TV movie

Duran Duran—Group whose "The Reflex" and "Ordinary World" were 1984 and 1993 hits, respectively

David Duval—Golfer whose 59 in 1999 at the Bob Hope Classic matched the best score in PGA history

LITERARY/FILM/TV/MUSIC D-D

Daffy Duck—Warner Brothers' cartoon drake known for saying "You're deth-picable"

Daily double—Opportunity on *Jeopardy!* to double your winnings by betting all of your money

Daisy Duck—Donald Duck's long-time girlfriend, his cousin

Daisy Duke*—Character Catherine Bach played on TV's *The Dukes of Hazzard*

Deadeye Dick—Kurt Vonnegut's 1982 novel whose title is the nickname of Rudy Waltz, the central character

Deadwood Dick—Hero of Edward L. Wheeler's 19th-century dime novels about the Wild West

"Delta Dawn"—Helen Reddy's No. 1 hit in 1973

(*The*) *Devil's Dictionary* —Ambrose Bierce's work first published as *The Cynic's Word Book*

Dewey Decimal (system)—Book classification system in libraries using 3-digit numbers, from 000 to 999, created by Melvil _____

Dick Deadeye—Deformed sailor and villain in Gilbert and Sullivan's operetta *H.M.S. Pinafore*

Dirty Dancing—1987 Jennifer Grey and Patrick Swayze film set at a Catskills resort

"Dirty Diana"—Michael Jackson's 1988 hit about rock-star groupies—from the album *Bad*

(*The*) *Dirty Dozen* —1967 film in which Lee Marvin is in charge of 12 military prisoners behind German lines

Doctor Dolittle—Fictional English veterinarian who lives in the town of Puddleby-on-the-Marsh

Doctor (Dr.) Dolittle—Film about the fictional English veterinarian created by Hugh Lofting, starring Rex Harrison in the 1967 version and Eddie Murphy in the 1998 remake

Doink! Doink!—Sound advertised as the one being made on TV's *Law and Order: Special Victims Unit* when the scene changes

Dr. Doom—Marvel's comic book arch-enemy of the Fantastic Four

Donald Duck—Disney character who wears a sailor shirt and whose identical triplet nephews are named Huey, Dewey, and Louie

Dudley Do-Right—Canadian mountie in the cartoons whose horse is named Horse

Dumb Dora—College-age comic strip character characterized by the line, "She ain't so dumb."

*The really short, form-fitting, cut-off jean shorts she wore in the series are now known as "Daisy Dukes."

POTPOURRI OF D-D

Da-da—Child's term for father

Daily double—Bet placed by choosing the winners in 2 designated races on the same program

Daily dozen—Gymnastic exercises, originally a series of 12, done on a regular basis

Dead drop—Slang term for the site where spies leave and pick up messages or other material

Dead drunk—Inebriated to the extent of being unable to move

Dead duck—Slang term for something totally worthless or doomed to failure or death
Decoration Day—Original name for Memorial Day, a day commemorating dead U.S. servicemen
Defensive driving—Efforts to avoid an accident by anticipating danger when behind the wheel of an automobile
Demolition derby—Event at which drivers crash old cars into one another until there is but one car left in running condition
Demon Deacons—Nickname of the atletic teams at Wake Forest
Derrick Dolls—Cheerleaders for the former NFL's Houston Oilers
Derring-do—Reckless courage
Designated driver—Person selected to drive others home because he has not consumed alcoholic beverages
Designer drug—Drug similar to a controlled narcotic but created by an underground chemist in order to avoid legal restrictions
Digital divide—Gap existing between people who have access to computers and those who don't
Din-din—Slang for dinner
Ding-dong—Sound of a bell or slang for a foolish person
Discovery Day*—Another name for Columbus Day
Dishonorable discharge—Dismissal from the U.S. military for a serious offense, such as murder, sabotage, espionage, or cowardice
Dog days—Hot, unpleasant days in July and August when the Dog Star, or Sirius, rises and sets with the sun
Dollar diplomacy—Use of (American) economic power and military and political muscle to create opportunities for (American) businessmen in the Far East and Latin America, a phrase derived from President Taft's fiscal foreign policy
Dominion Day—Former name for Canada Day, commemorating July 1, 1867
Done deal—Slang phrase for a plan that is a *fait accompli*, or an accomplished fact
Doo-doo—Slang for excrement or feces, or for trouble, as in the expression *in deep* _____
Doomsday Defense—1970s Dallas Cowboys defensive line
Double dagger—Symbol used as a reference mark
Double date—Social engagement shared by 2 couples
Double-dealing—Deceit or doing the opposite of what one pretends to do
Double-decker—Vehicle with an upper level, or a sandwich with two layers of filling
Double dipping—Slang for placing a cracker or chip into a dip for a second time after taking a bite from it or for receiving compensation from 2 sources, such as working at a government job while receiving a government pension
Double dribble—Bouncing a basketball in an illegal way
Double Dutch—Children's game of jumping rope in which 2 ropes are swung in a crisscross formation
Draft dodger—Person who avoids selection for military service, possibly by fleeing the country
(To) dress down—To scold, or to wear informal attire to work, on Friday for example
Dressing-down—Informal for a severe reprimand
Dry dock—Site where ships are serviced or repainted
(To) dumb down—Slang for to make less intelligent or less difficult
Dum-dum—Person considered stupid

*Or Discoverer's Day

Dum Dum (Dum-Dum)**—Town in West Bengal, India, headquarters of the Bengal artillery, 1783-1853, where _____ bullets were first made

Dust devil—Small whirlwind that raises powdery earth and litter in a narrow column

Dutch door—Entranceway closure with upper and lower halves that can be opened separately

**Dumdum bullets were first made there.

ATHLETES AND D-D NICKNAMES

Joe Louis (born Barrow)—Boxer known the "Dark Destroyer"

Juan Marichal—Giants pitcher known as the "Dominican Dandy"

Don Meredith—Dallas Cowboys quarterback known as "Dandy Don"

Doak Walker Jr.—Detroit Lions player known as "Dauntless Doak" and the "Little Man in Pro Football"

Shared Names

French resort town whose name came to stand for collaboration with the Nazis during the 2 years Germany occupied all of France—this town, which served as the capital of unoccupied France from 1940 to 1942, is known for a cold potato soup named after it and for its springs from which a natural sparkling mineral water was originally obtained
Answer: Vichy (a *Vichyite* was a "collaborator"; *vichyssoise* is the soup, and *Vichy water* is the mineral water).

FOUR OR MORE CLUES
Agate—Nebraska's _____ Fossil Beds National Monument; a former small 5½-point printing type; a hard semiprecious stone, with striped or clouded coloring; and a child's marble, especially the shooting marble used to bump other marbles out of the ring

Ariel—Procter & Gamble washing powder; a 1966 collection of poems by Sylvia Plath; a moon of Uranus; the airy sprite who is Prospero's servant in Shakespeare's *The Tempest*; and the mermaid princess in Disney's *The Little Mermaid*

Billy*—Kettle used in Australia for outdoor cooking; a club or heavy stick; a truncheon used by a policeman; and a male goat

Columbia—U.S. state capital; a university in New York; a major U.S. river; and a U.S. space shuttle

Emperor—Beethoven's Piano Concerto No. 5, in E flat; a brightly colored butterfly; the ruler of an empire; and the title conferred upon Charlemagne when he had himself crowned in A.D. 800

Equus—Company called _____ Computer Systems; a Peter Shaffer play about a young man who feels compelled to blind horses; the 1977 movie based on the Shaffer play; and a magazine about horses

Four Seasons—Prestigious Manhattan restaurant; a popular white singing group of the 1960s; a 1991 Alan Alda film; and Vivaldi's 4 best known violin concertos

Gold Coast—Elmore Leonard 1980 novel; a location where rich people live, especially along a shore; upscale area of Chicago along Lake Shore Drive; and the former British territory on the Gulf of Guinea today known as Ghana

Helter Skelter—Blues band started in 2000; haphazardly or in noisy and disorderly haste; a kind of spiral slide found at a British amusement park; a Beatles' song featuring this slide; Charles Manson's favorite phrase; and Vincent Bugliosi's book about the prosecution of Charles Manson in the Sharon Tate murders

Hobart—William McKinley's first Vice President, Garret _____; a company whose products include warewashers, mixers, and slicers; Geneva, New York's _____ and William Smith colleges; and Tasmania's capital

Kiwi—Flightless New Zealand bird that is the only one with nostrils at the tip of its bill; shoe polish; a type of fruit with an emerald-green pulp also known as a Chinese gooseberry; and informally a New Zealander

Lilith—Dr. _____ Sternin, Dr. Frasier Crane's wife on TV's *Cheers*, whom he later divorces; _____ Fair, an annual concert celebrating women in music; the devil's wife in Anne Rice's novel *Memnoch the Devil*; and a demon sometimes said to be the biblical Adam's first wife

*Australian word in full is *billycan*; the club is a *billy club*; a male goat is a *billy goat*.

Madison—U.S. state capital; a U.S. President; a New York City avenue; and a novelty dance once popular in France and mentioned in *The Rocky Horror Picture Show*

Marathon—Florida town in the Keys; an endurance contest; a plain nearby an ancient Greek village, site of a major victory over the Persians in 490 B.C.; and a 26-plus mile race

Orion—Lunar module for the *Apollo 16* mission; a Metallica instrumental song on their *Master of the Puppets* album; a handsome and energetic giant hunter in Greek mythology; and the brilliant constellation known as "the Hunter"

Pike—Controversial American Episcopal bishop James Albert _____; family of freshwater fish with sharp teeth and greedy appetite; tollgate or road on which a toll is charged; a long spear once used by foot soldiers; early 19th-century American general and explorer Zebulon M. _____; and a twisting, complicated mid-air diving maneuver

Range—Row, line, or series; a unit for cooking; a series of connected mountains; and a place for practice shooting at targets

Rogue—200-mile long river rising in Oregon's Cascade Range; a dishonest person or a scoundrel; a fun-loving, mischievous person; and an elephant or other animal that wanders from the herd

Santiago—Second largest city of the Dominican Republic; a South American capital city; a battle fought on July 1 in Cuba during the Spanish-American War with General Shafter leading the American forces; and an elderly Hemingway character who hooks a huge marlin

Shangri-La—Any imaginary, remote paradise, or utopia; FDR's answer to where the B-25s that bombed Tokyo in 1942 came from; Mark Knopfler's 2004 album; the Camp David presidential retreat prior to 1953; and the Himalayan mountain kingdom where James Hilton's novel *Lost Horizon* is set

Sol**—A Martian day, consisting of 24 hours, 37 minutes, and 22 seconds; a colloidal dispersion in a liquid in chemistry; Miami's former WNBA team; and the Roman sun god

Stud—Upright piece in the walls of a building; an earring consisting of a small ornament on a metal post; a form of poker; any male animal used for breeding; and a man considered as virile and sexually active

Tack—Short nail or pin with a flat head; a sewing stitch for marking darts from a pattern; a zigzag course in sailing; and a harness for a horse, including the saddle and bridle

Traffic—Buying and selling of goods, especially illegal goods, such as drugs; the 2000 film about the cocaine trade starring Michael Douglas and Benicio Del Toro; the flow of customers in a retail store or mall; and the movement of automobiles or pedestrians along a road

Wake—Coral atoll in the North Pacific between Midway and Guam; a trail left in the water by a moving ship; a viewing of a corpse before burial; and to come out of a sleep

Yankee Clipper—*Apollo 12* command module in 1969; Boeing's 314 flying boat, first airborne in 1938; Joe DiMaggio's nickname; and any of the tall-masted ships such as the *Lightning* built by Donald McKay

Zest—Procter & Gamble soap; keen enjoyment or gusto; a thin piece of orange or lemon peel used as flavoring; and something that gives flavor or piquancy

**The use of this Latin word for "sun" for a Martian day is probably based on the fact that its day is one rotation with respect to the sun.

THREE CLUES

Asylum—Place providing protection and shelter; protection from extradition granted to political refugees; and an institution for the mentally impaired

Bedrock—Basic principles; the town where the cartoon character Fred Flintstone lives; and solid rock beneath the earth

Bismarck—Germany's largest WWII battleship, severely damaged and sunk by British ships or scuttled by its crew on May 27, 1941; a U.S. state capital; and the Prussian chancellor of the German Empire, 1871-1890

Bonnet—Metal covering over a fireplace; an automobile hood in Britain; and a hat with a ribbon tied under the chin, worn by children and women

Braces—Suspenders in Britain; signs or symbols used to enclose words; and beams used as supports

Buck—Male deer; a high-spirited young man; and a dollar

Burgundy—Purplish red or reddish-brown; loosely, any dry red table wine; and a historical wine-producing region in eastern France whose chief town is Dijon

Cite—To summon to appear in a court of law; to mention as by way of proof; and to quote a passage from a speech or book

Davenport—East Iowa city on the Mississippi; a large sofa or couch; and a top U.S. female tennis player whose first name is Lindsay

Divinity—A deity; the study of religion; and a soft, white candy, usually with nuts

Echo—Soft repetition of a phrase in music; a nymph in Greek mythology who pines away from unrequited love, with only her voiced remaining; and the repetition of a sound by reflection of sound waves off a surface

Era (E-R-A)—Pitching statistic in baseball; a proposed amendment to the U.S. Constitution; and the largest division of geologic time

Eureka—Illinois college from which Ronald Reagan graduated; the motto of California; and the Greek word meaning "I have found it" that Archimedes supposedly used when he discovered how to test the purity of the king's golden crown

Ganymede—Name that Shakespeare's Rosalind takes in *As You Like It* when she assumes the disguise of a handsome young man; the boy taken by Zeus and made his cupbearer; and the Jupiter moon that is the largest in the solar system

Hull—Canadian city across the river from Ottawa; the NHL's "Golden Jet" Bobby _____; and _____ House, the famous settlement house founded in Chicago by Jane Addams and Ellen Gates Starr

Java—Programming language; a large Indonesian island; and a slang term for brewed coffee

Joe—In slang, "a fellow" or "guy" and "brewed coffee"; and a nickname for Joseph

John—Any man who is an easy mark; a prostitute's customer; and a toilet

Lurch—To roll or pitch suddenly to one side; *to leave someone in the* _____, meaning "to leave someone in a difficult situation"; and the butler on TV's *The Addams Family*

Macaroni—Caroline Kennedy's pony; pasta shaped like hollow tubes, often baked with cheese; and the feather Yankee Doodle stuck in his cap in an American Revolutionary War song

Midi—French word for "noon," the south of France, and a skirt or coat of mid-calf length

Moderator—Substance, such as heavy water, that slows down high-energy neutrons in a nuclear-reactor; the presiding officer of a governing body or at a town meeting or a debate; and someone who mediates disputes to solve problems

Nectar—Any delicious beverage; the sweetish liquid in many flowers gathered by bees for making honey; and the drink of the gods in Roman and Greek mythology

Nerd—Character in Dr. Seuss' *If I Ran the Zoo*; a person single-minded in pursuits such as computers but generally considered socially inept; and the rock band whose name is an acronym for *No One Ever Really Dies*

Outback—Any remote region; a popular American steakhouse chain; and Australia's sparsely settled, arid inland area

Panhandle—To beg, especially in the streets; a narrow strip of land extending between 2 states or territories; and West Virginia as known by its nickname "The _____ State"

Plaque—Deposit of fatty material on an arterial wall's inner lining; a thin, transparent film of mucus and bacteria on the surfaces of the teeth; and a wall tablet identifying a building

Providence—TV drama series featuring Dr. Sydney Hansen and Dr. Jim Hansen; God, as the guiding power of the universe; and the capital of Rhode Island

Raphael—Italian painter and architect known for *The Sistine Madonna*; one of the archangels; and a talk show host whose given name is Sally Jesse

Rank—Any of the rows of squares on a chess-board; an official grade or position; and a social division or class

Rook—European crow noted for its thievishness; a swindler; and a chess piece shaped like a castle tower

Seneca—Roman writer and statesman who was Nero's tutor; the largest of the 5 tribes of the Iroquois League; and the largest of the Finger Lakes

Silver bullets—Ammunition that could kill zombies and werewolves; all-women Colorado baseball team; and the fictional Lone Ranger's only ammunition

Solomon—Surname of the 4 aliens who landed on earth on TV's *3rd Rock from the Sun*; a group of islands in the southwest Pacific, east of New Guinea; and a king of Israel noted for his wisdom

Stephen—Last Norman king of England, who reigned from 1135 to 1154; the first king of Hungary, from 1001 to 1138; and the first Christian martyr, stoned to death in Jerusalem in A.D. 36

Tempest—Tchaikovsky's symphony-fantasy Opus 18; a violent storm; and a Shakespearean play

Urn—Sac in which the spores of a moss are produced; a large metal container with a faucet used for making tea or coffee; and a vase used to hold the ashes of a cremated body

Wattle—Wall, roof, or fencing material made of sticks or poles intertwined with twigs or branches; the bunch of golden blossoms that appears on Australia's coat of arms and is its national floral emblem; and the fleshy, wrinkled skin hanging from a turkey's chin

TWO CLUES

Ambrosia—Dessert made of oranges, shredded coconut, and some-times bananas or pineapple and the food of the gods in mythology

Calico—Cat with a mottled coat of black, brown, or orange, and printed cotton fabric originally first obtained in the city of Calicut, India

Cambric*—Very fine, thin linen named after a city in northern France and a hot drink of milk, sugar, and water or, often, weak tea, served to children

Carp—A freshwater fish and to complain in a petty or nagging manner

Flounder—A flatfish and to struggle awkwardly to move or speak in a confused manner

Gossamer—Filmy cobweb floating in the air and a very thin, delicate cloth whose name is related to a seasonal period called St. Martin's summer, a warm time in the fall when geese are in season and cobwebs are in the air

Grand prix—French for "great prize," or the highest award in a competition, and any of a series of races involving formula racing cars

Indomitable**—Not easily discouraged or defeated and the ship aboard which the fictional Billy Budd is impressed into service

Jock—Slang for both a male athlete and a disc jockey

*After the city of Cambrai **The ship is the HMS *Indomitable*.

Limbo—Place where the souls of infants or others dying in original sin but free of mortal sin abide temporarily according to some Christian theologies and a West Indies dance in which dancers try to pass beneath a bar that is placed lower and lower

Malaga (Málaga)—Spanish seaport on the Mediterranean and a large, white, oval grape commonly grown in California

Malagasy***—Former name of Madagascar, now used to designate those born or living there

Mimosa—Champagne and orange juice drink and a tree or shrub with small, white, yellow, or pink flowers

Nanny—Female goat and a child's nursemaid, especially one hired to live in the child's home

Pointers—2 outer stars in the Big Dipper that can be said to be almost in a direct line with the North Star, or Polaris, and long, tapered rods used by teachers or lecturers for directing attention to things on a blackboard or map

Prima donna—Italian for a temperamental or arrogant person or, more formally, the principal woman singer in an opera

Subordinate—Person or thing placed below another in rank and a grammatical clause that functions as a noun, adjective, or adverb in a sentence

Tangent—Metallic piece that produces a tone in a clavichord by hitting a string and remaining there as long as the player holds the key down and a line that touches a circle at just one point

Terminator—Line separating the illuminated and dark parts of the disk of the moon or a planet and the 1984 film in which Arnold Schwarzenegger plays a cyborg, or part-man, part machine

Topsy-turvy—Upside down, or confused and disorderly, and the 1999 film about Gilbert and Sullivan and the creation of their operetta, *The Mikado*

Vixen—Shrewish, malicious woman and a female fox

***The country was the Malagasy Republic.

NAME SHARING

Sam(uel) Adams—Brand of beer named after a brewer and patriot and this U.S. patriot who helped organize the Boston Tea Party

Angstrom*—Surname of a John Updike character and the unit of length named after a Swedish physicist

Apollo—NASA space program for lunar landings and the mythological Greek god of the sun

Aramis—One of the fictional Three Musketeers and a fragrance for men

Argus—Mythological giant with 100 eyes and the old dog of the epic hero Odysseus

Babe—Slugger George Herman Ruth and Paul Bunyan's blue ox

Birch**—Tree with a white bark that comes off in strips and John _____ Society, a right-wing, anti-Communist organization founded by Robert Welch

Black Hawk—Any member of the NHL team in Chicago and the Sauk Indian who led the 1832 war against the U.S. in Illinois named after him

Bran—Giant king of ancient Britain and the outer layers of cereal grain removed during the milling process

(James) Cook—British navigator who twice circumnavigated the world and a person who prepares meals

(Ichabod) Crane—Fictional schoolmaster in *The Legend of Sleepy Hollow* and a long-legged marsh bird

*Harry Angstrom is the Updike character. **John Birch Society

Eli—Automobile builder, Ransom _____ Olds, and a member of any athletic team at Yale

(Man) Friday—Day of the week and Robinson Crusoe's companion and servant

(Lady) Godiva—Brand of chocolate and the English woman who allegedly rode naked through town to protest her husband's imposition of taxes on the people

Hagar—Egyptian servant of the biblical Sarah and the name completing the title of the comic strip _____ the Horrible

Hannibal—Vice President _____ Hamlin, Lincoln's 1st Vice President, and the Carthaginian general who defeated the Romans at Cannae in 216 B.C.

Hawkeye—Natty Bumppo in Cooper's *The Leatherstocking Tales* and Capt. Benjamin Franklin Pierce on TV's *M*A*S*H*

Hero—Leander's beloved in mythology and the Phantom's horse in the comic strips

John Hancock—Statesman who signed the Declaration of Independence in big bold letters and a signature

John Henry—A signature and the "Steel driving man" who died competing against a steam engine

(Victor) Hugo—French author of *Les Misérables* and the annual award presented for the best science-fiction writing

Juggernaut—Any relentless, irresistible force and the title of the Hindu god Krishna, one of the incarnations of the god Vishnu

Luna—Roman goddess of the moon and a series of Soviet space probes

(Karl) Marx—Founder of modern socialism and a family of 5 comedic brothers

Mercury—Roman counterpart of Hermes and the closest planet to the sun

(Peter) Minuit—Dutch leader who purchased Manhattan Island from the Indians in 1626 for about $24 and the French word for "midnight"

Nebuchadnezzar (II)—King who conquered Jerusalem in 597 B.C. and again in 586 B.C. and the largest type of bottle used in champagne and Burgundy

Naiad—Water nymph who in myth ruled over streams, ponds, rivers, and lakes, and a girl or woman swimmer, especially an expert one

Panacea—Daughter of Asclepius, the Greek god of health, and a cure-all

Piccolo—Former Chicago Bears player Brian _____ and the smallest and the highest pitched woodwind instrument

Pistol—Braggart soldier and follower of Falstaff in several Shakespeare plays and a firearm held and fired with one hand

(Marco) Polo—Medieval Italian traveler to China and a game played on horseback

Rudolph—President Gerald Ford's middle name and a famous fictional reindeer

Saki—Cupbearer in the *Rubáiyát of Omar Khayyám* and the pen name of Hector Hugh Munro

Seti (I)***—4-letter name for both the pharaoh who was the father of Ramses II and, as an acronym, the project by which anyone with a personal computer may search for extraterrestrial intelligence

Swift—Surname of Jonathan _____, an English satirist, and an insect-eating, swallow-like bird noted for its speed

Triton—Mythological son of Poseidon and Amphitrite and Neptune's largest satellite

***SETI is the Search for Extraterrestrial Intelligence.

KIDDIE LIT

Author who in *Green Hills of Africa* said: "All modern literature comes from one book by Mark Twain called *Huckleberry Finn*"
Answer: Ernest Hemingway.

FICTIONAL CHARACTERS
Alice—Heroine who meets the March Hare and the Cheshire Cat in Lewis Carroll's *Alice's Adventures in Wonderland* and *Through the Looking Glass*
Arthur—Babar's cousin who lives with him and Celeste in the old lady's home in Jean de Brunhoff's *The Story of Babar, the Little Elephant*
Aslan—Noble talking lion who frees Narnia from the spell of the White Witch in C.S. Lewis' *The Lion, the Witch and the Wardrobe*
Auntie Em—Dorothy's hard-working aunt in L. Frank Baum's *The Wonderful Wizard of Oz*
Babar—Well-dressed elephant in a series of books by Jean de Brunhoff and his son Laurent de Brunhoff
Becky Thatcher—Tom Sawyer's sweetheart in Mark Twain's *The Adventures of Tom Sawyer*
Benjamin Bunny—Peter Rabbit's cousin whose adventures make up a Beatrix Potter tale
Big Bad Wolf—Wicked animal who huffs and puffs and tries to blow down houses in the fairy tale "The Three Little Pigs"
Black Beauty—Horse who tells the story of his life in Anna Sewell's book of the same name
Bob Cratchit—Tiny Tim's father who works for Ebenezer Scrooge in Charles Dickens' *A Christmas Carol*
Bobbsey twins—Two sets of twins (Bert and Nan and Freddie and Flossie) in Laura Lee's novel of the same name
Cassie Logan—Black girl who struggles to grow up in Mississippi during the Great Depression in Mildred D. Taylor's *Roll of Thunder, Hear My Cry*
Cat in the Hat—Charming cat who entertains 2 young children with his tricks in a Dr. Seuss tale
Celeste—Babar's cousin who becomes his queen in Jean de Brunhoff's *The Story of Babar, the Little Elephant*
Charlie Bucket—Good-natured young man who wins the best prize of all in Roald Dahl's popular fantasy about a chocolate factory
Charlotte A. Cavatica—Spider who befriends a pig in E.B. White's *Charlotte's Web*
Christopher Robin—Character A. A. Milne modeled after his son in a series of books telling of his adventures with his friend Edward Bear
Cinderella—Fairy tale heroine who escapes from her miserable life with 2 mean stepsisters and a cruel stepmother when she marries a prince after her foot fits the "glass" slipper she has left behind at a ball
Count of Monte Cristo*—Character imprisoned on a false charge who escapes, finds a hidden treasure, and uses it to get revenge on those who did him wrong in an Alexander Dumas novel of the same name
Curious George—Monkey who is always rescued from scrapes by the Man with the Yellow Hat in H.A. and Margaret Rey's tales

*His name is Edmond Dantès.

Darth Vader—Black-clad villain, the Dark Lord of the Sith and father of Luke Skywalker, in the *Star War* series—his former identity was Anakin Skywalker

Dr. Jekyll—Good, kind doctor who uses drugs that transform him into the brutal Henry Hyde in Robert Louis Stevenson's *The Strange Case of Dr. _____ and Mr. Hyde*

Dr. John Dolittle—Doctor who talks to the animals in the English village of Puddleby-on-the-Marsh in a series of books by Hugh Lofting

Dorothy Gale—Kansas girl who finds herself with her dog Toto in an enchanted kingdom after being carried off by a tornado in L. Frank Baum's *The Wonderful Wizard of Oz*

Ebenezer Scrooge—Stingy old London merchant who changes his mind about not celebrating Christmas after three scary visits from spirits in Charles Dickens' *A Christmas Carol*

Encyclopedia Brown**—10-year-old detective who solves crimes in the town of Idaville, where his father is chief of police, in a series of books by Donald Sobol

Fern—Young girl who saves Wilbur the pig from being slaughtered in E.B. White's *Charlotte's Web*

Frog prince—Fairy tale character who is to be released from the spell he is under by a beautiful lady who kisses him or is kind to him

Fudge—Nickname of Farley Drexel Hatcher, whose brother Peter considers him a big pain in Judy Blume's *Tales of a Fourth-Grade Nothing*

Ged—Character in Ursula Le Guin's *Earthsea Trilogy* who struggles with the forces of good and evil in an imaginary land

Goldilocks—Young girl who is discovered sleeping in baby bear's bed after eating the porridge in the story *The Three Bears*

Goody Two-Shoes—Poor girl who becomes very happy after she is given a pair of shoes in Oliver Goldsmith's book of the same name

(The) Grinch—Dr. Seuss's miserly character in *How the Grinch Stole Christmas*

Hans Brinker—Mary Mapes Dodge's Dutch boy who wins a great race and receives a pair of silver skates as a prize

Hardy Boys (Joe and Frank)—Sons of Fenton and Laura Hardy, who live in Bayport, in a series of detective stories begun by Edward Stratemeyer under the pseudonym Franklin W. Dixon in 1927

Harriet M. Welch—11-year-old who wants to see, do, and know everything so she can become a famous writer in Louise Fitzhugh's *Harriet the Spy* and other stories

Harry Potter—Orphaned bespectacled student wizard with a lightning-bolt-shaped forehead scar featured in a series of books by J.K. Rowling

Heidi—Swiss orphan girl who is raised in the Alps by her grandfather in Johanna Spyri's novel of the same name

Horton—Heroic elephant who is the only one to hear a tiny voice in a speck of dust in a Dr. Seuss book

Huckleberry Finn—Widow Douglas's ward who has a series of adventures on the Mississippi River with Jim, a runaway slave, in an 1884 novel by Mark Twain

Jacob Marley—Scrooge's partner who appears as a ghost in Dickens' *A Christmas Carol*

Jim—Escaped slave who accompanies Huckleberry Finn in his adventures in Mark Twain's *The Adventures of Huckleberry Finn*

Jim Hawkins—Cabin boy hero who thwarts the plans of the pirates to find the lost treasure in Robert Louis Stevenson's *Treasure Island*

Jody Tiflin—10-year-old boy who is the main character in John Steinbeck's "The Red Pony"

**In full, Leroy Encyclopedia Brown

John Henry—Negro laborer who according to legend died competing with a sledgehammer against a steam drill

Johnny Tremain—Boy with crippled hands who meets Paul Revere and John Hancock in Esther Forbes' *Johnny Tremain*

Jolly Green Giant—Large giant of American origin who says "Ho-Ho-Ho" as he helps to sell vegetable products

Kermit the Frog—Cute green muppet reporter created by Jim Henson

Lassie—Collie, "the best in Greenall Bridge," featured in a 1940 book by Eric Knight that later became the basis for a movie and TV series

Laura Ingalls—Curious daughter of the pioneer Ingalls family in a series of *Little House* books

The Little Prince—Curious prince from a distant asteroid in an Antoine de Saint-Exupéry tale

Little Red Hen—Folk tale character who by herself plants wheat, harvests it, and bakes bread, then refuses to share it with those who were unwilling to help her

Long John Silver—One-legged pirate leader and ship's cook who is searching for treasure in Robert Louis Stevenson's *Treasure Island*

Lucy Van Pelt—Charles Schulz's *Peanuts* comic strip character who is in love with Schroeder, an aspiring classical composer who admires Beethoven

Luke Skywalker—Young farmboy from the remote desert planet of Tatooine who becomes a Jedi Knight in the *Star Wars* series

Madeline—Little girl always out of step with her other 11 classmates in a convent school in Paris

Mary Ingalls—Laura Ingalls' older sister blinded by scarlet fever in a series of *Little House* books

Mary Lennox—Wilful young girl who goes to live in a manor house on the moor in Frances Hodgson Burnett's *The Secret Garden*

Mary Poppins—Nanny who guides Jane and Michael Banks through many adventures in Pamela L. Travers' *Mary Poppins*

Max—Boy wearing the wolf suit who is sent to bed without eating in Maurice Sendak's *Where the Wild Things Are*

Mickey Mouse—Walt Disney's most famous cartoon character, introduced in 1928 in *Plane Crazy*—his girlfriend is Minnie and his dog is Pluto

Miss Piggy—Vain, pretentious muppet with airs created by Jim Henson

Mother Goose—Imaginary narrator of a collection of Charles Perrault's tales

Mowgli—Indian boy who wanders away from his family and is raised by a pack of wolves in Rudyard Kipling's *Jungle Books*

Munchkins—Little people in L. Frank Baum's *The Wonderful Wizard of Oz*

Nancy Drew***—Teenage girl living in River Heights featured in a series of mystery and detective stories created by Edward L. Stratemeyer under the pseudonym Carolyn Keene in 1930

Nemo—Captain of the electric-powered submarine the *Nautilus* in Jules Verne's *Twenty Thousand Leagues Under the Sea*

Old Yeller—Loyal and brave dog who helps Little Arliss on the Texas frontier in a Fred Gipson tale

Paddington—Accident-prone honey bear wearing a shabby hat and yellow macintosh who lives with the Brown family in London in children's books by Michael Bond

Peter Pan—Young boy who never grows up in James Barrie's play of the same name

***Stratemeyer owned the syndicate that hired writers, and it was Mildred Wirt Benson who actually created this character.

Peter Rabbit—Character who is constantly going into Mr. McGregor's garden in Beatrix Potter's *The Tale of Peter Rabbit*

Phileas Fogg—Character who travels around the world to win a bet in Jules Verne's *Around the World in Eighty Days*

Pinocchio—Wooden puppet who wants to become a boy and whose nose grows longer every time he tells a lie in a story by Carlo Collodi

Pippi Longstocking—Free-thinking, strong-willed red-haired young girl with braids who lives in Villa Villekulla in a story by Astrid Lindgren

Puss in Boots—Red-booted fairy tale cat who through a series of clever tricks pleases the king and wins the princess's hand for his master

Raggedy Ann—Female rag doll created by Johnny Gruelle in a series of stories

Rapunzel—Fairy tale character whose long hair enables a prince to climb into a castle tower and free her from imprisonment

Rikki-Tikki-Tavi—Mongoose who kills a poisonous snake and saves lives in a Rudyard Kipling story

Rip Van Winkle—Washington Irving character who falls asleep for 20 years while hunting in the Catskill Mountains and is not recognized when he returns home

Robin Hood—Legendary outlaw and archer of 13th-century England who with the help of his band of Merry Men stole from the rich and gave to the poor

Robinson Crusoe—Character who survives 28 years on a deserted island following a shipwreck in Daniel Defoe's book of the same name

Rumpelstiltskin—Fairy tale dwarf who helps a young woman spin straw into gold in exchange for a promise to give him her firstborn child unless she can guess his name, which she does, prompting him to kill himself

Sleeping Beauty—Fairy tale princess released from a spell to sleep for 100 years when a handsome prince kisses her

Snoopy—Beagle who periodically fights his archenemy, the Red Baron, in Charles Schulz's *Peanuts* comic strip

Snow White—Fairy tale character poisoned by her wicked stepmother and awakened by a prince who later marries her

Sounder—Coon dog who gets shot trying to protect his master in a book by William Armstrong

Stuart Little—Two-inch-high mouse who is the second son of the Littles in an E.B. White novel of the same name

Superman—Jerry Siegel and Joe Shuster's comic book hero from the planet Krypton who is "faster than a speeding bullet, more powerful than a locomotive, (and) able to leap tall buildings at a single bound"

Tarzan—Hero reared by apes in the jungle and known for his strength and agility in a series of stories by Edgar Rice Burroughs

Tiny Tim—Crippled boy who is helped by Ebenezer Scrooge and remembered for saying, "God bless us, every one!" in Charles Dickens' *A Christmas Carol*

Tom Sawyer—Aunt Polly's nephew who gets into one scrape after another in Mark Twain's adventure novel published in 1876

Tom Thumb—Tiny fairy tale knight who never grows any bigger than his father's thumb and is killed while fighting a spider

Toto—Dorothy Gale's dog in L. Frank Baum's *The Wonderful Wizard of Oz*

Ugly Duckling—Hans Christian Andersen bird who is shunned by all the other animals but grows up to be a beautiful swan

Velvet Brown—Owner of the horse Piebald in an Enid Bagnold book

Velveteen Rabbit—Stuffed rabbit magically turned into a real rabbit in a 1922 book by Margery Williams

Wendy—Peter Pan's friend who sews his shadow back on in James Barrie's *Peter Pan*

Wilbur—Pig who is a loyal friend of Charlotte the spider in E.B. White's *Charlotte's Web*

Wild Things—Fantasy monster figures that Max tries to tame after being sent to his room in a Maurice Sendak story

Willy Wonka—Eccentric owner of the chocolate factory in Roald Dahl's *Charlie and the Chocolate Factory*

Winnie-the-Pooh—Edward Bear, the teddy bear of Christopher Robin in a series of books by A.A. Milne

Wizard of Oz—Seemingly brave, powerful character who says he will give Dorothy and her 3 friends what they are seeking but turns out to be a little old man with a bald head and a wrinkled face in L. Frank Baum's classic novel

LEGENDARY CREATURES/THINGS

Abominable snowman—Huge, hairy, manlike creature said to live in the Himalayas—also called a Yeti

Basilisk—Venom-spitting, lizardlike monster having the head and wings of a rooster and the body of a snake and allegedly fatal breath and glance

Big Foot—Huge, hairy, manlike creature with long arms said to lurk about the Pacific Northwest—also called Sasquatch

Borrowers, The—Very tiny race of people, completely dependent upon humans in Mary Norton's novel of the same name

Chitty-Chitty Bang-Bang—Amazing flying car in Ian Fleming's novel of the same name

Count Dracula—Vampire of Transylvania in Bram Stoker's novel *Dracula*

Dementor—Faceless gray-cloaked Azkaban prison guard able to sense any happy thought and suck the life from it or from his victims with a kiss in a Harry Potter novel by J.K. Rowling

Dragon—Mythical fire-breathing monster with wings and claws

Dwarf—Small, ugly, and sometimes malformed human, usually with magic powers

Elf—Small, prankish imaginary woodland creature having magical powers

Extraterrestrial (ET)—Creature from outside Earth's limits, especially one from another planet

Fairy—Very tiny and sometimes very delicate supernatural being with magic powers who can either help or harm humans—in medieval time, a creature of full human size

Ghost—Spirit of a dead person who appears to living people as a pale, shadowy form

Godzilla—Green, radioactive fire-breathing Japanese monster

Jinni (or genie)—Supernatural being of Muslim folklore who takes human or animal form to influence human relationships but is better known today as one who lives in a lamp or bottle and grants the wishes of whoever releases him

Leprechaun—Irish elf who allegedly if caught will reveal where a treasure is hidden, usually a crock of gold at the end of a rainbow

Loch Ness monster—Sea serpent also called "Nessie" said to live in a Scottish lake

Mermaid/merman—Sea creature with the head and upper body of a woman or man and the form of a fish from the waist down

Oompa Loompas—Mysterious tribe of little men living in tree houses that Willy Wonka has smuggled into the country from Loompaland in Roald Dahl's *Charlie and the Chocolate Factory*

Ogre—Man-eating monster or giant in fairy tales and folklore
Sandman—Fairy who induces sleep by dusting sand in children's eyes
Sorcerer—A wizard or one who uses magic or supernatural powers to affect humans, usually with the assistance of spirits
Sprite—Elflike supernatural being
Tooth fairy—Fairy who comes in the night and leaves money after taking a tooth
Vampire—Corpse that comes back to life and sucks the blood of sleeping persons at night
Werewolf—Person who is changed or can change into a wolf at will—also called a lycanthrope
Witch—Sorceress or woman said to have supernatural power and use a broom to fly
Wizard—Magician or sorcerer

HARRY POTTER

1) Name the first 6 novels in the Harry Potter series created by British author J.K. Rowling about a bespectacled orphaned youngster and student wizard.
Answer: *Harry Potter and the Sorcerer's Stone* (or *Harry Potter and the Philosopher's Stone*), *Harry Potter and the Chamber of Secrets*, *Harry Potter and the Prisoner of Azkaban*, *Harry Potter and the Goblet of Fire*, *Harry Potter and the Order of the Phoenix*, and *Harry Potter and the Half-Blood Prince*.

2) Identify the 4 houses that first-year students are divided into by means of the Sorting Hat at the Hogwarts School in the Harry Potter stories.
Answer: Gryffindor, Hufflepuff, Ravenclaw, and Slytherin (named after Godric Gryffindor, Helga Hufflepuff, Rowena Ravenclaw, and Salazar Slytherin).

Hogwarts—School of Witchcraft and Wizardry that Harry attends
9 3/4—King's Cross station platform where Harry and his friends set off on the train to return to school each year
(Lord) Voldemort—Wizard world's supreme villain who killed Harry Potter's parents and is referred to as "He-Who-Must-Not-Be-Named" or "You-Know-Who"
Albus Dumbledore—Headmaster at the School of Witchcraft and Wizardry
Ron Weasley—One of 6 brothers who becomes Harry's best friend after the two meet on the train
Muggle—Any ordinary person without magical powers
Hermione Granger—Smart girl born without magical powers who becomes Harry Potter's best female friend
Rubeus Hagrid—Keeper of the Keys and Grounds at the school who finds Harry, tells him he's a wizard, and gets him out of the Dursley household with whom he lives on 4 Privet Drive in a cupboard under the stairs after being orphaned
Quidditch—Soccer-like sport with 7 players and 4 balls played on flying broomsticks at which Harry excels at school
Sirius Black—Harry's godfather, whom Harry first discovers at the end of *Harry Potter and the Prisoner of Azkaban*

ROBIN HOOD

Merry Men—His band of men who helped this "outlaw"
Maid Marian—His beloved
Sherwood Forest—Forest in which they lived in Nottinghamshire

Little John—Member with an ironic name, since he was really large and mighty
Friar Tuck—Heavy-set monk in the Franciscan order who accompanied Robin and his men
Sheriff of Nottingham—Corrupt official who opposed Robin Hood and his men

PETER PAN
Wendy, John, and Michael—3 Darling children he persuades to go with him to a magic land
Nana—Dog who acts as a nursemaid to the Darling children
Never-Never-Land (Never Land)—Magic land of the Lost Boys, Indians, fairies, and pirates where Peter lives
Tinker Bell—Fairy who teaches Peter to fly
Piccaninnies—Indians who fight the pirates
Tiger Lily—Indian maiden, daughter of the chief of these Indians, who is rescued by Peter
Captain James Hook—Evil pirate leader of the pirate ship, who has a hook for the hand he lost to a crocodile
Jolly Roger—This evil pirate's ship

GIANT LUMBERJACK* IN AMERICAN FOLKLORE
Paul Bunyan—This legendary giant lumberjack with superhuman strength
Babe**—Large ox who is "twice as big as all outdoors and playful as a hurricane"
Blue—Color of this ox
10,000—Number of Minnesota lakes filled up by the tracks made the lumberjack and his ox
Bay of Fundy—Canadian bay in which this lumberjack caused a 70-foot tide when he stepped out of his cradle
Puget Sound—Body of water he created in Washington to float large logs to the mill
Great Lakes—Body of water he created to provide drinking water for his ox
Finger Lakes—11 elongated lakes in New York he created when he placed his hand on the earth
Johnny Inkslinger—Camp's head clerk who kept the books
Elmer—Name of all 7 of the lumberjack's axemen
Lucy—Purple Cow who wore green glasses and furnished dairy products for the camp
Sourdough Sam—One-armed camp cook who made everything except coffee from sourdough
Ole—Blacksmith known for making a huge griddle for flapjacks
Sport—The Reversible Dog, having been cut in two and sewn back together
Conveyor Belt—Bunyan's opponent in William Upson's short story "Paul Bunyan versus the _____," based upon an application of the Möbius strip

*The Minnesota towns of Bemidji and Brainerd have statues honoring him and his ox. **Also described as having grown to "twenty-four axe handles and a plug of tobacco wide between the eyes."

ADULT LIT

French mathematician, scientist, and philosopher who in *Le Discours de la méthode* said: "The reading of all good books is like a conversation with the finest men of past centuries"
Answer: René Descartes.

REAL NAMES/LITERARY PSEUDONYMS OR PEN NAMES
Isaac Asimov—Paul French
Charles Farrar Browne—Artemus Ward
Samuel Langhorne Clemens—Mark Twain, Sergent Fathom, Thomas Jefferson Snodgras
James Fenimore Cooper—Cornelius Littlepage, Amabel Penfeather
Patricia Cornwell—Patricia Daniels
Frederick Dannay and Manfred B. Lee—Ellery Queen, Barnaby Ross
Michael Donovan—Frank O'Connor
Benjamin Franklin—Richard Saunders, Alice Addertongue, Anthony Afterwit
Erle Stanley Gardner—A.A. Fair, Charles J. Kenny, Charles M. Green, Charleton Kendrake
Theodor Geisel—Dr. Seuss
Carolyn Gold Heilbrun—Amanda Cross
Evan Hunter—Ed McBain
Washington Irving—Diedrich Knickerbocker, Geoffrey Corson, Geoffrey Crayon (Gent.)
Margueritte Annie Johnson—Maya Angelou
(Everett) LeRoi Jones—(Imamu) Amiri Baraka
Stephen King—Richard Bachman
Frederick August Kittel—August Wilson
Ring Lardner—Jack Keefe
Kenneth Millar—(John) Ross MacDonald
Howard Allen O'Brien—Anne Rice, Anne Rampling, A.N. Roquelaure
Katherine O'Flaherty—Kate Chopin
Truman Streckfus Persons—Truman Capote
William Sidney Porter—O. Henry
Ezra Pound—Alfred Venison
Ayn Rand—Alisa Zinovievna Rosenbaum
Samuel Shepard Rogers—Sam Shepard
Henry Wheeler Shaw—Josh Billings
Frank Morrison Spillane—Mickey Spillane
Edward L. Stratemeyer—Carolyn Keene*
Gore Vidal—Edgar Box
Nathan Wallenstein Weinstein—Nathanael West
Edith Wharton—Edith Newbold Jones
Thomas Lanier Williams—Tennessee Williams
Chloe Anthony Wofford—Toni Morrison
Thomas Kennerly Wolfe Jr.—Tom Wolfe
Willard Huntington Wright—S.S. Van Dine

*In the Nancy Drew series (Because Stratemeyer founded a syndicate and hired others to write the stories, he is credited with more than 60 pen names. It was revealed in 1980 that Mildred Wirt Benson was the woman who created Nancy Drew. As Franklin Dixon, Stratemeyer wrote about the Hardy Boys; his other pen names include Victor Appelton for the Tom Swift series, Laura Lee Hope for the Bobbsey Twins series, and Arthur Winfield for tales about the Rover Boys. After his death, his daughter Harriet Stratemeyer Adams was credited with writing the Nancy Drew stories under the Carolyn Keene pseudonym).

FICTIONAL CHARACTERS

Ahab—Obsessed, one-legged captain of the whaling-ship *Pequod* who seeks revenge in capturing the white whale that cost him his leg in Herman Melville's *Moby-Dick*

Alice Adams—Ambitious small-town title character who easily falls in love in Booth Tarkington's 1921 novel

Anthony Adverse—Picaresque hero and title character of Hervey Allen's 1934 historical romance set in the Napoleonic era

Antonia Shimerda—Daughter of Bohemian immigrants who is the heroine in Willa Cather's 1918 novel *My Antonia*, which realistically portrays farm life in Nebraska

Arthur Dimmesdale—Minister with whom Hester Prynne has a child in Nathaniel Hawthorne's *The Scarlet Letter*

Arthur Gordon Pym—Hero of Edgar Allan Poe's novel about a man who stows away on a whaling ship and ends up at the South Pole

Atticus Finch—Widowed Southern lawyer with 2 children who defends a black man accused of the rape of a white woman in a Harper Lee novel

Bigger Thomas—Victim of racial prejudice from a Chicago slum condemned to death for a double murder in Richard Wright's *Native Son*

Billy Budd—Young sailor on a British warship who is falsely accused and hanged by Captain Vere for the slaying of Claggart in a Herman Melville novella

Billy Pilgrim—Hero who travels between the fire-bombing of Dresden in 1945 and the planet Tralfamadore in the distant future in Kurt Vonnegut's *Slaughterhouse-Five*

Carrie Meeber—Heroine who leaves a rural life to seek her fortune and after becoming an actress in New York rejects her lover George Hurstwood, leading to his suicide in Theodore Dreiser's naturalistic 1900 novel *Sister Carrie*

Cathy Ames Trask—Ex-prostitute who gives birth to twins but leaves Adam Trask and returns to her previous life in John Steinbeck's *East of Eden*

Celie—Black heroine who grows up in the Southern U.S. and suffers cruel treatment from her father and husband but finds a female friend in Alice Walker's *The Color Purple*

Chingachgook—Mohican Indian chief and longtime friend of Natty Bumppo in James Fenimore Cooper's Leatherstocking novels

Clyde Griffiths—Young man from a poor background who tries to succeed in New York but allows a girl to drown and is executed for her murder in Theodore Dreiser's *An American Tragedy*

Daisy Buchanan—Southern belle Jay Gatsby so loves that he moves to Long Island to be near her even though she has married another in an F. Scott Fitzgerald novel

Daisy Miller—Young American woman who is courted by Frederick Forsyth Winterbourne in Europe in a Henry James novel bearing her name

Deadwood Dick—Hero of Edward L. Wheeler's 19th-century dime novels about the Wild West

Elmer Gantry—Ex-football player turned evangelist to become rich in a Sinclair Lewis novel

Emily Webb—Smart, imaginative daughter of the newspaper editor in Grover's Corners, New Hampshire, who dies in childbirth in Thornton Wilder's *Our Town*

Ethan Frome—New England farmer who falls in love with his wife Zeena's cousin in a 1911 Edith Wharton novel

Eugene Gant—Hero of Thomas Wolfe's semi-autobiographical novels *Look Homeward, Angel: A Story of the Buried Life* and *Of Time and the River*

Frankie Addams—12-year-old Georgia tomboy who believes she will go with her brother and his bride on their honeymoon in Carson McCullers' *A Member of the Wedding*

Frederic Henry—Army lieutenant during WWII who falls in love with Catherine Barkley in Ernest Hemingway's *A Farewell to Arms*

George F. Babbitt—Real estate agent in Sinclair Lewis's *Babbitt*

Harry Angstrom—Anti-hero and car dealer nicknamed "Rabbit" in John Updike's *Rabbit, Run*; *Rabbit Redux*; and *Rabbit Is Rich*

Henry Fleming—Young soldier who becomes an unintentional hero in Stephen Crane's *The Red Badge of Courage*

Hester Prynne—Woman who has to wear a red letter *A* on her dress as punishment for her adultery in Nathaniel Hawthorne's *The Scarlet Letter*

Holden Caulfield—Rebellious 16-year-old who says he had a "lousy childhood" in J.D. Salinger's *The Catcher in the Rye*

Holly Golightly—Free-spirited heroine in Truman Capote's *Breakfast at Tiffany's*

Ichabod Crane—Tall, skinny schoolteacher frightened by an apparently Headless Horseman in Washington Irving's "The Legend of Sleepy Hollow"

Injun Joe—Half-breed who kills Dr. Robinson in Mark Twain's *The Adventures of Tom Sawyer*

Isabel Archer—Attractive woman who goes to Europe, is courted by many men, and makes a poor choice in marrying Gilbert Osmond in Henry James' 1881 *The Portrait of a Lady*

Ishmael—Narrator and only survivor of the *Pequod* in Herman Melville's *Moby-Dick*

Jabez Stone—Unfortunate New Hampshire farmer who said he would sell his soul to the devil in Stephen Vincent Benét's "The Devil and Daniel Webster"

Jack Burden—Willie Stark's aide who serves as the narrator in Robert Penn Warren's *All the King's Men*

Jaffrey Pyncheon—Judge who murders to gain control of the family fortune in Nathaniel Hawthorne's *The House of the Seven Gables*

Jake Barnes—WWII-wounded impotent hero of Ernest Hemingway's *The Sun Also Rises*

Jane Porter—Tarzan's beloved in Edgar Rice Burroughs' novel *Tarzan of the Apes* and its sequels

Jay Gatsby—Mysterious rich man living lavishly on Long Island who tries to revive his romance with Daisy Buchanan but is shot and killed in an F. Scott Fitzgerald novel

Jeeter Lester—Georgia cotton-farmer who lives in a beat-up shack in Erskine Caldwell's *Tobacco Road*

Jim—Runaway slave who embarks on a raft voyage down the Mississippi with Huck Finn in Mark Twain's *The Adventures of Huckleberry Finn*

Jim Burden—Narrator in Willa Cather's *My Antonia*

Jo March—Boyish heroine and aspiring writer who lives with her sisters, Meg, Beth, and Amy in Louisa M. Alcott's *Little Women*

Jody Baxter—12-year-old boy who makes friends with an orphaned fawn in the Florida woods in Marjorie Kinnan Rawlings' *The Yearling*

John Alden—Character who relays Miles Standish's proposal of marriage to Priscilla Mullens in a Henry Wadsworth Longfellow poem

John Singer—Deaf-mute who listens sympathetically to others in the boarding house in Carson McCullers' *The Heart Is a Lonely Hunter*

Katrina Van Tassel—Attractive young woman wooed by Brom Bones and Ichabod Crane in Washington Irving's "The Legend of Sleepy Hollow"

Kunta Kinte—West African shipped to America in the 18th century to be a slave in Alex Haley's "non-fiction" novel *Roots*

Lady Brett Ashley—British aristocrat who is in love with Jake Barnes but has a series of affairs in Ernest Hemingway's *The Sun Also Rises*

Lennie Small—Kind, half-witted giant of a man who is killed by his friend George Milton to keep a lynch mob from harming him in John Steinbeck's *Of Mice and Men*

Little Eva—Augustine St. Clare's daughter who dies in Harriet Beecher Stowe's *Uncle Tom's Cabin*—her full name is Evangeline St. Clare

Maggie Johnson—Slum child in Stephen Crane's novel subtitled *A Girl of the Streets*

Marmee—Name the girls call Mrs. March, their mother raising 4 daughters in Louisa M. Alcott's *Little Women*

Martin Arrowsmith—Small town idealistic doctor and medical researcher who later fights disease on a Caribbean island in Sinclair Lewis' 1925 novel *Arrowsmith*

Mattie Silver—Abandoned cousin who is taken in by the Fromes and becomes an invalid after attempting to end her life in a sledding accident with Ethan in Edith Wharton's 1911 novel *Ethan Frome*

Milo Minderbinder—Owner of M & M Enterprises who tries to run the war in Joseph Heller's *Catch-22*

Miss Amelia—Eccentric storeowner with a close relationship with Cousin Lymon in Carson McCullers' *The Ballad of the Sad Café*

Natty Bumpo—Frontiersman variously nicknamed Hawkeye, Pathfinder, Trapper, and Leatherstocking in James Fenimore Cooper's *The Leatherstocking Tales*

Nick Adams—Hero in Ernest Hemingway's short stories in the collections *In Our Time* and *Men Without Women*

Pearl—Hester Prynne's illegitimate child by the minister Arthur Dimmesdale in Nathaniel Hawthorne's *The Scarlet Letter*

Philip Nolan—Treasonous man who is sentenced to live the remainder of his life at sea, being transferred from ship to ship, in Edward Everett Hale's "The Man Without a Country"

Pollyanna—Pretty, well-behaved orphan known as the "Glad Girl" since she remains happy and cheerful in difficult times in an Eleanor Porter novel of the same name

Porgy—Crippled black hero in a DuBose Heyward novel about the Deep South rendered in operatic form by George Gershwin

Prince Edward—Prince who changes clothes with beggar Tom Canty in Mark Twain's *The Prince and the Pauper*

Queeg—Irrational captain of the minesweeper *Caine* in Herman Wouk's *The Caine Mutiny*

Quentin Compson—Suicidal offspring of the Compson family in Yoknapatawpha County in William Faulkner's *The Sound and the Fury* and *Absalom, Absalom!*

Queequeg—Polynesian harpooner and Ishmael's friend in Herman Melville's *Moby-Dick*

Randall Patrick McMurphy—Rebellious hero who is committed to a mental hospital but refuses sedation in Ken Kesey's novel *One Flew Over the Cuckoo's Nest*

Rhett Butler—Character who makes money running guns and supplies during the Civil War and becomes Scarlett O'Hara's third husband in Margaret Mitchell's *Gone With the Wind*

Rip Van Winkle—Washington Irving character who falls asleep for 20 years while hunting in the Catskill Mountains and is not recognized when he returns home

Robert Jordan—American who falls in love with Maria while fighting in the Spanish Civil War in Ernest Hemingway's *For Whom the Bell Tolls*

Roderick Usher—Mansion owner whose house splits apart and sinks into the tarn after he dies from shock upon the sudden appearance of his dead and buried sister in an Edgar Allan Poe short story

Roger Chillingworth—Hester Prynne's wronged and estranged husband who returns as her nemesis in Nathaniel Hawthorne's *The Scarlet Letter*

Scarlett O'Hara—Flirtatious, charming Southern belle who takes Rhett Butler as her third husband and saves her beloved plantation Tara in Margaret Mitchell's *Gone With the Wind*

Scout (Jean Louise) Finch—6-year-old girl who narrates the story of her attorney father's defense of a black man accused of the rape of a white woman in Harper Lee's *To Kill a Mockingbird*

Silas Lapham—Wealthy businessman who fails socially and economically but shows integrity and returns to Vermont in a William Dean Howells novel

Simon Legree—Cruel slave driver who whips Uncle Tom to death in Harriet Beecher Stowe's *Uncle Tom's Cabin*

Starbuck—God-fearing chief mate on the *Pequod* who tries to dissuade Captain Ahab in his quest for the white whale in Herman Melville's *Moby-Dick*

Studs Lonigan—Working-class Irish American who is the title character in James T. Farrell's trilogy

T.S. Garp—Novelist who loves wrestling and whose son loses an eye in a bizarre auto accident in John Irving's *The World According to Garp*

Tarzan—Hero reared by apes in the jungle and known for his strength and agility in a series of stories by Edgar Rice Burroughs—he is also known as John Clayton, Lord Greystoke

Tom Canty—Beggar who changes clothes with a prince and becomes king in Mark Twain's *The Prince and the Pauper*

Tom Joad—First-born son and hero of the family of Okies travelling to California seeking work in John Steinbeck's *The Grapes of Wrath*

Topsy—Orphan slave girl in Harriet Beecher Stowe's *Uncle Tom's Cabin* known for saying "I 'spect I growed"

Uncas—Principal Native American character in James Fenimore Cooper's *The Last of the Mohicans*

Uncle Remus—Black slave who tells the tales related by Joel Chandler Harris

Uncle Tom—Elderly black slave considered by others to be subservient to whites in Harriet Beecher Stowe's most famous novel

The Virginian—Nameless cowboy hero who when insulted by Trampas says, "When you call me that, smile," in Owen Wister's 1902 novel

Wang Lung—Hard-working Chinese peasant who is unfaithful to his loyal wife O'Lan with a dancing-girl in Pearl Buck's *The Good Earth*

Walter Mitty—Quiet, easy-going, timid man who dreams of glory and heroic actions in a story by James Thurber

Willie Stark—Corrupt Southern governor considered to be a fictional portrayal of real-life Huey Long in Robert Penn Warren's *All the King's Men*

Wizard of Oz—Seemingly brave, powerful character who says he will give Dorothy and her 3 friends what they are seeking but turns out to be a little old man with a bald head and a wrinkled face in L. Frank Baum's classic novel

Wolf Larsen—Ruthless ship captain in Jack London's *The Sea Wolf*

(John) Yossarian—Joseph Heller's anti-hero who tries to escape his absurd situation of being a pilot by pleading insanity in *Catch-22*

Zeena Frome—Ethan's wife who banishes Mattie Silver in Edith Wharton's 1911 novel *Ethan Frome*

FICTIONAL PLACES

Anopopei—Pacific island where Norman Mailer's *The Naked and the Dead* is set
Cimmeria—Homeland of Robert E. Howard's Conan the Barbarian
Emerald City—Capital of Oz in L. Frank Baum's *The Wonderful Wizard of Oz*
Gopher Prairie—Minnesota town that is the setting for Sinclair Lewis's *Main Street*
Gotham—Nickname for New York City, from Washington Irving's 1807 *Salmagundi Papers* and originally the name of a 13th-century village in Nottinghamshire, England, whose inhabitants became known as "wise fools" for feigning stupidity in order to thwart King John from building a castle that would have resulted in higher taxes and more restrictions
Graustark*—Imaginary kingdom in romantic novels by George Barr McCutcheon
Grover's Corners—Fictional New Hampshire town that is the setting for Thornton Wilder's *Our Town*
Mudville—Town where Casey strikes out in Ernest Lawrence Thayer's "Casey at the Bat"
Munchkinland—Land of the little people in L. Frank Baum's *The Wonderful Wizard of Oz*
Oz—Kingdom "somewhere over the rainbow" where Dorothy lands via a tornado in an L. Frank Baum story—it is divided into 4 parts, each ruled by a witch
Pianosa—Mythical Italian island that is the setting for Joseph Heller's *Catch-22*
Sleepy Hollow—Village in the Catskills where Brom Bones pulls off a disguise as the Headless Horseman in a Washington Irving story
Terabithia—Secret kingdom of Jesse Aarons and Leslie Burke in a Katherine Paterson novel
Tralfamadore—Planet on which Kurt Vonnegut's *Slaughterhouse-Five* is partially set
Yoknapatawpha County—Imaginary Mississippi county where William Faulkner set a number of his stories and novels
Zenith—Town in the State of Winnemac where Sinclair Lewis' *Babbitt* is set

*Its adjective form *Graustarkian* describes a never-never land of high romance or a very romantic piece of writing; this adjective form was used to describe the ornate and exaggerated costumes used by President Nixon in outfitting the White House Drum and Bugle Corps.

WORLD LITERATURE/CLASSICAL AUTHORS

Aeschylus—Greek playwright known for his *Oresteia* trilogy (consisting of *Agamemnon*, *The Libation Bearers*, and *The Eumenides* or *Furies*), *Seven Against Thebes*, and *Prometheus Bound*
Aesop—Greek slave known for his fables
Aristophanes—Greek "father of comedy" known for *Clouds*, *Wasps*, *Birds*, *Lysistrata*, *Frogs*, and *Plutus*
Cicero—Roman orator and statesman who introduced Greek ideas and technical terms into Latin and wrote the *Philippics*, 14 speeches attacking Mark Antony; *De Oratore*; and *De Republica*, a study of government
Euripides—Greek playwright whose 18 surviving plays include *Medea*, *Iphigenia in Aulis*, *Alcestis*, *Hippolytus*, *Andromache*, *Hecuba*, *Heracles*, *The Trojan Women*, and *Electra*
Herodotus—Greek historian who in 9 books traced the rise of the Persian Empire, the Persian invasion of Greece in 490 and 480 B.C., and the Greeks' resistance to that invasion
Hesiod—Father of Greek didactic poetry, author of *Works and Days*, which is filled with maxims for farmers, and *Theogony*, a genealogy of the Greek gods
Homer—Greek poet known for the *Iliad* and the *Odyssey*, epics about events during and after the Trojan War
Horace—Roman poet famous for his *Odes*, *Epodes* (a collection of odelike poems), *Epistles* (letters to his friends), and *Satires*

Flavius Joseph—Jewish historian who wrote *Jewish Antiquities*, a history of the Jews, and *The Jewish War*, a history of war between the Jews and Romans in the 1st century A.D.
Juvenal—Roman poet known for 16 satires ridiculing extravagances in Rome
Livy—Roman historian who wrote *History from the Founding of the City*, telling Rome's history up to 9 B.C., in 142 books, 35 of which survive
Martial—Roman author who developed the epigram into its modern form
Ovid—Roman poet known for his *The Art of Love* and other love poems and his *Metamorphoses*, describing the adventures and love affairs of Greek and Roman gods and heroes, both legendary and historical
Plutarch—Greek biographer known for his *Parallel Lives of Illustrious Greeks and Romans*
Sappho—Greek lyric poet from the island of Lesbos known for her 4-line stanza called the *Sapphic*
Sophocles—Greek playwright whose 7 surviving tragedies include *Ajax*, *Antigone*, *Oedipus Rex*, *Electra*, and *Oedipus at Colonus*
Tacitus—Roman historian who wrote *Histories* (a critical work about emperors Galba, Otho, and Vitellius), *Annals* (a history of Rome from Augustus to Nero), and *Germania* (a history of early German tribes)
Thucydides—Greek historian famous for his *History of the Peloponnesian War*, covering the war between Athens and Sparta from 431-411 B.C. (the war actually continued until 404 B.C.)
Virgil (Vergil)—Roman poet who wrote the *Aeneid* (story of Aeneas, the Trojan hero who survived the fall of Troy and whose ancestors founded Rome); the *Ecologues*, or *Bucolics*; and *Georgics* (a poem of advice to farmers)
Xenophon—Greek author whose *Anabasis* tells of the 1,500-mile march home made by 10,000 Greeks who chose him to lead them after all of their other leaders had been killed in a 401 B.C. battle

EPICS

Epic of Gilgamesh—c. 2500 B.C. Babylonian epic composed in southern Mesopotamia before 2000 B.C. containing an account like that of the biblical flood and telling about the champion Enkidu created by the gods to oppose the king
Iliad—Homer's 9th-century B.C. epic about the Trojan War
Odyssey—Homer's 9th-century B.C. epic about events after the Trojan War
Works and Days—Hesiod's 8th-century B.C. epic filled with maxims for farmers
Mahabharata—c. 5th-century B.C. 18-book Sanskrit epic, the world's longest poem, ascribed to the Hindu sage Vyasa and including the *Bhagavad-Gita*—its title means "Great King Bharata"
Ramayana—5th-century B.C. Hindu epic about the godlike Rama
Aeneid—Virgil's 1st-century B.C. epic poem that records some of the events before and after the Trojan War
Beowulf—8th-century Old English epic in which there is a monster named Grendel
Song of Roland*—11th-century French epic poem written about 1100 telling of Charlemagne's defeat by the Basques in Spain, especially about his nephew in command of the rear guard who fights to the end, blowing his horn for help only when it is too late

*or *Chanson de Roland*

Nibelungenlied—c. 12th-century German epic whose title means "Song of the Nibelungs," telling the story of the hero Siegfried, who has a cloak of invisibility and wants to marry Kriemhild

Poem of the Cid**—12th-century Spanish epic featuring the hero of the wars against the Moors in the 11th century

Reynard the Fox—Medieval beast-epic featuring the struggle for power between the fox Reynard and the wolf Isengrim

Divine Comedy—Dante's 14th-century epic about himself and the Roman poet Virgil taking a trip through Hell (*Inferno*), Purgatory (*Purgatorio*), and Paradise (*Paradiso*)

Orlando Furioso—Ludovico Ariosto's 16th-century Italian epic poem depicting the struggle between Christians and the Arab-Muslim tribes known as Saracens

Jerusalem Delivered—Torquato Tasso's 16th-century epic poem about the First Crusade (1096-1099)

Os Lusíadas****—Luis de Camoes' 16th-century epic dealing mainly with the exploits of Portuguese explorer Vasco da Gama and his "discovery" of India

The Faerie Queene—Edmund Spenser's 16th-century allegorical epic poem dedicated to Queen Elizabeth and featuring knights portraying different moral virtues

Don Quixote—Miguel de Cervantes' 17th-century epic novel about a crazed gentleman who sets out to redress the wrongs of the world

Paradise Lost******—John Milton's 17th-century epic poem telling the story "Of man's first disobedience and the fruit / Of that forbidden tree"

Kalevala—19th-century Finnish national epic, compiled from popular songs and oral tradition by Finnish philosopher Elias Lonnrott

Moby-Dick—Herman Melville's 1851 epic novel about a great white whale pursued by the monomaniacal Captain Ahab

War and Peace—Leo Tolstoy's 1864-1869 epic novel focusing on Napoleon's invasion of Russia in 1812 and Russia's resistance to the attack

Ulysses—James Joyce's 1922 epic novel about one day, June 16, 1904, in the life of its 3 leading characters

John Brown's Body—Stephen Vincent Benét's 1928 epic Civil War poem

The Grapes of Wrath—John Steinbeck's 1939 epic novel about the migration of Okies during the Dust Bowl era

The Lord of the Rings—J.R.R. Tolkien's 1954-1956 epic trilogy of novels set in Middle Earth

**or Cantar de mio Cid or Poeme del Cid ***or The Lusiads ****or Paradise Regained

WORLD AUTHORS/THEIR NATIONALITIES/THEIR WORKS

Aesop—Greek—*Fables*: "The Ant and the Grasshopper"; "Belling the Cat"; "The Dog in the Manger"; "The Fox and the Crow"; "The Fox and the Grapes"; "The Hare and the Tortoise"; "The Shepherd Boy and the Wolf"; "The Town Mouse and the Country Mouse"; "The Wolf in Sheep's Clothing"

Isabel Allende—Chilean—*The House of the Spirits; Eva Luna; Of Love and Shadows*

Hans Christian Andersen—Danish—*The Complete Fairy Tales and Stories*: "The Emperor's New Clothes"; "The Ugly Duckling"; "The Princess and the Pea"; "The Little Mermaid"; "The Red Shoes"; "The Little Match Girl"; "The Steadfast Tin-Soldier"

Thomas Aquinas—Italian—*Summa Theologica*

Ludovico Ariosto—Italian—*Orlando Furioso*

Miguel Angel Asturias—Guatemalan—*The President; Men of Maize*

Margaret Atwood—Canadian—*The Handmaid's Tale; Cat's Eye; Good Bones and Simple Murders*
St. Augustine—African-born—*The City of God; Confessions*
Honoré de Balzac—French—*The Human Comedy* (*La Comédie Humaine*); *Père Goriot; Eugénie Grandet*
Charles Baudelaire—French—*The Flowers of Evil* (*Les Fleurs du Mal*)
Pierre Augustin de Beaumarchais—French—*The Barber of Seville; The Marriage of Figaro*
Simone de Beauvoir—French—*She Came to Stay; The Mandarins; Second Sex*
Samuel Beckett—Irish—*Waiting for Godot; Endgame; Krapp's Last Tape*
Giovanni Boccaccio—Italian—*The Decameron*
Jorge Luis Borges—Argentinean—*El Aleph* (*The Aleph and Other Stories*); *Los conjurados* (*The Conspirators*); *Sietas Noches* (*Seven Nights*)
Bertolt Brecht—German—*The Threepenny Opera; Mother Courage and Her Children*
Albert Camus—French—*The Plague; L'Etranger*
Karel Capek—Czech—*R.U.R. = Rossum's Universal Robots*
Giovanni Jacopo Casanova—Italian—*Memoirs*
Miguel de Cervantes—Spanish—*Don Quixote*
François Chateaubriand—French—*Atala; René*
Anton Chekhov—Russian—*The Cherry Orchard; The Three Sisters; Uncle Vanya;* The Seagull
Jean Cocteau—French—*Les enfants terribles; The Infernal Machine; The Blood of a Poet* (a film); *Beauty and the Beast* (a film)
Colette—French—*Chérie; Gigi*
Carlo Collodi—Italian—*The Adventures of Pinocchio*
Joseph Conrad—Polish-born British—*Heart of Darkness; Lord Jim; Typhoon; Nostromo; The Nigger of the "Narcissus"*
Pierre Corneille—French—*The Cid* (*Le Cid*); *Horace; Cinna; Polyeucte; Tite et Bérénice*
Dante (Alighieri)—Italian—*Divine Comedy*
Guy De Maupassant—French—*Bel Ami; The Horla;* "The Diamond Necklace"; "The Piece of String"
Isak Dinesen—Danish—*Out of Africa*
Fyodor Dostoyevsky—Russian—*The Brothers Karamazov; Crime and Punishment; The Idiot*
Alexandre Dumas (fils)—French—*The Lady of the Camellias* (later adapted as *Camille*)
Alexandre Dumas (père)—French—*The Three Musketeers; The Count of Monte Cristo; The Man in the Iron Mask*
Umberto Eco—Italian—*The Name of the Rose*
Gustave Flaubert—French—*Madame Bovary; The Temptation of St. Anthony; Salammbô*
Jean de la Fontaine—French—*Fables*
Anne Frank—German—*The Diary of a Young Girl*
Carlos Fuentes—Mexican—*The Death of Artemio Cruz; The Hydra's Head; Terra Nostra; The Old Gringo; Where the Air Is Clear*
Federico García Lorca—Spanish—*Blood Wedding; Yerma; The House of Bernarda Alba; Lament for Ignacio Sanchez Mejías*
Gabriel José García Márquez—Colombian—*One Hundred Years of Solitude; Love in the Time of Cholera; Vivir Para Contrala* (*To Live to Tell the Tale*); *The Autumn of the Patriarch; The General in His Labyrinth*

Theophile Gautier—French—*Mademoiselle de Maupin*
Kahil Gibran—Syrian-American—*The Prophet*
Andre Gide—French—*The Counterfeiters; Strait Is the Gate; The Pastoral Symphony*
Jean Giraudoux—French—*Amphitryon 38; The Madwoman of Chaillot; Siegfried*
Johann Wolfgang Goethe—German—*The Sorrows of Young Werther; Faust; Iphigenia in Tauris*
Nikolai Gogol—Russian—*Dead Souls*
Nadine Gordimer—South African—*Burger's Daughter; My Son's Story; None to Accompany Me; A World of Strangers*
Maxim Gorki (Gorky)—Russian—*The Lower Depths; The Mother*
Günter Grass—German—*The Tin Drum; Cat and Mouse; Dog Years*
Jacob and Wilhelm Grimm—German—Fairy Tales: "Hansel and Gretel"; "Little Red Riding Hood"; "Rumpelstiltskin"; "Snow-White"; "Sleeping Beauty"; "Cinderella"; "Rapunzel"
Hermann Hesse—German—*Steppenwolf; Demian; Siddhartha; Narcissus and Goldmund* (also called *Death and the Maiden*); *Magister Ludi* (also called *The Glass Bead Game*)
Victor Hugo—French—*Les Misérables; The Hunchback of Notre Dame; Ruy Blas*
Henrik Ibsen—Norwegian—*A Doll's House; Ghosts; The Wild Duck; Hedda Gabbler; Peer Gynt*
Eugene Ionesco—Romanian-born French—*The Bald Soprano; The Chairs; The Killer; Rhinoceros; A Stroll in the Air*
James Joyce—Irish—*Dubliners; Ulysses; Finnegans Wake; A Portrait of the Artist as a Young Man*
Franz Kafka—Austrian-Czech—*The Trial; The Castle;* "The Metamorphosis"
Jerzy Kosinski—Polish—*The Painted Bird; Being There*
Alain-René Lesage (Le Sage)—French—*The Adventures of Gil Blas of Santillane*
Niccolò Machiavelli—Italian—*The Prince*
Maurice Maeterlinck—Belgian—*Pelléas et Mélisande; The Blue Bird*
Naguib Mahfouz—Egyptian—"The Cairo Trilogy"
André Malraux—French—*Man's Fate*
Thomas Mann—German—*The Magic Mountain; Death in Venice; Buddenbrooks; Doctor Faustus; Joseph and His Brothers*
José Julián Martí—Cuban—*Free Verses; Emerson; Whitman; Our America; Bolívar*
John McCrae—Canadian—"In Flanders Fields"
Colleen McCullough—Australian—*The Thorn Birds*
Gabriela Mistral—Chilean—"Sonnets of Death"; *Desolation; The Wine Press*
Molière—French—*The Misanthrope; Tartuffe, or The Imposter; The School for Wives; The Miser; The Would-Be Gentleman; The Imaginary Invalid; Don Juan, or The Stone Feast*
Michel de Montaigne—French—*Essays*
Lucy Maud Montgomery—Canadian—*Anne of Green Gables*
Shikibu Murasaki—Japanese—*The Tale of Genji*
Vladimir Nabokov—Russian-born—*Lolita; Pale Fire; Ada*
Pablo Neruda—Chilean—*Twenty Love Poems and a Song of Despair; Residence on Earth*
Omar Khayyám—Persian—*The Rubáiyát*
Baroness Orczy—Hungarian—*The Scarlet Pimpernel*
Boris Pasternak—Russian—*Doctor Zhivago*
Alan Paton—South African—*Cry, The Beloved Country*
Octavio Paz—Mexican—*Savage Moon; They Shall Not Pass!; Freedom Under Parole*

Petrarch—Italian—*Canzoniere; On Illustrious Men*
Marcel Proust—French—*Remembrance of Things Past* or *A la Recherche du Temps Perdu*
Alexander Pushkin—Russian—*Boris Godunov; Eugene Onegin; The Bronze Horseman*
François Rabelais—French—*Gargantua and Pantagruel*
Jean Racine—French—*Andromaque; Brittanicus; Bérénice; Phèdre*
Erich Maria Remarque—German—*All Quiet on the Western Front*
Mordecai Richler—Canadian—*Joshua Then and Now; The Apprenticeship of Duddy Kravitz*
José Enrique Rodó—Uruguayan—*Ariel*
Edmond Rostand—French—*Cyrano de Bergerac*
Jean Jacques Rousseau—French—*Les Confessions; Emile; The Social Contract*
Salman Rushdie—India-born—*The Satanic Verses; Midnight's Children; Shame*
Françoise Sagan—French—*A Certain Smile; Bonjour Tristesse*
Antoine de Saint-Exupéry—French—*The Little Prince; Wind, Sand, and Stars; Night Flight*
George Sand—French—*Lélia; Indiana*
Jean-Paul Sartre—French—*Being and Nothingness; No Exit; Nausea; The Flies; The Age of Reason*
Friedrich von Schiller—German—*Kabale und Liebe* (*Cabal and Love*); "An die Freude" ("Ode to Joy"); *Maria Stuart* (*Mary, Queen of Scots*); *Die Jungfrau von Orleans* (*The Maid of Orleans*); *Wilhelm Tell*
Robert Service—British-born Canadian—*The Law of the Yukon*; "The Shooting of Dan McGrew"
George Bernard Shaw—Irish—*Pygmalion; Man and Superman; Androcles and the Lion; Saint Joan; Caesar and Cleopatra; Arms and the Man; Mrs. Warren's Profession; Major Barbara*
Mikhail Sholokhov—Russian—*And Quiet Flows the Don*
Alexander Solzhenitsyn—Russian—*One Day in the Life of Ivan Denisovich; The Gulag Archipelago; Cancer Ward*
Johanna Spyri—Swiss—*Heidi*
Stendahl—French—*The Red and the Black; The Charterhouse of Parma*
August Strindberg—Swedish—*Miss Julie; The Dance of Death*
Thomas à Kempis—German—*Imitation of Christ*
Leo Tolstoy—Russian—*Anna Karenina; War and Peace;* "Where Love Is, There God Is Also"
Ivan Turgenev—Russian—*Fathers and Sons; A Sportsman's Sketches*
Mario Vargas Llosa—Peruvian—*The City and the Dogs; The War of the End of the War; The Green House; The Way to Paradise*
Lope de Vega—Spanish—*The Best Mayor, the King; Fuenteovejuna*
Jules Verne—French—*Around the World in Eighty Days; Twenty Thousand Leagues Under the Sea; From the Earth to the Moon; A Journey to the Center of the Earth*
François Villon—French—*Le Petit Testament; Le Testament;* "Ballade des Dames du Temps Jadis"
Voltaire—French—*Candide; Zadig; Micromégas*
Morris West—Australian—*The Devil's Advocate; The Shoes of the Fisherman*
Oscar Wilde—Irish—*The Picture of Dorian Gray; The Importance of Being Earnest; Lady Windermere's Fan;* "The Ballad of Reading Gaol"; "De Profundis"
Johann Wyss—Swiss—*The Swiss Family Robinson*
William Butler Yeats—Irish—"Sailing to Byzantium"; "The Second Coming"; "Among School Children"; "The Song of the Old Mother"; "The Lake Isle of Innisfree"; "Under Ben Bulben"; *The Countess Cathleen*
Emile Zola—French—"J'accuse"; *Germinal; Nana; Thérèse Raquin*

PUBLISHING: NEWSPAPERS AND MAGAZINES

Tabloid whose slogan is "Inquiring Minds Want to Know"
Answer: *The National Enquirer.*

U.S. CITIES AND THEIR NEWSPAPERS

Atlanta—*Journal-Constitution*
Baltimore—*Sun*
Birmingham—*News* and *Post-Herald*
Boston—*Globe, Herald, The Christian Science Monitor*
Charlotte—*Observer*
Chicago—*Sun-Times* and *Tribune*
Cincinnati—*Enquirer* and *Post*
Cleveland—*Plain Dealer*
Columbus (GA)—*Ledger-Enquirer*
Columbus (OH)—*Dispatch*
Dallas—*Morning News*
Denver—*Post* and *Rocky Mountain News*
Des Moines—*Register*
Detroit—*Free Press* and *News*
Fort Lauderdale—*Sun-Sentinel*
Fort Worth—*Star-Telegram*
Hartford—*Courant*
Houston—*Chronicle*
Indianapolis—*Star* and *News*
Jacksonville—*Times-Union*
Kansas City—*Star*
Los Angeles—*Times, Daily News,* and *La Opinión*
Louisville—*Courier-Journal*
Miami—*Herald*
Milwaukee—*Journal Sentinel*
Minneapolis—*Star Tribune*
Nashville—*Tennessean*
New Orleans—*Times-Picayune*
New York City—*Daily News, Post, Times, Wall Street Journal*
Newark—*Star-Ledger*
Omaha—*World-Herald*
Orlando—*Sentinel*
Philadelphia—*Inquirer* and *Daily News*
Phoenix*—*Republic* and *Gazette*
Pittsburgh—*Post-Gazette*
Portland—*Oregonian*
Sacramento—*Bee*
St. Louis—*Post-Dispatch*
St. Paul—*Pioneer Press*
St. Petersburg—*Times*
Salt Lake City—*Deseret News* and *Tribune*
San Diego—*Union-Tribune*
San Francisco—*Chronicle*
San Jose—*Mercury News*
Seattle—*Times* and *Post Intelligencer*
Tampa—*Tribune*
Vancouver—*Sun* and *Province*
Washington, D.C.—*Post*
Wichita—*Eagle*

*The newspapers are *The Arizona Republic* and *The Phoenix Gazette.*

WORLD CITIES AND THEIR NEWSPAPERS

Baghdad—*Al-Sabah*
Beijing—*Renmin Ribao* or *People's Daily*
Berlin—*Berliner Morgenpost, Berliner Zeitung, Der Tagesspiegel*
Buenos Aires—*La Nación, La Prensa*
Edinburgh—*The Scotsman*
Hamburg—*Bild-Zeitung, Die Welt, Die Zeit*
London—*Daily Mirror, Daily Telegraph, Evening Standard, The Financial Times, The Guardian, The Observer, The Times*
Madrid—*ABC, Cinco Dias, El Pais*
Mexico City—*Excélsior, Tiempos del Mundo*
Milan—*Corriere della Sera, Il Giorno*
Montreal—*Le Devoir, The Gazette, The Mirror, La Presse*
Moscow—*Pravda*
Ottawa—*The Citizen, The Sun*
Paris—*Le Figaro, Le Monde, Le Parisien*
Quebec—*Le Soleil*
Rome—*Il Messaggero, La Repubblica, Il Tempo*
Tokyo—*Asahi Shimbun, Nikkei Weekly, Yomiuri Shimbun*
Toronto—*Globe and Mail, The Star, The Sun*
Turin (Italy)—*La Stampa*
Vatican—*L'Osservatore Romano*

PUBLISHING HISTORY

Boston—City in which the first newspaper, *Publick Occurrences Both Forreign and Domestick*, was published in America in 1690 and suppressed after only one edition

John Campbell—Postmaster and bookseller who in 1704 published the *Boston News-Letter*, the first continuously-published newspaper—he shares his name with this book's author

Pennsylvania Gazette—Newspaper Benjamin Franklin began publishing in 1729, writing most of the material himself

John Peter Zenger—Publisher of the New York *Weekly Journal* in 1733 who after being acquitted for libel against William Cosby in 1735 published *A Brief Narrative of the Case and Tryal of John Peter _____*, covering the case

"Join, or Die"—Slogan Benjamin Franklin used in a *Pennsylvania Gazette* cartoon of a disjointed snake published before the 1754 Albany Congress to urge the separate colonies to unite against the French and Indians

The Hartford Courant—Nation's oldest continuously published newspaper, the Connecticut paper founded in 1764 whose slogan is "Older than the Nation"

Stamp Act—1765 act passed by the British Parliament requiring special tax stamps be placed on all newspapers

John Dickinson—So-called "Penman of the Revolution" who urged resistance to British taxation in his 12 newspaper pieces of 1767, later published as *Letters from a Farmer in Pennsylvania to the Inhabitants of the British Colonies*

Thomas Jefferson—Patriot who in a 1787 letter said, "The basis of our government being the opinion of the people . . . were it left to me to decide whether we should have a government without newspapers, or newspapers without a government, I should not hesitate a moment to prefer the latter."

The Federalist Papers—Series of 85 letters that Alexander Hamilton, James Madison, and John Jay sent to newspapers in 1787-1788 to urge ratification of the Constitution

Benjamin Lundy—Quaker editor who in 1821 published *The Genius of Universal Emancipation*, a newspaper advocating abolitionist principles

Freedom's Journal—First black newspaper in the U.S., begun on March 16, 1827, in New York

Sequoya*—Cherokee Indian who in 1828 founded in Georgia the *Cherokee Phoenix (and Indian Advocate)*, the first American newspaper published in an Indian language

Penny Press (Paper)**—2-word monetary term coined for the popular tabloid-style newspapers of the 1830s to 1860s because of their low cost

The Liberator—William Lloyd Garrison's abolitionist newspaper founded in 1831

New York Sun—Newspaper founded in 1833 by Benjamin Henry Day, the first successful penny newspaper in the U.S.

New York Herald—One-penny daily newspaper aimed at a mass audience launched in 1835 by James Gordon Bennett

New Orleans—Southern city where George W. Kendall and Francis Lumsden founded the *Picayune* in 1836, naming it for the coin at which it was sold

Illinois—State where newspaper editor Elijah Parish Lovejoy of the Alton *Observer* became a martyr to the antislavery movement in 1837 when he was killed by a mob wrecking his presses to stop his antislavery editorials

Horace Greeley—Newspaper editor who established the *New York Tribune* in 1841 and served as its editor for 30 years

*Also known as George Guess; to the Cherokees he was Sogwali **After 1860, these tabloid-style papers began publishing "news" instead of smears, lies, and gossip.

Margaret Fuller—Woman who in 1840 joined Emerson to edit *The Dial* and in 1844 joined the *New York Tribune*, becoming in 1846 America's first woman correspondent in Europe

Cassius Marcellus Clay—Founder of the antislavery newspaper *True American* in 1845 in Lexington, Kentucky (called the *Examiner* when he moved it to Louisville)

Rotary press—Kind of printing press using curved plates on cylinders instead of a flat plate that Richard Hoe developed in 1846, making it possible to print newspapers much faster and much cheaper

North Star—Antislavery newspaper Frederick Douglass founded in Rochester, New York, in 1847

Amelia Jenks Bloomer—Woman inventor of loose trousers who in 1849 founded *The Lily*, a newspaper for women, to promote her beliefs regarding temperance, liberal divorce laws, female suffrage, and dress reform

Thomas Edison—American inventor and industrial leader who at age 15 in 1862 published and sold a weekly newspaper called *The Weekly Herald* that he printed in the baggage car of a train

Ottmar Mergenthaler—German-U.S. inventor who in 1884 patented the linotype typesetting machine

International Herald Tribune—International newspaper founded in 1887 by New York *Herald* owner James G. Bennett and now completely owned by the New York *Times*

Daily Examiner—Ailing San Francisco newspaper William Randolph Hearst took over in 1887 and subsequently renamed the San Francisco *Examiner*

Wall Street Journal—Newspaper founded in 1889 when Dow, Jones, and Bergstresser of the Wall Street firm of Dow Jones & Co. converted a newsletter into an afternoon daily

Kansas—State where in 1895 William Allen White purchased the *Emporia Gazette*, for which he won a Pulitzer Prize for editing in 1923

New York Times—Newspaper that Henry J. Raymond founded in 1851, Adolph S. Ochs took over in 1896, and since 1897 has had the slogan "All the News That's Fit to Print" on page one—it's nicknamed the "Good Gray Lady"

Yellow journalism***—Use of cheaply sensational or distorted newspaper stories to attract readers

Yellow Kid—R.F. Outcault's 1895 comic strip character drawn for the New York *World* when yellow ink was used for the first time in the strip "Hogan's Alley" in order to attract readers' attention, thus the origin of the term "yellow journalism"

Frederic(k) Sackrider Remington—Newspaper artist who was sent to Cuba by the New York *Journal* editor in 1898 and allegedly filed the report: "Everything is quiet. There is no trouble here. There will be no war. Request to be recalled."

William Randolph Hearst—New York *Journal* publisher whose style of sensationalism was described as *yellow journalism* by critics and who allegedly sent to the newspaper artist in Cuba the response: "You furnish the pictures and I'll furnish the war. Please remain."

Joseph Pulitzer—Editor who acquired the New York *World* in 1883, founded the New York *Evening World* in 1887, and became known for using sensationalism to incite the public and attract readers

The Commoner—Weekly newspaper William Jennings Bryan founded and edited from 1901 to 1913

***Or yellow press

Theodore Roosevelt—U.S. President who used the biblical name Ananias, linked with cheating and hypocrisy, for a fictional club of newspaper reporters who published information from confidential sources they promised not to reveal

Mary Baker Eddy—Founder of the Church of Christ, Scientist who founded a newspaper in 1908

Christian Science Monitor—Daily newspaper this church founder established in 1908

Warren Harding—Owner and publisher of the Marion *Star* newspaper in Ohio who later became the U.S.'s 29th President

Baltimore Sun—Newspaper where H.L. Mencken worked as a reporter, columnist, and editor at intervals from 1906 to the end of his career

Hughes—Candidate named in many New York newspapers' early headline "THE PRESIDENT-ELECT—CHARLES EVANS ____," erroneously declaring him the winner over Woodrow Wilson in the 1916 presidential election

Pulitzer Prizes—Annual awards founded by Joseph ____ for achievements in American journalism, letters, and music and first presented in 1917 by Columbia University

New York *Daily News*—16-page, 4-column daily Joseph Patterson and Robert McCormick founded in 1919 emphasizing crime and sex and having 2,000,000 subscribers by the 1940s

Dorothy Day—Roman Catholic journalist and social worker who with Peter Maurin founded the *Catholic Worker* newspaper in 1933 to promote social programs to help the poor

Will Rogers—American humorist and social critic known for beginning his performances and newspaper column by saying: "All I know is what I read in the papers"

• **Eleanor Roosevelt**—First Lady who wrote a syndicated newspaper column called "My Day" from 1935 to 1962

Newsday—Newspaper founded in Long Island, New York, in 1940

William Randolph Hearst—Newspaper publisher on whose life Orson Welles's 1941 film *Citizen Kane* is loosely based

Walter Winchell—American journalist who made the gossip column a regular feature and began his radio broadcasts with the catch phrase: "Good evening, Mr. and Mrs. America and all the ships at sea. Let's go to press."

Chicago (*Sun-Times*)—City in which the *Times*, founded in 1929, combined with Marshall Field's *Sun* in 1948

Chicago Daily Tribune—Newspaper that on November 3, 1948, published the erroneous headline "DEWEY DEFEATS TRUMAN"

William F. Buckley Jr.—Yale University graduate and author known for his newspaper column *On the Right* syndicated in 1962

Pentagon Papers—U.S. Department of Defense top secret study from 1967 to 1969 officially called "History of the U.S. Decision-Making Process on Viet Nam Policy" and released by Daniel Ellsberg in 1971 to the New York *Times*

Washington Post—Katharine Graham's Washington newspaper whose reporters Robert Woodward and Carl Bernstein exposed in 1972 the coverup in the Watergate scandal

(Gerald) Ford—U.S. President named in the New York *Daily News*' 1975 headline "____ TO CITY: DROP DEAD" in reference to his response to New York's threatened bankruptcy

USA Today—Full-color newspaper called "The Nation's Newspaper" first published in Arlington, Virginia, by the Gannett Company in 1982

New York Post—Tabloid whose July 2004 headline erroneously claimed that John Kerry had picked Dick Gephardt as his running mate

POTPOURRI OF PUBLISHING

Associated Press—Full name of the AP, an organization founded in 1848 when representatives of 6 New York City newspapers banded together

• **Nellie Bly**—Pen name of Elizabeth Cochrane Seaman, the newspaper reporter who set out on November 14, 1889, to try to break Jules Verne's fictional hero Phileas Foggs' record of traveling around the world in 80 days, making it in 72 days, 6 hours, 11 minutes

Ben Bradlee—*Washington Post* editor when it cracked the Watergate scandal

Winston Churchill—British prime minister who earlier as a newspaper reporter in South Africa in 1899 had been captured by Louis Botha, a Boer officer and future South African prime minister

Charles A. Dana*—American newspaper editor to whom is attributed the 1882 remark in the New York *Sun*: "When a dog bites a man, that is not news, but when a man bites a dog, that is news."

Fleet Street—London street named as a metonym for the press in that many newspaper offices were located there

Fourth estate—2-word term including a number used as a metonym for newspapermen

Izvestia—Russian newspaper whose name means "News"

Robert Maxwell—British publishing magnate whose body was found off the coast of the Canary Islands in 1991

Paparazzi**—Freelance photographers who trail celebrities to capture candid shots to sell to newspapers and magazines, as known by a term of Italian origin literally meaning "scribblers or rummagers in old papers"

Pravda—Communist Party newspaper founded by V.I. Lenin in 1919 and named with the Russian for "truth"—it ceased publication in 1991

Reuters—Major world news service founded in London as a financial service by German-Jewish immigrant and journalist Paul Julius Baron de _____ in 1851

E.W. Scripps***—Journalist who founded the *Cleveland Penny Press* in 1878 and the United Press news service in 1907

The Stars and Stripes—Daily newspaper founded by soldiers for other soldiers during the Civil War, revived during WWI and WWII, and having the motto "Wherever You Go, We Go"

Toronto *Star*—Canada's largest newspaper

United Press International—Full name of UPI, an organization founded in 1958 when E.W. Scripps' association merged with Hearst's International News Service (1907)

The War Cry—Weekly newspaper of The Salvation Army

Emile Zola—French writer known for his famous 1898 newspaper letter entitled "J'accuse" demanding justice for Alfred Dreyfus

*Also attributed to John Bogart and Amos Cummings **Derived from Paparazzo, the photographer character in director Federico Fellini's 1960 movie *La Dolce Vita*. ***The founder of the first American newspaper chain.

FICTIONAL NEWSPAPERS

The Daily Bugle—Newspaper published by Spider-Man's nemesis, J. Jonah Jameson, in Marvel Comics

The Daily Fourth Gradian—Newspaper of Springfield Elementary School in *The Simpsons*

The Daily Globe—Newspaper that is the rival to J. Jonah Jameson's newspaper in Marvel Comics

The Daily Planet—Metropolis newspaper for which the fictional "mild-mannered" reporter Clark Kent works and whose motto is "Always First With the News"

The Daily Prophet—National newspaper of wizards in the Harry Potter series

Daily Sentinel—Newspaper published by Britt Reid in *The Green Hornet*

Gotham Gazette/Globe—Newspapers in *Batman* comics and movie, respectively

The Los Angeles Tribune—Newspaper in the TV series *Lou Grant*

New York Banner—Newspaper in Ayn Rand's *The Fountainhead* with Gail Wynand as publisher and Ellsworth Toohey as architecture critic

New York Herald—Newspaper of sportswriter Oscar Madison in the TV series *The Odd Couple*

MAGAZINES

Identify the women's magazines nicknamed "The Seven Sisters."
Answer: *Better Homes & Gardens*, *Family Circle*, *Good Housekeeping*, *Ladies' Home Journal*, *McCall's*, *Redbook*, and *Woman's Day*.

The Tatler—Famous English periodical founded by Richard Steele and published from 1709 to 1711 with the help of Joseph Addison

The Spectator—Famous English periodical published from 1711 to 1712 by essayists Joseph Addison and Richard Steele

The Gentleman's Magazine—English magazine founded by Edward Cave, published from 1731 to 1914, and subtitled *or, Trader's Monthly Intelligencer*

American Magazine—First magazine published in America, in 1741 in Philadelphia, subtitled *Or a Monthly View of the Political State of the British Colonies*

Farmer's Almanac*—U.S.'s oldest continuously annually published periodical, which released its 200th anniversary edition in 1991

Saturday Evening Post—Magazine published from 1821 to 1969 for which artist Norman Rockwell frequently served as its cover illustrator

Godey's Lady's Book—First American magazine for women, published by Louis A. Godey from 1830 to 1898

The Dial—Magazine published by Transcendentalists from 1840 to 1844, edited by Margaret Fuller and Ralph Waldo Emerson

Punch—Humor magazine founded in London in 1841 and subtitled *The London Charivari*

Harper's Magazine—Monthly, first published in New York City in 1850, whose drawings of the battlefront during the Civil War were provided by artist Winslow Homer

Atlantic Monthly—Monthly launched in 1857 in Boston and first edited by famous poet James Russell Lowell

The Nation—Liberal weekly periodical, founded in 1865, edited by Edward L. Godkin

Harper's Bazaar—Women's fashion magazine founded in 1867 as the first fashion magazine—part of its name was originally spelled *Bazar*

Puck Magazine—Magazine founded by a cartoonist in 1871 and named after the elfin character in Shakespeare's *A Midsummer Night's Dream*

Harvard Lampoon—Harvard's humor magazine, first published in 1876

The Watchtower—Periodical of the Jehovah's Witnesses, first published in 1879

Ladies' Home Journal—Women's magazine founded by Cyrus Curtis in 1883 as a women's supplement to the *Tribune and Farmer*

Cosmopolitan Magazine—Magazine founded in 1886 as "a first-class family magazine"

National Geographic—Magazine first published in 1888 by the world's largest nonprofit scientific and educational organization

*Or *The Old Farmer's Almanac*

McClure's Magazine—Magazine founded in 1893 that published Ida M. Tarbell's exposé entitled "Standard Oil Company" and Lincoln Steffens' "The Shame of the Cities" in 1902, and Ray Stannard Baker's "The Railroads on Trial" in 1906

The Smart Set—Magazine founded in 1890 and edited by H.L. Mencken and George Jean Nathan from 1914 to 1923—it ceased to exist in 1929

Popular Mechanics—Magazine whose first issue in January 1902 showed the inner workings of a submarine

Redbook Magazine—Magazine founded in 1903 to help young mothers find happiness and balance a busy life, so named for what was thought to be "the color of happiness"

Variety—Movie industry's "insider voice," founded in 1905

Mother Earth—Anarchist magazine Emma Goldman co-published with Alexander Berkman from 1906 to 1917

Boys' Life—Magazine of the Boy Scouts of America, first published in 1912 and having the Pedro the Mail Burro as its mascot

Vanity Fair—Sophisticated publication founded in 1914 and edited by Frank Crowninshield until 1935

Reader's Digest—Monthly magazine featuring condensed articles founded in 1922 by DeWitt and Lila Wallace

Time—First weekly news magazine, one founded by Henry R. Luce and Briton Hadden in 1923 (Luce founded *Life* in 1936 and *Sports Illustrated* in 1954)

American Mercury—Magazine H.L. Mencken and George Jean Nathan founded in 1924 to replace *The Smart Set*

Better Homes & Gardens—Magazine about the home and family that changed its name in 1924 from *Fruit, Garden and Home*

The New Yorker—Magazine founded in 1925 and edited by Harold Ross, who said it was to be for the "caviar sophisticates" and "not for the little old lady from Dubuque"

Fortune—Business magazine founded by Henry R. Luce in 1930

Newsweek—News magazine founded by Thomas J.C. Martyn in 1933 to compete with *Time* and having a hyphenated name and 7 different pictures on its first cover

Esquire—Premier men's magazine founded by Arnold Gingrich in 1933

Life—Magazine whose first cover in 1936 featured a picture of Montana's Fort Peck Dam taken by its photographer Margaret Bourke-White

Look—Popular general-interest magazine featuring photographs published from 1937 to 1971

Negro Digest—Magazine John H. Johnson began publishing in 1942 for African-American readers

Ebony—Magazine founded by the Johnson Publishing Company in 1945 to celebrate Black experience and given a name meaning "dark or black" and designating a hard, dark, durable wood

U.S. News & World Report—Weekly news magazine David Lawrence launched in 1948 as a merger of his 2 weeklies individually focusing on U.S. news and world news

Jet—Magazine founded in 1951 by John H. Johnson to celebrate the lives of African Americans

Mad Magazine—Humor magazine that debuted in 1952 as *Tales Calculated to Drive You Mad* and later featured Alfred E. Neuman, a curly-haired hero with a gap-toothed smile and the question "What? Me worry?"

Playboy—Magazine founded by Hugh Hefner whose first issue in 1953 featured Marilyn Monroe on its cover

Sports Illustrated—Magazine on whose first cover on August 16, 1954, Eddie Matthews was pictured at the plate
National Review—Conservative magazine founded in 1955 by William F. Buckley Jr.
Rolling Stone—Music magazine founded in San Francisco in 1967 by Jann Wenner and Ralph Gleason featuring John Lennon on its first cover
Ms.—Magazine for women started in 1972, cofounded by Gloria Steinem, and featuring Wonder Woman on its first cover
People—Magazine that debuted in 1974 and is known for its "The 50 Most Beautiful People in the World" and "The Best and Worst Dressed" lists
National Lampoon—Magazine begun in 1970 as an offshoot of the *Harvard Lampoon*
Mother Jones Magazine—Left-wing periodical founded in 1976 and named after Mary Harris Jones, a labor leader of the late 1800s and early 1900s who helped organize the IWW
Utne—Left-of-center periodical founded in 1984 by Eric _____
Lear—Frances Lear's 1988-1993 magazine with the slogan "for women over forty who weren't born yesterday"
George—John Kennedy Jr.'s political magazine founded in 1995
O—Oprah Winfrey's magazine that debuted in 2000
Mental Floss—Magazine founded primarily by Will Pearson in 2001 and designed to make "people feel smart again"

MAGAZINE POTPOURRI
Walter Annenberg—Founder of both *Seventeen* magazine (1944) and *TV Guide* (1953)
Richard Avedon—*Harper's Bazaar* photographer from 1945 to 1965 who published his first book of celebrity photographs, *Observations*, in 1959
Helen Gurley Brown—Woman who became editor of the failing *Cosmopolitan* magazine in 1965 and under whose leadership it featured a nude male, Burt Reynolds, in 1972
Joseph G. Cannon—U.S. Representative from North Carolina and the first person to appear on the cover of *Time* magazine, on March 3, 1923
Cindy Crawford—Model and actress who appeared dressed as George Washington on the first cover of *George* magazine
Daedalus—Magazine of the Academy of Arts and Sciences, named for the builder of the Labyrinth and father of Icarus in Greek myth
Princess Diana—Person most often featured on the cover of *People* magazine, at 52 times
Dr. Hook—Name completing _____ and the Medicine Show, the pop-country rock band whose hit song was "Cover of the Rolling Stone"
Esquire—Magazine known for its *Dubious Achievement Awards*, accompanied by a picture of a laughing Richard Nixon with the caption, "Why is this man laughing?"
Mia Farrow—Actress who was the first person on the cover of *People* magazine, in 1974
Larry Flint—Publisher who founded the sexually explicit magazine *Hustler* in 1974 and was convicted in Cincinnati in 1977 for promoting obscenity and involvement in organized crime
Mel Gibson—Actor who was the first Sexiest Man Alive for *People* magazine, in 1985
Sarah Josepha Hale*—Editor of *Ladies' Magazine*, the U.S.'s first successful women's magazine (1828-1837), and *Godey's Lady's Book* (1837-1877)
Bret Harte—First editor of the *Overland Quarterly*, the magazine founded in 1868 by Anton Roman, a San Francisco bookseller

*She also promoted the idea of a national Thanksgiving Day, prompting President Lincoln to proclaim the last Thursday in November as a day of thanksgiving in 1863; and she wrote the poem "Mary Had a Little Lamb."

Charles Lindbergh—First to appear on *Time* magazine's cover in 1928 as the first "Man of the Year"

Modern Maturity—Magazine of the AARP, or American Association of Retired Persons

Demi Moore—Actress who posed pregnant and nude on the cover of *Vanity Fair* in 1991, a magazine reinvigorated by Tina Brown in the late 1980s

Muckrakers—Theodore Roosevelt's pejorative label for journalists such as Lincoln Steffens and Ida M. Tarbell who targeted business and government for sensationalist exposés while writing for *Everybody's Magazine* and *McClure's Magazine*

J. Fred Muggs Award—Annual award presented by *TV Guide* "for people who made monkeys of themselves"

Condé Nast—Publisher who not only bought *Vogue* in 1909 and transformed it into a top fashion magazine but also turned *Vanity Fair* into a sophisticated and stylish one

National Geographic—First magazine ever to have an all-holographic cover, in its December 1988 issue on its 100th anniversary

The New Yorker—Magazine whose mascot, Eustace Tilley, appeared on its first cover in 1925 as a dandy peering at a butterfly through a monocle

Pegasus—Mythological winged creature used by *Reader's Digest* as its logo

The People vs. Larry Flynt—1996 Milos Forman film telling the story of Larry Flynt and his pornographic magazine *Hustler*

Little Rickie Ricardo**—Baby boy who was the first person on the cover of *TV Guide* magazine, in 1953

Smithsonian—One advertised as the "Magazine From Our Nations Attic"

Sports Illustrated—Magazine that has featured a "Swimsuit Issue" since 1964

Stern—West German magazine that rushed the forged Hitler diaries into publication in 1983

Vanity Fair—Magazine that in 2005 revealed FBI official W. Mark Felt as "Deep Throat" of the Watergate era

E.B. White—*The New Yorker* magazine humorist who began contributing to the "Notes and Comment" and "The Talk of the Town" columns in 1927 and headed the "One Man's Meat" department for *Harper's* from 1938 to 1943

**Born Desiderio Alberto Arnaz IV

MYTHOLOGY

4-letter word that completes the following statement from Oxford University professor Gilbert Ryle's book *The Concept of Mind*: "A _____ is, of course, not a fairy story. It is the presentation of facts belonging to one category in the idioms appropriate to another. To explode a myth is accordingly not to deny facts but to re-allocate them"
Answer: Myth.

GREEK AND ROMAN MYTHOLOGY
Greek—Roman—God/Goddess of
Aphrodite—Venus—Goddess of love and beauty
Apollo—Apollo—God of light, medicine, music, and poetry
Ares—Mars—God of war
Artemis—Diana—Goddess of the moon, the hunt, childbirth, and chastity
Asclepius—Aesculapius—God of healing and medicine
Athena—Minerva—Goddess of wisdom, war, and the liberal arts
Cronus (Cronos)—Saturn—God of the world and time in Greek mythology, god of agriculture in Roman mythology
Demeter—Ceres—Goddess of agriculture and fertility
Dionysus—Bacchus (Liber)—God of fertility, wine, and revelry
Eos—Aurora—Goddess of the dawn
Eris—Discordia—Goddess of discord and strife
Eros—Cupid (Amor)—God of love
Gaea (Gaia)—Terra—Goddess and personification of the earth
Hades (Pluto)—Pluto (Dis; Orcus)—God of the underworld
Helios—Sol—God of the sun
Hephaestus—Vulcan—God of fire and the forge; blacksmith for the gods
Hera—Juno—Goddess of women, marriage, and childbirth; queen of the gods
Hermes—Mercury—God of commerce and science; protector of travelers and thieves; messenger and herald for the other gods
Hestia—Vesta—Goddess of the hearth
Hygeia—Salus—Goddess of health
Hypnos—Somnus—God of sleep
Pan—Faunus—God of fields, herds, flocks, and the rustic and the pastoral life
Persephone—Proserpine (Proserpina)—Goddess of the underworld
Poseidon—Neptune—God of the sea; in Greek mythology, also god of earthquakes and horses
Rhea—Ops—Queen of the Titans as wife of Cronus or Saturn
Selene—Luna—Goddess of the moon
Tyche—Fortuna—Goddess of good fortune and luck
Uranus—Uranus (Coelus)—God of the sky and personification of the heavens
Zeus—Jupiter (Jove)—Supreme deity

"IN THE BEGINNING" IN GREEK AND ROMAN MYTHOLOGY
Hesiod—8th-century B.C. Greek poet who wrote the *Theogony*, or *Origin of the Gods*—he is called the "Father of Greek Didactic Poetry"

Chaos—Name Hesiod gave to the first "power" in the universe, the original and empty void that existed before the universe was created

Golden Age—First age when mankind was ideally happy and prosperous, prior to the rule of Zeus or Jupiter

Gaea (Gaia, Ge)—Mother Earth, or the life force that emerged somehow from the formless Chaos and gave birth to the Sky (Uranus), the Sea (Pontus), and the Mountains, along with the grass, flowers, trees, and the earth's animals

Nyx (Nox)—Wife of Chaos; the personification of night

Erebus—Mysterious darkness of the underworld that emerged when Chaos was dethroned by his son; the dark place through which the dead had to pass on their way to Hades

Tartarus—Lowest region of the underworld, born out of Chaos and located beneath Hades, where Zeus confined the defeated Titans

Uranus*—Earliest god of the sky, the original ruler of the universe who married his mother, Gaea, the earth

Cronus (Cronos)—Titan who dethroned his father Uranus by chaining him in Tartarus after castrating him with a sickle given him by his mother, Gaea

Hecatoncheires—Uranus and Gaea's offspring with 50 heads and 100 hands each who helped the Olympians wage war against Cronus

Titans—Enormous beings, offspring of Uranus and Gaea, considered the first generation of true gods who ruled before the Olympians and were imprisoned by their father before being defeated by Zeus and the other gods

Cyclopes—Uranus and Gaea's offspring with only one large eye in the middle of their foreheads, known for using their skill as smiths to produce the lightning bolts that helped Zeus defeat Cronus and the Titans

Olympians—Group under Zeus's leadership who defeated Cronus and the Titans, sending them to Tartarus after a fierce battle known as the Titanomachy (Titanomachia) that almost destroyed the universe and may have lasted 10 years

Giants—Set of beings who sprang from the blood that Uranus shed on Gaea after his castration, sometimes said to include the Titans, the Cyclopes, and the Hecatoncheires

Heracles (Hercules)—Zeus's son known as the "lion-skinned mortal," who arrived after the Olympians had weakened the Giants and finished them off

Typhon—Gaea's monster offspring, the largest of the Giants, defeated by Zeus with his thunderbolts and buried under Mount Aetna

Furies**—Vengeful, hideous creatures resembling old women produced from several drops of Uranus's blood when he was castrated by his son Cronus

Rhea—Daughter of Uranus and Gaea and wife and sister of Cronus

*He hated and feared his sons and either put them back into their mother, the Earth, or sent them to Tartarus. **Also called the Eumenides or Erinyes

MARKETPLACE MYTHS

Ajax—Colgate-Palmolive's all-purpose cleanser named for a heroic Greek warrior

Amazon—Online bookseller founded by Jeff Bezos who wanted an inventory as deep and as wide as a South American river named after a race of Greek women warriors

Ambrosia—Dessert consisting of oranges and coconut named for the food of the gods

Atlas—Tires, van line, and U.S. liquid-propelled intercontinental ballistic missile, all with the name of the Titan condemned to carry the world on his shoulders

Aurora—Oldsmobile mid-size car and the Roman goddess of dawn

Avalon—Toyota full-size car bearing the name of the island to which King Arthur and other heroes were taken after they died

Caduceus—U.S. Army medical branch's snake-wrapped insignia named for the snake-wrapped staff of Hermes and that of Asclepius, the god of medicine

Calypso—Jacques Cousteau's oceanographic ship and a type of Caribbean folk music sharing the name of Atlas' daughter who offered Odysseus immortality if he stayed with her on her island of Ogygia

Clio—Award given annually for special achievement in radio and TV advertising named for the Muse of history in Greek mythology

Cressida—Toyota full-size car bearing the name of the legendary Trojan woman who was unfaithful to Troilus, her lover

Cyclops—Tennis machine with an electronic eye used to determine whether a ball is in or out of bounds, named for the mythic giant having one eye in the middle of the forehead

Daedalus—Magazine of the Academy of Arts and Sciences bearing the name of the mythical Icarus' father, the builder of the Labyrinth

Echo—Toyota subcompact car bearing the name of the Greek nymph who pined away to nothing after Narcissus rejected her love

Eos—Line of Cannon cameras named for the Titan goddess of the dawn in Greek mythology

Halcion*—Tranquilizer/sleeping pill from the Upjohn Company named from the Greek word for the kingfisher who supposedly calmed the wind and the waves during a 14-day period while breeding in a nest on the sea

Helen of Troy—Brand of personal care products such as hair dryers named for the most beautiful woman in myth

Hermes**—Expensive scarves, handbags, and saddles bearing the shared surname of founder Thierry _____ and the Greek god of commerce and invention

Janus—Investment company bearing the name of the Roman god considered vigilant because he had 2 faces looking in opposite directions

Janus Films—Film distribution company bearing the name of the Roman god of beginnings, openings, doorways, and endings

Mercury—Auto brand of the Ford Motor Company named for the Roman god of commerce and messenger of the gods noted for his speed

Midas—Leader in exhaust services, such as mufflers, bearing the name of the king whom Dionysus enabled to turn what he touched into gold

Nike—Brand of athletic shoes and apparel named for the Greek winged goddess of victory

Odyssey—Honda 4-door minivan bearing the name of Homer's long epic poem describing the 10-year wanderings of Odysseus

Olympus—Maker of cameras and imaging systems that shares its name with the Greek home of the gods

Oracle—Computer software program bearing the name of the ancient Greek shrine where priests/priestesses foretold the future

Orion—Former motion picture company named for the famous giant and handsome hunter whom Artemis killed and placed among the stars

Saturn—U.S. auto or space-vehicle booster having the name of the Greek god of agriculture and harvest

Siren—Whistle with a loud, piercing sound named for the sweet-singing monsters who lured sailors to destruction by their sound and from whom Odysseus protected his men by putting wax in their ears

Taurus—Ford mid-size car sharing the name of the mountain range in Asia Minor in which the mythical Prometheus was chained for giving fire to man

*After *halcyon* **Thierry's surname is spelled *Hermès*.

Thunderbird—Ford mid-size luxury car and an inexpensive fortified wine bearing the name of the enormous bird said to affect the weather in America Indian mythology

Titanic—Ill-fated ship that sank in 1912 whose name is the adjective meaning "having great size and strength" and derived from the giant children of Uranus and Gaea

Triton—Ford V-8 engine design and Mitsubishi truck sharing the name of the Greek sea god who was the son of Poseidon and Amphitrite

Trojan—Brand of condoms sharing the name of a strong, determined person with stamina derived from the name for the inhabitants of the ancient city that fought the Greeks

Valhalla—Louisville, Kentucky, golf club bearing the name of Asgard's great hall with 540 doors where Odin received and feasted the souls of the warriors slain in battle in Norse mythology

Venus Pencils—World's "largest selling quality drawing pencil," named for the Roman goddess of beauty

Vulcanization—Charles Goodyear's rubber-strengthening process named for the Roman god of fire and metalworking

Vulcan Productions—Independent film production company named after the Roman god of fire and metal-working

Zephyrhills***—Bottled spring water named in part for the west wind, whose name comes from its personification as a god in Greek mythology

***Zephyr, from *Zephyrus*, identifies the Burlington Silver Streak Zephyr train that set a speed record on May 26, 1934, making the trip from Denver to Chicago in 13 hours; the Lincoln Zephyr auto was named after the train.

GEOGRAPHY MYTHS

Achilles—Virginia town named after the sulking heroic warrior of Homer's *Iliad*

Amazon River—World's 2nd longest river, named after a tribe of warlike women who lived in Scythia, near the Black Sea

Apollo—Pennsylvania town named after the god of the sun, prophecy, music, medicine, and poetry

Arcadia—California town named after a pastoral region in the central Peloponeseus where Heracles frightened away the Stymphalian birds

Argo—Alabama town named after Jason's ship that sailed in search of the Golden Fleece

Argusville—North Dakota town named after the 100-eyed giant who guarded Io

Athena—Oregon town named after the Greek goddess of wisdom and the arts

Athens—Greek capital named after the goddess of wisdom, its patron goddess

Atlas—North African mountains named for the Titan condemned to carry the world on his shoulders

Aurora—Cities near Denver and Chicago named after the Roman goddess of the dawn

Calypso—North Carolina town named after Atlas' daughter on whose island, Ogygia, Odysseus shipwrecked and stayed 7 years

Castor—Louisiana town named after the twin brother of Pollux in Greek myth

Ceres—California town named after the Roman goddess of agriculture

Champs-Élysées—Famous boulevard in Paris named for the mythological Elysian Fields

Charybdis—Sierra Nevada peak named after the whirlpool on the Italian side of the Strait of Messina

Corinth—Georgia and New York towns named after a city of ancient Greece from which Oedipus fled

Crete—Illinois town named after a Mediterranean Sea island on which Rhea hid Zeus in a secret cave on Mount Ida or Mount Dicte

Daphne—Alabama town named after the woman turned into a laurel tree to escape Apollo
Delphi—Indiana town named after the seat of an oracle of Apollo
Diana—West Virginia town named after the Roman goddess of the hunt
(Mount) Erebus—Antarctic mountain located on Ross Island, an active volcano named for the dark place through which the souls of the dead had to pass on their way to Hades
Eros—Louisiana town named after the Greek god of love
Europe—Continent named after Agenor's beautiful daughter with whom Zeus fell in love when he saw her in a meadow
Flora—Mississippi town named for the Greek goddess of flowers and gardens
Griffin—Georgia town named after the half-eagle, half-lion creature of Greek mythology
Hector—Arkansas town named for Priam's son whom Achilles killed during the Trojan War
Hercules—California town named after the "lion-skinned mortal," son of Zeus, who completed 12 labors
Hesperia—California town whose name is the ancient Greek name meaning "land of the evening," as used by Aeneas for Italy and by the Romans for Spain
Hesperus—Colorado town whose name identifies the evening star, Venus
Homer—Alaskan town named after the poet who wrote the *Iliad* and *Odyssey*
Irene—South Dakota town named after the Greek goddess of peace
Ithaca—New York city named for Odysseus' homeland, the site of Cornell University
Juno Beach—Florida town named after the wife and sister of Jupiter
Karnak—Illinois town named after a village on the Nile where the solar deity Montu in Egyptian mythology was worshipped
Luna—New Mexico town named after the Roman goddess of the moon
Marathon—Florida town named after the Greek plain on which Theseus captured the bull unleashed by Poseidon
Memphis—Tennessee town named after the capital of ancient Egypt
Mentor—Ohio town named after the guardian and teacher of Telemachus
Minerva—Ohio town named after the Roman goddess of wisdom and the arts
Neptune Beach—Florida town named after the Roman god of the sea
Olympia—Washington's capital named for the home of the gods in Greek myth
Palladium—Famous London music hall whose name comes from that of the goddess Pallas Athena
Pandora—Ohio town named after the first mortal woman in Greek mythology
Paris—French capital named after the Trojan prince who ran away with Helen of Troy, prompting the Trojan War
Parthenon—Arkansas town named after the famous temple to Athena built on the Acropolis in Athens
Phoenix—U.S. state capital named for a creature that consumed itself in fire, then resurrected itself from its ashes
Pluto—West Virginia town named after the Roman god of the dead and ruler of the underworld
Pomona—California city named after the Roman goddess of fruit and fruit trees
Rhodes—Iowa and Michigan towns named after the largest of the Dodecanese islands where the 100-foot-high statue called the Colossus was located
Rome—Towns in Georgia and New York named after the ancient city founded by Romulus
Romulus—Michigan town named after the son of Mars who was raised by a she-wolf and later became Rome's first king
Sabine River—U.S. river with the same name as an ancient Italian tribe whose females were allegedly seized and raped by Roman soldiers during the reign of Romulus

Scylla—Sierra Nevada peak named after the female sea monster that ate sailors who escaped the danger of the whirlpool called Charybdis
Sparta—Georgia and Kentucky towns named after the ancient city-state of which Menelaus was king
Thebes—Illinois city named after the ancient Greek city of which Oedipus was king
Thor—Iowa town named after the god of thunder in Norse mythology
Troy—New York town named for an ancient city in Asia Minor where a major war was fought, a city celebrated in Homer's and Virgil's epics
Vesta—Georgia and Nebraska towns named for the Roman goddess of the hearth
Ulysses—Kansas and Nebraska towns using the Latin name for Odysseus, the king of Ithaca and leader of the Greeks during the Trojan War

FOOD

William Shakespeare play that opens with Orsino saying, "If music be the food of love, play on!"
Answer: *Twelfth Night, or What You Will.*

BRITISH
Banger—Slang word for a sausage
Beef Wellington—Steak filet filled with paté de foie gras, then wrapped in pastry and baked, named after the 1st Duke of _____
Bubble and squeak—Cabbage and potatoes fried together, so named from the noise it makes while cooking
Cheddar—Hard, smooth cheese, from a town in Somerset, England, where it originated
Dorset—Blue cheese named after a county in England on the English Channel
Flapjack—Griddlecake made from rolled oats and syrup
Gloucester—Hard yellow cheese named after an English city on the Severn
Haggis—Pudding-like concoction of sheep innards, oatmeal, suet, herbs, and spices boiled in the lining of a sheep's stomach and served especially in Scotland
Humble pie—Pie made from a deer's inner parts, known as *umbles*
Kippers—Fish, especially herring or salmon, that has been split, salted, dried, and smoked and served especially in Scotland
Mince pie—Pie with a filling of chopped apples, raisins, spices, suet, etc., and sometimes meat
Sandwich—Slices of bread with a filling between them named after John Montagu, the 4th Earl of _____, who ordered one made so he wouldn't have to leave the gambling table
Scones—Small, biscuit-like filled pastry that Scottish poet Robert Burns described as "the wale [best] o' food"
Stilton—Blue-veined cheese named after a village in England
Welsh rarebit (rabbit)—Melted cheese mixed with beer and served on toast
Worcestershire—Meat sauce of soy, vinegar, and spices named after a former county in England
Yorkshire pudding—Dish consisting of a batter of eggs, flour, milk, baked in drippings of roast beef, named after a former county in northern England on the North Sea

FRENCH
Aspic—Molded cold jelly of meat juice or tomato juice
Béarnaise—Creamy sauce similar to Hollandaise named after the French region Béarn
Béchamel—Basic white sauce made of flour, butter, and milk to which egg yolk, lemon juice, and sometimes parsley are added, named after Louis de _____, Louis XIV's chef who created it
Bisque—Thick, creamy soup made from shellfish or rabbit
Blancmange—Cold sweet jelly-like pudding made with milk or cornstarch
Brie—Ripened, soft cheese named after a region in northern France
Calvados—Apple brandy named after a department in northwestern France
Camembert—Soft, creamy cheese named after a town in Normandy, France
Canapé—Small piece of bread or cracker, spread with spiced meat, fish, cheese, etc., served as an appetizer

Chateaubriand—Very thick tender cut of beef tenderloin, named for François-René de _____, the French author of *Atala* and *René*, by his chef
Consommé—Clear soup made of meat or vegetable stock or both
Coquilles St. Jacques—Appetizer of diced scallops in a wine and cream sauce topped with grated cheese and browned, named after the scallop shell emblem of St. James of Compostela and the emblem worn by pilgrims to his shrine
Crêpe—Very thin pancake
Crêpe suzette—Thin pancake rolled in an orange-flavored sauce and often served with a flaming brandy sauce
Croissant—Crescent-shaped flaky roll that's a traditional part of breakfast
Fondu (fondue)—Dish consisting of melted cheese, chocolate, or other sauce into which bread, fruit, or other food is dipped, named from the French for "to melt"
Hollandaise—Sauce of egg yolks, butter, lemon juice, and seasonings, from the French for "Dutch sauce"
Hors d'oeuvre—Small portion of a tasty food served as an appetizer before a meal, especially at a cocktail party, named from the French meaning "outside of the work"
Julienne—Clear broth garnished with vegetables cut into strips, or any meat or vegetable cut into thin strips, possibly after a French chef who prepared the dish
Madeleine—Small rich tea cake, or something that summons nostalgia, possibly after _____ Paulnier, a cook, or a contraction of the French *gâteau à la* _____
Mousse—Chilled dessert pudding made with eggs, gelatin, and whipped cream, and frequently chocolate
Muenster—Mild, semisoft cheese named after Munster, France
Napoleon—Pastry with crisp, flaky layers filled with custardlike filling, named after a French leader
Neufchâtel—Soft white cheese prepared from whole or skim milk, named after a town in northern France
Paté de foie gras—Spread made of the livers of fattened geese
Petits pois—Small green peas
Port du Salut—Creamy cheese named after a French Trappist monastery where it was made
Quiche Lorraine—Quiche made with cheese and crisp bacon bits named after a region in northeastern France
Ragoût—Highly seasoned stew of meat, poultry, or fish and vegetables
Ratatouille—Vegetable stew with eggplant, zucchini, tomatoes, and onions, flavored with garlic and simmered in olive oil
Roquefort—Dressing or blue cheese named after a town in Southern France
Salade niçoise—Salad of tuna, tomatoes, green beans, potatoes, anchovies, hard-boiled eggs, and black olives served with a garlic vinaigrette, named for the resort city of Nice
Vichyssoise—Thick, creamy potato soup flavored with leeks or onions and usually served cold, from the name of a city in central France

GERMAN
Bavarian cream—Dessert made with gelatin, fruit, and whipped cream named after a state in Germany
Braunschweiger—Smoked liver sausage named with the German for Brunswick
Frankfurter—Cooked smoked sausage named after the city of Frankfurt
Hamburger—Ground beef named after a seaport and state

Hasenpfeffer—Dish of rabbit meat marinated in vinegar and cooked in its marinade, whose name literally means "pepper rabbit"
Kirsch(wasser)—Clear brandy distilled from black cherries used to flavor foods such as fondue, whose name literally means "cherry water"
Kn(a)ockwurst—Short, thick, highly seasoned sausage, especially with garlic
Pumpernickel—Coarse, dark, sour bread made of rye and wheat flour, often flavored with molasses
Sauerbraten—Pot roast marinated in vinegar, etc., before browning then simmering in its marinade
Sauerkraut—Shredded cabbage fermented in salt and spices
Strudel—Pastry of a thin dough sheet covered with fruit such as apple or cherry, cheese, rolled up and baked—similar to phyllo
Wiener Schnitzel—Breaded veal cutlet garnished with lemon slices, anchovies, and capers, named with the German for "Viennese cutlet"

GREEK
Baklava—Dessert made of thin, flaky layers of filo pastry with chopped nuts, sugar, honey, and cloves
Dolmades—Grape leaves or cabbage leaves cooked with a filling of ground meat, herbs, or rice
Dolmathes—Vegetable leaves filled with rice and ground beef
Feta—Crumbly white soft goat or sheep cheese used for salads
Gyro—Minced lamb or beef or both roasted on a spit, sliced, and topped with grilled onions, or a sandwich made of layers of this meat with onion and tomato, usually on pita bread
Moussaka—Sliced eggplant and ground lamb or beef arranged in layers, covered with a béchamel sauce and cheese, then baked
Olive—Primary kind of oil used for frying and dressing salads
Ouzo—Strong, licorice-flavored drink derived from resinated Greek wine
Phyllo (filo)—Thin layers of pastry dough used in sweet dishes such as baklava
Soupa Avgolemono—Lemon-flavored chicken soup
Souvlaki(a)—Marinated lamb or pork chunks skewered between vegetable chunks and cooked over a grill, usually served inside a pita

ITALIAN
Antipasto—Assortment of smoked meats, cheese, salted fish, and marinated vegetables served as an appetizer, named from the Italian meaning "before the food"
Bologna—Large smoked sausage named after a commune in Italy where first made
Calamari—Seafood delicacy known in English as squid, whose Italian name comes from a word for "reed pen," possibly because of the ink-like fluid it secretes or because of its pen-shaped skeleton
Cannoli—Tube of pastry, deep-fried, and filled with ricotta cheese, chocolate, fruit, nuts, etc.
Cantaloupe—Melon named after the former papal summer estate, near Rome, Italy, where it was grown
Chicken Marengo—Chicken cooked in a tomato sauce with garlic and wine, named after a village in Italy's Piedmont region where it originated
Gelato*—Ice cream
Gorgonzola—White, blue-veined cheese named after a northern Italian town

*Gelateria is an ice cream parlor.

Marzipan—Confection made of ground almonds and sugar
Minestrone—Thick vegetable soup containing vermicelli or macaroni, dried beans, barley, etc., in a meat broth
Mozzarella—Soft, mild, white cheese used in cooking and often melted on pizza
Parmesan—Hard, sharp, dry cheese named after Parma, Italy
Pasta primavera—Pasta dish part of whose name means "spring" that is prepared with fresh vegetables in a light cream sauce
Pesto—Uncooked sauce of ground fresh basil, garlic, pine nuts, and parmesan cheese mixed with olive oil
Pizza—Flattened bread dough covered with tomato sauce, grated cheese, etc., whose name literally means "pie" or "cake"
Polenta—Corn meal mush boiled in water or stock
Prosciutto—Spicy ham, seasoned by salt, cured by drying, and thinly sliced
Provolone—Firm, mild cheese, frequently smoked and molded into a pear shape
Raddichio—Red-leaf variety of chicory, used as a salad ingredient
Risotto—Rice cooked with olive oil and chicken broth and served with grated cheese and tomato sauce
Salami—Highly spiced, salty sausage
Saltimbocca—Thinly sliced veal and prosciutto flavored with sage, rolled, and sautéed in butter, then braised in white wine
Scaloppine—Thinly sliced meat, usually veal, sautéed with herbs and usually served with a wine or tomato sauce
Spumoni—Italian ice cream having layers of different flavors and often containing fruits and nuts, named from the Italian for "foam"
Tiramisu (tiramisù)—Spongecake pieces soaked in coffee and liqueur and layered with cheese and topped with chocolate, named from the Italian meaning "pick me up"
Tournedos Rossini—Slices of filet mignon, or tournedos, often bound in bacon and named for the composer of the opera *Otello*
Zabaglione—Dessert made by beating eggs, sugar, and wine together to make a light, foamy custard

ITALIAN PASTA
Cannelloni—Literally "little tubes," for tubular casings of boiled pasta filled with meat, cheese, or vegetables and baked in a tomato or cream sauce
Farfalle—Literally "butterfly," for pasta in the shape of bow ties
Fettuccine—Literally "little ribbons," for thin, flat strips of pasta
Linguini(e)—Literally "little tongues," for thin, flat, narrow pasta
Macaroni—Literally "dumplings," for tube-like pasta that is often baked with cheese or ground meat
Manicotti—Literally "sleeves," for pasta in long, broad tubes, boiled, stuffed with meet or cheese, covered with a sauce and baked
Ravioli—Literally "turnips," for small square pasta filled with meat, cheese, etc., and often served in a tomato sauce
Rigatoni—Literally "stripes" or "lines," for pasta in short, wide tubes, with long ridges
Spaghetti—Literally "little chords," for long, thin strings of pasta, usually boiled or steamed and served with a meat sauce
Tortellini—Literally "little flat cakes," for ring-shaped pasta filled with meat, cheese, or vegetables
Vermicelli—Literally "little worms," for spaghetti-like pasta

JAPANESE

Donburi—Bowl of cooked rice with other food on top, named from the Japanese for "bowl"
Miso—Thick soybean paste used in making soup and sauces
Norimake—Sushi rice and seafood rolled in dried seaweed sheets
Sashimi—Thinly sliced, raw fish served with soy sauce and wasabi
Shiitake—Edible, golden or dark brown mushroom
Soba—Noodles made of wheat flour or buckwheat flour
Sukiyaki—Thinly sliced meat fried with onions and other vegetables, flavored with soy sauce
Sushi—Small cakes of cold cooked rice flavored with vinegar and usually garnished with raw fish or cooked vegetables
Tempura—Dish of fish, seafood, or vegetables dipped in batter and fried in deep fat
Teriyaki—Fish or meat grilled over an open fire and basted with soy sauce and sake until glazed
Tofu—Soybean paste used in soup and other cooked dishes
Tsukemono—Pickled vegetables
Wasabi—Herb used like horseradish and having the form of a green paste for seasoning sushi or sashimi

MEXICAN

Arroz con pollo—Chicken and rice dish seasoned with garlic, saffron, paprika, and other spices
Burrito—Flour tortilla wrapped around a beef, bean, or cheese filling
Chili—Bell pepper relative that must be handled carefully because its oils can burn the eyes, hands, and mouth, or a thick soup made with meat or beans in a tomato paste
Chili con carne—Very spicy dish made of red peppers, meat, and usually beans, named from the Spanish for "hot peppers with meat"
Chorizo—Pork sausage seasoned with cayenne pepper, garlic, and paprika
Enchilada—Tortilla filled with cheese or meat and topped with a chili sauce
Fajita—Grilled strips of marinated beef or chicken, served wrapped in a tortilla with vegetables
Guacamole—Thick paste of mashed avocado served with many Mexican dishes or sometimes as a dip or in salads
Jalapeño—Small, dark green hot pepper
Kidney bean—Popular bean used in chili con carne and so named for its shape resembling a body organ
Mole—Spicy sauce served with meat or chicken and made with chilies, chocolate, tomatoes, and spices
Pico de gallo—Garnish made from chopped tomato, onion, and chiles, named from the Spanish for "rooster's beak"
Pinto bean—Popular bean named with the Spanish word for "spotted" because of its appearance—also called red Mexican beans
Refried beans—Beans that have been cooked and then mashed and fried and seasoned
Quesadilla—Flour tortilla filled with cheese or a spicy mixture, then folded in half and deep-fried
Salsa—Hot sauce made with chili peppers, onions, and tomatoes
Taco—Fried, folded corn tortilla filled with chopped meat and shredded lettuce
Tamale—Minced meat, tomato sauce, and crushed red peppers rolled in cornmeal dough and then baked or steamed
Tortilla—Round, flat cake of unleavened cornmeal baked on a griddle and used as the basis for various dishes
Tostada—Tortilla fried until crisp, then topped with beans, meat, and cheese

Mmm-Mmm Good

Company whose candy bars, including Mounds and Almond Joy, feature the slogan "Indescribably delicious"
Answer: Peter Paul.

1) Name the candy advertised by the slogan "The milk chocolate melts in your mouth . . . not in your hand," adopted in 1954.
Answer: M&Ms (first produced as brown-coated chocolate-covered peanuts).

2) Name the American poet of light verse who wrote the lines: "Candy / Is dandy / But liquor / Is quicker."
Answer: Ogden Nash.

Andes—Mint thins that share their name with the world's longest chain of mountains above sea level
Baby Ruth—Candy bar named after the daughter of President Grover Cleveland
Bar None—Candy bar whose name is a 2-word phrase meaning "without exception"
Bavarian—Mints named for the German state whose capital is Munich
Bazooka—Bubble gum named with the word for a weapon of metal tubing that fires armor-piercing rockets
Big Red—"America's No. 1 Cinnamon Gum" bearing Man o'War's nickname
Boston Baked Beans—Candy-coated peanuts whose name includes that of the Massachusetts capital and designates the food Puritan women prepared every Saturday and served for Sunday dinner
Bugles—Crispy corn snacks whose name designates brass instruments lacking keys or valves and used mainly for military calls and signals
Butterfinger—Candy bar whose name when made plural is a colloquial term for a person who frequently fumbles or drops things
Chessmen—Pepperidge Farm butter cookies named for the pieces in chess
Chunky—Milk chocolate candy bar with nuts and raisins whose name is an adjective meaning "short and thick" or "stocky"
Crunch—Candy bar whose name means "to bite with a noisy, crackling sound"
Dots—Assorted fruit-flavored gumdrops whose name designates the opposite of dashes in Morse Code
Dove—Candies or candy bar whose name designates the bird that is a symbol of peace
Dream—Candy bar whose name designates a fantasy or an aspiration
Extra—Sugarfree chewing gum whose name means "a special addition of a newspaper" or "an additional charge"
Fast Break—Reese's milk chocolate peanut butter with soft nougats candy bar whose name designates a basketball play moving quickly down court ahead of the defense
5th Avenue—Candy bar whose name designates the New York City street famous as a shopping district
Fig Newtons—Nabisco fruit chewy cookies named after either a town in Massachusetts or Sir Isaac Newton

Ghirardelli—Candy bar bearing the name of a famous chocolate factory that once stood on the site of a shopping center now named for it near Fisherman's Wharf in San Francisco

Graham*—Crackers named after a 19th-century Presbyterian minister who campaigned against white flour and developed instead this dry sweet cracker made of un-sifted whole-wheat flour

Heath (bar)—English toffee bar whose name designates a tract of open wasteland covered with heather

Hot Tamales—Chewy cinnamon candies whose name designates a hot Mexican food of minced meat, tomato sauce, and red peppers rolled in cornmeal

Icebreakers—Breath-savers whose name designates strong, powerful ships designed to cut channels through heavy ice or anything serving to open a conversation

Kit Kat—Candy bar whose name designates the 1931 Berlin nightclub where Liza Minnelli, in the role of Sally Bowles, sang in the 1972 movie *Cabaret*

Kudos—Granola bar whose name in Greek means "credit or praise for an achievement"

Lido—Pepperidge Farm dark chocolate cookies named for a popular beach resort near Venice, Italy

LifeSavers—Candies whose name designates persons or things that give aid in time of need

Lorna Doone—Shortbread cookies whose name is also the title of an R.D. Blackmore novel about a kidnapped child who is an heiress of a noble family

Marathon—Snickers energy bar whose name designates a long distance race

Mars**—Candy bar whose name designates the Roman god of war and the planet 4th in distance from the sun

Milky Way—Candy bar bearing the name of the spiral galaxy containing our sun

Mr. Goodbar—Candy bar whose name completes the title of Judith Rossner's 1975 novel *Looking for* _____

Mon Chéri—Chocolates whose name is French for "my dear"

Mounds—Dark chocolate-covered coconut cream bars whose name designates banks of earth built by early Indians as burial places and as platforms for monuments, temples, and houses for their chiefs

Munch—Candy bar whose name means "to chew steadily with a crunching sound" and is the surname of the Norwegian artist of *The Scream*

Nerds—Tiny, tangy, crunchy candy whose name is a slang term for people considered dull and bookish

Nuggets—Hershey's candies whose name designates lumps of gold

Oh Henry!***—Peanutty, caramel fudge bar in rich milk chocolate whose name is pronounced the same as William Sydney Porter's pen name

100 Grand—Candy bar whose name is a slang term for a hundred thousand dollars

Payday—Candy bar whose name designates the day on which wages are paid

Poppycock—Butter-almond pecan crunch whose name is a colloquial term meaning "foolish talk" or "nonsense"

Pot of Gold—Candy bar of roasted almonds in fine milk chocolate whose name designates the riches to be found at the spot where a rainbow touches the earth

Rippled—Potato chips whose name means "wavy, like the surface of water broken by small waves"

Ritz—Crackers whose name completes the phrase *putting on the* _____, meaning "to show off" and alluding to the grand style of 3 lavish hotels named for the Swiss entrepreneur who built them

*After Sylvester Graham (1794-1851) **The company's founder is Franklin Mars. ***His pen name is O. Henry.

Ruffles—Potato chips whose name designates strips of cloth gathered in pleats and used for trimming

Runts—Chewy fruit-shaped candy whose name designates the smallest animals of a litter

Skittles—Candies whose name identifies a British form of ninepins and completes the phrase "(not) all beer and ____," meaning "(not) pure pleasure"

Snickers—Candy bar whose name means "sly, or partly stifled laughs"

Sonic Boom—Bubble gum whose name designates the sound produced when the shock wave caused by an airplane flying at supersonic speed hits the ground

Spree—Chewy candy whose name means "a noisy frolic" or "a period of uninhibited activity"

Starburst—Fruit chews whose name designates something shaped like the bursting forth of a star's rays

Sugar Daddy—Milk-caramel pop whose name is a slang term for a rich, older man who lavishes gifts on a younger woman

Switzer—Licorice candy whose name is the surname of Barry ____, the coach who won a college football championship at Oklahoma and a Super Bowl with the Dallas Cowboys

Symphony—Candy bar whose name designates an extended composition for a full orchestra

Take 5—Hershey's pretzel, caramel, peanuts, peanut butter, and milk chocolate candy bar that shares its name with a 1962 Dave Brubeck jazz composition

3 Musketeers—Candy bar whose name designates Alexander Dumas's characters Athos, Porthos, and Aramis

Town House—Crackers whose name designates a 2- or 3-story city dwelling connected on its side to other similar dwellings

Trident****—Brand of sugarless gum whose name identifies the 3-pronged spear carried by Poseidon or Neptune

Turtles—Chocolate candies packaged 3 to a bar named for the reptiles they resemble—the only reptiles with a shell

Whatchamacallit—Candy bar whose name is another colloquial term for "thingamajig"

Whoppers—Malted milk balls whose name is a colloquial term meaning "things extraordinarily large" or "great lies"

Willy Wonka—Division of Sunmark that makes Nerds candy and bears the name of the Chocolate Factory owner in a Roald Dahl story

York—Peppermint patties bearing the name of the ruling family of England from 1461 to 1485

Zero—Candy bar whose name is a synonym for "cipher" and "naught" and designates the freezing point of water on a Centigrade scale

****Trident is also the name of the U.S. submarine-launched missiles first tested in the 1980s.

POTPOURRI OF ONLYS

Only convicted cannibal in U.S. history, whose 1874 act of cannibalism was verified by scientists in 1989 and for whom a university grill is named
Answer: Alferd Packer (the University of Colorado at Boulder named its grill after him).

1) Identify the only 3 people outside the monarchy to have been granted state funerals in Great Britain, specifically, a government leader in the 20th century and 2 military leaders in the 19th.
Answer: Winston Churchill, Duke of Wellington, and Lord Nelson.

2) Name the only 3 films in which James Dean starred.
Answer: *East of Eden*, *Rebel Without a Cause*, and *Giant*.

Aeschylus—Author of the only surviving Greek tragic trilogy from ancient times, the *Oresteia*, written in 458 B.C.
Alfred—Only English king called "the Great"
Barbary Ape—Only wild monkey now living in Europe, one that lives on the British dependency of Gibraltar
John Bardeen—Only American to have won 2 Nobel prizes in physics
Ludwig van Beethoven—Composer whose music is the only music Schroeder, a character in the comic strip *Peanuts*, wishes to play on his piano
Anne Boleyn—Henry VIII's wife who was at least allegedly the only royal figure with 6 fingers on one hand
Bromine—Only nonmetallic element that is liquid at standard temperature and pressure
Samuel Chase—Only U.S. Supreme Court Justice to be impeached
Cleopatra—Only African queen in the title of a Shakespearean play
Charles DeGaulle—Only president of France to serve 2 non-consecutive terms—1944-1946 and 1959-1969
Abe Fortas—Only Supreme Court justice to resign under the threat of impeachment for his allegedly unethical conduct
Friday*—Only day of the week named after a mythological goddess
Gallaudet University—Washington, D.C., school that is the world's only liberal arts college for the deaf
General Assembly—Only major organ of the U.N. in which all members are represented
Ginkgo—Deciduous tree of China and Japan, also called a maidenhair tree, that is a "living fossil," the only remaining species of a large order of gymnosperms that existed in the Triassic Period
Oliver Goldsmith—Irish writer whose only novel is *The Vicar of Wakefield*
Matthew Henson—Black who was the only American to accompany Robert E. Peary when the explorer allegedly reached the North Pole
Impeachment case—Only case in which the President cannot issue a pardon
Homo sapiens—Only surviving species of the primate family *Hominidae*
Houston (Texas)**—U.S. city named after the only person to be governor of 2 states
Japan—Only country whose monarch has the title of emperor
Bobby Tyre Jones Jr.***—Georgian who was the first and only golfer to win the Grand Slam of Golf, doing so in 1930

*After the Norse goddess, Frigga (whose identity is also linked with Freya, the Norse goddess of love and beauty) **Sam Houston was governor of Texas and Tennessee. ***He won the U.S. Open, the British Open, the U.S. Amateur, and the British Amateur; today the grand slam consists of the Masters, the U.S. Open, the British Open, and the PGA, or Professional Golfers Association Championship, and no golfer has won all 4 in the same calendar year.

John Luther "Casey" Jones—Only person to die in the wreck of the *Cannonball Express* on April 30, 1900

Ben Jonson—Dramatist and poet who is the only person buried in London's Westminster Abbey in a standing position

Judas (Iscariot)—Apostle who was the only non-Galilean—he was elected by his fellow disciples to handle the funds from the common purse

Kiwi—Only known bird with nostrils in the tip of its bill

Henry Wadsworth Longfellow****—Poet who is the only American honored with a memorial bust in the Poet's Corner of Westminster Abbey

Luxembourg—Only country ruled by a duke, by Grand Duke Henri since 2000

Mars—Only planet whose surface can be seen in detail from the earth

Mary (I; "Bloody Mary")—Only one of the 6 children of Catherine of Aragon and Henry VIII who lived into adulthood

John Mitchell—President Nixon's attorney general who in 1975 became the only U.S. attorney general convicted of illegal activities and imprisoned

Montreal Canadiens—Only NHL team to win 5 consecutive Stanley Cups, from 1956-1960

The Mystery of Edwin Drood—Charles Dickens's unfinished novel published posthumously in 1870 is his only true mystery story

Naked mole-rat—Small rodent with wrinkled skin that is the only known mammal whose social behavior resembles that of bees, ants, and termites

Eugene O'Neill—Only American dramatist to win the Nobel Prize in literature, in 1936

Opossum (possum)—Only marsupial native to North America

Linus Pauling—Only American to win 2 unshared Nobel prizes, one in chemistry in 1954 and the other in peace in 1962

Jeannette Rankin—Only person to vote against U.S. entry into WWII and the only legislator to oppose U.S. involvement in both World Wars

Franklin Roosevelt—Only one in the 20th century who after being defeated as a Vice Presidential candidate later became U.S. President

Julius and Ethel Rosenberg—Only U.S. citizens executed for espionage in the U.S., in 1953

Saturday—Only day of the week named after a mythological Roman god

George Bernard Shaw—Only person to have won both a Nobel Prize and an Oscar, one in 1925 in literature and the other in 1938 for the screenplay *Pygmalion*

3—Only positive whole number that is the sum of the 2 positive whole numbers immediately preceding it

2—Only even prime number

U Thant—Of the secretaries-general of the U.N., only one with one name since the *U* with his name is a title of respect, with a meaning similar to *Mister*

Van Cliburn—Only classical musician ever honored with a New York City ticker-tape parade, in 1958 after winning a Tchaikovsky Competition in Moscow

Giuseppe Verdi—Italian composer whose final opera and only true comedy is *Falstaff*

Vito Corleone—Only role for which 2 performers have won Academy Awards: Marlon Brando as Best Actor in *The Godfather* and Robert De Niro as Best Supporting Actor in *The Godfather Part II*

Vulcan—Only major Roman god who was physically imperfect—he was the son of Jupiter and Juno, and some say he was born lame and thrown into the sea by his mother

Mary Edwards Walker—First female surgeon in the U.S. Army, and the first and only woman ever to receive the Medal of Honor, awarded after she spent 4 months in a Confederate prison

****Westminster Abbey honorees T.S. Eliot and Henry James both became British subjects.

LONELYs

Pop-rock singer/songwriter/guitarist known for his 1960 hit "Only The Lonely (Know the Way I Feel)"
Answer: Roy Orbison.

Paul Anka—Ottawa-born Canadian singer known for the 1959 hit "Lonely Boy"
The Beatles—Singing group known for their *Sgt. Pepper's Lonely Hearts Club Band*
Ray Bradbury—Acclaimed science fiction author who late in his career wrote the hard-boiled detective novel *Death Is a Lonely Business*, published over three decades after his *Martian Chronicles*
Benjamin Britten—British composer whose central operatic character, fisherman Peter Grimes, goes mad because of the desperate and lonely circumstances of his life
Lord Byron*—British poet who wrote the lines: "There is a pleasure in the pathless woods, / There is rapture on the lonely shore . . . / I love not man the less, but Nature more" in his *Childe Harold's Pilgrimage*
Joseph Conrad—Author who wrote the line "The ship, a fragment detached from the earth, went on lonely and swift like a small planet" in *The Nigger of the Narcissus*
Cuba—Country from which people are fleeing in J. Joaquin Fraxedas's novel *The Lonely Crossing of Juan Cabrera*
Don Giovanni—Mozart opera in which the title character meets Donna Elvira, his old flame, on a lonely road near Seville in Scene 2
"Eleanor Rigby"—Beatles' song that includes the line, "All the lonely people, where do they all belong?"
Harlow—1965 film whose theme song is "Lonely Girl" sung by Bobby Vinton
"Heartbreak Hotel"—Elvis Presley song including the lines: "I found a new place to dwell / Well, it's down at the end of lonely street / At _____ Hotel"
Ernest Hemingway—Writer whose short story "A Clean, Well-Lighted Place" features a lonely, drunken old man, and whose *Islands in the Stream* features a lonely painter
Edward Hopper—20th-century American artist known for his stark, realistic paintings of New York City and New England, often featuring lonely, isolated individuals, as in the painting *Nighthawks*
In a Lonely Place—1950 film featuring Humphrey Bogart as Dixon Steele, a Hollywood screenwriter
Janet Jackson—Gary, Indiana-born singer known for 1998's hit "I Get Lonely"
James Weldon Johnson—Poet who wrote the lines: "And God stepped out on space, / And He looked around and said, / 'I'm lonely / I'll make me a world'" in his poem "The Creation"
Louis L'Amour—Master of the modern western novel, author of *The Lonely Men* and *The Lonesome Gods*
Lonely Are the Brave—1962 Western starring Kirk Douglas and Gena Rowlands
Lonelyhearts—Having to do with single people who are looking for companionship, as in a column in the newspaper
Lonesome—Having a lonely feeling, as in the title of Larry McMurtry's book _____ *Dove*

*The *Byronic hero* is lonely, rebellious, and brooding.

Long Distance Runner—Words completing the title of the 1962 film *The Loneliness of the* _____, based on a short story by Alan Sillitoe

John Masefield—British poet who wrote the lines: "I must down to the seas again, to the lonely sea and the sky, / And all I ask is a tall ship and a star to steer her by" in his poem "Sea Fever"

John D. MacDonald—Author who wrote *The Lonely Silver Rain*, featuring Travis McGee living on a Florida houseboat

Carson McCullers—Columbus, Georgia, author who wrote *The Heart Is a Lonely Hunter*

Miss Lonelyhearts—Nathanael West's 1933 novel about a man who gets sick from the strain of writing an "advice to the lovelorn" column and is finally murdered by one of the men he tries to help

"Mrs. Robinson"—Paul Simon song that includes the lines: "Where have you gone, Joe DiMaggio? / Our nation turns its lonely eyes to you"

Only the Lonely—Title of a biography of Roy Orbison, a stage musical, and a 1991 film starring John Candy, Maureen O'Hara, and Ally Sheedy

Philip Carey—Club-footed hero who overcomes a lonely childhood to become a doctor in W. Somerset Maugham's *Of Human Bondage*

Mickey Spillane—Author whose novel *One Lonely Night* features detective Mike Hammer

Alfred, Lord Tennyson—British poet of "The Eagle," which includes these lines: "He clasps the crag with crooked hands; / Close to the sun in lonely lands, / Ringed with the azure world, he stands"

J.R.R. Tolkien—Author whose Lonely Mountain is a Dwarven stronghold located northeast of Rhovanion

The Twilight Zone—Rod Serling's science fiction series whose story *The Lonely* is about a man on a prison asteroid who falls in love with a feminine android

Bobby Vinton—Singer known for his "There! I've Said It Again" and "Mr. Lonely," No. 1 hits in 1964

Walt Whitman—19th-century poet named in Allen Ginsberg's line: "I saw you, _____, childless, lonely old grubber, porking among the meats in the refrigerator and eying the grocery boys," in the poem "A Supermarket in California"

William Wordsworth—British poet who wrote "I Wandered Lonely as a Cloud"

Wuthering Heights—Novel featuring Heathcliff as a disruptive influence in the Earnshaw's lonely moorland home

U.S. GEOGRAPHY

Folk singer known for his song having the following lines: "This land is your land, / This land is my land, / From California / To the New York Island, / From the redwood forest, / To the Gulf Stream waters, / This land was made for you and me"
Answer: Woodrow Wilson "Woody" Guthrie (song is titled "This Land Is Your Land").

STATES AND THEIR CAPITALS

Alabama—Montgomery
Alaska—Juneau
Arizona—Phoenix
Arkansas—Little Rock
California—Sacramento
Colorado—Denver
Connecticut—Hartford
Delaware—Dover
Florida—Tallahassee
Georgia—Atlanta
Hawaii—Honolulu
Idaho—Boise
Illinois—Springfield
Indiana—Indianapolis
Iowa—Des Moines
Kansas—Topeka
Kentucky—Frankfort
Louisiana—Baton Rouge
Maine—Augusta
Maryland—Annapolis
Massachusetts—Boston
Michigan—Lansing
Minnesota—St. Paul
Mississippi—Jackson
Missouri—Jefferson City
Montana—Helena
Nebraska—Lincoln
Nevada—Carson City
New Hampshire—Concord
New Jersey—Trenton
New Mexico—Santa Fe
New York—Albany
North Carolina—Raleigh
North Dakota—Bismarck
Ohio—Columbus
Oklahoma—Oklahoma City
Oregon—Salem
Pennsylvania—Harrisburg
Rhode Island—Providence
South Carolina—Columbia
South Dakota—Pierre
Tennessee—Nashville
Texas—Austin
Utah—Salt Lake City
Vermont—Montpelier
Virginia—Richmond
Washington—Olympia
West Virginia—Charleston
Wisconsin—Madison
Wyoming—Cheyenne

STATES AND THEIR NICKNAMES

Alabama—Cotton State; Cornucopia of the South; Heart of the Deep South; Heart of Dixie; Star of the South; Yellowhammer State
Alaska—Arctic Treasureland; Gibraltar of the North; Great Land; Land of the Midnight Sun; Land Where the Summer Sun Never Sets; The Last Frontier
Arizona—Apache State; Aztec State; Grand Canyon State; Italy of America; Jewel in the West; Sunset State; Valentine State (February 14, 1912)
Arkansas—Bear State; Bowie State; Hot Water State; Land of Majestic Beauty; Land of Opportunity; Nation's Cool Green Paradise; Wonder State
California—Cornucopia of the World; Eureka State; El Dorado State; Gateway to the Pacific; Golden State; Sunshine Empire; Sunshine State; Wine Land of America
Colorado—Centennial State (1876); Highest State; Land of Contrasts; Rocky Mountain Empire; Silver State; Ski Country U.S.A.; Switzerland of America; Top of the Mountain State
Connecticut—Arsenal of the Nation; Blue Law State; Brownstone State; Constitution State; Insurance State; Land of Steady Habits; Nutmeg State; Provision State
Delaware—Blue Hen State; Diamond State; First State; New Sweden; State that Started a Nation; Uncle Sam's Pocket Handkerchief
Florida—Alligator State; Everglade State; Gulf State; Land of Sunshine and Flowers; Orange State; Peninsula State; Sunshine State

Georgia—Buzzard State; Cracker State; Empire State of the South; Goober State; Land of Adventure; Land of Peanuts, Pecans, and Peaches; Peach State; Yankee Land of the South

Hawaii—Aloha State; Crossroads of the Pacific; Gateway to the Orient (Pacific); 50th State of Enchantment; Gem (Paradise, Playground) of the Pacific; Island State

Idaho—Gem of the Mountains; Gem State; Panhandle State; Spud State; State of Shining Mountains

Illinois—Corn Belt State; Egypt Land; Garden of the West; Heart (Hub) of the Nation; Land of Lincoln; Prairie State; Tall State

Indiana—Center of the Commercial Universe; Crossroads of America; Hoosier State; Peerless State; State of Surprises

Iowa—Breadbasket of the Nation; Corn State; Food Market of the World; Hawkeye State; Land of the Rolling Prairie; Land Where the Tall Corn Grows

Kansas—Battleground of Freedom; Cyclone State; Breadbasket of America; Garden of the West; Jayhawker State; Midway U.S.A.; Salt of the Earth; Sunflower State; Wheat State

Kentucky—Bluegrass State; Corncracker State; Dark and Bloody Ground State; Hemp State; Pioneer Commonwealth; Tobacco State

Louisiana—Bayou State; Child of the Mississippi River; Creole State; Holland of America; Magnolia State; Nature's Cornucopia; Pelican State; Sportsman's Paradise; Sugar State

Maine—Angler's Paradise; Border State; Lobsterland; Lumber State; Pine Tree State; Polar Star State; Vacationland

Maryland—America in Miniature; Cockade State; Free State; Monumental State; Old Line State; Oyster State; Queen State; Star-Spangled Banner State; Terrapin State

Massachusetts—Baked Bean State; Bay State; Birthplace of American Freedom; Custodian of the Nation's Heritage; Hub of the Universe; Old Colony State; Puritan State

Michigan—Automobile State; Great Lake State; Lady of the Lakes; Peninsula State; Wolverine State; Wonderland of 11,000 Lakes

Minnesota—Bread and Butter State; Gopher State; Land of 10,000 Lakes; Land of Sky-Blue Waters; New England of the West; North Star State

Mississippi—Bayou State; Border-Eagle State; Gateway to the Southland; Hospitality State; Magnolia State; Mud-Cat State; Tadpole State

Missouri—Center State; Gateway to the West; Heartland of Hospitality; Iron Mountain State; Mother of the West; Pennsylvania of the West; Show Me State

Montana—Big Sky (Ski) Country; Bonanza State; Land of Enchantment; Land of Shining Mountains; Land of Scenic Splendor; Treasure State

Nebraska—Antelope State; Beef State; Cornhusker State; Cowboy Country; Land of the Pioneer; Land Where the West Begins; Tall Corn State; Tree Planters State

Nevada—Battle-Born State; Entertainment Capital of the World; Sagebrush State; Silver State; State Where Man and Nature Gamble

New Hampshire—Granite State; Land of Peace and Beauty; Mother of Rivers; Old Man of the Mountain State; White Mountain State; Yankee Playground

New Jersey—Armpit of the Nation; Cockpit of History (of the Revolution); Crossroads State; Garden State; Hub of Commerce; Industrial Park State; Pathway of the Revolution; Workshop of the Nation

New Mexico—Cactus State; Land of Enchantment; Space Age Research Center for the Free World; Sunshine State; Unspoiled Empire

New York—Apple State; Empire State; Excelsior State; Knickerbocker State; Nation's Showcase; Seat of Empire

North Carolina—Graveyard of the Atlantic; First in Freedom; Ireland of America; Land of Beginnings; Old North State; Tar Heel State; Year-Round Mid-South

North Dakota—Flickertail State; Gateway to the Big Country; Land of the Dakotas; Land of Theodore Roosevelt and General Custer; Sioux State

Ohio—Buckeye State; Gateway to the Northwest Territory; Modern Mother of Presidents; Oldest State West of the Thirteen Original Colonies

Oklahoma—Boomer State; Buckle of the Sunbelt; Heart of Cow Country; Land of the Red Men; Sooner State

Oregon—Beaver State; End of the Trail; Land of Exciting Contrasts; Pacific Wonderland; Sunset State; Web-foot State

Pennsylvania—Birthplace of a Nation; Coal State; Keystone State; Quaker State; State Where American Industry Began; Workshop of the World

Rhode Island—American Venice; Land of Roger Williams; Little Rhody; Ocean State; Plantation State; Smallest State

South Carolina—Keystone of the South Atlantic Seaboard; Palmetto State; Swamp State; Wonderful Iodine State

South Dakota—Artesian State; Blizzard State; Coyote State; Land of Infinite Variety; Pheasant Capital of the World; Sunshine State

Tennessee—Big Bend State; Butternut State; Hog and Hominy State; Lion's Den State; Mother of Southwestern Statesmen; Volunteer State

Texas—Beef State; Blizzard State; Jumbo State; Lone Star State; State of the Confederacy; World Cotton Center

Utah—Beehive State; Deseret State; Honey State; Land of the Saints; Mormon State; Salt Lake State

Vermont—Beckoning State; Country with a Heritage; Green Mountain State; Land of Marble, Milk, and Honey; Ski State of the East

Virginia—Battlefield of the Civil War; Birthplace of 8 Presidents; Birthplace of the Nation; Cavalier State; Commonwealth; Mother of Presidents; Mother of States and Statesmen; Old Dominion

Washington—Chinook State; Clam State; Evergreen State; Gateway to Alaska and the Orient; State of Exciting Contrasts

West Virginia—Appalachian State; Free State; Fuel State; Glass Center of the World; Mountain State; Panhandle State; Switzerland of America

Wisconsin—America's Dairyland; Badger State; Cheese Capital of the Nation; Copper State; Land o' Lakes; Playground of the Middle West

Wyoming—Cowboy State; Equality State; Land of Cattle, Sheep, Song, and Story; Land of the Purple Sage; Sagebrush State; Sanctuary of Peace

STATE CAPITALS

1) Which 4 state capitals are named after U.S. Presidents?
Answer: Jefferson City, Missouri; Madison, Wisconsin; Jackson, Mississippi; and Lincoln, Nebraska.

2) Name the 4 state capitals that begin with the same letter as the first letter of their state.
Answer: Dover, Delaware; Honolulu, Hawaii; Indianapolis, Indiana; and Oklahoma City, Oklahoma.

3) Identify the 4 state capitals with the most letters in their names.
Answer: Jefferson City (Missouri); Salt Lake City (Utah); Indianapolis (Indiana); and Oklahoma City (Oklahoma).

4) Identify the 4 state capitals whose names include the word "city."
Answer: Jefferson City (Missouri); Carson City (Nevada); Oklahoma City (Oklahoma); and Salt Lake City (Utah).

(Listed alphabetically)
Albany, New York—Capital on the Hudson River nicknamed "Cradle of the Union" after Benjamin Franklin presented his plan to form a self-governing federation under the British crown at the Congress held there in 1754
Annapolis, Maryland—Capital on the Severn River that is the home of the U.S. Naval Academy
Atlanta, Georgia—Capital known as "The Dogwood City," the home of the High Museum of Art, the Carter Library, and the Martin Luther King Jr., tomb—during the Civil War, most of its buildings were burned
Augusta, Maine—Capital on the Kennebec River that replaced Portland as the capital in 1832
Austin, Texas—Capital on the Colorado River formerly named Waterloo and renamed after Stephen A. _____, the earliest leader of the state's independence movement
Baton Rouge, Louisiana—Capital on the east bank of the Mississippi River that derives its name from a red pole placed to mark the boundary between Indian and French territory—its name means "red stick" in French
Bismarck, North Dakota—Capital originally named Edwinton and renamed after a German chancellor in order to attract German capital to finance the building of the Northern Pacific Railway
Boise, Idaho—Capital nicknamed "The City of Trees" that derives its name from the French for "wooded river"
Boston, Massachusetts—Capital founded in 1630 by English Puritans at the mouth of the Charles and Mystic rivers, named after an English town in Lincolnshire and nicknamed "The Cradle of Liberty"
Carson City, Nevada—Capital named after a famous frontier scout, a notorious Wild West town during the silver boom in the 1800s
Charleston, West Virginia—Capital at the confluence of the Elk and Kanawha rivers in a state that was part of Virginia until it voted against secession in 1861
Cheyenne, Wyoming—Capital known for its annual "Frontier Days" festival, the capital of he first state to allow women to vote
Columbia, South Carolina—Capital named after an explorer and located on the Congaree River, just below the junction of the Broad and Saluda rivers
Columbus, Ohio—Capital named after an explorer and located at the junction of the Olentangy and Scioto rivers
Concord, New Hampshire—New England capital first named Penacook, or Penny Cook—its present name may have been chosen to mark a "peaceful" agreement between 2 factions
Denver, Colorado—Capital on the South Platte River and Cherry Creek formerly called Auraria, then, following its merger with 2 other towns, renamed after a governor of the territory, the home of a U.S. mint
Des Moines, Iowa—Capital that takes its name from the French derivative of the Indian name meaning "river of the mounds"—its name may also be derived from the name meaning "river of the monks"

Dover, Delaware—Capital on the St. Jones River nicknamed "The First City of the First State," so called because its state was the first of the original 13 to ratify the U.S. Constitution

Frankfort, Kentucky—Capital called "The Bluegrass Capital," the site of Daniel Boone's grave

Harrisburg, Pennsylvania—Capital, nicknamed "Heart of the Commonwealth," that was named after an English Quaker whose son founded the city where his father had operated a ferry across the river

Hartford, Connecticut—Capital on the Connecticut River known as "The Insurance City, the site of the Mark Twain House and the Wadsworth Athenaeum

Helena, Montana—Capital formerly called "Last Chance Gulch" and now claiming to have more millionaires per capita than any other U.S. city

Honolulu, Hawaii—Capital called "The Crossroads of the Pacific," the site of the Iolani Palace, the only royal palace in the U.S.

Indianapolis, Indiana—Capital that considers itself to be the amateur sports capital of the U.S.—it is also the site of the National Track and Field Hall of Fame and Benjamin Harrison's Memorial Home

Jackson, Mississippi—Capital on the Pearl River nicknamed "Crossroads of the South," first called LeFleur's Bluff, then renamed for a U.S. President in 1792

Jefferson City, Missouri—Capital on the Missouri River named after a U.S. President and having murals by Thomas Hart Benton in its statehouse

Juneau, Alaska—Capital where miners landed on their way to search for Northern gold, in area the largest capital in the U.S.

Lansing, Michigan—Capital that lies at the junction of the Grand and Red Cedar rivers and was named by settlers after a New York village

Lincoln, Nebraska—Capital named after a U.S. President and known as "The Cornhusker Capital City," the site of the William Jennings Bryan Home

Little Rock, Arkansas—Capital on the Arkansas River that has a capitol patterned after the U.S. Capitol—this city is also known as "The City of Three Capitols"

Madison, Wisconsin—Only capital built on an isthmus and located between Lakes Monona and Mendota and named after a U.S. President

Montgomery, Alabama—Capital nicknamed "The Cradle of the Confederacy," where Southerners established the Confederate States of America in 1861

Montpelier, Vermont—New England capital on the Winooski River that is the least populous state capital

Nashville, Tennessee—Capital called "Music City, U.S.A.," the site of the Country Music Hall of Fame and Museum and the Grand Ole Opry House

Oklahoma City, Oklahoma—Capital on the North Canadian River that is known for its National Softball Hall of Fame, its National Cowboy Hall of Fame and Western Heritage Center, and the statue called "The Cowboy"

Olympia, Washington—Capital located on the southern point of Puget Sound

Phoenix, Arizona—Capital that is one of the fastest growing urban areas in the U.S. and is named for a mythological bird

Pierre, South Dakota—Capital bearing the first name of a French fur trader, a name translated as "Peter" in English

Providence, Rhode Island—Capital so named by Roger Williams in 1636 because he believed God had guided him there

Raleigh, North Carolina—Capital named after the English soldier and explorer who named an entire region "Virginia" in honor of Elizabeth, "The Virgin Queen"

Richmond, Virginia—Capital where Patrick Henry gave his 1775 "liberty or death" speech in Saint John's Episcopal Church and probably named after an English town on the Thames

Sacramento, California—Capital that was known in the 1860s as the last point on the Pony Express Line

St. Paul, Minnesota—Capital on the north and south banks of the Mississippi River originally named Pig's Eye because the city's founder, Pierre Parrant, was so nicknamed

Salem, Oregon—Capital that shares its name with a city in Massachusetts—the English Puritans derived this city's name from a Hebrew name taken to mean "peace"

Salt Lake City, Utah—Capital where the headquarters of the Church of Jesus Christ of Latter Day Saints and the Pioneer Trail State Park are located with its "This Is the Place" monument

Santa Fe, New Mexico—Capital that was settled by the Spaniards in 1609 and has been a seat of government longer than any other U.S. capital city

Springfield, Illinois—Capital in which Abraham Lincoln lived from 1837 to 1861

Tallahassee, Florida—Only capital east of the Mississippi that didn't fall to the Union during the Civil War

Topeka, Kansas—Capital in which the Menninger Foundation, a noted psychiatric training center, is located

Trenton, New Jersey—Capital on the east bank of the Delaware River that served as the U.S. capital in 1784—its motto is, "_____ Makes—the World Takes"

ONLYS IN U.S. GEOGRAPHY

Only state without a national park
Answer: Delaware.

1) Name the only 3 state capitals located on the Missouri River.
Answer: Bismarck (North Dakota), Pierre (South Dakota), and Jefferson City (Missouri).

2) Name the only 2 state capitals on the Mississippi River.
Answer: St. Paul (Minnesota) and Baton Rouge (Louisiana).

3) Identify the only 2 state capitals whose names begin and end with the letter *A*.
Answer: Atlanta (Georgia) and Augusta (Maine).

Acadia—Only national park located in New England, in Maine
Alaska—Only state touching 2 oceans
Aleutian Islands—Lengthy group of islands stretching west from the tip of the Alaskan Peninsula where the only chain of active volcanoes in the U.S. is located
Arkansas—Only state with a major diamond mine opened to the public, located in Crater of the Diamonds State Park near Murfreesboro
Bronx—Only one of New York City's 5 boroughs that is part of the mainland
Crater Lake—Only national park located in Oregon
Delaware—Only state in which counties are divided into hundreds
Enterprise—Only town with a monument to an insect—the Boll Weevil Monument in Alabama
Florida—Only state that touches the Atlantic Ocean and the Gulf of Mexico
Georgia—Only state bordering North Carolina and South Carolina
Hawaii—Only state with a statewide, unified public school system
Hot Springs—Only U.S. city, one in Arkansas, that has almost all of a national park within its city limits
Indianapolis—Only state capital whose one-word name includes the state's name
Iolani Palace—Only royal palace used as an official residence by a reigning monarch in the U.S., located in Honolulu
Iowa—Only state whose name begins with 2 vowels
Juneau—Only state capital accessible only by plane or boat and not by outside roads
Louisiana—Only state that calls its counties "parishes"
Maine—Only state having a one-syllable name
Maryland*—Only state whose state bird bears the name of its major city
Michigan—Only state that touches 4 of the 5 Great Lakes
Mobile—Alabama's only port city
Montana—Only state on which 3 Canadian provinces border
Nevada—Only state that is located entirely in the Pacific time zone but doesn't border the Pacific Ocean
New Mexico—Only state named for another country
New York—Only state that touches the Atlantic Ocean and the Great Lakes
Petrified Forest—Only national park with the word *forest* in its name—it is located in Arizona

*The bird is the Baltimore Oriole.

Pierre (South Dakota)—Only state capital with a one-syllable name
Rhode Island—Only state whose name is derived from the Dutch language
Theodore Roosevelt—Only U.S. national park named after a U.S. President—it is located in North Dakota
Tallahassee—Only state capital whose name has 3 sets of double letters
Texas—Only state to have had 6 different national flags fly over it during 8 changes of sovereignty
Utah—State in which the only monument to a bird, a sea gull, which saved the Mormons from a cricket plague, is located in the capital
Vermont—Only New England state that does NOT border the Atlantic Ocean
Washington—Only state named after a U.S. President
Yellowstone—Only National Park located in 3 states
New York—Only state named after a Duke
Hawaii—Only state that was once an independent monarchy
Maine—Only state bordered by a single state
Michigan—Only Great Lake located entirely in the U.S.
Hawaii—Only state lying south of the Tropic of Cancer
Louisiana—Only state bisected by the Mississippi River
Hawaii—Only state that lies outside of North America
Pierre (South Dakota)—Only state capital that does not share any letters with its state
Hawaii—Only state that grows both bananas and coffee
Florida—Only state that has the U.S. motto, "In God We Trust," as its state motto
Louisiana—Only state whose laws are based on France's Napoleonic Code
Montana—Only U.S. state bordering Alberta, Canada

WORLD GEOGRAPHY

Completion of the title of the popular computer geography game *Where in the World is Carmen ____?*
Answer: **Sandiego**.

NATIONS AND THEIR CAPITALS (Arranged by continent)
AFRICA
Algeria—Algiers
Angola—Luanda
Benin—Porto-Novo (official); Cotonou (de facto)
Botswana—Gaborone
Burkina Faso—Ouagadougou
Burundi—Bujumbura
Cameroon—Yaoundé
Cape Verde—Praia
Central African Republic—Bangui
Chad—N'Djamena
Comoros—Moroni
Congo, Republic of the—Brazzaville
Congo, Democratic Republic of—Kinshasha
Djibouti—Djibouti
Egypt—Cairo
Equatorial Guinea—Malabo
Eritrea—Asmara
Ethiopia—Addis Ababa
Gabon—Libreville
The Gambia—Banjul
Ghana—Accra
Guinea—Conakry
Guinea-Bissau—Bissau
Ivory Coast (Côte d'Ivoire)—Yamoussoukro (official); Abidjan (administrative)
Kenya—Nairobi
Lesotho—Maseru
Liberia—Monrovia
Libya—Tripoli
Madagascar—Antananarivo
Malawi—Lilongwe
Mali—Bamako
Mauritania—Nouakchott
Mauritius—Port Louis
Morocco—Rabat
Mozambique—Maputo
Namibia—Windhoek
Niger—Niamey
Nigeria—Abuja
Rwanda—Kigali
São Tomé and Príncipe—São Tomé
Senegal—Dakar
Seychelles—Victoria
Sierra Leone—Freetown
Somalia—Mogadishu
South Africa—Cape Town (legislative); Pretoria* (administrative); Bloemfontein (judicial)
Sudan—Khartoum
Swaziland—Mbabane (administrative); Lobamba (legislative)
Tanzania—Dodoma**
Togo—Lomé
Tunisia—Tunis
Uganda—Kampala
Zambia—Lusaka
Zimbabwe—Harare

*It is expected to be renamed Tshwane. **The transition from Dar es Salaam is still in progress.

ASIA
Afghanistan—Kabul
Armenia—Yerevan
Azerbaijan (Asian)—Baku
Bahrain—Manama
Bangladesh—Dhaka (Dacca)
Bhutan—Thimphu
Brunei—Bandar Seri Begawan
Cambodia (Kampuchea)—Phnom Penh
China, People's Republic of—Beijing (Peking)
   Hong Kong—Victoria
   Macau (Macao)—Macau (Macao)
Cyprus—Nicosia
East Timor—Dili
Egypt (Asian)—Cairo
Georgia (Asian)—Tbilisi
India—New Delhi
Indonesia—Jakarta
Iran—Teheran
Iraq—Baghdad
Israel—Jerusalem*

*Most nations maintain their embassies in Tel Aviv.

Japan—Tokyo
Jordan—Amman
Kazakhstan (Asian)—Astana
Korea, North—Pyongyang
Korea, South—Seoul
Kuwait—Kuwait
Kyrgyzstan—Bishkek
Laos—Vientiane
Lebanon—Beirut
Malaysia—Kuala Lumpur
Maldives—Male
Mongolia—Ulan Bator (Ulaanbaator)
Myanmar (Burma)—Yangon (Rangoon)
Nepal—Kathmandu
Oman—Muscat
Pakistan—Islamabad
Philippines—Manila
Qatar—Doha
Russia (Asian)—Moscow
Saudi Arabia—Riyadh
Singapore—Singapore
Sri Lanka—Colombo
Syria—Damascus
Taiwan (Republic of China)—Taipei
Tajikistan—Dushanbe
Thailand—Bangkok
Turkey (Asian)—Ankara
Turkmenistan—Ashgabat
United Arab Emirates—Abu Dhabi
Uzbekistan—Tashkent
Vietnam—Hanoi
Yemen—Sana

EUROPE
Albania—Tirana (Tiranë)
Andorra—Andorra la Vella
Austria—Vienna
Azerbaijan (European)—Baku
Belarus—Minsk
Belgium—Brussels
Bosnia-Herzegovina—Sarajevo
Bulgaria—Sofia
Croatia—Zagreb
Czech Republic—Prague
Denmark—Copenhagen
OUTLYING TERRITORIES
Faeroe Islands—Thorshavn
Greenland (Kalaallit Nunaat)—Nuuk
Estonia—Tallinn
Finland—Helsinki
France—Paris
OVERSEAS DEPARTMENTS AND TERRITORIES
Corsica—Ajaccio
French Guiana (Guyane)—Cayenne
Guadeloupe—Basse-Terre
Martinique—Fort-de-France
Réunion—Saint-Denis
Mayotte—Mamoutzou
St. Pierre and Miquelon—St. Pierre
French Polynesia—Papeete (on Tahiti)
New Caledonia—Nouméa
Wallis and Futuna Islands—Mata Uta (on Uvéa)
Georgia (European)—Tbilisi
Germany—Berlin
Greece—Athens
Hungary—Budapest
Iceland—Reykjavik
Ireland—Dublin
Italy—Rome
ITALIAN ISLANDS
Sardinia—Cagliari
Sicily—Palermo
Kazakhstan (European)—Astana
Latvia—Riga
Liechtenstein—Vaduz
Lithuania—Vilnius
Luxembourg—Luxembourg
Macedonia—Skopje
Malta—Valletta
Moldova—Chisinau
Monaco—Monaco
Netherlands (Holland)—Amsterdam; The Hague (seat of government)
DEPENDENCIES
Netherlands Antilles—Willemstad, Curaçao
Aruba—Oranjestad
Norway—Oslo
Poland—Warsaw
Portugal—Lisbon
Romania—Bucharest
Russia (European)—Moscow
San Marino—San Marino
Slovakia—Bratislava
Slovenia—Ljubljana
Spain—Madrid
Sweden—Stockholm
Switzerland—Bern
Turkey (European)—Ankara
Ukraine—Kiev

United Kingdom of Great Britain and Northern Ireland—London
   England—London
   Northern Ireland—Belfast
   Scotland—Edinburgh
   Wales—Cardiff
   DEPENDENCIES OF THE UNITED KINGDOM
   Anguilla—The Valley
   Bermuda—Hamilton
   British Virgin Islands—Road Town
   Cayman Islands—Georgetown
   Channel Islands
      Jersey—St. Helier
      Guernsey—St. Peter Port
   Falkland Islands—Stanley
   Gibraltar—Gibraltar
   Isle of Man—Douglas
   Montserrat—Plymouth
   Pitcairn Island—Adamstown
   Saint Helena—Jamestown
   Turks and Caicos Islands—Grand Turk
Vatican City—
Serbia and Montenegro—Belgrade

NORTH AMERICA
Antigua and Barbuda—St. John's
Bahamas—Nassau
Barbados—Bridgetown
Belize—Belmopan
Canada—Ottawa
   PROVINCES AND TERRITORIES
   Alberta—Edmonton
   British Columbia—Victoria
   Manitoba—Winnipeg
   New Brunswick—Fredericton
   Newfoundland—St. John's
   Nova Scotia—Halifax
   Ontario—Toronto
   Prince Edward Island—Charlottetown
   Quebec—Quebec
   Saskatchewan—Regina
   Nunavut—Iqaluit
   Northwest Territories—Yellowknife
   Yukon Territory—Whitehorse
Costa Rica—San José
Cuba—Havana
Dominica—Roseau
Dominican Republic—Santo Domingo
El Salvador—San Salvador
Grenada—St. George's
Guatemala—Guatemala City
Haiti—Port-au-Prince
Honduras—Tegucigalpa
Jamaica—Kingston
Mexico—Mexico City
Nicaragua—Managua
Panama—Panama City
St. Kitts and Nevis—Basseterre
St. Lucia—Castries
St. Vincent and the Grenadines—Kingstown
Trinidad and Tobago—Port-of-Spain
United States—Washington, D.C.
   TERRITORIES AND DEPENDENCIES
   American Samoa—Pago Pago
   Guam—Agana
   Northern Mariana Islands—Saipan
   Puerto Rico—San Juan
   Virgin Islands—Charlotte Amalie

SOUTH AMERICA
Argentina—Buenos Aires
Bolivia—La Paz; Sucre
Brazil—Brasília
Chile—Santiago
Colombia—Bogotá
Ecuador—Quito
Guyana—Georgetown
Paraguay—Asunción
Peru—Lima
Suriname—Paramaribo
Uruguay—Montevideo
Venezuela—Caracas

OCEANIA'S INDEPENDENT COUNTRIES
Australia—Canberra
   STATES/TERRITORIES
   Capital Territory—Canberra
   New South Wales—Sydney
   Northern Territory—Darwin
   Queensland—Brisbane
   South Australia—Adelaide
   Tasmania—Hobart
   Victoria—Melbourne
   Western Australia—Perth
Fiji—Suva
Kiribati—Tarawa
Marshall Islands—Majuro
Micronesia, Federated States of—Palikir
Nauru—Yaren
New Zealand—Wellington
Palau—Koror
Papua New Guinea—Port Moresby
Samoa—Apia
Solomon Islands—Honiara
Tonga—Nukualofa
Tuvalu—Fongafle (on Funafuti Island)*
Vanuatu (New Hebrides)—Vila

*Funafuti is sometimes listed as the capital.

WORLD GEOGRAPHY

CONTINENTS
(Listed from largest to smallest)

1) **Asia**
2) **Africa**
3) **North America**
4) **South America**
5) **Antarctica**
6) **Europe**
7) **Australia**

SEVEN SUMMITS OF THE WORLD

CONTINENT—SUMMIT and LOCATION
Asia—Mount Everest, 29,035 feet, in the Himalayas on Nepal-Tibet border
South America—Mount Aconcagua, 22,834 feet, in the Andes in Argentina
North America—Mount McKinley, 20,231 feet, in the Alaska Range in Alaska
Africa—Mount Kilimanjaro, 19,563 feet, in Tanzania
Europe—Mount Elbrus, 18,481 feet, in the Caucasus Mountains in Russia
Antarctica—Vinson Massif, 16,066 feet, in the Sentinel Range of the Ellsworth Mountains in Antarctica
Australia*—Mount Kosciusko, 7,310 feet—in the Australian Alps in New South Wales
*Mount Carstensz (Pyramid, also called Puncak Jaya and Djaja Peak) at 16,502 feet in the Sudirman Range in Irian Jaya, Indonesia, is the highest in Australasia/Oceania.

LONGEST RIVERS BY CONTINENT

North America—Mississippi
South America—Amazon
Europe—Volga
Africa—Nile
Asia—Yangtze or Chang Jiang
Australia—Darling

LARGEST COUNTRIES BY CONTINENT

North America—Canada
South America—Brazil
Europe—Russia
Africa—Sudan
Asia—Russia
Australia—Australia

15 LARGEST COUNTRIES IN AREA
(Listed from largest to smallest in square miles*)

1) **Russia** (6.6 million)
2) **Canada** (3.9 million)
3) **China** (3.6 million)
4) **United States** (3.5 million)
5) **Brazil** (3.2 million)
6) **Australia** (2.9 million)
7) **India** (1.3 million)
8) **Argentina** (1.1 million)
9) **Kazakhstan** (1,050,000)
10) **Sudan** (967,000)
11) **Algeria** (919,000)
12) **Democratic Republic of the Congo** (905,000)
13) **Saudi Arabia** (830,000)
14) **Mexico** (761,000)
15) **Indonesia** (741,000)

*Sources do not agree on total area.

ONLYS IN WORLD GEOGRAPHY

Only country that is also a continent
Answer: Australia.

1) Identify the only 2 Canadian provinces whose names begin and end in the same letter.
Answer: Alberta and Ontario.

2) Identify the only 2 independent South American countries named after famous men.
Answer: Bolivia and Colombia (after Simón Bolívar and Christopher Columbus).

3) Identify the only 2 independent countries in the Western Hemisphere where French is an official language.
Answer: Canada and Haiti.

4) Identify the only 2 South American countries that do not border Brazil.
Answer: Chile and Ecuador.

5) Identify the only 2 rivers in Africa that are longer than the Niger.
Answer: Nile and Congo.

Andorra*—Only country that was until 1993 a coprincipality, governed by the bishop of Urgel, Spain, and the president of France
Antarctica—Only continent through which the International Date Line passes
Bolivia—Only South American country with 2 capitals, La Paz and Sucre
British Columbia—Only Canadian province that borders both Alaska and the lower 48 states—it is also the only one that borders the Pacific Ocean
Congo River—Only major river that flows both north and south of the equator—it is the world's 5th longest river and is second to the Amazon in the volume of water it carries
Cyprus—Only country with a map of the country depicted on its national flag
French Guiana—Only region in South America that is an overseas department of France
Guatemala—Only Central American country that borders 4 other countries
Halifax (Nova Scotia)—Only Canadian capital whose name ends in an -x
Hormuz—Strait that is the Persian Gulf's only outlet to the sea
Istanbul (Turkey)—Only major city located on 2 continents—Asia and Europe—on both sides of the Bosporus
K2—Only mountain known by a single letter and number—it is the world's 2nd highest and is also known as Mount Godwin Austen and Dapsang
Laos—Of the 3 countries that were part of French Indochina and to which France granted self-government after WWII, only one that is landlocked
Libya—Only country whose national flag is a single plain color—green
Luxembourg—Only country in which the head of state is a grand duke (or duchess)
Mauritius—Only island country in which the extinct flightless dodo bird is believed to have ever lived
Monrovia (Liberia)—Only foreign capital named after a U.S. President

*In 1993, Andorra adopted its first constitution, making its elected officials responsible for governing although the "princes," or former co-rulers, still must approve certain treaties and other matters.

Montreal—North American city that lies on an island and is the only city on the continent built around a mountain
Nepal—Only country whose flag is neither rectangular nor square, one consisting of 2 crimson triangular pennants one above the other
Nepal—Only country whose official religion is Hinduism
Ontario—Only Canadian province that touches 4 of the 5 Great Lakes
Panama—Only Central American country that borders just one other Central American country and one other South American country
Prince Edward Island—Only Canadian province that is entirely separated from the North American mainland
Prince Edward Island—Only national park in Canada that shares its name with a province
Quebec—Canadian city that is the only preserved and maintained walled city in North America
Rwanda**—Only country whose flag once featured a single letter—an *R*
Surinam—Only South American country whose official language is Dutch
Switzerland—Only U.N. country with a square flag, one with a white cross on a red background
Taiwan (Nationalist China)—Only country officially expelled from the U.N., in 1971
Thailand—Only nation in Southeast Asia that has never been ruled by a Western power
Toronto—Only Canadian capital on the shore of one of the Great Lakes
United States—Only country whose national anthem begins with a question
Vatican City—Only non-U.N. country with a square flag, one featuring St. Peter's keys supporting a papal crown
Venezuela***—Only South American country named for an Italian city
Vesuvius—Only active volcano on the mainland of Europe

**This flag now has 3 horizontal stripes—blue, yellow, and green—and features a sun. ***Named for the city of Venice.

COUNTRIES BORDERING ONLY ONE OTHER COUNTRY
United States—Only country Canada borders
Senegal—Only country Gambia borders
South Africa—Only country Lesotho borders
France—Only country Monaco borders
Spain—Only country Portugal borders
Saudi Arabia—Only country Qatar borders
Italy—Only country San Marino borders
North Korea—Only country South Korea borders
Italy—Only country Vatican City borders

TOPONYMS
(Names Derived from a Place or Region)

Author who wrote the book *Oh, the Places You'll Go!*
Answer: Dr. Seuss.

U.S. RELATED
Americium—Man-made radioactive element whose atomic number is 95, after America by analogy with Europium, the corresponding rare earth element
Baltimore chop—High bouncing batted ball in baseball that becomes a hit, after the home of the Orioles
Baltimore clipper—Small clipper ship, after the Maryland city where it was first made in its Chesapeake Bay in the 1800s
Baltimore oriole—Bird with an orange body and black markings on its head, wings, and tail, after the English lord who was the colonial proprietor of Maryland, so named for having the colors of his coat of arms
Berkelium—Man-made radioactive element whose atomic number is 97, after a California city by analogy with terbium, an element named for the Swedish town of Ytterby
Boston arm—Battery-powered artificial arm, after the New England capital where it was first developed
Boston terrier—Breed of small dog with a smooth coat of black with white markings, after a New England capital city
Bikini—2-piece bathing suit, after an atoll in the Marshall Islands suggestive of the suit's eruptive effect on the beholder
Californium—Man-made radioactive element whose atomic number is 98, after the state of California
Charleston—Fast ballroom dance in 4/4 time popular in the 1920s, after a seaport in South Carolina
Chautauqua—Adult educational movement offering lectures, concerts, and other cultural activities, after the resort village in New York where the movement began
Chesapeake Bay Retriever—One of the 5 recognized breeds of retrievers, after a large bay that is an arm of the Atlantic Ocean
Chinook—Warm, dry wind blowing over the Rocky Mountains, after a North American Indian tribe
Conestoga wagon—Heavy covered wagon, after a region in Pennsylvania where wagons of this type were made
Denver boot—Metal clamp locked in place on the wheel of an illegally-parked car to prevent it from moving, after a western city, one of the first to use the device
Gila monster—Venomous lizard, after a river in Arizona where this lizard can be found
Hollywood—U.S. film industry or its life-style, after the city where many film studios are located
Jimson weed*—Poisonous weed of the nightshade family, after a colonial Virginia town where British soldiers used this weed while stopping Bacon's Rebellion
Kodiak bear—Largest land carnivore or largest brown bear (also called Alaska brown bear), after an island in Alaska

*Alteration of *Jamestown weed*

Legionnaires' disease—Form of pneumonia caused by bacterial infection, after an American Legion convention held in a Philadelphia hotel

Louisville Slugger—Baseball bat, after the Kentucky city in which it was first crafted

Lyme disease—Acute inflammatory disease caused by a tick-borne virus, after a town in Connecticut

Mackinaw—Heavy, woolen cloth used to make blankets, after Mackinac Island, Michigan

Motown—1960s style of rhythm and blues with a strong, even beat, from the trade name for a company that published musical records and tapes, from "Motor Town," a nickname for Detroit

Quonset hut—Prefabricated building of corrugated metal, after a Naval Air Station in Rhode Island where the hut was first manufactured

Rhode Island Red—Breed of domestic chicken raised for its meat, after a small Atlantic coast state

Saratoga trunk—Large lady's trunk, after _____ Springs, a city in New York

Shasta daisy—Any of a variety of daisylike chrysanthemum, after a volcanic peak in California's Cascade Range where such flowers grow

Springfield rifle—Breechloading .30-caliber magazine-fed rifle adopted by the U.S. Army in 1903, after a town in Massachusetts where an armory was located

Stogy (stogie)—Cheap cigar, after *Conestoga*, a Pennsylvania-made wagon whose drivers liked to smoke cheap cigars

Texas leaguer—Fly ball in baseball that falls between the infield and outfield, after one of the minor leagues

Tularemia—Infectious disease caused by bacterium affecting rodents, especially wild rabbits and some birds, after Tulare, a county in California where it originated—also called rabbit fever

Tuxedo—Formal black dinner jacket for men, after a country club named for a village in New York where it was first worn

Virginia reel—Country dance, after Virginia, the state where it originated

FOOD AND DRINK IN THE U.S.

Baked Alaska—Dessert cake with ice cream and beaten egg whites browned in an oven, after the state of Alaska

Boston baked beans—Beans such as Navy ones baked for hours over low heat with salt pork, seasonings, and brown sugar, after a capital city where Puritan women prepared them every Saturday to be served on Sunday

Blue point—Small oyster, usually eaten raw, after a Long Island location where beds of such oysters originated

Boston cream pie—Two-layer cake with whipped cream or cream filling, after the New England capital where it was created

Bourbon—Whiskey, after a county in Kentucky

Brunswick stew—Stew of chicken, rabbit, or squirrel cooked with vegetables, after a county in Virginia

Key lime pie—Custardlike pie made with condensed milk, lime juice, eggs, and sugar, after Key West, a Florida city

Manhattan—Cocktail made of sweet vermouth, whiskey, and a dash of bitters, after a New York City borough

Monterey Jack—Semisoft white cheese, after a town in California

Parker House roll—Yeast-leavened roll, after a hotel in Boston where it was first served

Thousand Island dressing—Salad dressing of mayonnaise, catchup, and relishes, after a group of New York-Ontario islands in the St. Lawrence River

Waldorf salad—Salad with apples, celery, and nuts mixed with mayonnaise, after a hotel in New York City where it was first prepared

WORLD RELATED

Alpine hat—Red or green soft felt hat decorated with a feather, after the Alps where Swiss guides and others wear them

Alpine skiing—Downhill or slalom skiing, after a European mountain system

Australian crawl—Swimming stroke, after the country of Australia where it originated

Badminton—Court game originating in India, after the English estate of the Duke of Beaufort

Bangalore torpedo—Explosive device, after a city in India

Bollywood—Nickname of India's film industry, centered in Bombay

Carthusian—Member of a strict religious order founded at Chartreuse, France, after the Latin name for Chartreuse

Caucasian—Member of the white race, after people living in the Caucasus Mountains, a region between Asia and Europe

Cistercian—Member of a strict religious order, after Cistercium, now Cîteaux, France

Cologne—Perfumed toilet water, after a city in Germany

Conga—Latin American line dance, possibly after the Congo, its country of origin and associated with Cuba, where it was popularized

Damascus steel—Hard, flexible steel decorated with wavy lines, after the Syrian city in which it was made

Delft—Blue-and-white glazed pottery, after a city in the Netherlands

Dresden china—Fine porcelain produced in Meissen, after a German city near which it is made

Dumdum—Soft-nosed bullet, after an arsenal near Calcutta, India

Faience*—Opaquely glazed earthenware, resembling Majolica, after Faenza, Italy

Fiacre—Small carriage for hire, after the Hôtel de St. _____, in Paris, where such vehicles were first rented

Flamenco—Dance of gypsy origin in Andalusia, after the Spanish word for Flemish

Fleet Street—London press, after the street where many British newspapers were long headquartered

Gamboge—Gum resin or a yellow or a yellowish-orange color, from the Latin name of Cambodia (*cambugium, gambogium*), the former name of Kampuchea

Guinea—Former English gold coin, after a coastal region of Africa where the gold used to make it came

Havana cigar—Cigar, especially a fine quality one, after the capital of Cuba

Highland fling—Lively folk dance of the Highlands of Scotland

India ink**—Black permanent ink, formerly made chiefly in China and Japan

Indigo—Reddish blue, after a dyestuff first produced from plants in India

Italic—Typeface, after Italy where it was first used by an Italian printer in Venice

Karst—Limestone plateau featuring underground drainage, rolling surfaces, caverns, and sinkholes, after a limestone region in Slovenia near Trieste

Landau—4-wheeled covered carriage, after the town in Germany where it was made

Limoges porcelain—Fine porcelain, after a city in France near where kaolin was discovered in 1760

*French name for Faenza, Italy **Also called Chinese ink

Lincoln green—Olive green, after the color of a fabric originally made in a former English county for which it is named

Magenta—Purplish red, or purplish-red dye, after the Italian town where it was discovered and where a bloody battle was fought in 1859

Majolica—Enameled, glazed, and richly-decorated Italian earthenware, after the Spanish island of Majorca where it was made

Malacca cane—Elegant walking cane made of rattan, after a state in Malaysia

Manila—Hemp, paper, and rope, after the largest city in the Philippines

Mongoloid—Loosely, a member of the *yellow race*, distinguished by physical characteristics of a Mongol, having yellowish-brown skin, straight black hair, and dark eyes, after any of the traditionally nomadic peoples of Mongolia

Nassau system—Scoring system or type of bet in golf, after the capital of the Bahamas

Ottoman—Upholstered sofa or low, large footstool, after a Turkish empire

Parchment—Originally animal skin used as writing paper, after Pergamum, in present-day Turkey

Polka—Folk dance, from "half-step" in Bohemia, the Czech Republic, where it originated, although its name may mean "Polish woman"

Polonaise—Stately dance, after Poland

Prussian blue—Dark blue, or dark blue dye, after the historic region of Europe including what is now Germany, where it was made by an 18th-century color-maker in Berlin

Rhinestone—Artificial gem, after *caillou du Rhin*, so called because it was made at Strasbourg, France, located on the Rhine

Rialto—Theatre district or marketplace area, after an island in Venice, Italy, that was formerly a center of business and trade

Rugby—Team sport played with a ball, after a school in central England

Sèvres porcelain—Fine porcelain, after a suburb of Paris and originally made at Vincennes

Shillelagh—Club or cudgel, after a village in Ireland

Surrey—Light 4-wheeled horse-drawn carriage with 2 or 4 seats, after a county in England

Tarantella—Fast dance for couples in 6/8 time, after the Italian seaport of Taranto

Toledo—Finely tempered sword or sword blade, after the Spanish city in which it was made

Turquoise—Gemstone, after Turkey, first called *la pierre* _____ or "the Turkish stone" by the French

Umber—Brownish, after the brownish earth in Umbria, Italy where it was found

Windsor chair—Wooden chair with a curved back, after an English city known for a castle with the same name

ARTICLES OF CLOTHING AND FABRIC

Afghan—Soft blanket or shawl done in a colorful geometric pattern, after the country of Afghanistan

Antimacassar—Small covering placed on the backs of chairs and sofas to prevent soiling, after the oil made in Makassar, a city in Indonesia

Argyle—Diamond-shaped pattern, or socks made with a tartan-like pattern, after a clan tartan in a former county in Scotland

Ascot—Necktie or scarf, after an English site where famous horse races were held

Balaclava—Knitted head and neck covering worn by soldiers in the Crimean War, after a seaport in the Crimea

Balmoral—Woolen petticoat, a round, brimless cap, or a shoe that laces up, after a castle in Aberdeen, Scotland

Bangkok—Straw hat, after the capital of Thailand

Bengaline—Heavy cloth, after the Indian region of Bengal from which it was first imported

Calico—Plain-woven cotton cloth with figured pattern, after the Indian city of Calicut where it was first obtained

Cambric—Delicate linen fabric, after the city of Cambrai, France, where it was first made (a tea is so named because it is thin and white like the fabric)

Carnaby Street—London fashion industry, after the London street noted as a center for new clothing fashions

Cashmere—Fine wool made from goat hair, after the old spelling of the region disputed between India and Pakistan since 1947

Cordovan—Soft leather, or shoes made from such leather, after Córdoba, a city in Spain

Cravat—Scarf or necktie, after Croatia as applied by the French to the scarves they saw the Croatian soldiers wearing

Damask—Linen or cotton fabric with a patern formed by weaving, after the Syrian city of Damascus

Denim—Durable twilled fabric, after the town of (de) Nîmes in France

Duffel bag—Large, cloth bag made of canvas, after a Flemish village near Antwerp, Belgium, where the coarse fabric for the bags was made

Eton collar—Wide flat white collar, after a town in Berkshire, England, site of a private preparatory school for boys

Eton jacket—Short, black jacket with wide lapels, after a town in Berkshire, England

Fez—Brimless felt hat, after a Moroccan city

Gauze—Thin, light, transparent cloth, or a fabric used in bandages, after Gaza, a town in Palestine

Glengarry—Men's cap, after a valley in Scotland

Hessian—Knee-high boot, or a coarse, strong cloth, after a state in Germany

Homburg—Men's stiff felt hat with a dented crown and brim, after a town in Prussia where it was first made

Inverness—Loose overcoat with a detachable cape, after a city and county in Scotland

Jean—Sturdy cotton cloth, after the Italian town of Genoa

Jersey—Pullover shirt, after the largest of the Channel Islands

Jodhpurs—Riding breeches, after a city in India

Kendal green—Coarse, woolen cloth, after the city of Kendal in England where it was originally made

Lisle—Fine, very-strong cotton thread, after the French town of Lille

Madras—Cotton cloth, usually striped or plaid, after the Indian town now named Chennai

Mantua—Loose gown or cloak, after an Italian city whose name may have been derived from the French *manteau*, meaning "mantle"

Mocha—Soft, velvety leather, after the name of a seaport on the Red Sea in Yemen

Morocco—High quality leather made of goatskin, after a North African country

Muslin—Woven cotton fabric, used especially for sheets, after the city of Mosul, Iraq, where it was first made

Nankeen (nakin)—Brownish-yellow, sturdy cotton cloth, from Nanking, China

Oxford—Shoe or cotton fabric used for shirts, after an English university

Paisley—Soft woolen fabric or silk printed with colorful, swirled designs, after a city in Scotland where wool shawls in this pattern were originally made

Panama hat*—Straw hat, after the Central American country bordering Colombia

*Named for Panama possibly from where they were shipped but made in Ecuador, Peru, and Colombia.

Pekin—Silk fabric, after the capital of China, where it was first made
Sisal—Strong fiber derived from a fleshy plant, after a former seaport in Yucatán, Mexico
Suede—Leather, after the French name for Sweden
Tulle—Gauze-like material for veils and scarves, after a city in France
Tweed—Wool fabric with a rough surface, from a misreading of the Scottish *tweel* or *twill* for a river so named
Tyrolean cap—Man's soft felt hat with a flat conical crown, creased at the top and featuring a decorative feather, after Tyrol, a region of the eastern Alps
Windsor tie—Loosely knotted tie, after an English city known for a castle with the same name
Worsted wool—Smooth, firmly twisted thread or yarn made from long-stapled wool, after Worstead, England, where it was first made

FOOD AND DRINK WORLDWIDE (See FOOD chapter for more)
Benedictine—Sweet liqueur, named after the monks at Fécamp, France, where it originated in 1510
Burgundy—Any dry red wine, after a historical region in eastern France
Casaba—Variety of winter melon, after a city in Turkey
Cayenne—Hot pepper, after the capital of French Guiana
Champagne—Any effervescent white wine, after a northeastern French region
Chartreuse—Yellow or green liqueur, after the liqueur produced at *La Grande* _____, a Carthusian monastery, in France
Chianti—Dry red wine, after a mountainous region of Tuscany, Italy, where it is produced
Chicken Kiev—Dish of boned, flattened chicken breasts rolled around butter, breaded, then fried, after the capital of Ukraine, where it originated
Cognac—Brandy, after a region in France where it was first distilled from wine
Curaçao—Liqueur made by flavoring distilled spirits with the dried peel of bitter oranges, after the largest island of the Netherlands Antilles
Daiquiri—Cocktail made of rum, sugar, and lemon juice, after the Cuban town whose rum was first used for this drink
Damson—Small plum, after the Syrian city of Damascus
Darjeeling—Black tea, after a district in northeast India
Dijon mustard—Pale, grayish-yellow mustard with a sharp flavor from a city in France, whose best known variety is Grey Poupon
Edam—Medium yellow cheese covered with red wax, after a town in western Netherlands
Evian—Bottled mineral water, after a fashionable health resort in France
Gouda—Medium firm pale yellow cheese, after a city in the Netherlands
Gruyère—Light, yellow cheese made with whole milk, after a district in Switzerland
Java—Coffee or a domestic chicken, after a large island in Indonesia
Lima bean—Common variety of bean, after a city in Peru where it was native
Limburger—Semisoft wgite cheese with a strong odor and taste, after a province in Belgium
Madeira—Fortified dessert wine, after the Portuguese island off the west coast of Morocco
Madrilène—Consommé made with tomatoes, often served jellied and chilled, after Madrid, Spain
Mocha—High-quality coffee or flavoring agent made from coffee, after a seaport on the Red Sea in Yemen
Peking duck—Chinese dish of roasted duck, after the capital of China
Perrier—Mineral water in a green bottle, after a spring in southern France

Port—Sweet, usually dark-red, fortified wine, after Oporto, Portugal, where it originated

Scallion—Green onion or spring onion, after the city of Ascalon in the ancient country of Philistia in Palestine

Seltzer—Naturally effervescent mineral water, or any carbonated water, often flavored with fruit juices, from Selters, after Niederselters, a village in Germany

Sherry—Fortified wine, after Xeres, now Jerez, Spain

Tabasco—Trademark for a very hot sauce, after a state in Mexico

Tangerine—Hybrid mandarin orange, after Tangier(s), Morocco

Worcestershire—Spicy sauce for meat, after a former county in England

MEDICINE AND HUMAN ANATOMY

Ancient Greek physician whose oath begins as follows: "I swear by Apollo the Physician, by Asclepius, by Health, by Panacea, and by all the gods and goddesses, making them my witnesses, that I will carry out, according to my ability and judgment, this oath and this indenture"
Answer: Hippocrates (known as the Hippocratic Oath or Physician's Oath)

1) Name the body's 5 senses.
Answer: Hearing, sight, smell, taste, and touch.

2) Identify the 4 generally-accepted kinds of taste the human tongue is able to distinguish.
Answer: Sweet, sour, salt, and bitter.

3) Name the 4 types of teeth in the human mouth.
Answer: Incisors, canines (or cuspids), premolars (or bicuspids), and molars.

4) Give the English names for the 3 little bones of the middle ear.
Answer: Hammer, anvil, and stirrup.

5) Give the Latin names for the 3 little bones of the middle ear.
Answer: Malleus, incus, and stapes.

6) Name the 4 bones in the human leg.
Answer: Femur (thigh bone), patella (kneecap), fibula, and tibia (shinbone).

7) Name the 3 bones that meet at the elbow and are the 3 bones of the human arm.
Answer: Humerus (upper arm), ulna and radius (lower arm).

8) Name the 5 excretory organs of the body represented by the mnemonic device SKILL.
Answer: Skin, kidneys, intestines, liver, and lungs.

9) Name the 5 largest organs in the human body.
Answer: Skin, liver, brain, lungs, and heart.

10) Name the 3 major parts of the small intestine.
Answer: Duodenum, jejunum, and ileum.

11) Name the 3 diseases for which immunization in infancy is recommended and provided for by a vaccine referred to as MMR.
Answer: Measles, mumps, and rubella (chickenpox, which is also on the list for vaccination in infancy, has a separate vaccine).

12) Name the 3 diseases against which a DPT shot will protect a child.
Answer: Diphtheria, pertussis (or whooping cough), and tetanus (lockjaw).

13) Identify the letters that designate the 4 basic types of human blood.
Answer: A, B, AB, and O (in order from most common to least common are as follows: O, A, B, and AB).

14) Name both the watery liquid and the 3 types of cells that are the 4 main parts of blood.
Answer: Plasma, red blood cells (or erythrocytes), white blood cells (or leukocytes), and platelets.

EYE
Sclera (sclerotica)—Tough, "white," fibrous outer membrane that covers most of the eyeball and helps the eye keep its spherical shape
Conjunctiva—Membrane covering this tough, "white," fibrous outer membrane
Iris—Round, pigmented membrane surrounding the pupil and located behind the cornea
Pupil—Apparently black circular opening in the center of the round, pigmented membrane
Cornea—Transparent tissue forming the outer part of the eyeball and covering the iris and the pupil
Retina—Light-sensitive membrane that lines the inner eyeball and changes light rays into electrical signals
Vitreous humor—Clear substance inside the eyeball
Aqueous humor—Watery fluid in the space between the cornea and the lens
Lens—Transparent part between the iris and the vitreous humor that focuses light rays upon the retina
Optic nerve—Nerve that conducts impulses from the retina to the brain
Rods and cones—Two types of light receptors in the retina of the eye

TEETH
Canines (cuspids)—Teeth used to tear off pieces of food
Deciduous (milk teeth)—Term for the teeth that fall out at an early age and are replaced by permanent teeth
Incisors—Main teeth used to bite
Molars—Back teeth that grind food
Premolars (bicuspids)—Teeth with 2 points that grind and crush food—they are located between the molars and canines
Pulp—Innermost layer of the tooth
Dentin—Hard, yellow substance that surrounds this layer
Enamel—Tooth's top layer, the body's hardest substance

BODY PARTS
Ball-and-socket joint—Type of joint where the femur meets the hipbone
Cochlea—Latin for "snail" for the spiral-shaped cavity of the inner ear shaped like a snail shell
Femur (or thigh bone)—Body's longest and strongest bone
Eardrum (tympanic membrane)—Thin membrane that separates the middle ear from the outer ear
Eustachian tube—Narrow canal connecting the pharynx to the middle ear
Sartorius—Longest muscle in the human body, a narrow thigh muscle named from the Latin for "tailor"
Tendons (sinews)—Strong cords of tissue by which muscles are attached to the bones

BONES OF THE BODY
Calcaneus—Heelbone
Carpus—Wrist
Clavicle—Collarbone
Coccyx—Tailbone
Cranium—Skull
Femur—Upper leg or thigh
Fibula—Outer and thinner bone of the lower leg
Hallux—Big toe
Humerus—Upper arm bone
Hyoid—U-shaped bone at the base of the tongue
Mandible—Lower jaw bone
Maxilla—Upper jaw bone
Metacarpus—5 bones of the hand between wrist and fingers
Metatarsus—Bones between ankle and toes
Olecranon—Part of the ulna behind the elbow joint
Patella—Kneecap
Pelvis—Basin-shaped cavity formed by the hipbones and lower part of the backbone
Phalanges—Bones forming the fingers or toes
Pollex—Thumb
Radius—Bone of the forearm on the thumb side
Rib—One of the 24 curved bones around the chest
Sacrum—Triangular bone at the lower end of the spine
Scapula—Shoulder blade
Spine—Spinal column of bone along the middle of the back
Sternum—Breastbone
Talus—Anklebone
Tarsus—Ankle
Tibia—Shinbone
Ulna—Thinner, longer bone of the forearm
Vertebrae—Bones making up the spinal column, or backbone
Zygoma (zygomatic bone)—Cheekbone

ADJECTIVES PERTAINING TO PARTS OF THE BODY
Abdominal—Abdomen
Buccal—Mouth
Cardiac—Heart
Cardiopulmonary—Heart and lungs
Carpal—Wrist
Colorectal—Colon and rectum
Cranial—Skull
Dorsal—Back
Encephalitic—Brain
Gastric—Stomach
Gustatory—Taste
Guttural—Throat
Hepatic—Liver
Lingual—Tongue
Nasal—Nose
Nephritic—Kidney
Optical—Eye
Ossiferous—Bone
Otic—Ear
Pectoral—Abdomen or chest
Pulmonary—Lungs
Rectal—Rectum
Renal—Kidney
Sagittal—Parietal bones of the skull
Tarsal—Foot or ankle
Ventral—Belly or abdomen

INFLAMMATORY CONDITIONS
Adenitis—Lymph node or gland
Angiitis—Blood or lymph vessel
Appendicitis—Vermiform appendix
Arteritis—Artery
Arthritis—Joint
Blepharitis—Eyelid
Bronchitis—Bronchial tube
Bursitis—Bursa, especially in the shoulder, elbow, or knee joint
Carditis—Heart
Cheilitis—Lip or lips
Cholecystitis—Gall bladder
Chondritis—Cartilage
Colitis—Colon, or large intestine
Conjunctivitis—Conjunctiva, or transparent membrane covering the front of the eyeball
Coxitis—Hip joint
Cystitis—Bladder
Dermatitis—Skin
Diverticulitis—Diverticula, or abnormal pouches or sacs protruding from the wall of the intestinal tract
Encephalitis—Brain
Enteritis—Intestinal tract, especially the small intestine
Enterocolitis—Colon and small intestine
Esophagitis—Esophagus
Gastritis—Stomach
Gastroenteritis—Mucous membrane of the intestines and stomach
Gingivitis—Gum
Glossitis—Tongue
Gnathitis—Jaw
Hepatitis—Liver
Hyalitis—Vitreous humor of the eye
Keratitis—Cornea
Laryngitis—Larynx
Lymphadenitis—Lymph gland
Mastitis—Female breast or udder
Mastoiditis—Mastoid cells
Meningitis—Meninges, especially as the result of infection by bacteria or viruses
Meningomyelitis—Spinal cord and its surrounding membranes
Metritis—Uterus
Myelitis—Spinal cord
Myositis—Muscle
Myringitis—Tympanic membrane, or eardrum
Nephritis—Kidney
Neuritis—Nerve or group of nerves
Omphalitis—Navel
Oophoritis—Whole eye
Ophthalmitis—Eyeball or conjunctiva
Orchitis—One or both testes
Osteitis—Bone
Osteochondritis—Bone and cartilage
Osteomyelitis—Bone and marrow
Otitis—Ear
Pancarditis—Heart
Pancreatitis—Pancreas
Parotitis—Parotid (supply salvia to the mouth)
Pericarditis—Pericardium, or tissue covering the heart
Periodontitis—Periodontal tissue, or the area around the tooth
Peritonitis—Peritoneum, or membrane lining the abdominal organs
Pharyngitis—Pharynx, or tube connecting the mouth and nasal passages
Phlebitis—Vein
Pneumonitis—Lung tissue
Poliomyelitis—Gray matter of the spinal cord
Pyelonephritis—Kidney
Pyonephritis—Kidney accompanied by the presence of pus
Rachitis—Spine
Rectitis—Rectum
Rhinitis—Mucus membrane of the nose
Sclerotitis—Sclera (white or outer coat of the eye)
Sinusitis—Sinus
Sphenoiditis—Air cavity of the sphenoid bone (large bone at the base of the skull)
Stomatitis—Soft tissue of the mouth
Tendinitis—Tendon
Tonsillitis—Tonsil
Tracheitis—Trachea
Tympanitis—Eardrum
Typhlitis—Caecum (cecum—the pouch at the beginning of the large intestine)
Ulitis—Gums
Uteritis—Womb

SPECIALIZED LANGUAGE

Achromatopsia—Color blindness
Acne—Chronic skin disease
Alopecia—Baldness
Amputation—Removal of a limb
Anacusis—Total deafness
Annulary—Ring finger
Anosmia—Lack of a sense of smell
Aphasia—Loss of the ability to understand or use words
Apnea—Temporary cessation of breathing
Apraxia—Inability to perform fine motor acts
Axilla—Armpit
Bleb—Blister
Borborygmus—Stomach rumbling
Bradycardia—Slow heartbeat
Bulla—Large blister
Byssinosis—Brown lung disease
Cacodontia—Bad teeth
Cardialgia—Heartburn
Caries—Tooth decay
Cephalalgia—Headache
Cerumen—Earwax
Cicatrix—Scar
Circadian dysrhythmia—Jet lag
Claudication—Limping
Colostomy—Surgical formation of an artificial anal opening
Comedo—Blackhead
Contusion—Bruise
Coryza—Head cold
Deglutition—Swallowing
Diaphoresis—Profuse perspiration
Diarrhea—Excessive bowel movement
Diplopia—Double vision
Dysarthria—Speech impairment
Dysostosis—Defective bone information
Dyspepsia—Indigestion
Dysphagia—Difficulty in swallowing
Dyspnea—Shortness of breath
Dysuria—Painful urination
Ecchymosis—Black-and-blue mark
Emesis—Vomiting
Encephalon—Brain
Enuresis—Involuntary bed-wetting
Epistaxis—Nosebleed
Eructation—Belching
Flatulence—Gas
Furuncle—Boil
Gastralgia—Stomach ache
Gingivae—Gums
Gluteus—Buttock
Graphospasm—Writer's cramp
Gravidity—Pregnancy
Halitosis—Bad breath
Harelip—Congenital cleft in the lip
Hematoma—Swelling containing blood
Hepatoma—Cancer of the liver
Horripilation—Goose bumps
Hydrocephalus—Water on the brain
Hyponatremia—Water intoxication
Hypothermia—Very low body temperature
Larynx—Voice box
Lesion—Injury in an organ or body tissue
Lumbago—Low back pain
Lunule (lunula)—Half-moon area at base of fingernail
Mastectomy—Removal of a breast
Medius—Middle finger
Minimus—Smallest digit on human hand and foot
Myalgia—Muscle pain
Nares—Nostrils
Nasion—Space between the eyes where several bones meet
Nasus—Nose
Neonate—Newborn
Nephrolith—Kidney stone
Neuralgia—Pain along a nerve
Nevus—Birthmark, mole
Occiput—Back of the head
Ophthalmia—Inflammation of the eye, especially of the conjunctiva
Ossification—Transformation into bone
Otalgia—Earache
Papule—Pimple
Parotitis—Mumps
Philtrum—Indentation above the upper lip
Placebo—Harmless drug given to humor a patient
Postprandial—After eating
Prosthesis—Artificial limb
Pruritus—Itching
Psoriasis—Chronic skin disease
Ptomaine poisoning—Food poisoning

Pyorrhea—Discharge of pus
Pyrexia—Fever
Pyrosis—Heartburn
Renal calculus—Kidney stone
Rhinoplasty—Plastic surgery on the nose
Rhinorrhea—Runny nose
Rhytidectomy—Face lift
Sclera—White of the eye
Scurf—Dandruff
Singultus—Hiccups
Somnambulism—Sleepwalking
Sternutation—Sneeze, or the act of sneezing
Suture—Process of joining together an incision or wound by stitching
Syncope—Fainting
Tachycardia—Rapid heartbeat
Thenar—Bulge or mass of flesh at the base of the thumb; palm of the hand
Thrombosis—Formation of a blood clot
Toxin—Poisonous compound
Trachea—Windpipe
Tragus—Fleshy protrusion at the front of the external ear
Tussis—Cough
Urticaria—Hives
Varicella—Chicken pox
Variola—Smallpox
Vertigo—Dizziness

VITAMINS
A—Called *retinol* and important for good eyesight, healthy bones and teeth, and preventing night blindness
C—Known as *ascorbic acid* and important for healthy bones, teeth, and gums, and for preventing and curing scurvy
D—Known as the "sunshine vitamin" and important for healthy bones and teeth and for the prevention of rickets
E—Needed for maintaining cell membranes
K—Essential for blood clotting and the only one produced by bacteria in the human intestine

B Group
B_1—Called *thiamine* and needed for carbohydrate metabolism and the functioning of the heart nerves and preventing beriberi
B_2—Called *riboflavin* and needed for healthy skin, growth, and eye functioning
B_{12}—Called *folic acid* and needed for development of red blood cells, especially for treating certain anemias
Niacin—Called *nicotinic acid* and needed for healthy skin and the functioning of the stomach, intestine, and nerves, especially for the treatment of pellagra

MEDICAL SPECIALISTS
Anesthesiologist—M.D. who administers anesthesia
Cardiologist—M.D. who is a heart specialist
Chiropodist—M.D. who treats disorders of the foot
Chiropractor—Licensed practitioner who manipulates body joints to restore the body to normal nerve function
Dermatologist—M.D. who specializes in the skin and its diseases
Endodontist—Dentist who specializes in work on the tooth pulp and in root-canal therapy
Exodontist—Dentist who specializes in tooth extraction
Gynecologist—M.D. who specializes in the care and disease of women
Hematologist—M.D. who specializes in the treatment of blood diseases
Neurologist—M.D. who specializes in the nervous system and its disorders
Neurosurgeon—M.D. who performs surgery on any part of the nervous system

Medicine And Human Anatomy

Obstetrician—M.D. who specializes in delivering babies
Oncologist—Specialist in dealing with tumors
Ophthalmologist (oculist)—M.D. who treats disorders of the eye
Optician—Specialist in making corrective lenses
Optometrist—Specialist in correction of vision with lenses or other methods not requiring license as a physician
Orthodontist—Specialist in diagnosing, correcting, and preventing irregularities of the teeth
Orthopedist—M.D. who treats disorders of bones, joints, and muscles
Osteopath—M.D. who treats diseases by manipulating the bones and muscles
Pathologist—Specialist in the study of the nature of disease in tissue
Pediatrician—M.D. who specializes in the treatment of children and infants
Periodontist—Specialist who treats disorders of the gum
Podiatrist—M.D. who treats disorders of the foot
Proctologist—M.D. who treats disorders affecting the colon, rectum, and anus
Psychiatrist—M.D. who treats disorders of the mind
Psychologist—Specialist who treats disorders of the mind
Urologist—M.D. who treats disorders of the urinary tract

POTPOURRI
Amyotrophic lateral sclerosis—Medical term for Lou Gehrig's Disease
Anemia—Blood condition known as "tired blood"
Conjunctivitis—Eye inflammation also called "pink eye"
Decompression sickness—Serious problem known as the bends or caisson disease
Diarrhea—Loose bowel movements called Mexican quickstep or Montezuma's revenge
Hansen's Disease—Chronic infectious disease also called leprosy
Hemophilia—Disease called the "Royal disease"
Hydrophobia—Disease also called rabies
Mononucleosis—Disease known as the "kissing disease"
Polio (poliomyelitis)—Disease sometimes called "infantile paralysis"
Rubella—Disease also known as German measles
Rubeola—Disease known simply as measles
Scarlet Fever—Disease known as scarlatina
Tetanus—Medical name for lockjaw
Tuberculosis—Disease known as "consumption" and "the white plague"
Variola—Group of diseases including smallpox, cowpox, and horsepox
Zits—Slang term for acne

Just Trivia

Epithet for the mythological Diana and Hecate because they were protectors of the crossroads of 3 roads
Answer: Trivia (they were the goddesses of the "crossing of 3 roads," a site at which only unimportant talk was engaged in).

Albatross—British term for a double eagle or three under par on a single hole
Area 51*—Nevada secret military facility associated with UFO and conspiracy stories
Dr. Joseph Bell**—Noted medical school professor who was the inspiration for the fictional Sherlock Holmes
Edgar Bergen—Only ventriloquist to receive an Oscar, a special one in 1937 for his dummy Charlie McCarthy
Bibendum***—Latin word for "drink" that is the name of the Michelin Man
Bookkeeper—Only word in the English language with 3 adjacent pairs of double letters—a word designating an occupation
Nadia Comaneci—14-year-old after whom the theme song of the TV soap *The Young and the Restless* was renamed following the 1976 Olympic Games
Brandi Chastain—Scorer of the victorious shootout goal in the 1999 Women's World Cup Soccer finals to defeat China
Dixville Notch—New Hampshire town that is traditionally the first site to vote in the presidential election, opening just after midnight and closing as soon as the 30-odd residents have voted
Dolores Haze—Lolita's real name in a Vladimir Nabokov novel
W. Mark Felt—Former No. 2 official at the FBI revealed in 2005 to be "Deep Throat," the code name for the secretive Watergate informant of the 1970s
Glimmerglass—Name James Fenimore Cooper gave to Otsego Lake in Cooperstown, New York, as the site for his novel *The Deerslayer*
Archie Griffin—Ohio State running back who is the only player to have won the Heisman Trophy twice
Hephastion—Alexander the Great's lifelong companion
Honorificabilitudinitatibus—Longest word in a Shakespeare work, meaning "the state of being able to achieve honors," spoken by the clown Costard in *Love's Labours Lost*
Hot Springs—New Mexico town renamed Truth or Consequences after the radio/TV game show
Cal Hubbard—Only person elected to both the Baseball Hall of Fame (as an umpire) and the Pro Football Hall of Fame (as a player)
Jim "Catfish" Hunter—First former Little League player inducted into the Baseball Hall of Fame, in 1987
Hyoid bone—U-shaped bone at the root of the tongue that is the only bone in the body not connected to another bone
King Kong—1933 movie whose set on MGM's Culver City studio lot was set on fire by the *Gone With the Wind* crew to re-create the Civil War burning of Atlanta
Ladies Love (Cool) James—Meaning of the letters in the name of rap singer L.L. Cool J
Hedy Lamarr—Actress who devised a jam-proof radio communications system for the military in 1941 that is still in use today

*Also known as Groom Lake **Holmes, however, was named for a cricket player with the name Sherlock and for Oliver Wendell Holmes. ***From the early Michelin slogan *Nunc est Bibendum*, meaning "Now is the time to drink," which the French misinterpreted, possibly as "Here is Bibendum."

Anne Morrow Lindbergh—First licensed female glider pilot in the U.S.

Lucille—Nickname of B.B. King's Gibson guitar

My Pet Goat—Book President Bush read to school children even after being told that planes had hit the World Trade Center on 9/11 and that America was under attack

"Nearer My God to Thee"—Hymn the band played aboard the *Titanic* as it was sinking on April 15, 1912

New Hampshire—First U.S. state to have a lottery, in 1964

Nina—Caricaturist Al Hirschfeld's daughter's name that he hid in all of his drawings after her birth in 1945

Pansy—Name that Margaret Mitchell originally used as a first name for Scarlett O'Hara in *Gone With the Wind*

Pilobolus—Cow dung fungus whose name also designates an American dance company that developed from a 1971 dance class at Dartmouth College and is known for its extraordinary acrobatics

Pococurante—Italian word meaning "caring little" that names a character in Voltaire's *Candide* and was the 15th and last word in the 2003 National Spelling Bee finals

Qwerty—Standard typewriter keyboard, as named from the first 6 letters at the upper left, as opposed to the Dvorak, which has the vowels *a, e, i, o*, and *u* on the home row

Rappahannock—River across which George Washington allegedly threw a silver dollar

Brad Rutter—Contestant who defeated both Ken Jennings and Jerome Vered to win the Ultimate Tournament of Champions and its $2,000,000 prize on TV's *Jeopardy!*

Walter M. Schirra—3rd American to orbit the Earth and the only one to fly 3 different types of spacecraft, aboard *Mercury*, in 1962, *Gemini* in 1965, and *Apollo*, in 1968

7UP—Soft drink invented by C.L. Grigg in St. Louis that celebrated its 75th anniversary in 2004, originally called Bib-Label Lithiated Lemon-Lime Soda

666—Total if all the numbers from 1 to 36 around the circumference of a roulette wheel are added—the other 2 symbols on the wheel are 0 and 00

Bernadette Soubirous—French girl in Lourdes, France, to whom the Virgin Mary is said to have appeared 18 times in 1858, or the role for which Jennifer Jones won a Best Actress Oscar in the 1943 film *The Song of Bernadette*

Sparky—Cartoonist Charles Schulz's childhood nickname from the name of Spark Plug, Barney Google's horse in the comics

Speedwell—Boat that set out with the *Mayflower* from Southampton but accompanied it only as far as Plymouth, England, since it proved to be unseaworthy to travel to the New World

Sphygmomanometer—Instrument to measure blood pressure

Stag Party—Original working title of *Playboy* magazine

Thunderhead Mountain—South Dakota mountain on which sculptor Korczack Ziolkowski began his 563-foot high memorial to Sioux warrior Crazy Horse

Tweedledum/Tweedledee—Names John Byrom used for rival composers Handel and Bononcini in his 1725 satirical poem emphasizing how alike they were despite their rivalry

Typewriter—Device known as a "literary piano" invented by Christopher Sholes in 1872

Johnny Vander Meer—Only pitcher to throw consecutive no-hitters, against the Boston Braves on June 11, 1938, and then against the Brooklyn Dodgers on June 15

Wizard of Oz—Fictional title character whose full name is Oscar Zoroaster Phadrig Isaac Norman Henkle Emmanuel Ambroise Diggs****

Lynette Woodard—Woman inducted into Basketball Hall of Fame in 2004 who was the first woman to play for the Harlem Globetrotters

****The initial letters of the names make the acronym Oz Pinhead.

Wright—Surname of the father-son pair who became the first pair ever to have both won Pulitzers in poetry, the father James in 1972 for his *Collected Poems* and the son Franz in 2004 for his *Walking to Martha's Vineyard*

Yen Sid*****—Sorcerer in "The Sorcerer's Apprentice" in the Disney film *Fantasia*

Nancy Zerg—Woman who defeated Ken Jennings on *Jeopardy!* when he missed a question about H&R Block after having won 74 consecutive games and earned $2,520,700

Zog I—Albania's last king, who ruled from 1928 to 1939

Zuzu—George Bailey's daughter whose flower petals he finds in his pocket, making him realize that he is not dead after all in the movie *It's a Wonderful Life*

*****Yen Sid is *Disney* spelled backwards.

THIRTY-THREE THREES

Which 3 adjectives complete the following Robert Frost lines in "Stopping by Woods on a Snowy Evening": "The woods are _____, _____ and _____. / But I have promises to keep, / And miles to go before I sleep, / And miles to go before I sleep"?
Answer: "lovely, dark and deep."

1) Which 3 words complete the proverb "_____, _____, and be _____, for tomorrow we die," derived from the Old Testament's books of Ecclesiastes and Isaiah, meaning "enjoy yourself because death may come early"?
Answer: "Eat, drink, and be merry."

2) Give the 3 generally accepted names of the Three Wise Men of the East, the Three Kings of the Orient, or the Magi who came to worship the baby Jesus in Bethlehem.
Answer: Melchior (or Melichior, meaning "King of Light"); Balthasar (or Balthazar, meaning "The Lord of the Treasures"); and Gaspar (or Caspar; meaning "The White One").

3) Identify the 3 gifts the Three Wise Men, or Magi, brought to the Christ child.
Answer: Gold, frankincense, and myrrh.

4) Which 3 words, each beginning with the prefix *omni-*, are used by most religions to describe their god as "all-knowing," "all-powerful," and "present in all places at the same time"?
Answer: Omniscient, omnipotent, and omnipresent.

5) Name the 3 characters who want the Wizard to give them brains, heart, and courage in the 1939 film *The Wizard of Oz*.
Answer: Scarecrow, Tin Woodman, and Cowardly Lion, respectively.

6) Name the 3 actors who play the Scarecrow, the Tin Woodman, and the Cowardly Lion in the film *The Wizard of Oz*.
Answer: Ray Bolger, Jack Haley, and Bert Lahr, respectively.

6) Identify the 3 chipmunks created by David Seville.
Answer: Alvin, Simon, and Theodore.

7) Name the 3 Good Fairies in the Disney film *Sleeping Beauty*.
Answer: Mistress Flora, Mistress Fauna, and Mistress Merryweather.

8) Name the 3 nephews of Donald Duck.
Answer: Huey, Dewey, and Louie.

9) Name the 3 nieces of Daisy Duck.
Answer: April, May, and June.

10) Identify the 3 warnings on the care and feeding of gremlins in the 1984 film *Gremlins*.
Answer: Do not get wet, do not feed after midnight, and keep out of bright light.

11) Identify the song from the 1953 musical *Kismet* whose 3 main words begin with the letter *B*.
Answer: "Baubles, Bangles, and Beads."

12) Identify the 3 entertainment industry awards represented by the initials TOE.
Answer: Tony, Oscar, and Emmy.

13) Identify the 3 films that have won 11 Oscars each.
Answer: *Ben-Hur* (12 nominations), *Titanic* (14 nominations), and *The Lord of the Rings: The Return of the King* (the last of which in 2004 became the third movie after *Gigi* and *The Last Emperor* to sweep every nominated category with 11 out of 11; *Gigi* and *The Last Emperor* were 9 out of 9).

14) Name the 3 famous tenors who performed before the World Cup soccer finals in 1990, in Rome, in 1994, in Los Angeles, and again in 1998, in Paris.
Answer: Jose Carreras, Placido Domingo, and Luciano Pavarotti.

15) Name the 3 Confederates immortalized on Georgia's Stone Mountain.
Answer: Jefferson Davis, General Robert E. Lee, and General Thomas J. "Stonewall" Jackson.

16) Name the 3 words in the English language that end in *-ceed*.
Answer: Exceed, proceed, and succeed.

17) Which 3 parts of the body are treated by a specialist known as an *otorhinolaryngologist* or *otolaryngologist*?
Answer: Ear, nose, and throat.

18) Name Peter Rabbit's 3 sisters in *The Tale of Peter Rabbit* written by Beatrix Potter.
Answer: Flopsy, Mopsy, and Cottontail.

19) Name the 3 novels in J.R.R. Tolkien's *The Lord of the Rings* trilogy that continues the story of *The Hobbit*, a work set in a mythical past.
Answer: *The Fellowship of the Ring*, *The Two Towers*, and *Return of the King*.

20) Identify Eugene Field's 3 fishermen who one night "Sailed off in a wooden shoe / . . . on a river of crystal light, / Into a sea of dew."
Answer: Wynken, Blynken, and Nod.

21) Name the 3 who "all jumped out of a rotten potato" in the nursery rhyme "Rub-a-dub-dub, / Three men in a tub."
Answer: Butcher, Baker, and Candlestick Maker.

22) According to the nursery rhyme, what 3 things are little boys are made of?
Answer: "Snakes and snails and puppy dog tails."

23) According to the nursery rhyme, what 3 things are little girls made of?
Answer: "Sugar and spice and everything nice."

24) Name the 3 rock 'n' roll stars who died in a plane crash in a cornfield near Mason City, Iowa, on February 3, 1959, the so-called "Day the Music Died" in singer Don McLean's song "American Pie."
Answer: Charles Hardin "Buddy" Holly, Ritchie Valens (known for "La Bamba"), and J.P. Richardson (called "The Big Bopper"; Waylon Jennings, who originally planned to join the group, did not board the plane).

25) In the song "If I Had a Hammer," what 3 things would be hammered out "all over this world"?
Answer: "danger," "warning," and "love between my brothers and my sisters."

26) Identify the names for the rain, the wind, and the fire in an Alan Jay-Lerner-Frederick Loewe song from the musical *Paint Your Wagon*.
Answer: "The rain is Tess, the fire is Joe (or Jo or Jove), and they call the wind Mariah."

27) Name the 3 isotopes of hydrogen.
Answer: Protium, deuterium (or heavy hydrogen), and tritium.

28) Which 3 gases make up almost 100% of the atmosphere?
Answer: Nitrogen (78%), oxygen (21%), and argon (1%; with small amounts of other gases).

29) Identify the 3 "ages," or periods, into which human cultures are divided according to archeological finds.
Answer: Stone Age, Bronze Age, and Iron Age.

30) Identify the 3 Latin words that make up the Olympic motto.
Answer: *Citius, Altius, Fortius*.

31) Give the 3-word English version of the Olympic motto *Citius, Altius, Fortius*.
Answer: "Faster, higher, stronger" (or "swifter, higher, braver").

32) Identify the 3 players that made up the famous double-play combination for the Chicago Cubs in the early part of the 20th century.
Answer: (Joe) Tinker to (Johnny) Evers to (Johnny) Chance (the phrase *Tinkers to Evers to Chance* designates "a routine double play"; they averaged only about 14 double plays a year but are all in the Hall of Fame primarily because of Franklin P. Adams' poem singing their praise).

33) What 3 phrases were used by Washington Senators fans to fondly describe their consistently last-place baseball team?
Answer: First in war, first in peace, and last in the American League (the team moved to Texas in 1972 and became the Texas Rangers; in 2005, the Washington Nationals became the new team in D.C.).

ORDER FORM

Order From:
PATRICK'S PRESS
P.O. Box 5189
Columbus, Georgia 31906

E-mail Address: patrickspress@patrickspress.com
For free color catalog, call 1-800-654-1052

NAME _____
ADDRESS _____
CITY_____ STATE____ ZIP_____
PHONE (_____)_____

Method of Payment: Check one (To avoid delay, payment must accompany order)

____ CHECK OR MONEY ORDER ENCLOSED (payable to Patrick's Press, Inc.)
____ M/C ____ VISA ____ AMEX Card #__ __ __ __ __ __ __ __ __ __ __ __ __ __ __ __
                                              (include all digits)
_____ Expiration Date __ __ __ __
           Signature (for charge cards)

Books	Unit Price	Qty	Total
Let's Git Nekkid Trivia****	$17.95	_____	_____
Campbell's 2501 Quiz Questions*	$15.95	_____	_____
Campbell's High School/College Book of Lists***	$20.95	_____	_____
Campbell's Constant Quiz Companion**/***	$24.95	_____	_____
Campbell's 3001 Quiz Questions***	$17.95	_____	_____
Campbell's Potpourri V of Quiz Questions***	$16.95	_____	_____
Campbell's Potpourri VI of Quiz Questions***	$16.95	_____	_____
Campbell's 2004 Quiz Questions***	$15.95	_____	_____
Campbell's 2005 Quiz Questions***	$15.95	_____	_____
Campbell's 213 Lightning Rounds***	$15.95	_____	_____
Campbell's 214 Lightning Rounds***	$15.95	_____	_____
Campbell's 2701 Quiz Questions**	$17.95	_____	_____
Campbell's Middle School Quiz Book #3**	$16.95	_____	_____
Campbell's Middle School Quiz Book #4**	$16.95	_____	_____
Campbell's 176 Lightning Rounds**	$15.95	_____	_____
Campbell's 177 Lightning Rounds**	$15.95	_____	_____
Campbell's Elementary School Quiz Book #1*	$13.95	_____	_____
Campbell's Elementary School Quiz Book #2*	$15.95	_____	_____
Campbell's 2501 Quiz Questions*	$15.95	_____	_____

*Elementary school (5th-6th) **Middle school ***High school ****General public

Shipping & Handling _____
$5.00+*
GA residents, add appropriate sales tax _____
TOTAL _____

*$5.00 for orders under $50.00. Add $1.00 for each increment of $50.00.

John Campbell has a B.A. in history from Loyola College as well as an M.A. in French from Middlebury College. After serving two years in the Peace Corps, he taught high school French and coached boys and girls soccer, and since 1981, has been self-publishing quiz books.

Triv* says, "The path to quiz show success is through Patrick's Press."
*Triv is the little nekkid guy on the book's cover.